Examining Quantum Algorithms for Quantum Image Processing

HaiSheng Li
Guangxi Normal University, China

A volume in the Advances
in Computer and Electrical
Engineering (ACEE) Book Series

Published in the United States of America by
IGI Global
Engineering Science Reference (an imprint of IGI Global)
701 E. Chocolate Avenue
Hershey PA, USA 17033
Tel: 717-533-8845
Fax: 717-533-8661
E-mail: cust@igi-global.com
Web site: http://www.igi-global.com

Library of Congress Cataloging-in-Publication Data

Names: Li, HaiSheng, 1974- author.
Title: Examining quantum algorithms for quantum image processing / HaiSheng
    Li.
Description: Hershey, PA : Engineering Science Reference, an imprint of IGI
    Global, [2020] | Includes bibliographical references and index. |
    Summary: "This book provides a comprehensive introduction to quantum
    image algorithms to establish frameworks of quantum image processing"--
    Provided by publisher.
Identifiers: LCCN 2019059580 (print) | LCCN 2019059581 (ebook) | ISBN
    9781799837992 (hardcover) | ISBN 9781799851608 (paperback) | ISBN
    9781799838005 (ebook)
Subjects: LCSH: Image processing--Mathemaics. | Quantum optics. | Quantum
    computing. | Algorithms.
Classification: LCC TA1637.5 .L53 2020 (print) | LCC TA1637.5 (ebook) |
    DDC 006.3/843--dc23
LC record available at https://lccn.loc.gov/2019059580
LC ebook record available at https://lccn.loc.gov/2019059581

This book is published in the IGI Global book series Advances in Computer and Electrical Engineering (ACEE) (ISSN: 2327-039X; eISSN: 2327-0403)

British Cataloguing in Publication Data
A Cataloguing in Publication record for this book is available from the British Library.

All work contributed to this book is new, previously-unpublished material.
The views expressed in this book are those of the authors, but not necessarily of the publisher.

For electronic access to this publication, please contact: eresources@igi-global.com.

Advances in Computer and Electrical Engineering (ACEE) Book Series

ISSN:2327-039X
EISSN:2327-0403

Editor-in-Chief: Srikanta Patnaik, SOA University, India

MISSION

The fields of computer engineering and electrical engineering encompass a broad range of interdisciplinary topics allowing for expansive research developments across multiple fields. Research in these areas continues to develop and become increasingly important as computer and electrical systems have become an integral part of everyday life.

The **Advances in Computer and Electrical Engineering (ACEE) Book Series** aims to publish research on diverse topics pertaining to computer engineering and electrical engineering. **ACEE** encourages scholarly discourse on the latest applications, tools, and methodologies being implemented in the field for the design and development of computer and electrical systems.

COVERAGE

- Microprocessor Design
- Electrical Power Conversion
- Power Electronics
- Analog Electronics
- Algorithms
- VLSI Design
- Digital Electronics
- VLSI Fabrication
- Computer Science
- Circuit Analysis

IGI Global is currently accepting manuscripts for publication within this series. To submit a proposal for a volume in this series, please contact our Acquisition Editors at Acquisitions@igi-global.com or visit: http://www.igi-global.com/publish/.

Titles in this Series

For a list of additional titles in this series, please visit:
http://www.igi-global.com/book-series/advances-computer-electrical-engineering/73675

Research Advancements in Smart Technology, Optimization, and Renewale Energy
Pandian Vasant (University of Technology Petronas, Malaysia) Gerhard Weber (Poznan University of Technology, Poland) and Wonsiri Punurai (Mahidol University, Thailand)
Engineering Science Reference • © 2021 • 407pp • H/C (ISBN: 9781799839705) • US $225.00

HCI Solutions for Achieving Sustainable Development Goals
Fariza Hanis Abdul Razak (Universiti Teknologi MARA (UiTM), Malaysia) Masitah Ghazali (Universiti Teknologi Malaysia (UTM), Malaysia) Murni Mahmud (International Islamic University Malaysia, Malaysia) Chui Yin Wong (Multimedia University, Malaysia) and Muhammad Haziq Lim Abdullah (Universiti Teknikal Malaysia, Melaka, Malaysia)
Engineering Science Reference • © 2021 • 300pp • H/C (ISBN: 9781799849360) • US $195.00

Innovations in the Industrial Internet of Things (IIoT) and Smart Factory
Sam Goundar (The University of the South Pacific, Fiji) J. Avanija (Sree Vidyanikethan Engineering College, India) Gurram Sunitha (Sree Vidyanikethan Engineering College, India) K Reddy Madhavi (Sree Vidyanikethan Engineering College, India) and S. Bharath Bhushan (Sree Vidyanikethan Engineering College, India)
Engineering Science Reference • © 2020 • 300pp • H/C (ISBN: 9781799833758) • US $225.00

Advancements in the Design and Implementation of Smart Grid Technology
Ravi Samikannu (Botswana International University of Science and Technology, Botswana) Karthikrajan Senthilnathan (VIT University, India) Balamurugan Shanmugam (Quants IS & CS, India) Iyswarya Annapoorani (VIT University, India) and Bakary Diarra (Institute of Applied Sciences University of Sciences, Techniques and Technologies of Bamako, Mali)
Engineering Science Reference • © 2020 • 300pp • H/C (ISBN: 9781799836575) • US $205.00

For an entire list of titles in this series, please visit:
http://www.igi-global.com/book-series/advances-computer-electrical-engineering/73675

701 East Chocolate Avenue, Hershey, PA 17033, USA
Tel: 717-533-8845 x100 • Fax: 717-533-8661
E-Mail: cust@igi-global.com • www.igi-global.com

Table of Contents

Preface

Quantum image processing is an interdisciplinary field combining quantum information, quantum computation and image processing. It devotes to the development of novel quantum algorithms for storing, processing, and retrieving visual information. The purpose of this book is to give a valuable resource and useful methods for graduate students and researchers interested in quantum computation, quantum image processing, quantum algorithm, and emerging interdisciplinary field. Especially, this book provides quantum Fourier transform, quantum wavelet transform, and quantum wavelet packet transform as tool algorithms in image processing and quantum computation.

This book is divided into seven chapters as follows.

The introduction briefly describes the background of quantum image processing, which includes advantages of quantum image processing, the steps of quantum image processing, and topics related to quantum image processing.

Chapter 1 briefly describes the basic concepts and principles of quantum computation. These contents provide the necessary theoretical basis for subsequent chapters.

Chapter 2 describes some typical examples of quantum image representations of three categories, which solve how to store an image in a quantum system, and to retrieve the image from the quantum system. In addition, this chapter introduces the type conversions for quantum images, quantum real-valued images and complex-valued images.

Chapter 3 provides quantum algorithms to realize geometric transformations (including two-point swapping, symmetric flip, local flip, orthogonal rotation, and translation). These transformations are implemented using quantum circuits based on basic quantum gates, which are constructed with polynomial numbers of single-qubit and double-qubit gates.

Chapter 4 designs four circuits of 1D quantum Fourier transform and its inverse by using perfect shuffle permutations and generalized tensor products. Meanwhile, 2D and 3D quantum Fourier transforms are proposed for images and videos, respectively.

Chapter 5 describes the iteration equations of quantum wavelet transforms, and designs the implementation circuits of Haar quantum wavelet transform, Daubechies D4 quantum wavelet transform and their inverses.

Chapter 6 describes multi-level and multi-dimensional quantum wavelet packet transforms, and introduces quantum image compression for 2D quantum wavelet packet transforms.

Chapter 7 introduces quantum edge detection algorithm and quantum image segmentation based on generalized Grover search algorithm, respectively.

The conclusion discusses open challenges and future research directions in the field of quantum image processing.

In addition, the reader can experience algorithms proposed in this book using simulation codes in Appendix 2. The relationship between chapters is shown in Figure 1.

The bibliography contains a listing of all reference materials cited in the text of the book. My apologies to any researcher whose work we have inadvertently omitted from citation.

Dr. Fan Ping (East China JiaoTong University, China), Prof. Zhou RiGui (Shanghai Maritime University), Dr. Xia Haiying (Guangxi Normal University, China), Prof. Song Shuxiang (Guangxi Normal University, China), Prof. Long

Figure 1. The frame of chapters

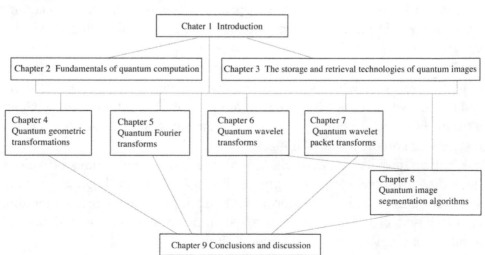

Guilu (Tsinghua University, China), and Prof. He Xiangjian (University of Technology, Sydney, Australia) offered suggestions for the improvement of the manuscript. Graduate students Li Chunyu, Chen Xiao, Xue Fan, Xu Yusi, Quan Jinhui, Wu Rongyu, Lu Jianheng provided some materials and necessary works. This book also quoted works of some scholars. To all these people, I extend my sincere thanks.

This book is supported in part by the National Natural Science Foundation of China under Grant Nos. 61462026 and 61762012, in part by the Science and Technology Project of Guangxi under Grant No. 2018JJA170083.

Quantum image processing is still in its infancy, and the author's knowledge is limited, therefore, flaws and omissions are unavoidable. The author welcomes reader's criticism and suggestions.

HaiSheng Li
Guangxi Normal University, China
June 24, 2020

Introduction

THE GENERATION OF QUANTUM IMAGE PROCESSING

Quantum principles enables fast quantum algorithms for factorization (Shor, 1994), database search (Grover, 1996), quantum simulation (Feynman, 1982; Lloyd, 1996). There have been rapid progress in quantum computation hardware (Arute et al., 2019), and classical emulation of quantum computers as well (Xin, 2019). It is promising that quantum computation may be used in solving problems with practical significance.

One possible area of application of quantum computation is quantum image processing. The massive amount of data storage in classical image processing can be greatly reduced. Meanwhile, the number of gate operations is also drastically reduced. Quantum image processing is a discipline devoted to the development of novel quantum algorithms for storing, processing, and retrieving visual information (Venegas-Andraca, 2015). The field of quantum image processing was born with the publications (Vlasov, 1997; Venegas-Andraca, & Bose, 2003; Beach, Lomont, & Cohen, 2003).

The Steps of Quantum Image Processing

The first step of quantum image processing is to store a classical image in quantum systems. In the second step, the quantum image is operated by quantum algorithms. In the third step, the classical image is retrieved from quantum systems using quantum measurement methods. These steps are given in Figure 1.

Quantum Image Storage and Retrieval

Quantum image representation is a stored pattern by which images are stored in a quantum system. Venegas-Andraca and Bose proposed the quantum

Figure 1. The steps of quantum image processing.

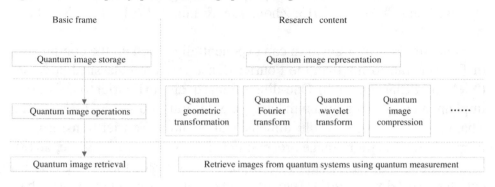

lattice representation to store a classical image in a quantum system, and gave a retrieval method (Venegas-Andraca & Bose, 2003). Some quantum image representations and the corresponding retrieval methods were proposed, for instance, a flexible representation of quantum images (FRQI) (Le, Dong, & Hirota, 2011), the model of a normal arbitrary superposition state (NASS) (Li, Zhu, Zhou, Li, Song, & Ian, 2014), and a novel enhanced quantum representation (NEQR) (Zhang, Lu, Gao, & Wang, 2013). Surveys of quantum image representations were given (Yan, Iliyasu, & Venegas-Andraca, 2016; Jiang, 2016; Ranjani, 2019; Yan, & Venegas-Andraca, 2020).

Quantum Image Operations

In the past decade, many quantum image operations (i.e., quantum image algorithms) have been proposed, such as quantum geometric transformation, quantum Fourier transform, quantum wavelet transform, quantum wavelet packet transform, quantum image compression, quantum image segmentation, quantum image feature extraction, quantum image scrambling, quantum image encryption and decryption, and quantum machine learning.

Quantum geometric transformations were implemented for different quantum image representations. Le et al. proposed two-point swapping, flip, orthogonal rotation, and restricted geometric transformation, are applied to images based on FRQI (Le, Iliyasu, Dong, & Hirota, 2010, 2011). Quantum geometric transformations based on NASS were proposed to implement two-point swapping, symmetric flip, local flip, orthogonal rotation, and translations (Fan, Zhou, Jing, & Li, 2016). Using nearest neighbor interpolation, Jiang and Wang implemented quantum image scaling based on the improved novel enhanced quantum representation (Jiang, & Wang, 2015). Linear cyclic translation transformations were proposed using quantum modular adder (Wang, Jiang, & Wang, 2015; Zhou, Tan, & Ian, 2017; Li, Fan, Xia, Peng, & Long, 2020).

Quantum Fourier transform can exponentially speed up the computation of Fourier transforms than the Fourier transforms on a classical computer (Nielsen, & Chuang, 2000). One-dimensional quantum Fourier transform was implemented by using quantum basis gates (Karafyllidis, 2003; Wang, Zhu, Zhang, & Yeon, 2011). Multi-dimensional quantum Fourier transform was proposed for quantum image processing (Li, Fan, Xia, Song, & He, 2018).

Quantum wavelet transform is exponentially faster than their classical counterparts (Hoyer, 1997). Two different quantum wavelet transforms have been developed, which are Haar quantum wavelet transform and Daubechies D4 quantum wavelet transform, respectively (Fijany & Williams, 1998; Li, Fan, Xia, & Song, 2019).

Quantum wavelet packet transform can be classified with one-dimensional or multi-dimensional according to the types of data it acts on are one-dimension or multi-dimension. One-dimensional quantum wavelet packet transform has been proposed (Hoyer, 1997; Fijany & Williams, 1998; Klappenecker, 1999). Images are naturally represented in 2-dimensions. By now, 2-dimensional quantum wavelet packet transform was proposed for 2-dimensiona Data (Li, Fan, Xia, Song, & He, 2018).

Quantum image compression was proposed to reduce the number of quantum measurements to reconstruct images (Li, Zhu, Zhou, Li, Song, & Ian, 2014).

Quantum image segmentation is still in its infancy, and the relevant research results are rare. Venegas-Andraca and Ball used maximally entangled qubits to store binary geometrical shapes, and found out these maximally entangled qubits from quantum systems to realize image segmentation (Venegas-Andraca & Ball, 2010). An edge detection algorithm was given to detect the edge information of an image, which completes the edge detection with only one single-qubit operation, independent of the size of the image (Yao et al., 2015). Using quantum search algorithm, Li et al. gave a quantum image segmentation algorithm (Li, Zhu, Zhou, Song, & Yang, 2014).

Quantum image feature extraction was proposed to extract local feature point from a quantum image (Zhang, Lu, Xu, Gao, & Wilson, 2015).

Quantum image scrambling is an important method of quantum encryption, which includes quantum Arnold image scrambling (Jiang, & Wang, 2014), quantum Hilbert image scrambling (Jiang, Wang, & Wu, 2014), quantum Fibonacci image scrambling (Jiang, Wu, & Wang, 2014), and a block-based quantum image scrambling (Li, Chen, Song, Liao, & Fang, 2019).

Quantum image encryption and decryption is a fruitful direction in quantum image processing (Jiang, 2016). Many scholars proposed different algorithms of quantum image encryption and decryption (Akhshani, Akhavan, Lim, & Hassan, 2012; Zhou, Wu, Zhang, & Shen, 2013; Song, Wang, El-Latif, & Niu, 2014; Zhou, Hua, Gong, Pei, & Liao, 2015; Li, Li, Chen, & Xia, 2018). Yan et al. described quantum image security technologies (Yan, Iliyasu, & Le, 2017; Yan, & Venegas-Andraca, 2020). Heidari et al. proposed quantum image histogram to quantum image security performance (Heidari, Abutalib, Alkhambashi, Farouk, & Naseri, 2019).

Quantum machine learning bridges the gap between abstract developments in quantum computation and the applied research on machine learning, and explores how to devise and implement quantum software that could enable machine learning that is faster than that of classical computers (Biamonte, et al., 2017).

CONCLUSION

This was an introduction to quantum image processing and discussed the main issues in previous and current up to date work. Compared with classical image processing, the research results of quantum image processing are still too few. The researchers still need to make continuous efforts to gradually enrich the quantum image processing.

REFERENCES

Akhshani, A., Akhavan, A., Lim, S. C., & Hassan, Z. (2012). An image encryption scheme based on quantum logistic map. *Communications in Nonlinear Science and Numerical Simulation*, *17*(12), 4653–4661. doi:10.1016/j.cnsns.2012.05.033

Arute, F., Arya, K., Babbush, R., Bacon, D., Bardin, J. C., Barends, R., Biswas, R., Boixo, S., Brandao, F. G. S. L., Buell, D. A., Burkett, B., Chen, Y., Chen, Z., Chiaro, B., Collins, R., Courtney, W., Dunsworth, A., Farhi, E., Foxen, B., ... Martinis, J. M. (2019). Quantum supremacy using a programmable superconducting processor. *Nature*, *574*(7779), 505–510. doi:10.103841586-019-1666-5 PMID:31645734

Beach, G., Lomont, C., & Cohen, C. (2003). Quantum image processing. *Proceedings of The 2003 IEEE Workshop on Applied Imagery Pattern Recognition*, 39–44. 10.1109/AIPR.2003.1284246

Biamonte, J., Wittek, P., Pancotti, N., Rebentrost, P., Wiebe, N., & Lloyd, S. (2017). Quantum machine learning. *Nature*, *549*(7671), 195–202. doi:10.1038/nature23474 PMID:28905917

Fan, P., Zhou, R. G., Jing, N., & Li, H. S. (2016). Geometric transformations of multidimensional color images based on NASS. *Information Sciences*, *340*, 191–208. doi:10.1016/j.ins.2015.12.024

Feynman, R. P. (1982). Simulating physics with quantum computers. *International Journal of Theoretical Physics*, *21*(6), 467–488. doi:10.1007/BF02650179

Fijany, A., & Williams, C. P. (1998). Quantum wavelet transforms: Fast algorithms and complete circuits. *NASA International Conference on Quantum Computing and Quantum Communications*, 10-33.

Grover, L. (1996). A fast quantum mechanical algorithm for database search. *Proc. 28th Annual ACM Symposium on the Theory of Computing*, 212-219. 10.1145/237814.237866

Heidari, S., Abutalib, M. M., Alkhambashi, M., Farouk, A., & Naseri, M. (2019). A new general model for quantum image histogram (QIH). *Quantum Information Processing*, *18*(6), 175. doi:10.100711128-019-2295-5

Hoyer, P. (1997). *Efficient quantum transforms*. arXiv preprint quant-ph/9702028

Jiang, N. (2016). *Quantum image processing*. Tsinghua University Press.

Jiang, N., & Wang, L. (2014). Analysis and improvement of the quantum Arnold image scrambling. *Quantum Information Processing*, *13*(7), 1545–1551. doi:10.100711128-014-0749-3

Jiang, N., & Wang, L. (2015). Quantum image scaling using nearest neighbor interpolation. *Quantum Information Processing*, *14*(5), 1559–1571. doi:10.100711128-014-0841-8

Jiang, N., Wang, L., & Wu, W. Y. (2014). Quantum Hilbert image scrambling. *International Journal of Theoretical Physics*, *53*(7), 2463–2484. doi:10.100710773-014-2046-4

Jiang, N., Wu, W. Y., & Wang, L. (2014). The quantum realization of Arnold and Fibonacci image scrambling. *Quantum Information Processing*, *13*(5), 1223–1236. doi:10.100711128-013-0721-7

Karafyllidis, I. G. (2003). Visualization of the quantum Fourier transform using a quantum computer simulator. *Quantum Information Processing*, *2*(4), 271–288. doi:10.1023/B:QINP.0000020076.36114.13

Klappenecker, A. (1999). *Wavelets and wavelet packets on quantum computers*. arXiv preprint quant-ph/9909014

Le, P. Q., Dong, F., & Hirota, K. (2011). A flexible representation of quantum images for polynomial preparation, image compression, and processing operations. *Quantum Information Processing*, *10*(1), 63–84. doi:10.100711128-010-0177-y

Le, P. Q., Iliyasu, A. M., Dong, F., & Hirota, K. (2010). Fast Geometric Transformations on Quantum Images. *International Journal of Applied Mathematics*, *40*(3), 113–123.

Le, P. Q., Iliyasu, A. M., Dong, F., & Hirota, K. (2011). Strategies for designing geometric transformations on quantum images. *Theoretical Computer Science*, *412*(15), 1406–1418. doi:10.1016/j.tcs.2010.11.029

Li, H. S., Chen, X., Song, S., Liao, Z., & Fang, J. (2019). A Block-Based Quantum Image Scrambling for GNEQR. *IEEE Access: Practical Innovations, Open Solutions*, *7*, 138233–138243. doi:10.1109/ACCESS.2019.2942986

Li, H. S., Fan, P., Xia, H. Y., Peng, H., & Long, G. L. (2020). Efficient quantum arithmetic operation circuits for quantum image processing. *Science China. Physics, Mechanics & Astronomy*, *63*(8), 280311. doi:10.100711433-020-1582-8

Li, H. S., Fan, P., Xia, H. Y., Song, S., & He, X. (2018). The quantum Fourier transform based on quantum vision representation. *Quantum Information Processing*, *17*(12), 333. doi:10.100711128-018-2096-2

Li, H. S., Fan, P., Xia, H. Y., Song, S., & He, X. (2018). The multi-level and multi-dimensional quantum wavelet packet transforms. *Scientific Reports*, *8*(1), 13884. doi:10.103841598-018-32348-8 PMID:30224678

Li, H. S., Fan, P., Xia, H. Y., & Song, S. X. (2019). Quantum multi-level wavelet transforms. *Information Sciences*, *504*, 113–115. doi:10.1016/j. ins.2019.07.057

Li, H. S., Li, C., Chen, X., & Xia, H. Y. (2018). Quantum image encryption algorithm based on NASS. *International Journal of Theoretical Physics*, *57*(12), 3745–3760. doi:10.100710773-018-3887-z

Li, H. S., Zhu, Q., Zhou, R. G., Li, M. C., Song, L., & Ian, H. (2014). Multidimensional color image storage, retrieval, and compression based on quantum amplitudes and phases. *Information Sciences*, *273*, 212–232. doi:10.1016/j.ins.2014.03.035

Li, H. S., Zhu, Q., Zhou, R. G., Song, L., & Yang, X. J. (2014). Multidimensional color image storage and retrieval for a normal arbitrary quantum superposition state. *Quantum Information Processing*, *13*(4), 991–1011. doi:10.100711128-013-0705-7

Lloyd, S. (1996). Universal quantum simulators. *Science*, *273*(5278), 1073–1078. doi:10.1126cience.273.5278.1073 PMID:8688088

Nielsen, M. A., & Chuang, I. L. (2000). *Quantum Computation and Quantum Information*. Cambridge University Press.

Ranjani, J. J. (2019). Quantum Image Processing and Its Applications. In Handbook of Multimedia Information Security: Techniques and Applications. Springer.

Shor, P. W. (1994). Algorithms for quantum computation: Discrete logarithms and factoring. *Proc. 35th Annual Symposium on Foundations of Computer Science*, 124-134. 10.1109/SFCS.1994.365700

Song, X. H., Wang, S., El-Latif, A. A. A., & Niu, X. M. (2014). Quantum image encryption based on restricted geometric and color transformations. *Quantum Information Processing*, *13*(8), 1765–1787. doi:10.100711128-014-0768-0

Venegas-Andraca, S. E. (2015). Introductory words: Special issue on quantum image processing published by Quantum Information Processing. *Quantum Information Processing*, *14*(5), 1535–1537. doi:10.100711128-015-1001-5

Venegas-Andraca, S. E., & Ball, J. L. (2010). Processing images in entangled quantum systems. *Quantum Information Processing*, *9*(1), 1–11. doi:10.100711128-009-0123-z

Venegas-Andraca, S. E., & Bose, S. (2003). Storing, processing and retrieving an image using quantum mechanics. *Proceedings of the SPIE Conference Quantum Information and Computation*, 137-147. 10.1117/12.485960

Vlasov, A. Y. (1997). *Quantum Computations and Image Recognition.* arXiv:quant-ph/9703010

Wang, H. F., Zhu, A. D., Zhang, S., & Yeon, K. H. (2011). Simple implementation of discrete quantum Fourier transform via cavity quantum electrodynamics. *New Journal of Physics, 13*(1), 013021. doi:10.1088/1367-2630/13/1/013021

Wang, J., Jiang, N., & Wang, L. (2015). Quantum image translation. *Quantum Information Processing, 14*(5), 1589–1604. doi:10.100711128-014-0843-6

Xin, T. (2019). A novel approach for emulating quantum computers on classical platforms. *Quantum Engineering, 1*(2), e18. doi:10.1002/que2.18

Yan, F., Iliyasu, A. M., & Le, P. Q. (2017). Quantum image processing: A review of advances in its security technologies. *International Journal of Quantum Information, 15*(03), 1730001. doi:10.1142/S0219749917300017

Yan, F., Iliyasu, A. M., & Venegas-Andraca, S. E. (2016). A survey of quantum image representations. *Quantum Information Processing, 15*(1), 1–35. doi:10.100711128-015-1195-6

Yan, F., & Venegas-Andraca, S. E. (2020). *Quantum image processing.* Singapore: Springer Nature Singapore Company.

Yao, X. W., Wang, H., Liao, Z., Chen, M. C., Pan, J., Li, J., ... Zheng, W. (2017). Quantum image processing and its application to edge detection: Theory and experiment. *Physical Review X, 7*(3), 031041. doi:10.1103/PhysRevX.7.031041

Zhang, Y., Lu, K., Gao, Y., & Wang, M. (2013). NEQR: A novel enhanced quantum representation of digital images. *Quantum Information Processing, 12*(8), 2833–2860. doi:10.100711128-013-0567-z

Zhang, Y., Lu, K., Xu, K., Gao, Y., & Wilson, R. (2015). Local feature point extraction for quantum images. *Quantum Information Processing, 14*(5), 1573–1588. doi:10.100711128-014-0842-7

Zhou, N. R., Hua, T. X., Gong, L. H., Pei, D. J., & Liao, Q. H. (2015). Quantum image encryption based on generalized Arnold transform and double random-phase encoding. *Quantum Information Processing, 14*(4), 1193–1213. doi:10.100711128-015-0926-z

Zhou, R. G., Tan, C., & Ian, H. (2017). Global and local translation designs of quantum image based on FRQI. *International Journal of Theoretical Physics*, *56*(4), 1382–1398. doi:10.100710773-017-3279-9

Zhou, R. G., Wu, Q., Zhang, M. Q., & Shen, C. Y. (2013). Quantum image encryption and decryption algorithms based on quantum image geometric transformations. *International Journal of Theoretical Physics*, *52*(6), 1802–1817. doi:10.100710773-012-1274-8

Chapter 1
Fundamentals of Quantum Computation

ABSTRACT

This chapter briefly describes the basic concepts and principles of quantum computing. Firstly, the concepts of qubit, quantum coherence, quantum decoherence, quantum entanglement, quantum density operators, linear operators, inner products, outer products, tensor products, Hermite operators, and unitary operators are described. Then, the four basic assumptions of quantum mechanics are introduced, focusing on the measurement assumptions of quantum mechanics. Finally, the definition of commonly used quantum logic gates is given including single qubit gates, double qubit gates, and multiple qubit gates. These contents provide the necessary theoretical basis for subsequent chapters.

INTRODUCTION

On December 14, 1900, Planck proposed the quantization hypothesis of energy at the annual meeting of the physical society, thus establishing the concept of quantum. After that, a group of outstanding physicists, such as Einstein, Heisenberg and Schrodinger, established the theory of quantum mechanics (Long, Pei, & Zeng, 2007; Cong, 2006). Quantum computation based on quantum mechanics has many new characteristics different from classical computation. This chapter briefly introduces the basic concepts and principles of quantum computation. Related mathematics backgrounds

DOI: 10.4018/978-1-7998-3799-2.ch001

are shown in Appendix A. The implementation codes of controlled gates are seen in Appendix B.

BASIC CONCEPTS OF QUANTUM COMPUTATION

Basic concepts of quantum computation are described, such as qubit, tensor products, inner products, and outer products.

Qubit

A classical bit has a state: either 0 or 1. In quantum computation, information elements are represented by qubits (Schumacher, 1995), which have two possible states $|0\rangle$ and $|1\rangle$, which are called basis states. Any two-level quantum system can be used to implement qubits. For instance, the ground and excited states of electrons in a hydrogen atom, and the two different polarizations of a photon, can be called as $|0\rangle$ and $|1\rangle$, respectively. Dirac uses the symbol $|\bullet\rangle$ to represent a quantum state, also known as a ket, which is equivalent to a column vector. $\langle\bullet|$ called a bra, is equivalent to a row vector and is a dual vector of $|\bullet\rangle$, which can be simply understood as a conjugate transpose vector of a vector (Dirac, 1947). A qubit can also be a linear combination of two basis states, often called superposition states:

$$|\psi\rangle = \alpha|0\rangle + \beta|1\rangle, \tag{2.1}$$

where the numbers α and β are complex numbers, satisfying $|\alpha|^2 + |\beta|^2 = 1$. Therefore, they are called the probability amplitude. When the quantum state $|\psi\rangle$ is measured, it collapses to $|0\rangle$ with a probability of $|\alpha|^2$, and collapses to $|1\rangle$ with a probability of $|\beta|^2$. Hence a qubit can contain both $|0\rangle$ and $|1\rangle$, which is quite different from classical bits.

The special basis states $|0\rangle$ and $|1\rangle$ are also called computation basis states. Their vector forms are

$$|0\rangle = \begin{bmatrix} 1 \\ 0 \end{bmatrix}, |1\rangle = \begin{bmatrix} 0 \\ 1 \end{bmatrix}, \tag{2.2}$$

and their dual vectors are

$$\langle 0| = [1 \quad 0], \langle 1| = [0 \quad 1]. \tag{2.3}$$

It is known from (2.2) that the states of a qubit are unit vectors in a two-dimensional vector space (Rudin, 1999), which can also be in states $\frac{1}{\sqrt{2}}|0\rangle + \frac{1}{\sqrt{2}}|1\rangle$ and $\frac{1}{\sqrt{2}}|0\rangle - \frac{1}{\sqrt{2}}|1\rangle$. The two states are also called basis states, denoted as |+⟩ and |-⟩, respectively.

A qubit also has a useful geometric representation, i.e., Bloch sphere representation (Nielsen & Chuang, 2000)

$$|\psi\rangle = \cos\frac{\theta}{2}|0\rangle + e^{i\varphi}\sin\frac{\theta}{2}|1\rangle, \tag{2.4}$$

where numbers θ and φ define a point on the unit three-dimensional sphere. It provides a useful means of visualizing the state of a single qubit, and often serves as an excellent testbed for ideas about quantum computation and quantum information.

Tensor Products and Multiple Qubits

The tensor product is a way of putting small vector spaces together to form larger vector spaces, represented by the symbol $\otimes$. Suppose U and V are two complex matrices,

$$U = \begin{bmatrix} u_{00} & u_{01} \\ u_{10} & u_{11} \end{bmatrix}, V = \begin{bmatrix} v_{00} & v_{01} & v_{02} \\ v_{10} & v_{11} & v_{12} \end{bmatrix}, \tag{2.5}$$

their tensor product is

$$U \otimes V = \begin{bmatrix} u_{00}V & u_{01}V \\ u_{10}V & u_{11}V \end{bmatrix} = \begin{bmatrix} u_{00}v_{00} & u_{00}v_{01} & u_{00}v_{02} & u_{01}v_{00} & u_{01}v_{01} & u_{01}v_{02} \\ u_{00}v_{10} & u_{00}v_{11} & u_{00}v_{12} & u_{01}v_{10} & u_{01}v_{11} & u_{01}v_{12} \\ u_{10}v_{00} & u_{10}v_{01} & u_{10}v_{02} & u_{11}v_{00} & u_{11}v_{01} & u_{11}v_{02} \\ u_{10}v_{10} & u_{10}v_{11} & u_{10}v_{12} & u_{11}v_{10} & u_{11}v_{11} & u_{11}v_{12} \end{bmatrix}. \tag{2.6}$$

Figure 1. Bloch spherical representation of quantum bits

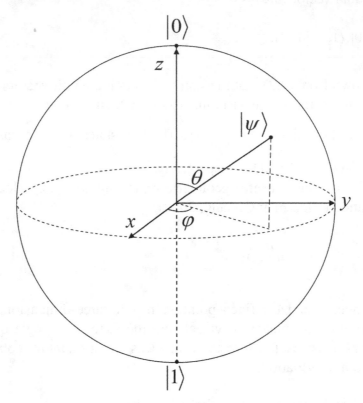

The tensor product of two states $|u\rangle \otimes |v\rangle$ is often abbreviated to $|uv\rangle$ or $|u,v\rangle$. For instance, for the basic states |0⟩ and |1⟩, their tensor product can be expressed as

$$|0\rangle \otimes |1\rangle = |0\rangle |1\rangle = |01\rangle = \begin{bmatrix} 1 \\ 0 \end{bmatrix} \otimes \begin{bmatrix} 0 \\ 1 \end{bmatrix} = \begin{bmatrix} 0 \\ 1 \\ 0 \\ 0 \end{bmatrix}. \tag{2.7}$$

For n times of the tensor product $U \otimes U \cdots \otimes U$ of the matrix U, it can be abbreviated as $U^{\otimes n}$ and be realized by Code B.2 in Appendix B. Similarly, $|u\rangle^{\otimes n}$ means the tensor product of |u⟩ with itself k times.

A double qubit can be synthesized by two single qubit tensor operations with four basis states $|00\rangle$, $|01\rangle$, $|10\rangle$, and $|11\rangle$. Therefore, a double qubit state can be described as

$$|\psi\rangle = a_{00}|00\rangle + a_{01}|01\rangle + a_{10}|10\rangle + a_{11}|11\rangle, \tag{2.8}$$

where results $|00\rangle$, $|01\rangle$, $|10\rangle$, and $|11\rangle$ occur with probabilities $|a_{00}|^2$, $|a_{01}|^2$, $|a_{10}|^2$, and $|a_{11}|^2$, respectively. The normalized condition

$$|a_{00}|^2 + |a_{01}|^2 + |a_{10}|^2 + |a_{11}|^2 = 1$$

is satisfied.

If a quantum system consists of n qubits, which have 2^n mutually orthogonal basis states $|i_1 i_2 \ldots i_n\rangle$, $i_1, i_2, \ldots, i_n \in \{0,1\}$, and the 2^n basis states are used to construct a 2^n dimensional Hilbert space. Therefore, a state in a quantum system can be expressed as

$$|\psi\rangle = \sum_{i=0}^{2^n-1} a_i|i\rangle, \tag{2.9}$$

where $i = i_1 i_2 \ldots i_n$ is the binary expansion of an integer i, and $\sum_{i=0}^{2^n-1}|a_i|^2 = 1$.

Linear Operators, Eigenvectors and Eigenvalues

Let U and V be vector spaces, for the function $A: U \rightarrow V$, if

$$A\sum_i a_i|u_i\rangle = \sum_i a_i A|u_i\rangle, \tag{2.10}$$

then, A is a linear operator between vector spaces U and V.

If $A|u\rangle = |u\rangle$ is true for all vectors $|u\rangle$, then A is called the identity operator, usually denoted by the symbol I.

An eigenvector of the linear operator A on the quantum state $|v\rangle$ is non-zero vector $|v\rangle$ such that $A|v\rangle = \lambda|v\rangle$, where λ is a complex number known as the eigenvalue of the operator A corresponding to the vector $|v\rangle$.

Inner Products and Outdoor Products

An inner product is a binary complex function on a vector space, which takes as input two vectors $|u\rangle$ and $|v\rangle$ from a vector space and produces a complex number as output. It shall be convenient to write the inner product as $\langle u|v\rangle$.

Suppose that $|u\rangle = \begin{bmatrix} u_1 & \cdots & u_n \end{bmatrix}^T$ and $|v\rangle = \begin{bmatrix} v_1 & \cdots & v_n \end{bmatrix}^T$, then, the matrix form of the inner product is

$$\langle u|v\rangle = \begin{bmatrix} u_1^* & \cdots & u_n^* \end{bmatrix} \begin{bmatrix} v_1 \\ \vdots \\ v_n \end{bmatrix}, \tag{2.11}$$

where the dual vector $\langle u| = \begin{bmatrix} u_1^* & \cdots & u_n^* \end{bmatrix}$ is the conjugate transpose vector of the vector $|u\rangle$.

Vectors $|u\rangle$ and $|v\rangle$ are orthogonal if their inner product is zero. The norm of a vector $|u\rangle$ is defined by $\||u\rangle\| = \sqrt{\langle u|u\rangle}$.

A unit vector is a vector $|u\rangle$ such that $\||u\rangle\| = 1$. If each vector is a unit vector, and distinct vectors in the set are orthogonal, that is, $\langle i|j\rangle = \delta_{ij}$, then the basis $|i\rangle$ ($i=0,1,\ldots,n-1$) is a standard orthogonal basis in an n-dimensional vector space.

Suppose that $|w\rangle$ and $|v\rangle$ are vectors in inner product spaces W and V, respectively, we define the outer product $|w\rangle\langle v|$ as a linear operator from V to W,

$$(|w\rangle\langle v|)(|u\rangle) = |w\rangle(\langle v|u\rangle) = \langle v|u\rangle|w\rangle, \tag{2.12}$$

where $|u\rangle$ is a vector in the inner product space V.

Hermite Operators

If the adjoint of a linear operator A is $A^\dagger = A$, where $A^\dagger = \left(A^*\right)^T$, the symbols $*$ and $(\ )^T$ indicate a complex conjugation operation and a transpose operation, respectively, then A is called as a Hermite operator.

An important class of Hermite operators is the projectors. Suppose that W is a k-dimensional vector subspace of the n-dimensional vector space V, and $|0\rangle,\ldots,|n-1\rangle$ is an orthogonal basis for V, hence the projector P onto the subspace W is defined as

$$P = \sum_{i=0}^{k-1}|i\rangle\langle i|, \tag{2.13}$$

where $|0\rangle,\ldots,|k-1\rangle$ is an orthogonal basis for W. The orthogonal complement of P is the operator $i(i=1,2,\ldots,n)$ which is the vector space spanned by $|k\rangle,\ldots,|n-1\rangle$.

Hermite operators have the following properties:

- The eigenvalues of Hermite operator are real numbers;
- The eigenstates are orthogonal corresponding to different eigenvalues;
- The eigenstates of Hermite operators span into a complete vector space.

Unitary Operators

If $AA^\dagger = A^\dagger A = I$, then the operator A is said to be unitary. A unitary operator is usually called unitary transformation or unitary operation, which is a very significant transformation and has the following properties:

- Unitary transformations remain the norm of the quantum state unchanged, that is, the normalized property of the quantum state does not change;
- Unitary transformations ensure that the logical operations in quantum computation are reversible, so quantum systems can solve the energy consumption problems in classical computation (Landauer, 1961);
- Unitary transforms do not change the inner product of the two states;
- Unitary transformations do not change eigenvalues of an operator;

7

- Unitary transformations do not change the algebraic relationship of operators.

Coherence and Decoherence

Coherence is closely related to the concept of superposition. A quantum system is said to be coherent if it is in a linear superposition of basis states. Coherence states in the quantum system are also called coherent superposition states. The realization of quantum parallelism essentially utilizes quantum coherence, then, the superiority of quantum computation disappears when it loses quantum coherence (Duan & Guo, 1998). When the quantum coherent system interacts with the environment in which it is located, causing quench energy dissipation or relative phase change, and finally degenerating from a coherent superposition state to a mixed state or a single state, this phenomenon is called decoherence or collapse.

Entanglement

Suppose that a quantum system is in one of a number of states $\left\{\left|\psi_i\right\rangle\right\}$ with respective probabilities $\left\{p_i\right\}$, then, the density operator for the system is defined by

$$\rho = \sum_i p_i \left|\psi_i\right\rangle\left\langle\psi_i\right|. \tag{2.14}$$

A quantum state in two subsystems cannot be written as a tensor product of quantum states in two subsystems, which is called a quantum entanglement state. It has important applications in quantum computation. For example, quantum entangled states can be used for quantum key distribution, quantum teleportation and quantum error correction codes (Yi & Han, 2013; Zhou & Guo, 2000).

In a two-particle quantum system, Bell states, also known as EPR states, refer to the following four entangled states,

$$
\left[
\begin{aligned}
|\beta_{00}\rangle &= \frac{1}{\sqrt{2}}\big(|00\rangle + |11\rangle\big), \\
|\beta_{01}\rangle &= \frac{1}{\sqrt{2}}\big(|01\rangle + |10\rangle\big), \\
|\beta_{10}\rangle &= \frac{1}{\sqrt{2}}\big(|00\rangle - |11\rangle\big), \\
|\beta_{11}\rangle &= \frac{1}{\sqrt{2}}\big(|01\rangle - |10\rangle\big),
\end{aligned}
\right.
\tag{2.15}
$$

In the three-particle quantum system, the most important entanglement state is the GHZ state,

$$
|GHZ\rangle = \frac{1}{\sqrt{2}}\big(|000\rangle + |111\rangle\big).
\tag{2.16}
$$

Both Bell states and the GHZ state are the largest entangled states (Vedral, Plenio, Rippin, & Knight, 1997), and there are some partially entangled quantum states, such as the following state (Zhou, 2007),

$$
|\psi\rangle = \frac{1}{\sqrt{3}}\big(|00\rangle + |01\rangle + |11\rangle\big).
\tag{2.17}
$$

The corresponding density operator can be expressed as

$$
\rho = |\psi\rangle\langle\psi| = \frac{1}{3}
\begin{bmatrix}
1 & 1 & 0 & 1 \\
1 & 1 & 0 & 1 \\
0 & 0 & 0 & 0 \\
1 & 1 & 0 & 1
\end{bmatrix},
\tag{2.18}
$$

which can be partially decomposed into

$$\rho = \frac{1}{\sqrt{3}} \left(\begin{bmatrix} 1 & 1 \\ 1 & 1 \end{bmatrix} \otimes \begin{bmatrix} 0 & 0 \\ 0 & 1 \end{bmatrix} \otimes \begin{bmatrix} 1 & 1 & 0 & 1 \\ 1 & 0 & 0 & 0 \\ 0 & 0 & 0 & 0 \\ 1 & 0 & 0 & 0 \end{bmatrix} \right). \tag{2.19}$$

BASIC POSTULATES OF QUANTUM MECHANICS

Basic postulates of quantum mechanics are put forward after a lot of experiments and failures, which are also the cornerstone of constructing the mathematical framework of quantum theory.

State Space Postulate

The first postulate of quantum mechanics is the state space postulate, which is described as follows.

Postulate 2.1. For any independent physical system, there is a Hilbert space associated with it, and this Hilbert space is called the system state space. Also, the physical system can be described by the unit vector of the Hilbert space (Nielsen & Chuang, 2000).

The postulate implies that the linear combination of state vectors is also a state vector, which is known as the principle of quantum state superposition (Dirac, 1947). In particular, any state vector $n=3$ can be represented by a superposition state which consists of a set of basis states $\{|e_i\rangle\}$, i.e.,

$$|\psi\rangle = \sum_i c_i |e_i\rangle. \tag{2.20}$$

where $|111\rangle$ is a complex number.

Evolutionary Postulate of Closed Quantum Systems

The second postulate of quantum mechanics is the evolutionary postulate of closed quantum systems, describing how the state of the system changes over time (Nielsen & Chuang, 2000).

Postulate 2.2 (Unitary operator description). The evolution of a closed quantum system is described by a unitary transformation. The state of the system at time t_2 is related to the state of the system at time t_1 by a unitary operator U, i.e.,

$$\left|\psi(t_2)\right\rangle = U\left|\psi(t_1)\right\rangle.$$ (2.21)

Quantum Measurement Postulate

The influence of a classical measurement on the measured object is negligible, but in quantum mechanics, quantum measurement is a counter-intuitive process. The influence on the measured object is generally not negligible because the measurement destroys the closure of the quantum system, that is, quantum systems no longer follow the evolutionary postulate. To describe the effects of measurements on quantum systems, quantum measurement postulate has been introduced (Nielsen & Chuang, 2000).

Postulate 2.3. A set of measurement operators $\{M_m\}$ is used to describe quantum measurements. These are operators acting on the state space of the system being measured. The obtained index m corresponds to different measurement results. The observations corresponding to the measurement results may be physically measurable such as position, energy, and momentum. Suppose that $|.\rangle$ is the quantum state to be measured, then

$$p(m) = \left\langle \psi \left| M_m^+ M_m \right| \psi \right\rangle,$$ (2.22)

which is the probability with the measurement result m. The state of the system after the measurement is

$$\frac{M_m\left|\psi\right\rangle}{\sqrt{\left\langle \psi \left| M_m^+ M_m \right| \psi \right\rangle}}.$$ (2.23)

The measurement operators satisfy the completeness condition, i.e., $\sum_m M_m^+ M_m = I$, which ensures the probability sum is 1:

$$\sum_m \left\langle \psi \left| M_m^+ M_m \right| \psi \right\rangle = \sum_m p(m) = 1.$$ (2.24)

The projective measurement is to measure the quantum state into an eigenvector space of the observable Hermite operator M (Deutsch, 1985). The observable has a spectral decomposition,

$$M = \sum_i m_i P_i , \qquad (2.25)$$

where $P_i = |i\rangle\langle i|$ is the projector onto the eigenspace of M with the eigenvalue m_i, $|i\rangle$ is the eigenvector corresponding to the eigenvalue m_i.

Assuming that $|\psi\rangle$ is the quantum state to be measured, the probability of the measurement m_i is given by

$$p(i) = \langle \psi | P_i | \psi \rangle , \qquad (2.26)$$

and the measured quantum state is

$$|\psi\rangle_{P_i} = \frac{P_i|\psi\rangle}{\sqrt{p(i)}} . \qquad (2.27)$$

$P_i^+ P_i = P_i$ and $\sum_i P_i = I$ hold, so projective measurements are a special case of Postulate 2.3. The projective measurement is actually equivalent to the general quantum measurement postulate (Nielsen & Chuang, 2000).

Since the projector of the projective measurement satisfies $P_i P_i = P_i$, i.e., $P_i P_i |\psi\rangle = P_i |\psi\rangle$. In other words, repeated measurements do not change the result of the measurement. This is the principle of consistency in measurement.

Let us consider an example of a single qubit projective measurement. Suppose that the observable measurement of the projective measurement is $M = -P_0 + P_1$, where the two measurement operators are $P_0 = |0\rangle\langle 0|$ and $P_1 = |1\rangle\langle 1|$, the eigenvalues of M are -1 and 1, and the corresponding eigenvectors are $|0\rangle$ and $|1\rangle$, respectively. Suppose that the quantum state to be measured is $|\psi\rangle = \alpha|0\rangle + \beta|1\rangle$, where $|\alpha|^2 + |\beta|^2 = 1$. Then, the probability with the measurement result -1 is $p(0) = \langle \psi | P_0 | \psi \rangle = |\alpha|^2$, the measured quantum state is $|0\rangle$, and the probability with the measurement result 1 is $p(1) = \langle \psi | P_1 | \psi \rangle = |\beta|^2$, the measured quantum state is $|1\rangle$.

The quantum measurement methods used in subsequent chapters of this book are mainly projective measurements.

Composite System Postulate

The fourth postulate of quantum mechanics is the composite system postulate, which describes how to construct a state space of a composite system from the state space of multiple systems (Nielsen & Chuang, 2000).

Postulate 2.4. The tensor product of the state space of multiple subsystems constitutes the state space of the composite system. If $|\psi_1\rangle, |\psi_2\rangle, ..., |\psi_n\rangle$ are state vectors for n subsystems, then

$$|\psi_T\rangle = |\psi_1\rangle \otimes |\psi_2\rangle \otimes \cdots \otimes |\psi_n\rangle$$

is the state vector of the composite system.

The postulate helps us understand the concept of entangled states: an entangled state cannot be written as a tensor product of the quantum states of the subsystem.

QUANTUM CIRCUITS AND QUANTUM GATES

The evolutionary postulate of quantum mechanics ensures the evolution of quantum systems is a reversible process. Therefore, different models of reversible quantum systems have been proposed, such as quantum Turing machine model (Benioff, 1982; Peres, 1985; Feynman, 1986), quantum circuit model (Deutsch, 1989; Lloyd, 1993), Cellular automata model (Liu, 2008). Quantum circuit model is more understandable than the other models, but the function is equivalent (Yao, 1993; Fredkin & Toffoli, 1982), so this book mainly introduces and studies quantum circuit models.

Quantum Circuits

A quantum circuit consisting of a set of quantum gates, which can approximate any unitary operation with arbitrary precision, then the set of quantum gates is universal. For example, three-qubit Toffoli gates and Fredkin gates (Sleator & Weinfurter, 1995) are universal gates. Toffoli gates and Fredkin gates can be implemented with some double-qubit logic gates (Chau & Wilczek, 1995;

DiVincenzo, 1995), i.e., a finite number of double-qubit logic gate is universal (Barenco et al., 1995). A more important class of universal gates are single qubit gates and controlled NOT gates (CNOT gates) (Boykin, Mor, Pulver, Roychowdhury, & Vatan, 1999), i.e., quantum gates can be composed of single qubit gates and CNOT gates. A specific example is Hadamard gates, phase gates,

$$|0\rangle \otimes |1\rangle = |0\rangle|1\rangle = |01\rangle = \begin{bmatrix} 1 \\ 0 \end{bmatrix} \otimes \begin{bmatrix} 0 \\ 1 \end{bmatrix} = \begin{bmatrix} 0 \\ 1 \\ 0 \\ 0 \end{bmatrix}$$

gates, and CNOT gates are universal (Nielsen & Chuang, 2000). This section describes single qubit gates, double qubit gates, and multiple qubit gates.

Single Qubit Gates

Qubit gates can be conveniently represented in matrix form, then, single qubit gates can be represented by a unitary matrix $U \otimes U \cdots \otimes U$

We refer to the U gate represented by the unitary matrix U. Its symbol is shown in Figure 2.

Figure 2. Symbolic representation of a single qubit U gate.

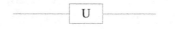

Apply the U gate to the quantum state $|\psi\rangle = \alpha|0\rangle + \beta|1\rangle$ to get

$$U|\psi\rangle = \left(\alpha u_{00} + \beta u_{01}\right)|0\rangle + \left(\alpha u_{10} + \beta u_{11}\right)|1\rangle. \tag{2.28}$$

A symbolic representation of a specific single qubit gate can be obtained by replacing the matrix U in Figure 2.2 with a specific matrix. The names, symbols and corresponding matrix representations of some single qubit gates are shown in Figure 2.3. The matrices corresponding to I, X, Y, Z and H gates in Figure 2.3 are both Hermite and unitary matrices, so their squares are equivalent to the unit matrix I, such as $X^2=I$, $H^2=I$. The quantum gates in Figure 2.3 satisfy the algebraic relationship: $H = (X + Z)/\sqrt{2}$, and $X = V_x^2$. Substituting the gate X into (2.28), we get

$$X|\psi\rangle = X(\alpha|0\rangle + \beta|1\rangle) = \beta|0\rangle + \alpha|1\rangle.$$

2-Qubit Gates

The most important gate of double qubits is the controlled-U gate, where U is an arbitrary unitary matrix of $|11\rangle$. It has two input qubits, known as the control qubit and the target qubit, respectively. When the control bit is 1 or 0, we name the controlled-U gate as $C_1^1(U)$ or $C_1^0(U)$ shown in Figure 4.

Figure 3. Some single qubit gates.

Gate	Symbol	Matrix
I		$\begin{bmatrix} 1 & 0 \\ 0 & 1 \end{bmatrix}$
Pauli-X(X)	X	$\begin{bmatrix} 0 & 1 \\ 1 & 0 \end{bmatrix}$
Pauli-Y(Y)	Y	$\begin{bmatrix} 0 & -i \\ i & 0 \end{bmatrix}$
Pauli-Z(Z)	Z	$\begin{bmatrix} 1 & 0 \\ 0 & -1 \end{bmatrix}$
Hadamard(H)	H	$\frac{1}{\sqrt{2}}\begin{bmatrix} 1 & 1 \\ 1 & -1 \end{bmatrix}$
V_x	V_x	$\frac{1}{2}\begin{bmatrix} 1-i & 1+i \\ 1+i & 1-i \end{bmatrix}$

Figure 4. Controlled U gates of double qubits.

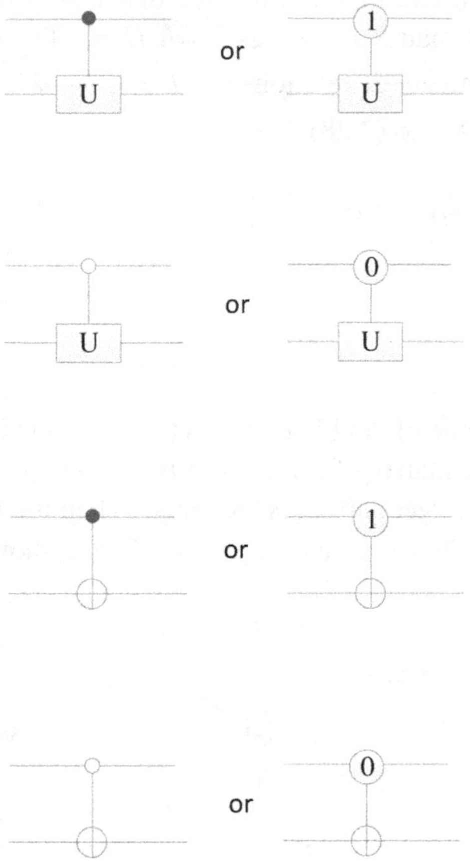

$C_1^1(U)$ or $\begin{bmatrix} 1 & 0 & 0 & 0 \\ 0 & 1 & 0 & 0 \\ 0 & 0 & u_{00} & u_{01} \\ 0 & 0 & u_{10} & u_{11} \end{bmatrix}$

$C_1^0(U)$ or $\begin{bmatrix} u_{00} & u_{01} & 0 & 0 \\ u_{10} & u_{11} & 0 & 0 \\ 0 & 0 & 1 & 0 \\ 0 & 0 & 0 & 1 \end{bmatrix}$

$C_1^1(X)$ or $\begin{bmatrix} 1 & 0 & 0 & 0 \\ 0 & 1 & 0 & 0 \\ 0 & 0 & 0 & 1 \\ 0 & 0 & 1 & 0 \end{bmatrix}$

$C_1^0(X)$ or $\begin{bmatrix} 0 & 1 & 0 & 0 \\ 1 & 0 & 0 & 0 \\ 0 & 0 & 1 & 0 \\ 0 & 0 & 0 & 1 \end{bmatrix}$

Applying $C_1^1(U)$ and $C_1^0(U)$ on the quantum states $|\phi\rangle = c|0\rangle + d|1\rangle$ and $|\psi\rangle = \alpha|0\rangle + \beta|1\rangle$, respectively, the results are

$$C_1^1(U)\left(|\phi\rangle|\psi\rangle\right) = c|0\rangle|\psi\rangle + d|1\rangle\left(U|\psi\rangle\right), \qquad (2.29)$$

and

$$C_1^0(U)\left(|\phi\rangle|\psi\rangle\right) = c|0\rangle\left(U|\psi\rangle\right) + d|1\rangle|\psi\rangle, \qquad (2.30)$$

where 2^n is shown in (2.28).

Let $U=X$, then the two gates $C_1^1(X)$ and $C_1^0(X)$ are called **CNOT** gates, which implement

$$C_1^1(X)\big(\big|\phi\big\rangle\big|\psi\big\rangle\big) = c\big|0\big\rangle\big|\psi\big\rangle + d\big|1\big\rangle\big(X\big|\psi\big\rangle\big)$$

and

$$C_1^0(X)\big(\big|\phi\big\rangle\big|\psi\big\rangle\big) = c\big|0\big\rangle\big(X\big|\psi\big\rangle\big) + d\big|1\big\rangle\big|\psi\big\rangle.$$

Swap gate is also a double qubit gate, the symbol of which is represented as shown in Figure 5.

Figure 5. Swap gate and its equivalent representation

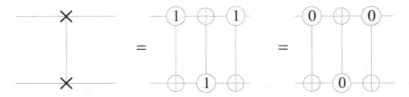

Applying Swap gate to the quantum state

$$\big|\phi\big\rangle\big|\psi\big\rangle = \big(c\big|0\big\rangle + d\big|1\big\rangle\big)\big(\alpha\big|0\big\rangle + \beta\big|1\big\rangle\big),$$

we obtain $Swap\big(\big|\phi\big\rangle\big|\psi\big\rangle\big) = \big|\psi\big\rangle\big|\phi\big\rangle.$

Multiple Qubit Gates

The evolution of a closed quantum system is described by a unitary transformation, therefore quantum operations can be simulated using unitary matrices. We describe that how to calculate the matrices of controlled gates.

Suppose that $|k\rangle$ is a basis state in a 2^n dimensional Hilbert space for $k = 0,1,\dots 2^n - 1$, the state $|k\rangle$ and its dual state $\langle k|$ are

$$A^{\dagger} = \left(A^{*}\right)^{T} \cdot \begin{cases} |k\rangle = |k_{n-1}\rangle \otimes |k_{n-2}\rangle \otimes \dots \otimes |k_0\rangle, \\ \langle k| = \langle k_{n-1}| \otimes \langle k_{n-2}| \otimes \dots \otimes \langle k_0|, \end{cases} \tag{2.31}$$

where $k = \sum_{j=1}^{n} k_j \times 2^j$, $k_1, k_2, \dots, k_n \in \{0,1\}$, and $\otimes$ is the symbol of tensor product. We often use the abbreviated notations $|k_n\rangle |k_{n-1}\rangle \cdots |k_1\rangle$ or $|k_n k_{n-1} \dots k_1\rangle$ for the tensor product $|k_n\rangle \otimes |k_{n-1}\rangle \otimes \dots \otimes |k_1\rangle$. The implementation code of $|k\rangle$ is seen in Code B.1.

Let U be a $2^m \times 2^m$ unitary matrix, two $(n+m)$-qubit controlled-U gates in Figure 2.6 (c) and (d) can be calculated by (see Code B.3 and Code B.4)

$$\begin{cases} V_n^i(U) = (U \otimes |i\rangle\langle i|) + \sum_{j=0, j \neq i}^{2^n - 1} (I^{\otimes m} \otimes (|j\rangle\langle j|)), \\ C_n^i(U) = (|i\rangle\langle i|) \otimes U + \sum_{j=0, j \neq i}^{2^n - 1} ((|j\rangle\langle j|) \otimes I^{\otimes m}). \end{cases} \tag{2.32}$$

Figure 6. Notations of controlled-U gates. (a) $V_1^1(U)$. (b) $V_1^0(U)$. (c) $V_n^t(U)$. (d) $C_n^t(U)$. In (a) and (b), the numbers 1 and 0 can be replaced by black and white points on control qubits. In (c) and (d), $t_n \dots t_2 t_1$ is the binary expansion of integer t, i.e., $t = \sum_{i=1}^{n} t_i \times 2^{i-1}$.

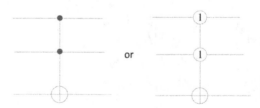

For instance, we obtain the matrices of the gates in Figure 6 (a) and (b) as follows,

$$V_1^1(X) = \begin{bmatrix} 1 & 0 & 0 & 0 \\ 0 & 0 & 0 & 1 \\ 0 & 0 & 1 & 0 \\ 0 & 1 & 0 & 0 \end{bmatrix}, Swap = \begin{bmatrix} 1 & 0 & 0 & 0 \\ 0 & 0 & 1 & 0 \\ 0 & 1 & 0 & 0 \\ 0 & 0 & 0 & 1 \end{bmatrix}. \tag{2.33}$$

When $n=3$, $U=X$ and $i_1=i_2=1$, the three-qubit controlled gate is the famous Toffoli gate shown in Figure 7.

Figure 7. Toffoli gate.

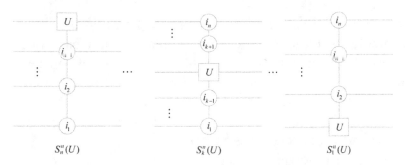

$$S_n^n(U) \qquad S_k^n(U) \qquad S_1^n(U)$$

These n-qubit controlled-U gates with the target qubit in the k-th ($k=$ $1,1,\ldots,n$) qubit, abbreviated as $S_k^n(U)$, are shown in Figure 8, where U is a single-qubit gate.

Figure 8. n-qubit controlled-U gate

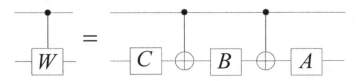

Applying the $S_k^n(U)$ gate to the quantum state $\left| j_n \cdots j_{k+1} j_k j_{k-1} \cdots j_1 \right\rangle$, we have

$$S_k^n(U)\left| j_n \cdots j_{k+1} j_k j_{k-1} \cdots j_1 \right\rangle = \left| j_n \cdots j_{k+1} \right\rangle (U^f \left| j_k \right\rangle)\left| j_{k-1} \cdots j_1 \right\rangle, \qquad (2.34)$$

where $U^0=I$, $U^1=U$. If

$$j_n \cdots j_{k+1} j_k j_{k-1} \cdots j_1 = i_n \cdots i_{k+1} i_k i_{k-1} \cdots i_1,$$

then $f=1$, otherwise $f=0$. For instance, suppose $n=3$, $i_1=i_3=1$, and $S_2^3(X)$ are applied to the quantum state $|111\rangle$, then $S_2^3(X)|111\rangle=|101\rangle$.

The Complexity of Quantum Gates

A basic operation is a single qubit gate or a CNOT gate. When a quantum gate is implemented by basic operations, the number of these basic operations is the complexity of the quantum gate. The complexities of some elementary gates have been given (Barenco, et al., 1995). We introduce some lemmas and corollaries as follows.

A special unitary group consists of 2×2 unitary matrices with unity determinant, which is denoted as SU(2).

We define the following matrices:

$$R_r(\theta) = \begin{bmatrix} \cos\theta/2 & \sin\theta/2 \\ -\sin\theta/2 & \cos\theta/2 \end{bmatrix}, R_z(\alpha) = \begin{bmatrix} e^{i\alpha/2} & 0 \\ 0 & e^{-i\alpha/2} \end{bmatrix}, \Phi(\delta) = \begin{bmatrix} e^{i\delta} & 0 \\ 0 & e^{i\delta} \end{bmatrix}, \sigma_x = \begin{bmatrix} 0 & 1 \\ 1 & 0 \end{bmatrix},$$

(2.35)

where α, θ, and δ are real valued, and $i = \sqrt{-1}$.

Lemma 2.5. Every 2×2 unitary matrix can be expressed as $\Phi(\delta)R_z(\alpha)R_r(\theta)R_z(\beta)$, where δ, α, θ, and β are real valued. Moreover, any element in the group SU(2) can be expressed as $R_z(\alpha)R_r(\theta)R_z(\beta)$.

Proof. Since a matrix is unitary if and only if its row vectors and column vectors are orthonormal, every 2×2 unitary matrix is of the form

$$\begin{bmatrix} e^{i(\delta+\alpha/2+i\beta/2)}\cos\theta/2 & e^{i(\delta+\alpha/2-i\beta/2)}\sin\theta/2 \\ -e^{i(\delta-\alpha/2+i\beta/2)}\sin\theta/2 & e^{i(\delta-\alpha/2-i\beta/2)}\cos\theta/2 \end{bmatrix},$$

(2.36)

where δ, α, θ, and β are real valued, and $i = \sqrt{-1}$. The first factorization above now follows immediately. Since any element in the group SU(2) is a 2×2 unitary matrix with unity determinant, the determinant of the matrix $\Phi(\delta)$ must be 1, which implies $e^{i\delta} = \pm1$. Thus, $\Phi(\delta)$ in the product $\Phi(\delta)R_z(\alpha)R_r(\theta)R_z(\beta)$ can be absorbed into the second one. **Lemma 2.6.** For any matrix W in SU(2), there exists matrices A, B, and C in SU(2) such as $ABC=I$, and $W = A\sigma_x B\sigma_x C$, where I is a 2×2 identity matrix.

Proof. By Lemma 2.5, there exit α, θ, and β such that $W = R_z(\alpha)R_r(\theta)R_z(\beta)$. Set

$$A = R_z(\alpha)R_r(\theta/2), \ B = R_r(-\theta/2)R_z[-(\alpha+\beta)/2], \text{ and } C = R_z[(\beta-\alpha)/2].$$

Then, we obtain $ABC=I$ and $W = A\sigma_x B\sigma_x C$. **Lemma 2.7.** For any matrix W in SU(2), a 2-qubit controlled-U gate, such as $C_1^1(U)$, can be simulated by a network in Figure 9.

Figure 9. The simulated network of the gate $C_1^1(W)$.

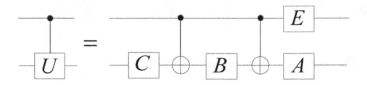

Proof. Let A, B, C be as in Lemma 2.6. Since quantum circuit is executed from left to right, when the value of the first (top) qubit bit is $|0\rangle$, then $ABC=I$ is applied to the second qubit. If the value of the first qubit is $|1\rangle$, then $A\sigma_x B\sigma_x C = W$ is applied to the second qubit.

Corollary 2.8. For any 2×2 unitary matrix U, a 2-qubit controlled-U gate, such as $C_1^1(W)$, can be simulated by at most six basic gates: four single qubit gates and two CNOT gates.

Proof. Let

$$E = \begin{bmatrix} 1 & 0 \\ 0 & e^{i\delta} \end{bmatrix}, \tag{2.37}$$

then, we have

$$E \otimes I = \begin{bmatrix} 1 & 0 & 0 & 0 \\ 0 & 1 & 0 & 0 \\ 0 & 0 & e^{i\delta} & 0 \\ 0 & 0 & 0 & e^{i\delta} \end{bmatrix} = C_1^1(\Phi(\delta)). \tag{2.38}$$

By Lemma 2.5, any 2×2 unitary matrix U can be expressed as $U = \Phi(\sigma)W$, where $W \in SU(2)$. Therefore, the gate $C_1^1(U)$ can be implemented by

$$C_1^1(U) = C_1^1(\Phi(\sigma)W) = C_1^1(\Phi(\sigma))C_1^1(W) = (E \otimes I)C_1^1(W). \tag{2.39}$$

Using Lemma 2.7, we obtain the network of the gate $C_1^1(U)$ shown in Figure 10.

Figure 10. The simulated network of the gate $C_1^1(U)$.

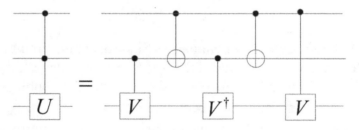

Clearly, the gate $C_1^1(U)$ can be simulated by at most six basic gates. **Lemma 2.9.** For any 2×2 unitary matrix U, a 3-qubit controlled-U gate, such as $C_2^3(U)$, can be simulated by a network in Figure 11.

Figure 11. The simulated network of the gate $C_2^3(U)$. Here, V is unitary.

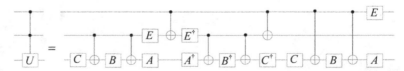

Proof. Let V be such that $V^2=U$. If the first qubit or the second qubit is $|0\rangle$, then the transformation applied to the third qubit is either I or $V^\dagger V = I$ where $V^\dagger$ denotes the conjugate transpose of V. If the first two qubits are both $|1\rangle$, then the transformation applied to the third qubit is $V^2=U$.

Corollary 2.10. For any 2×2 unitary matrix U, a 3-qubit controlled-U gate, such as $C_2^3(U)$, can be simulated by at most fourteen basic gates: eight single qubit gates and six CNOT gates.

Proof. We combine Lemma 2.9 with Corollary 2.8 to obtain a network of $C_2^3(U)$ shown in Figure 12.

Figure 12. The simulated network of the gate $C_2^3(U)$ with basic gates.

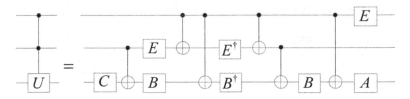

Since $A^\dagger A = I$ and $CC^\dagger = I$, the number of these gates in Figure 2.12 can reduce to 16. The following equation

Figure 13. The simplified network of the gate $C_2^3(U)$.

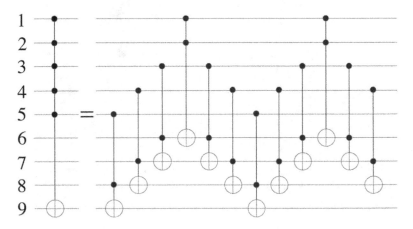

$$\Phi(\delta)\sigma_x = \begin{bmatrix} 0 & e^{i\delta} \\ e^{i\delta} & 0 \end{bmatrix} = \sigma_x \Phi(\delta) \tag{2.40}$$

shows that the two gates $C_1^1(\Phi(\delta))$ and CNOT are commutative, i.e., the $E \otimes I$ gate and the CNOT gate are commutative. The three consecutive CNOT gates in Figure 2.12 can be replaced by just two CNOT gates. The network in Figure 2.12 can be simplified to a new network shown in Figure 13.

Thus, the gate $C_2^3(U)$ can be simulated by at most fourteen basic gates. We adopt the notation $\Lambda_m(U)$ to denote an n-qubit controlled-U gate with m control qubits, where U is a 2×2 unitary matrix. we give two examples shown in Figure 2.14 and Figure 2.15 to illustrate Lemma 2.11 and Lemma 2.12, respectively.

Lemma 2.11. If $n \geq 5$ and $m \in \left\{ 3, 4, \ldots, \lceil n/2 \rceil \right\}$, where $\lceil n/2 \rceil$ rounds $n/2$ to the nearest integer more than or equal to itself, then a $\Lambda_m(\sigma_x)$ gate can be simulated by a network consisting of $4(m-2)$ Toffoli gates.

Figure 14. The network of $\Lambda_m(\sigma_x)$ gate with $n=9$ and $m=5$.

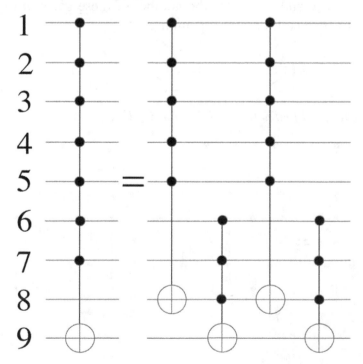

Figure 15. The network of $\Lambda_{n-2}(\sigma_x)$ *gate with n=9 and m=5.*

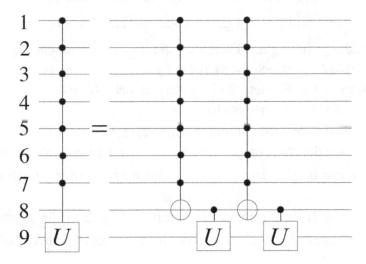

Lemma 2.12. For $n \geq 5$ and $m \in \{2,3,\ldots,n-3\}$, a $\Lambda_{n-2}(\sigma_x)$ can be simulated by two $\Lambda_m(\sigma_x)$ gates and two $\Lambda_{n-m-1}(\sigma_x)$ gates.

Corollary 2.13. When $n \geq 7$, a $\Lambda_{n-2}(\sigma_x)$ gate can be simulated by a network consisting of $8(n-5)$ Toffoli gates.

Figure 16. The simulated network of a $\Lambda_m(U)$ *gate illustrated for n=9 and m=8.*

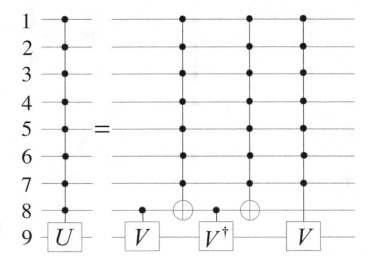

Proof. First apply Lemma 2.11 with $m_1 = \lceil n/2 \rceil$ and $m_2 = n - m_1 - 1$ to simulate $\Lambda_{m_1}(\sigma_x)$ and $\Lambda_{m_2}(\sigma_x)$ gates. Then combine these by Lemma 2.12 to simulate the $\Lambda_{n-2}(\sigma_x)$ gate. Therefore, the $\Lambda_{n-2}(\sigma_x)$ gate can be simulated by $8(m_1 - 2) + 8(m_2 - 2) = 8(n - 5)$ Toffoli gates.

Corollary 2.14. For any 2×2 unitary matrix U, when $m < n - 1$, the complexity of a $\Lambda_m(U)$ gate is $O(n)$.

Proof. When $m < n - 1$, combining Lemma 2.11, Lemma 2.12 with Corollary 2.13, we obtain that the complexity of a $\Lambda_m(\sigma_x)$ gate is $O(n)$. Meanwhile, a $\Lambda_m(U)$ gate can be simulated by an n-qubit network of the form in Figure 16.

Therefore, a $\Lambda_m(U)$ gate can be simulated by 2 $\Lambda_m(\sigma_x)$ gates and 2 controlled-U gates with 2 qubits. We conclude that the complexity of a $\Lambda_m(U)$ gate is $O(n)$.

Lemma 2.15. For any 2×2 unitary matrix U, a $\Lambda_{n-1}(\sigma_x)$ gate can be simulated by a network of the form in Figure 17.

Proof. The proof is very similar to that of Lemma 2.9, setting V so that $V^2 = U$.

Corollary 2.16. For any 2×2 unitary matrix U, the complexity of a $\Lambda_{n-1}(U)$ gate is $O(n^2)$.

Figure 17. The simulated network of a $\Lambda_{n-1}(\sigma_x)$ gate illustrated for n=9. Here, V is unitary.

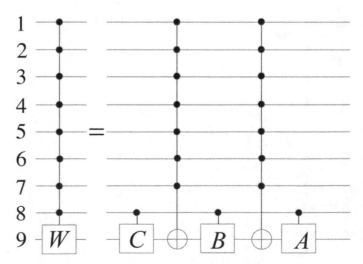

Proof. This is a recursive application of Lemma 2.15. Let C_{n-1} denote the complexity of simulating a $\Lambda_{n-1}(U)$ gate. Consider the simulation in Lemma 2.15. The complexity of simulating the 2-quit controlled-V and controlled-$V^{\dagger}$ gates is $O(1)$ by Corollary 2.8. The complexity of simulating the two $\Lambda_{n-2}(\sigma_x)$ gates is $O(n)$ by Corollary 2.13. The complexity of simulating the $\Lambda_{n-2}(U)$ gates is C_{n-2} by a recursive application of Lemma 2.14. Therefore, C_{n-1} satisfies

$$C_{n-1} = C_{n-2} + O(n), \tag{2.41}$$

which implies that $C_{n-1} = O(n^2)$.

Lemma 2.17. For any matrix W in SU(2), a $\Lambda_{n-1}(W)$ gate can be simulated by a network of the form in Figure 18.

Figure 18. The simulated network of a $\Lambda_{n-1}(W)$ gate illustrated for n=9. Here, $A, B, C \in$ SU(2).

Proof. The proof is very similar to that of Lemma 2.7, referring to Lemma 2.6.

Corollary 2.18. For any matrix W in SU(2), the complexity of a $\Lambda_{n-1}(W)$ gate is $O(n)$.

Proof. Consider the simulation in Lemma 2.17. The complexity of simulating the three gates $C_1^1(A)$, $C_1^1(B)$ and $C_1^1(C)$ is $O(1)$ by Corollary 2.8. The complexity of simulating the two $\Lambda_{n-2}(\sigma_x)$ gates is $O(n)$ by Corollary 2.13. Therefore, the complexity of a $\Lambda_{n-1}(W)$ gate is $O(n)$.

CONCLUSION

To make it easy for readers to understand the subsequent image processing algorithms in this book, this chapter described the basic concepts and principles of quantum computation, which include qubit, tensor products, linear operators, inner products, outer products, Hermite operators, unitary operators, coherence and decoherence, entanglement, four basic postulates of quantum mechanics, quantum circuits and quantum gates. In addition, the complexity of quantum gates has been introduced.

REFERENCES

Barenco, A., Bennett, C. H., Cleve, R., DiVincenzo, D. P., Margolus, N., Shor, P., Sleator, T., Smolin, J. A., & Weinfurter, H. (1995). Elementary gates for quantum computation. *Physical Review A.*, *52*(5), 3457–3467. doi:10.1103/PhysRevA.52.3457 PMID:9912645

Benioff, P. (1982). Quantum mechanical Hamiltonian models of Turing machines. *Journal of Statistical Physics*, *29*(3), 515–546. doi:10.1007/BF01342185

Boykin, P. O., Mor, T., Pulver, M., Roychowdhury, V., & Vatan, F. (1999). *On universal and fault-tolerant quantum computing.* arXiv preprint quant-ph/9906054

Chau, H. F., & Wilczek, F. (1995). Simple Realization of the Fredkin Gate using a Series Of Two-Body Operators. *Physical Review Letters*, *75*(4), 748–750. doi:10.1103/PhysRevLett.75.748 PMID:10060104

Cong, S. (2006). *Introduction to Quantum Mechanical System Control.* Science Press.

Deutsch, D. (1985). Quantum theory, the Church-Turing principle and the universal quantum computer. *Proceedings of the Royal Society of London A: Mathematical, Physical and Engineering Sciences, 400*(1818), 97-117.

Deutsch, D. (1989). Quantum computational networks. *Proceedings of the Royal Society of London A: Mathematical, Physical and Engineering Sciences, 425*(1868), 73-90.

Dirac, P. A. M. (1947). *The Principles of Quantum Mechanics.* Oxford University Press.

DiVincenzo, D. P. (1995). Two-bit gates are universal for quantum computation. *Physical Review A.*, *51*(2), 1015–1022. doi:10.1103/PhysRevA.51.1015 PMID:9911679

Duan, L. M., & Guo, G. S. (1998). Lecture on Quantum Information: Quantum Computers. *Physics (China)*, *27*(1), 53–58.

Feynman, R. P. (1986). Quantum mechanical computers. *Foundations of Physics*, *16*(6), 507–531. doi:10.1007/BF01886518

Fredkin, E., & Toffoli, T. (1982). Conservative Logic. *International Journal of Theoretical Physics*, *21*(3), 219–253. doi:10.1007/BF01857727

Landauer, R. (1961). Irreversibility and heat generation in the computing process. *IBM Journal of Research and Development*, *5*(3), 183–191. doi:10.1147/rd.53.0183

Liu, Y. (2008). *Database processing in quantum computers*. Tsinghua University.

Lloyd, S. (1993). A potentially realizable quantum computer. *Science*, *261*(5128), 1569–1571. doi:10.1126cience.261.5128.1569 PMID:17798117

Long, G. L., Pei, S. Y., & Zeng, J. Y. (2007). *Recent Progress in Quantum Mechanics* (4th ed.). Tsinghua University Press.

Nielsen, M. A., & Chuang, I. L. (2000). *Quantum Computation and Quantum Information*. Cambridge University Press.

Peres, A. (1985). Reversible logic and quantum computers. *Physical review A*, *32*(6), 3266–3276. doi:10.1103/PhysRevA.32.3266 PMID:9896493

Rudin, W. (1999). *Real and complex analysis* (3rd ed.). McGraw-Hill Book Company.

Schumacher, B. (1995). Quantum coding. *Physical Review A.*, *51*(4), 2738–2747. doi:10.1103/PhysRevA.51.2738 PMID:9911903

Sleator, T., & Weinfurter, H. (1995). Realizable universal quantum logic gates. *Physical Review Letters*, *74*(20), 4087–4090. doi:10.1103/PhysRevLett.74.4087 PMID:10058409

Vedral, V., Plenio, M. B., Rippin, M. A., & Knight, P. L. (1997). Quantifying entanglement. *Physical Review Letters*, *78*(12), 2275–2279. doi:10.1103/PhysRevLett.78.2275

Venegas-Andraca, S. E. (2005). Discrete *Quantum Walks and Quantum image processing* (Unpublished doctoral dissertation). Oxford University, Oxford, UK.

Yao, A. C. (1993). Quantum circuit complexity. *34th Annual Symposium on Foundations of Computer Science*, 352-361.

Yi, H., & Han, Y. (2013). *Principle and Technology of Quantum Communication*. Publishing House of Electronics Industry.

Zhou, R. G. (2007). *Research of Quantum Neural Network* (Doctoral dissertation). Nanjing, China: Nanjing University of Aeronautics and Astronautics.

Zhou, Z. W., & Guo, G. S. (2000). Lecture on Quantum Information: Quantum entanglement. *Physics (China)*, *29*(11), 695–699.

Chapter 2
The Storage and Retrieval Technologies of Quantum Images

ABSTRACT

Quantum image processing represents an emerging image processing technology by taking advantage of quantum computation. Quantum image processing faces the first question: How is an image stored in and retrieved from a quantum system? To solve the issue, the authors provide six quantum image representations, which can be divided into three categories. The first, second, and third categories store color information using amplitudes, phases, and basis states, respectively. Next, they design their circuits to implement the storage of quantum image. Then, retrieval methods are introduced. The storage and retrieval technologies of quantum image are the basis and premise condition to process quantum images.

INTRODUCTION

Quantum image representation (QIR) is a stored pattern by which images are stored in a quantum system. Compared with classical image representations (Cohen & Weiss, 2012), quantum image representation has displayed the enormous storage capacity (Le, Dong, & Hirota, 2011; Li, Zhu, Zhou, Li, Song, & Ian, 2014).

DOI: 10.4018/978-1-7998-3799-2.ch002

The amplitudes or phases of a quantum state were used to store information (Long, & Sun, 2001). For the convenience to retrieve accurately images, basis states were used to store information (Zhang, Lu, Gao, & Wang, 2013). Therefore, quantum image representations are classified into three categories. The first, second, and third categories store color information using amplitudes, phases, and basis states, respectively (Li, Song, Fan, Peng, Xia, & Liang, 2019).

The first category of QIRs includes: Qubit Lattice (Venegas-Andraca & Bose, 2003, 2010), flexible representation of quantum images (Le, Dong, & Hirota, 2011), quantum states for M colors and quantum states for N coordinates (Li, Zhu, Song, Shen, Zhou & Mo, 2013), multi-channel representation for quantum images (Sun, Iliyasu, Yan, Dong, & Hirota, 2013), the model of a normal arbitrary superposition state (Li, Zhu, Zhou, Li, Song, & Ian, 2014), a simple quantum representation of infrared images (Yuan, Mao, Xue, Chen, Xiong, & Compare, 2014), the model of a normal arbitrary quantum superposition state (Li, Zhu, Zhou, Song, & Yang, 2014), the model of a normal arbitrary superposition state with three components (Li, Zhu, Zhou, Li, Song, & Ian, 2014).

The second category of QIRs has a flexible quantum representation for gray-level images (Yang, Xia, Jia, & Zhang, 2013), and a normal arbitrary superposition state with relative phases (Li, Zhu, Zhou, Li, Song, & Ian, 2014).

The third category of QIRs includes: a novel enhanced quantum representation (NEQR) (Zhang, Lu, Gao, & Wang, 2013), quantum image representation for log-polar images (Zhang, Lu, Gao, & Xu, 2013), Improved NEQR (Sang, Wang, & Niu, 2016), a flexible representation of quantum audio (Yan, Iliyasu, & Guo, 2018), quantum image representation based on bitplanes (Li, Chen, Xia, Liang, & Zhou, 2018), generalized NEQR (GNEQR) (Li, Fan, Xia, Peng, & Song, 2019), quantum representation of real-valued digital signals and quantum representation of complex-valued digital signals (Li, Fan, Xia, Peng, & Song, 2019).

This chapter discusses the storage and retrieval technologies of quantum images by using some typical examples of QIRs of three categories.

QUBIT LATTICE

As the first of quantum image representation, Qubit Lattice stores a

$$\rho = |\psi\rangle\langle\psi| = \frac{1}{3}\begin{bmatrix} 1 & 1 & 0 & 1 \\ 1 & 1 & 0 & 1 \\ 0 & 0 & 0 & 0 \\ 1 & 1 & 0 & 1 \end{bmatrix},$$

color image in quantum systems with

$$\rho = \frac{1}{\sqrt{3}}\left(\begin{bmatrix} 1 & 1 \\ 1 & 1 \end{bmatrix} \otimes \begin{bmatrix} 0 & 0 \\ 0 & 1 \end{bmatrix} \otimes \begin{bmatrix} 1 & 1 & 0 & 1 \\ 1 & 0 & 0 & 0 \\ 0 & 0 & 0 & 0 \\ 1 & 0 & 0 & 0 \end{bmatrix}\right).$$

qubits (Venegas-Andraca & Bose, 2003, 2010). Qubit Lattice uses frequency of the physical nature of color to represent a color instead of the RGB model other HIS model, so a color could be represented by only a 1-qubit quantum state, i.e.,

$$|q\rangle = \cos(\frac{\theta}{2})|0\rangle + e^{i\gamma}\sin(\frac{\theta}{2})|1\rangle, \tag{3.1}$$

where γ is a constant, and the real number $\theta \in [0,\pi]$ represents a color.

An $n_1 \times n_2$ image is stored in a qubit lattice Q,

$$Q = \{|q\rangle_{i,j}\}, i \in \{1,2,...,n_1\}, j \in \{1,2,...,n_2\}. \tag{3.2}$$

A set of qubit lattices Z is defined as

$$Z = \{Q_k\}, k \in \{1,2,...,n_3\}. \tag{3.3}$$

Each lattice $Q_k \in Z$ will be used to store a copy of the image so that, Z will be a set of n_3 lattices all of which have been prepared identically.

Qubit Lattice uses the frequency of the wave's physical properties to represent color, therefore, the method can store a color in a single qubit state without worrying about the color quality requirements, which are difficult to be achieved in classical computers. In a classic computer, the only way to make an image's color more realistic is to use more bits to store a color. However, this method is only suitable for the monochromatic wave, and cannot deal with many mixed colors in the nature.

THE MODEL OF QUANTUM STATES FOR M COLORS AND QUANTUM STATES FOR N COORDINATES

The image storage algorithm presented in (Venegas-Andraca & Bose, 2003) was extended into a set of quantum states for M colors (QSMC) and a set of quantum states for N coordinates (QSNC) (Li, Zhu, Song, Shen, Zhou & Mo, 2013). In this section, the model of QSMC and QSNC is used to describe single qubit quantum state image representation, storage and retrieval.

The Representation of Colors and Coordinates

The procedure of creating QSMC is explained in Algorithm 3.1. A quantum rotation gate $R_y(\theta)$ is defined as

$$R_y(\theta) = \begin{bmatrix} \cos\theta & -\sin\theta \\ \sin\theta & \cos\theta \end{bmatrix},$$

(3.4)

where $\theta \in [0,\pi]$. Applying the rotation gate on $|0\rangle$, we obtain

$$R_y(\theta)|0\rangle = \cos\theta|0\rangle + \sin\theta|1\rangle.$$

Algorithm 3.1 A set of quantum states for M colors (QSMC)

Step 1. Sort M different colors to create a color set

$Color = \{color_1, color_2, \cdots, color_M\}.$

Step 2. Define an ordered set of angles A_ϕ as

$$A_\phi = \{\phi_1, \phi_2, \cdots, \phi_M\}, \phi_i = \frac{\pi(i-1)}{2(M-1)},$$

(3.5)

where $i=1,2,...,M$.

Step 3. Define a bijective function F_1 from a color set to an angle set,

$$F_1 : Color \leftrightarrow A_\phi,$$ (3.6)

where $F_1(color_i) = \phi_i$, and $F_1^{-1}(\phi_i) = color_i$.

Step 4. Create M quantum states $|v_1\rangle, |v_2\rangle, \cdots, |v_M\rangle$, where

$$|v_i\rangle = \cos\alpha_i |0\rangle + \sin\alpha_i |1\rangle, \ \alpha_i \in A_\phi, \ i=1,2,...,M.$$

Specifically, the quantum state $|v_i\rangle$ is created by applying the rotation operator $R_y(2\alpha_i)$ on $|0\rangle$.

Algorithm 3.1 (QSMC) is suitable for binary images, grayscale images and color images. For binary images, $M=2$, the color set is $Color=\{color_1,color_2\}$, where $color_1$ and $color_2$ are white and black, respectively. Elements of the ordered set of angles $A_\phi = \{\phi_1,\phi_2\}$ are defined as $\phi_1=0$, $\phi_2=\pi/2$.

For grayscale images, $M=256$, colors are sorted in ascending order by the gray values, i.e.,

$$Color = \{color_1, color_2, \cdots, color_{256}\},$$

where $color_i(i=1,2,...,256)$ is a color with gray value $i-1$. Elements of the ordered set of angles $A_\phi = \{\phi_1,\phi_2,\cdots,\phi_{256}\}$ are calculated by $\phi_i = \pi(i-1)/(2\times255)$.

For RGB color images, $M=2^{24}$, let x,y,z be the gray values of the three components of the color $color_i$, respectively, we define

$$i = 256 \times 256 \times x + 256 \times y + z + 1,$$ (3.7)

and obtain the ordered color set

$$Color = \{color_1, color_2, \cdots, color_{2^{24}}\}.$$

For instance $color_1$ and $color_{2^{24}}$ are the RGB colors (0,0,0) and (255,255,255). Using (3.5), we obtain the angle ϕ_i for $color_i$,

$$\phi_i = \frac{\pi(i-1)}{2\times(2^{24}-1)}.$$ (3.8)

Similarly with Algorithm 3.1, we design the algorithm QSNC to store N coordinates.

Algorithm 3.2 A set of quantum states for N coordinates (QSNC)

Step 1. Define an ordered coordinate set

$$Coordinate = \{coo_1, coo_2, \cdots, coo_N\}$$

for an $n_1 \times n_2$ image, where $N = n_1 \times n_2$, and coo_i corresponds to the coordinate (x,y) with $i = n_2(x-1)+y$.

Step 2. Define a bijection function from a coordinate to an angle F_2: $Coordinate \leftrightarrow A_\gamma$, where

$$A_\gamma = \{\gamma_1, \gamma_2, \cdots, \gamma_N\}, \gamma_i = \pi(i-1)\big/2(N-1), i \in \{1,2,\ldots,N\}.$$

Step 3. Create N quantum states $|u_1\rangle, |u_2\rangle, \cdots, |u_N\rangle$, where

$$|u_i\rangle = \cos\theta_i |0\rangle + \sin\theta_i |1\rangle,$$

and $\theta_i \in A_\gamma$, Specifically, the quantum state $|u_i\rangle$ is created by applying the rotation operator $R_y(2\theta_i)$ on $|0\rangle$.

We explain Algorithm 3.2 (QSNC) with a 3×3 image in Figure 2 as an example. Quantum state $|u_1\rangle = \cos\theta_1 |0\rangle + \sin\theta_1 |1\rangle$ represents coo_1 which is the coordinate of the first pixel in the image, namely, $coo_1=(,1,)$. Quantum state $|u_9\rangle = \cos\theta_9 |0\rangle + \sin\theta_9 |1\rangle$ represents coo_9 which is the coordinate of the ninth pixel in the image, namely, $coo_9(3,3)$.

Figure 1. Representation of pixel coordinates in a 3×3 image

	1	2	3
1	$coo_1 = (1,1)$	$coo_2 = (1,2)$	$coo_3 = (1,3)$
2	$coo_4 = (2,1)$	$coo_5 = (2,2)$	$coo_6 = (2,3)$
3	$coo_7 = (3,1)$	$coo_8 = (3,2)$	$coo_9 = (3,3)$

y

x

Storing an Image in a Quantum System

Using Algorithms 3.1 and 3.2, we store a pixel in the following state,

$$|\psi_i\rangle = |v_i\rangle|u_i\rangle, \tag{3.9}$$

where $|v_i\rangle$ and $|u_i\rangle$ represent the color and coordinate of the *i*-th pixel.

Thus an image with *N* pixels can store in the set $Q = \{|\psi_1\rangle, |\psi_2\rangle, ..., |\psi_N\rangle\}$. Compared with Qubit Lattice, this method requires the storage of coordinate information. However, it is convenient for only storing few pixels in an image. For instance, we can use $Q = \{|\psi_1\rangle, |\psi_5\rangle, |\psi_9\rangle\}$ to store the first, fifth, and ninth pixel of the image in Figure 1.

Because measurement makes a superposition state collapse into a basis state, many identical states are necessary, which store copies of the same image. In order to reduce the number of the identical quantum states for retrieving an image, Algorithm 3.3 is designed to store an image in a quantum system by modifying the image storage algorithm in the reference (Li, Zhu, Song, Shen, Zhou & Mo, 2013).

A bijective function F_3 is defined as

$$F_3 : Number \leftrightarrow A_\eta, \tag{3.10}$$

where *Number*=$\{1,2,...,\lambda\}$ is an integer set, and $A_\eta = \{\eta_1, \eta_2, \cdots, \eta_\lambda\}$ is an angle set with $\eta_i = \pi(i-1)/2(\lambda-1)$, $i\in\{1,2,...,\lambda\}$. if $\lambda=1$, let $\eta_1=0$.

Algorithm 3.3 Storing a $n_1 \times n_2$ image in a quantum system

Step 1. Suppose that λ is the number of different colors of an image, we store the *m* different colors in a quantum queue Q_1 using Algorithm 3.1.

Step 2. Apply the rotation $R_y(2\beta_i)$, $(i=1,2,...,\lambda)$ on $|0\rangle$ to create successively λ quantum states $|w_1\rangle, |w_2\rangle, \cdots |w_\lambda\rangle$, where $|w_i\rangle = \cos\beta_i |0\rangle + \sin\beta_i |1\rangle$ stores an integer *i*, and $\beta_i \in A_\eta$ in (3.10).

Step 3. Assume that the color of the pixel in the coordinate (x,y) is stored in the *jth* position of Q_1, we store $|\varphi_i\rangle = |w_j\rangle$ in another quantum queue Q_2, where $i= n_2(x-1)+y$. Let $N=n_1 \times n_2$, thus $Q_2 = \left\{ |\varphi_1\rangle, |\varphi_2\rangle, ..., |\varphi_N\rangle \right\}$ and Q_1 store the image of *N* pixels.

We explain Algorithm 3.3 by using a 3×3 image shown in Figure 2 as an example. There are only two colors (green and red), therefore, $\lambda=2$. Suppose $|v_j\rangle$ and $|v_k\rangle$ store the two color by using Algorithm 3.1, and the positions of which in Q_1 are $|w_1\rangle$ and $|w_2\rangle$, respectively, we obtain that $|w_1\rangle = |0\rangle$ and $|w_2\rangle = |1\rangle$. Meanwhile, we obtain that $|\varphi_i\rangle = |0\rangle$, $i \in \{1,5,7,8\}$, and $|\varphi_j\rangle = |1\rangle$, $j \in \{2,3,4,6,9\}$. Because the quantum states in Q_2 are some basis states in this case, a quantum state in Q_2 is retrieved by a single measurement.

Figure 2. The storage of a 3x3 image

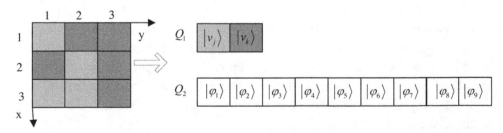

Algorithm 3.3 shows that a 24-bit RGB color image with *N* pixels is stored in a quantum system with $N+m$ qubits, and stores an image with 2^n pixels

and λ different colors in a quantum system by using $(2^n+\lambda)$ 1-qubit gates. For an image of 2^n pixels, $\lambda \leq 2^n$, so the complexity of Algorithm 3.3 is $O(2^n)$.

Retrieving an Image from a Quantum System

The involved basic probability theory in this section is shown in Appendix A. We define an observable operator on projection measurement

$$P = \sum_{i=1}^{2} m_i P_i,$$

(3.11)

where $P_1 = |0\rangle\langle 0|, P_2 = |1\rangle\langle 1|, m_1 = +1, m_2 = -1$. We retrieve the image in quantum queues Q_1 and Q_2 using the observable operator P. For example, we describe how to retrieve colors form $\cos\phi_j |0\rangle + \sin\phi_j |1\rangle$ in quantum queue Q_1 in Figure 2.

Result is +1 with probability

$$p(+1) = \cos^2 \phi_j,$$

(3.12)

then, we calculate

$$\phi_j = \arccos(\sqrt{p(+1)}).$$

(3.13)

Result is -1 with probability

$$p(-1) = \sin^2 \phi_j,$$

(3.14)

thus, we obtain

$$\phi_j = \arcsin(\sqrt{p(-1)}).$$

(3.15)

The number of measurements is finite, so the statistical results for the probability of +1 or -1 are only estimates of the probability. Suppose that the numbers of +1 and -1 are n_1 and n_2 in n measurements, respectively, so

$\hat{p}(+1) = n_1/n$ is the estimate of $p(+1)$, and $\hat{p}(-1) = n_2/n$ is the estimate of $p(-1)$.

Substituting $\hat{p}(+1)$ for $p(+1)$ in (3.13) to get

$$\hat{\phi}_j = \arccos(\sqrt{\hat{p}(+1)})\,. \tag{3.16}$$

Similarly, we obtain

$$\hat{\phi}_j = \arccos(\sqrt{\hat{p}(+1)})\,. \tag{3.17}$$

We calculate $\hat{\phi}_j$ using (3.16) or (3.17). Assuming that a quantum state is measured successfully with the probability of $1-\alpha$ with n_{max} measurements at most, now, we describe how to get the value of n_{max}.

Let us define

$$X = \begin{cases} 0, \text{result of measurment is} +1, \\ 1, \text{result of measurment is} -1. \end{cases} \tag{3.18}$$

Results of measurements are only divided into two categories (+1 and -1), so X is either 1 or 0. Thus X is a Bernoulli random variable. The probability mass function of the random variable X is given by

$$\begin{cases} p(0) = P\{X = 0\} = 1 - p, \\ p(1) = P\{X = 1\} = p, \end{cases} \tag{3.19}$$

where $p = p(-1) = \sin^2 \phi_j$. The expectation μ and variance σ of X are $\mu = p$ and $\sigma^2 = p(1 - p)$, respectively.

Suppose that $X_1, X_2, \ldots, X_n$ are n samples of X and n is sufficiently large, then

$$\frac{\sum\limits_{i=1}^{n} X_i - np}{\sqrt{np(1 - p)}} = \frac{n\bar{X} - np}{\sqrt{np(1 - p)}} \tag{3.20}$$

has approximately a standard normal distribution by the Central Limit Theorem. Thus, we have

$$P\left\{\left|\frac{n\bar{X}-np}{\sqrt{np(1-p)}}\right|<Z_{\alpha/2}^2\right\}\approx 1-\alpha,\tag{3.21}$$

where $1-\alpha$ is a confidence level (the value of $Z_{\alpha/2}$ can be found in standard normal distribution look-up tables: e.g., when $1-\alpha=0.95$, we can obtain $Z_{\alpha/2}=1.96$).

Solving the inequality

$$\left|\frac{n\bar{X}-np}{\sqrt{np(1-p)}}\right|<Z_{\alpha/2}^2,\tag{3.22}$$

we obtain that the confidence interval of p is $[p_{min},p_{max}]$ with approximate confidence level $1-\alpha$. p_{min} and p_{max} are expressed as follows,

$$p_{min}=\frac{2n\bar{X}+m-\sqrt{(2n\bar{X}+m)^2-4(n+m)n\bar{X}^2}}{2n+2m},\tag{3.23}$$

and

$$p_{max}=\frac{2n\bar{X}+m+\sqrt{(2n\bar{X}+m)^2-4(n+m)n\bar{X}^2}}{2n+2m},\tag{3.24}$$

where $m=Z_{\alpha/2}^2$.

Let

$$\hat{p}_{min}=p_{min}-\left(m\sqrt{p(1-p)}/\sqrt{n}\right)$$

and

$$\hat{p}_{\max} = p_{\max} + \left(m\sqrt{p(1-p)} \middle/ \sqrt{n}\right),$$

we have

$$p \in \left[p_{\min}, p_{\max}\right] \subset \left[\hat{p}_{\min}, \hat{p}_{\max}\right]. \tag{3.25}$$

From (3.22), we obtain

$$\bar{X} \in \left[\hat{p}_{\min}, \hat{p}_{\max}\right]. \tag{3.26}$$

Set $\Delta p = \hat{p}_{\max} - \hat{p}_{\min}$, and calculate

$$\Delta p = \frac{\sqrt{4nm\bar{X} - 4nm\bar{X}^2 + m^2}}{n+m} + \frac{2m\sqrt{p(1-p)}}{\sqrt{n}}. \tag{3.27}$$

We define

$$\begin{cases} \theta_{\max} = \arcsin\sqrt{\hat{p}_{\max}}, \\ \theta_{\min} = \arcsin\sqrt{\hat{p}_{\min}}, \end{cases} \tag{3.28}$$

and obtain

$$\sin(\Delta\theta) = \sqrt{\hat{p}_{\max}(1-\hat{p}_{\min})} - \sqrt{\hat{p}_{\min}(1-\hat{p}_{\max})} \leq \sqrt{\hat{p}_{\max}(1-\hat{p}_{\min}) - \hat{p}_{\min}(1-\hat{p}_{\max})} = \sqrt{\Delta p},$$
$$\tag{3.29}$$

where $\Delta\theta = \theta_{\max} - \theta_{\min}$. Since $\hat{p}(-1) = \bar{X}$ and $p(-1)=p$, i.e.,

$$\hat{\phi}_j = \arcsin\sqrt{\hat{p}(-1)} = \arcsin\sqrt{\bar{X}}$$

and

$$\phi_j = \arcsin \sqrt{p(-1)} = \arcsin \sqrt{p} \,,$$

we conclude

$$\begin{cases} \phi_j \in \left[\theta_{\min}, \theta_{\max}\right], \\ \hat{\phi}_j \in \left[\theta_{\min}, \theta_{\max}\right], \end{cases} \tag{3.30}$$

and

$$\left| \phi_j - \hat{\phi}_j \right| \leq \Delta\theta \,. \tag{3.31}$$

According to Algorithm 2.1, we have

$$\Delta\phi = \left| \phi_{i+1} - \phi_i \right| = \frac{\pi}{2(M-1)} \,. \tag{3.32}$$

where $i \in \{1,2,\ldots(M-1)\}$ and $M=2^{24}$.
   Suppose

$$\sqrt{\Delta p} < \sin(\Delta\phi) \,, \tag{3.33}$$

from (3.22), we obtain

$$\Delta\theta < \Delta\phi \,. \tag{3.34}$$

When $\phi_j \leq \theta_{\max} \leq \phi_{j+1}$ and $\Delta\theta = \theta_{\max} - \theta_{\min} < \Delta\phi$, we conclude that $\phi_{j-1} \leq \theta_{\min} \leq \phi_j$. Thus $\Delta\theta$, $\Delta\phi$, $\phi_j, \hat{\phi}_j$ $\theta_{\min}$ and $\theta_{\max}$ are shown in Figure 3. When measured result $\phi_{j-1} \leq \hat{\phi}_j \leq \phi_{j+1}$, the quantum state which is measured in this case is $\phi_j |0\rangle + \sin\phi_j |1\rangle$.
   Using (3.23), we infer

$$\sqrt{p(1-\mathrm{p})} \leq \sqrt{\overline{X} - \overline{X}^2 + \frac{m^2}{4n}} + \frac{m}{2\sqrt{n}} \leq \sqrt{\overline{X} - \overline{X}^2} + \frac{m}{\sqrt{n}} \,, \tag{3.35}$$

Figure 3. The relation of $\Delta\theta$, $\Delta\phi$, $\phi_j, \hat{\phi}_j$, ϕ_{min} and ϕ_{max}

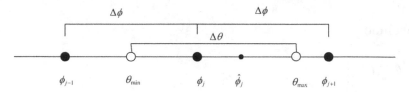

i.e.,

$$\frac{2m\sqrt{p(1-\mathrm{p})}}{\sqrt{n}} \leq \frac{2m\sqrt{n}\sqrt{\overline{X} - \overline{X}^2} + 2m^2}{n}. \tag{3.36}$$

From (3.27), (3.33) and (3.36), we calculate

$$\Delta p \leq \frac{\sqrt{4nm\overline{X} - 4nm\overline{X}^2 + m^2}}{n+m} + \frac{2m\sqrt{n}\sqrt{\overline{X} - \overline{X}^2} + 2m^2}{n} < \frac{\sqrt{4nm\overline{X} - 4nm\overline{X}^2 + m^2}}{n}$$

$$+ \frac{2m\sqrt{n}\sqrt{\overline{X} - \overline{X}^2} + 2m^2}{n} \leq \frac{2(m + \sqrt{m})\sqrt{\overline{X} - \overline{X}^2}\sqrt{n} + 2m^2 + m}{n}, \tag{3.37}$$

therefore, when

$$\frac{2(m + \sqrt{m})\sqrt{\overline{X} - \overline{X}^2}\sqrt{n} + 2m^2 + m}{n} \leq \sin^2(\Delta\phi), \tag{3.38}$$

the formula (3.33) holds. Solving (3.38), we conclude that the formula (3.33) holds, when

$$n \geq \frac{\left(2(m + \sqrt{m})\sqrt{\overline{X} - \overline{X}^2} + \sin(\Delta\phi)\sqrt{(2m^2 + m)}\right)^2}{\sin^4(\Delta\phi)}. \tag{3.39}$$

Thus, we retrieve a color in the quantum queue Q_1 after at most

$$n_{\max} = \frac{\left[2(m + \sqrt{m})\sqrt{\overline{X} - \overline{X}^2} + \sin(\Delta\phi)\sqrt{(2m^2 + m)} \right]^2}{\sin^4(\Delta\phi)} \tag{3.40}$$

measurements with the approximate probability of $1 - \alpha$.

If the sample size n is large enough, $\overline{X} \approx p = \sin^2 \phi_j$. Substituting $2\sqrt{\overline{X} - \overline{X}^2} \approx \sin(2\phi_j)$ into (3.40) gives

$$n_{\max} \approx \frac{\left((m + \sqrt{m})\sin(2\phi_j) + \sin(\Delta\phi)\sqrt{(2m^2 + m)} \right)^2}{\sin^4(\Delta\phi)}. \tag{3.41}$$

When the probability $1 - \alpha > 0.95$, then $m = Z_{\alpha/2}^2 > (1.96)^2$, and

$$n_{\max} < \frac{4Z_{\alpha/2}^4 \left(\sin(2\phi_j) + \sin(\Delta\phi) \right)^2}{\sin^4(\Delta\phi)} < \frac{16Z_{\alpha/2}^4}{\sin^4(\Delta\phi)}. \tag{3.42}$$

When $M \gg 1$, such as $M = 2^{24}$ for a RGB color image,

$$\sin(\Delta\phi) \approx \Delta\phi = \pi/2(M - 1).$$

We have

$$n_{\max} < \frac{256Z_{\alpha/2}^4 (M - 1)^4}{\pi^4}. \tag{3.43}$$

Through the above analysis, we conclude that a color in quantum queue Q_1 can be retrieved by $O(M^4)$ measurements, where M is the size of the color set *Color* in (3.5).

Similarly, we retrieve information from $\cos \eta_i |0\rangle + \sin \eta_i |1\rangle$ in the quantum queue Q_2 after at most

$$n_{\max 2} = \frac{\left((Z_{\alpha/2}^2 + Z_{\alpha/2})\sin(2\eta_j) + \sin(\Delta\eta)\sqrt{(2Z_{\alpha/2}^4 + Z_{\alpha/2}^2)}\right)^2}{\sin^4(\Delta\eta)} < \frac{16Z_{\alpha/2}^4}{\sin^4(\Delta\eta)}$$

$$(3.44)$$

measurements with the approximate probability of $1 - \alpha$. That is, a state in quantum queue Q_1 can be retrieved by $O(1/\sin^4(\Delta\eta))$ measurements, where $\Delta\eta = \pi/2(\lambda - 1)$, and λ is the number of different colors of an image.

Therefore, we retrieve an image from quantum queues Q_1 and Q_2 using $O(2^n/\sin^4(\Delta\eta)) + O(\lambda M^4)$ measurements. Since Qubit Lattice stores 2^n RGB colors in quantum systems, these colors can be retrieved by $O(2^n M^4)$ measurements. For a RGB color image of 2^n pixels, generally $\lambda \ll M$, i.e., $\Delta\eta \gg \Delta\phi$, therefore, $O(2^n/\sin^4(\Delta\eta)) \ll O(2^n M^4)$, and $O(\lambda M^4) \ll O(2^n M^4)$. Thus, we retrieve an image from quantum queues Q_1 and Q_2 using fewer measurements than Qubit Lattice.

FLEXIBLE REPRESENTATION OF QUANTUM IMAGES

Flexible representation of quantum images (FRQI) was proposed to store a $2^n \times 2^n$ image with $2n+1$ qubits (Le, Dong, & Hirota, 2011). In this section, we introduce the representation, storage and retrieval of images based on FRQI.

Representation of an Image Based on FRQI

FRQI is defined as

$$|I\rangle = \frac{1}{2^n} \sum_{i=0}^{2^{2n}-1} |c_i\rangle \otimes |i\rangle ,$$

$$(3.45)$$

and

$$|c_i\rangle = \cos\theta_i |0\rangle + \sin\theta_i |1\rangle ,$$

$$(3.46)$$

where $|i\rangle$ ($i=0,1,\ldots,2^{2n} - 1$) encodes a coordinate of an $2^n \times 2^n$ image, and $|c_i\rangle$ represents the color on the coordinate $|i\rangle$.

Thus, $|I\rangle$ can represents a $2^n \times 2^n$ image. For instance, a 2×2 image is shown in Figure 4.

Figure 4. A simple image and its FRQI state

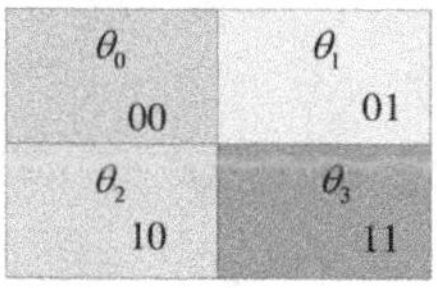

$$|I\rangle = \frac{1}{2}[(\cos\theta_0|0\rangle + \sin\theta_0|1\rangle) \otimes |00\rangle + (\cos\theta_1|0\rangle + \sin\theta_1|1\rangle) \otimes |01\rangle$$
$$+ (\cos\theta_2|10\rangle + \sin\theta_2|1\rangle) \otimes |10\rangle + (\cos\theta_3|0\rangle + \sin\theta_3|1\rangle) \otimes |11\rangle]$$

The Implementation Circuit of FRQI

Applying Hadamard transforms on the initial states $|0\rangle^{\otimes 2n+1}$ products the state $|H\rangle$,

$$(I \otimes H^{\otimes 2n})|0\rangle^{\otimes 2n+1} = \frac{1}{2^n}|0\rangle \otimes \sum_{i=0}^{2^{2n}-1}|i\rangle = |H\rangle. \tag{3.47}$$

The rotation matrixes $R_y(\theta_i)$ with $i=0,1,\ldots,2^{2n}-1$,

$$R_y(\theta_i) = \begin{bmatrix} \cos\theta_i & -\sin\theta_i \\ \sin\theta_i & \cos\theta_i \end{bmatrix}, \tag{3.48}$$

are substituted for U in (2.32) to get

$$V_{2n}^i(R_y(\theta_i)) = R_y(\theta_i) \otimes (|i\rangle\langle i|) + \sum_{i=0,j\neq i}^{2^{2n}-1}(I \otimes (|j\rangle\langle j|)). \tag{3.49}$$

Applying $V_{2n}^i(R_y(\theta_i))$ on $|H\rangle$ gives

$$V_{2n}^i(R_y(\theta_i))|H\rangle = \frac{1}{2^n}\left[|0\rangle \otimes \sum_{j=0,j\neq i}^{2^{2n}-1}|j\rangle + (\cos\theta_i|0\rangle + \sin\theta_i|1\rangle) \otimes |i\rangle\right]. \tag{3.50}$$

Therefore, an image is stored in a quantum system by using

$$\left[\prod_{i=0}^{2^{2n}-1} V_{2n}^i (R_y(\theta_i)) \right] \left| H \right\rangle = \left| I \right\rangle, \tag{3.51}$$

its implementation circuit is as shown in Figure 5.

Figure 5. An implementation circuit of FRQI

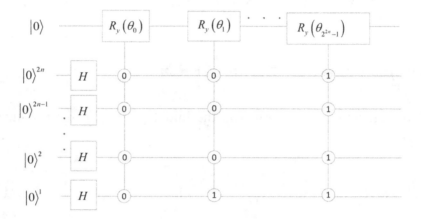

The complexity of the implementation circuit of FRQI for a $2^n \times 2^n$ image can be calculated as $O(2^{4n})$ (Le, Dong, & Hirota, 2011). However, it actually has less complexity than $O(2^{4n})$. Since the determinant of matrices $R_y(\theta_i)$ is one, i.e., $R_y(\theta_i) \in SU(2)$, then the complexity of $V_{2n}^i(R_y(\theta_i))$ is $O(n)$ by Corollary 2.8. The implementation circuit of FRQI consists of 2^{2n} gates for a $2^n \times 2^n$ image, so its complexity is $O(n2^{2n})$.

Image Retrieval Based on FRQI

Define an observable operator M_1

$$M_1 = \sum_{j=0}^{2^{2n}-1} m_j P_j, \tag{3.52}$$

where $P_j = I \otimes |j\rangle\langle j|$. Apply M_1 to measure the FRQI state $|I\rangle$, and obtain the coordinate $|j\rangle$ with probability $1/2^{2n}$. That is, the coordinate $|j\rangle$ can be retrieved by 2^{2n} measurements. The state after measurement is

$$\frac{P_j \left| I \right\rangle}{2^n} = \left| c_j \right\rangle \left| j \right\rangle. \tag{3.53}$$

Next, using the method in the model of QSMC and QSNC, we can retrieve the color of the pixel on the coordinate $\left| j \right\rangle$ from the state $\left| c_j \right\rangle \left| j \right\rangle$ after $O(M^4)$ measurements, where M is the size of the color set *Color* in (3.5).

A color and a coordinate of an image based on FRQI can be retrieved by $O(2^{2n}M^4)$ measurements.

THE MODEL OF A NORMAL ARBITRARY SUPERPOSITION STATE

The model of a normal arbitrary superposition state (NASS) was proposed to store a multi-dimensional image (Li, Zhu, Zhou, Li, Song, & Ian, 2014). In this section, we describe the representation, storage and retrieval of images and videos based on NASS, and provide simulated codes in Appendix B (see Code B.5-Code B.12).

Representation of Images and Videos Based on NASS

A quantum superposition state in 2^n dimensional Hilbert space can be expressed as

$$\left| \psi_a \right\rangle = \sum_{i=0}^{2^n-1} a_i \left| i \right\rangle, \tag{3.54}$$

where $\left| i \right\rangle = \left| i_n \cdots i_2 i_1 \right\rangle$, $i = \sum_{j=1}^{n} i_j \times 2^j$, $i_1, i_2, \ldots, i_n \in \{0,1\}$, and a_i is an arbitrary real. Let a_i be an element in the angle set ϕ in (3.5), then $a_i \in \phi$ represents the color. To represent colors and coordinates of 2^n pixels, then state $\left| \psi_a \right\rangle$ can be modified into $\left| \psi_\phi \right\rangle$ as follows,

$$\left| \psi_\phi \right\rangle = \sum_{i=0}^{2^n-1} a_i \left| i \right\rangle = \sum_{i=0}^{2^n-1} a_i \left| i_n \cdots i_2 i_1 \right\rangle, \tag{3.55}$$

where $\left|i\right\rangle=\left|i_n\cdots i_2 i_1\right\rangle$ are the coordinate of the i-th pixel, and $a_i\in\phi$ represents the color of the pixel on the coordinate $|i\rangle$.

To normalize the state $\left|\psi_\phi\right\rangle$, we set

$$\theta_i=a_i\Big/\sqrt{\sum_{y=0}^{2^n-1}a_y^2}\,,\tag{3.56}$$

thus, a normal state $\left|\psi\right\rangle$ represents colors and coordinates of 2^n pixels,

$$\left|\psi\right\rangle=\sum_{i=0}^{2^n-1}\theta_i\left|i\right\rangle=\sum_{i=0}^{2^n-1}\theta_i\left|i_n\cdots i_2 i_1\right\rangle.\tag{3.57}$$

Substituting $\left|i\right\rangle=\left|x_m\right\rangle\left|y_k\right\rangle$ into (3.52), we obtain a normal state $\left|\psi_2\right\rangle$ to represent an image,

$$\left|\psi_2\right\rangle=\sum_{i=0}^{2^n-1}\theta_i\left|i\right\rangle=\sum_{i=0}^{2^n-1}\theta_i\left|x_m\right\rangle\left|y_k\right\rangle=\sum_{i=0}^{2^n-1}\theta_i\left|i_n\cdots i_{k+1}\right\rangle\left|i_k\cdots i_1\right\rangle,\tag{3.58}$$

where $\left|x_m\right\rangle=\left|i_n\cdots i_{k+1}\right\rangle$ and $\left|y_k\right\rangle=\left|i_k\cdots i_1\right\rangle$ are the X-axis and Y-axis of the image, and $n=m+k$. For instance, when $n=5$, $k=2$, and $m=3$, the following state

$$\left|\psi_2^{3,2}\right\rangle=\sum_{i=0}^{2^5-1}\theta_i\left|i_5 i_4 i_3\right\rangle\left|i_2 i_1\right\rangle=\theta_0\left|000\right\rangle\left|00\right\rangle+\theta_1\left|000\right\rangle\left|01\right\rangle+\cdots+\theta_{30}\left|111\right\rangle\left|10\right\rangle+\theta_{31}\left|111\right\rangle\left|11\right\rangle\tag{3.59}$$

can represent an 8×4 color image shown in Figure 6.

Substituting $\left|i\right\rangle=\left|x_m\right\rangle\left|y_k\right\rangle\left|t_h\right\rangle$ into (3.57), we obtain a normal state $\left|\psi_3\right\rangle$ to represent a video,

$$\left|\psi_3\right\rangle=\sum_{i=0}^{2^n-1}\theta_i\left|i\right\rangle=\sum_{i=0}^{2^n-1}\theta_i\left|x_m\right\rangle\left|y_k\right\rangle\left|t_h\right\rangle=\sum_{i=0}^{2^n-1}\theta_i\left|i_n\ldots i_{h+k+1}\right\rangle\left|i_{h+k}\ldots i_{h+1}\right\rangle\left|i_h\ldots i_1\right\rangle,\tag{3.60}$$

where $|m\rangle$, $|y_k\rangle$ and $|t_h\rangle$ are the X-axis, Y-axis and time-axis of the video, and $n=m+k+h$. For instance, when $n=5$, $h=2$, $k=1$, and $m=2$, the following state

Figure 6. A 8x4 color image

	00	01	10	11	
000	θ_0	θ_1	θ_2	θ_3	y_2
001	θ_4	θ_5	θ_6	θ_7	
010	θ_8	θ_9	θ_{10}	θ_{11}	
011	θ_{12}	θ_{13}	θ_{14}	θ_{15}	
100	θ_{16}	θ_{17}	θ_{18}	θ_{19}	
101	θ_{20}	θ_{21}	θ_{22}	θ_{23}	
110	θ_{24}	θ_{25}	θ_{26}	θ_{27}	
111	θ_{28}	θ_{29}	θ_{30}	θ_{31}	

x_3

$$
\begin{aligned}
\left| \psi_3^{2,1,2} \right\rangle &= \sum_{i=0}^{2^5-1} \theta_i \left| i_5 i_4 \right\rangle \left| i_3 \right\rangle \left| i_2 i_1 \right\rangle \\
&= \theta_0 \left| 00 \right\rangle \left| 0 \right\rangle \left| 00 \right\rangle + \theta_1 \left| 00 \right\rangle \left| 0 \right\rangle \left| 01 \right\rangle + \cdots + \theta_{31} \left| 11 \right\rangle \left| 1 \right\rangle \left| 11 \right\rangle,
\end{aligned} \tag{3.61}
$$

can represent a video with four frames shown in Figure 7, where each frame is a 4×4 image.

Figure 7. A video with four frames

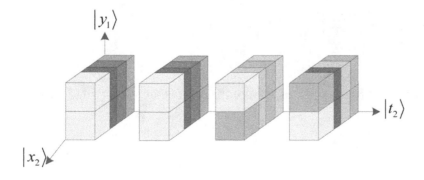

The Implementation Circuit of NASS

A unitary matrices is defined as (Long, & Sun, 2001),

$$R_x(\theta) = \begin{bmatrix} \cos\theta & \sin\theta \\ \sin\theta & -\cos\theta \end{bmatrix},$$

(3.62)

where $\theta \in [0, 2\pi]$.

A sequence of angles is given as follows (Long, & Sun, 2001),

$$\begin{cases} \alpha_j = \arctan\sqrt{\dfrac{\sum_{i_{n-1}\cdots i_1}\left|\theta_{1i_{n-1}\cdots i_1}\right|^2}{\sum_{i_{n-1}\cdots i_1}\left|\theta_{0i_{n-1}\cdots i_1}\right|^2}}, & j = 1, \\[4mm] \alpha_{j,i_n\cdots i_{n-j+1}} = \arctan\sqrt{\dfrac{\sum_{i_{n-j}\cdots i_1}\left|\theta_{i_n\cdots i_{n-j+2}1i_{n-j}\cdots i_1}\right|^2}{\sum_{i_{n-j}\cdots i_1}\left|\theta_{i_n\cdots i_{n-j+2}0i_{n-j}\cdots i_1}\right|^2}}, & 2 \le j \le n, \end{cases}$$

(3.63)

here, suppose that $0i_{n-1}\cdots i_1, 1i_{n-1}\cdots i_1, i_n\cdots i_{n-j+2}0i_{n-j}\cdots i_1$ and $i_n\cdots i_{n-j+2}0i_{n-j}\cdots i_1$ are the binary expansions for integers g, h, x and y, respectively, then $\theta_{0i_{n-1}\cdots i_1} = \theta_g$, $\theta_{1i_{n-1}\cdots i_1} = \theta_h$, $\theta_{i_n\cdots i_{n-j+2}0i_{n-j}\cdots i_1} = \theta_x$ and $\theta_{i_n\cdots i_{n-j+2}1i_{n-j}\cdots i_1} = \theta_y$.

For instance, when $j=2$, the equation (3.63) is rewritten as

$$\begin{cases} \alpha_{2,0} = \arctan\sqrt{\dfrac{\sum_{i_{n-2}\cdots i_1}\left|\theta_{01i_{n-2}\cdots i_1}\right|^2}{\sum_{i_{n-2}\cdots i_1}\left|\theta_{00i_{n-2}\cdots i_1}\right|^2}}, \\[4mm] \alpha_{2,1} = \arctan\sqrt{\dfrac{\sum_{i_{n-2}\cdots i_1}\left|\theta_{11i_{n-2}\cdots i_1}\right|^2}{\sum_{i_{n-2}\cdots i_1}\left|\theta_{10i_{n-2}\cdots i_1}\right|^2}}. \end{cases}$$

(3.64)

Set $U = R_x(\alpha_{j,i})$ and $n=j$, the controlled-U gate $C_n^i(U)$ in (2.32) is changed into

$$C_{j-1}^i[R_x(\alpha_{j,i})] = (|i\rangle\langle i|) \otimes R_x(\alpha_{j,i}) + \sum_{j=0, j\neq i}^{2^j-1} (|j\rangle\langle j|) \otimes I, \tag{3.65}$$

where $j \geq 2$.

Unitary operations R_j with $j=1,2,\ldots,n$ are defined as

$$\begin{cases} R_1 = R_x(\alpha_1) \otimes I^{\otimes(n-1)}, & j=1, \\ R_j = \prod_{i=0}^{2^{j-1}-1} \{C_{j-1}^i[R_x(\alpha_{j,i})] \otimes I^{\otimes(n-j)}\}, & 2 \leq j \leq n. \end{cases} \tag{3.66}$$

By applying the unitary operations R_j successively on the initial state $|0\rangle^{\otimes n}$, we obtain

$$(\prod_{j=1}^n R_j)|0\rangle^{\otimes n} = \sum_{i=0}^{2^n-1} \theta_i|i\rangle = |\psi\rangle, \tag{3.67}$$

that is, the initial state $|0\rangle^{\otimes n}$ is changed into the NASS state $|\psi\rangle$ in (3.57). The implementation circuit is as shown in Figure 8, named as RNASS (Realization of NASS) shown on the right. $|0\rangle_n |0\rangle_{n-1} \cdots |0\rangle_2 |0\rangle_1$ is an input of n qubits, which is also notated as $|0\rangle^{\otimes n}$ in (3.67). Dashed boxes $j(j=1,2,\ldots,n)$ correspond to the implementations of R_j. The output of the circuit is the state $|\psi\rangle$.

Figure 8. The implementation circuit of NASS

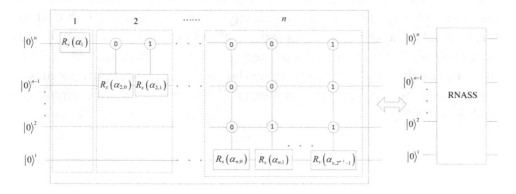

Substituting $(\pi/2 - \alpha_{j,i})$ for θ of $R_r(\theta)$ in (2.35), we give

$$R_r\left(\pi/2 - \alpha_{j,i}\right) = \begin{bmatrix} \cos(\pi/4 - \alpha_{j,i}/2) & \sin(\pi/4 - \alpha_{j,i}/2) \\ -\sin(\pi/4 - \alpha_{j,i}/2) & \cos(\pi/4 - \alpha_{j,i}/2) \end{bmatrix}, \tag{3.68}$$

and its transpose matrix is

$$R_r^T\left(\pi/2 - \alpha_{j,i}\right) = \begin{bmatrix} \cos(\pi/4 - \alpha_{j,i}/2) & -\sin(\pi/4 - \alpha_{j,i}/2) \\ \sin(\pi/4 - \alpha_{j,i}/2) & \cos(\pi/4 - \alpha_{j,i}/2) \end{bmatrix}, \tag{3.69}$$

where $\alpha_{j,i}$ is seen in (3.63).

Since

$$R_x(\pi/2 - \alpha_{j,i})XR_r^T(\pi/2 - \alpha_{j,i}) = R_x(\alpha_{j,i})$$

and

$$R_x(\pi/2 - \alpha_{j,i})R_r^T(\pi/2 - \alpha_{j,i}) = I$$

hold, where X is the matrix of a NOT gate, then, the controlled gate $C_{j-1}^i[R_x(\alpha_{j,i})] \otimes I^{\otimes(n-j)}$ can be implemented by two 1-qubit gates and a controlled-NOT gate with j qubits, which is shown in Figure 9.

When $j<n$, combining Figure 9 with Corollary 2.14, we obtain the complexity of the controlled gate $C_{j-1}^i[R_x(\alpha_{j,i})] \otimes I^{\otimes(n-j)}$ is $O(n)$. For $j=n$, the complexity of the gate in Figure 9, i.e., $C_{n-1}^i[R_x(\alpha_{n,i})]$ can is $O(n^2)$ by Corollary 2.16. For $k<n$, the k-th dashed box in Figure 9 includes 2^k gates, and every gate's complexity is $O(n)$. The complexity of the circuit in the k-th dashed box is $O(n2^k)$. Therefore, the complexity of the circuit in the first $n-1$ dashed boxes is $O(n^2 2^n)$. The complexity of every gate in the last dashed box is $O(n^2)$, thus, the circuit complexity in the dashed box is $O(n^2 2^n)$. Through the analysis above, we conclude that the complexity of the implementation circuit of NASS is $O(n^2 2^n)$.

Figure 9. The implementation of the controlled gate $C_{j-1}^i[R_x(\alpha_{j,i})] \otimes I^{\otimes(n-j)}$

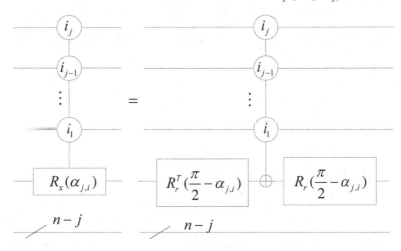

Image and Video Retrieval Based on NASS

Using the observable operator M

$$M = \sum_{j=0}^{2^n-1} m_j P_j, P_j = |j\rangle\langle j| \tag{3.70}$$

on the state $|\psi_2\rangle$ in (3.58), we obtain the result m_j with probability $p(m_j) = \langle\psi_2|P_j|\psi_2\rangle = \theta_j^2$, i.e.,

$$\theta_j = \sqrt{p(m_j)}. \tag{3.71}$$

Thus, we can retrieve an image stored in the state $|\psi_2\rangle$ by repeated measurements.

Similarly, applying the operator M on the state $|\psi_3\rangle$ in (3.60) retrieves a video by repeated measurements.

Suppose that θ_j can be retrieved with the probability of $1 - \alpha$ with n_{max}, then, we describe how to get n_{max}, i.e., how many measurements are necessary to obtain the accurate value of θ_j.

Let n_s be measurement sample size, and the occurrence number of m_j be n_j, then $\hat{p}(m_j) = n_j/n_s$. Since n_s is finite, $\hat{p}(m_j)$ is the estimate value of $p(m_j)$. Substituting $\hat{p}(m_j)$ for $p(m_j)$ in (3.71), we obtain the estimate value of θ_j,

$$\hat{\theta}_j = \sqrt{\hat{p}(m_j)} . \tag{3.72}$$

Set

$$Z = \begin{cases} 0, \text{the result of measurement isn't } m_j, \\ 1, \text{the result of measurement is } m_j. \end{cases} \tag{3.73}$$

Since Z is either 1 or 0, Z is a Bernoulli random variable. The probability mass function of the random variable Z is given by

$$\begin{cases} p(\widetilde{m_j}) = P\{Z = 0\} = 1 - p, \\ p(m_j) = P\{Z = 1\} = p, \end{cases} \tag{3.74}$$

where $\widetilde{m_j}$ indicates that the measurement result is not m_j.

The expectation μ and variance σ of Z are $\mu = p$ and $\sigma^2 = p(1-p)$, respectively. Suppose that $Z_1, Z_2, \cdots Z_{n_s}$ are n_s samples of Z and that n_s is sufficiently large, let $\overline{Z}$ be the average of n_s samples of Z, then

$$\frac{\sum_{i=1}^{n_s} Z_i - n_s p}{\sqrt{n_s p(1-p)}} = \frac{n_s \overline{Z} - n_s p}{\sqrt{n_s p(1-p)}} \tag{3.75}$$

has an approximately standard normal distribution according to the Central Limit Theorem. Therefore, we have

$$P\left\{\left|\frac{n_s \overline{Z} - n_s p}{\sqrt{n_s p(1-p)}}\right| < Z_{\alpha/2}^2\right\} \approx 1 - \alpha, \tag{3.76}$$

where 1 - α is the confidence level (the value of $Z_{\alpha/2}$ can be found in standard normal distribution look-up tables, e.g., when α=0.05, $Z_{\alpha/2} = 1.96$).

Solving the inequality

$$\left| \frac{(n_s \overline{Z} - n_s p)}{\sqrt{n_s p(1-p)}} \right| < Z_{\alpha/2}^2, \tag{3.77}$$

obtains that the confidence interval of p is $[p_{min}, p_{max}]$ with an approximate confidence level of $1 - \alpha$. p_{min} and p_{max} are expressed as follows,

$$p_{min} = \frac{2n_s \overline{Z} + \lambda - \sqrt{(2n_s \overline{Z} + \lambda)^2 - 4(n_s + \lambda)n_s \overline{Z^2}}}{2n_s + 2\lambda}, \tag{3.78}$$

and

$$p_{max} = \frac{2n_s \overline{Z} + \lambda + \sqrt{(2n_s \overline{Z} + \lambda)^2 - 4(n_s + \lambda)n_s \overline{Z^2}}}{2n_s + 2\lambda}, \tag{3.79}$$

where $\lambda = Z_{\alpha/2}^2$.

From (3.77), we have

$$\left| \overline{Z} - p \right| < \frac{Z_{\alpha/2}^2 \sqrt{p(1-p)}}{\sqrt{n_s}}. \tag{3.80}$$

Set

$$\hat{p}_{min} = p_{min} - \left(Z_{\alpha/2}^2 \sqrt{p(1-p)} \middle/ \sqrt{n_s} \right),$$

$$\hat{p}_{max} = p_{max} + \left(Z_{\alpha/2}^2 \sqrt{p(1-p)} \middle/ \sqrt{n_s} \right).$$

From (3.80), we obtain

$$\overline{Z} \in \left[\hat{p}_{\min}, \hat{p}_{\max}\right], \ p \in \left[p_{\min}, p_{\max}\right] \subset \left[\hat{p}_{\min}, \hat{p}_{\max}\right]. \tag{3.81}$$

The size of the confidence interval $[p_{\min}, p_{\max}]$ is

$$\Delta p = p_{\max} - p_{\min} = \frac{\sqrt{4n_s \lambda \overline{Z} - 4n_s \lambda \overline{Z}^2 + \lambda^2}}{n_s + \lambda}. \tag{3.82}$$

Define

$$\begin{cases} \theta_{\max} = \sqrt{\hat{p}_{\max}}, \\ \theta_{\min} = \sqrt{\hat{p}_{\min}}, \end{cases} \tag{3.83}$$

then, we infer

$$\Delta\theta = \theta_{\max} - \theta_{\min} = \sqrt{\hat{p}_{\max}} - \sqrt{\hat{p}_{\min}} \le \sqrt{\hat{p}_{\max} - \hat{p}_{\min}} = \sqrt{\Delta p}. \tag{3.84}$$

Since

$$\begin{cases} \hat{\theta}_j = \sqrt{\hat{p(m_j)}} = \sqrt{\overline{Z}}, \\ \theta_j = \sqrt{p(m_j)} = \sqrt{p}, \end{cases}$$

then the formula

$$\begin{cases} \theta_j \in \left[\theta_{\min}, \theta_{\max}\right], \\ \hat{\theta}_j \in \left[\theta_{\min}, \theta_{\max}\right], \\ \left|\theta_j - \hat{\theta}_j\right| \le \Delta\theta, \end{cases} \tag{3.85}$$

holds by (3.81), (3.83) and (3.84). Therefore, we give

$$\begin{cases} a_j, \hat{a}_j \in \left[G_\phi \theta_{\min}, G_\phi \theta_{\max}\right], \\ \left|\hat{a}_j - a_j\right| \le G_\phi \Delta\theta, \end{cases} \tag{3.86}$$

where $G_\phi = \sqrt{\sum_{y=0}^{2^n-1} a_y^2}$, $a_j = \theta_j G_\phi$ (see (3.56)), and $\hat{a}_j = \hat{\theta}_j G_\phi$.

According to (3.5), we calculate

$$\Delta\phi = \left|\phi_{i+1} - \phi_i\right| = \frac{\pi}{2(M-1)}, \tag{3.87}$$

where $i \in \{1,2,\ldots,(M-1)\}$ and $M \in \{2, 256, 2^{24}\}$.

Suppose that

$$\sqrt{\Delta p} < \frac{\Delta\phi}{G_\phi}, \tag{3.88}$$

and define $\Delta\hat{\phi} = \left|a_j - \hat{a}_j\right|$, from (3.84), (3.86) and (23.88), we can see that

$$\Delta\hat{\phi} \le G_\phi \Delta\theta \le \sqrt{\Delta p}\, G_\phi \le \Delta\phi. \tag{3.89}$$

Therefore, $\Delta\hat{\phi}$, $\Delta\phi$, a_j, $\hat{a}_j$, $G_\phi \theta_{\min}$, $G_\phi \theta_{\max}$, and $G_\phi \Delta\theta$ are shown in Figure 10. When $\hat{\theta}_j \in \Delta\theta$ (i.e., $\hat{a}_j \in G_\phi \Delta\theta$), we conclude $a_j = \phi_j$ from the figure, that is, the color of the pixel on coordinate $|j\rangle$ is retrieved.

Figure 10. Relationships between $\Delta\hat{\phi}$, $\Delta\phi$, a_j, $\hat{a}_j$, $G_\phi \theta_{\min}$, $G_\phi \theta_{\max}$, and $G_\phi \Delta\theta$

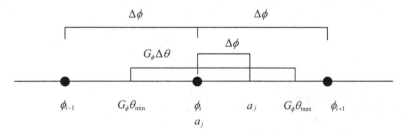

According to (3.80), we have

$$\frac{2Z_{\alpha/2}^2 \sqrt{p(1-p)}}{\sqrt{n_s}} \leq \frac{2m\sqrt{n_s}\sqrt{\overline{X} - \overline{X}^2} + 2Z_{\alpha/2}^4}{n_s}. \tag{3.90}$$

Combining (3.82) with (3.90), we obtain

$$\Delta p \leq \frac{2(Z_{\alpha/2}^2 + Z_{\alpha/2})\sqrt{\overline{X} - \overline{X}^2}\sqrt{n_s} + 2Z_{\alpha/2}^4 + Z_{\alpha/2}^2}{n_s}. \tag{3.91}$$

Therefore, the formula (3.88) will hold as long as the following inequation

$$\frac{2(Z_{\alpha/2}^2 + Z_{\alpha/2})\sqrt{\overline{Z} - \overline{Z}^2}\sqrt{n_s} + 2Z_{\alpha/2}^4 + Z_{\alpha/2}^2}{n_s} \leq \left(\frac{\Delta\phi}{G_\phi}\right)^2 \tag{3.92}$$

is satisfied.

Solving (3.86), we obtain a feasible solution

$$\sqrt{n_+} = \frac{(Z_{\alpha/2}^2 + Z_{\alpha/2})\sqrt{\overline{Z} - \overline{Z}^2}G_\phi^2}{(\Delta\phi)^2} + \frac{\sqrt{(Z_{\alpha/2}^2 + Z_{\alpha/2})^2(\overline{Z} - \overline{Z}^2)G_\phi^4 + (\Delta\phi)^2 G_\phi^2 (2Z_{\alpha/2}^4 + Z_{\alpha/2}^2)}}{(\Delta\phi)^2}$$

$$\leq \frac{2(Z_{\alpha/2}^2 + Z_{\alpha/2})\sqrt{\overline{Z} - \overline{Z}^2}G_\phi^2}{(\Delta\phi)^2} + \frac{G_\phi(2Z_{\alpha/2}^4 + Z_{\alpha/2}^2)}{\Delta\phi}, \tag{3.93}$$

i.e.,

$$n_{\max} = \left(\frac{2(Z_{\alpha/2}^2 + Z_{\alpha/2})\sqrt{\overline{Z} - \overline{Z}^2}G_\phi^2}{(\Delta\phi)^2} + \frac{G_\phi(2Z_{\alpha/2}^4 + Z_{\alpha/2}^2)}{\Delta\phi}\right)^2. \tag{3.94}$$

Thus, we can obtain the correct angle θ_j after at most $\theta_{\max}$ measurements with an approximate probability of $1 - \alpha$.

Setting $\bar{a} = \sum_{i=0}^{2^n-1} a_i^2 / 2^n$ gives $G_\phi = \sqrt{\sum_{y=0}^{2^n-1} a_y^2} = \sqrt{2^n}\sqrt{\bar{a}}$. If the sample size n_s is large enough, $\bar{z} \approx p = \theta_j^2 = a_j^2 / G_\phi^2$. Then, the formula (3.94) is changed into

$$n_{max} \approx 2^n \left[\frac{2(Z_{\alpha/2}^2 + Z_{\alpha/2})a_j \sqrt{\bar{a}}\sqrt{1 - a_j^2/2^n\bar{a}}}{(\Delta\phi)^2} + \frac{\sqrt{\bar{a}}(2Z_{\alpha/2}^4 + Z_{\alpha/2}^2)}{\Delta\phi} \right]^2. \qquad (3.95)$$

Since $a_j \in [0, \pi/2]$, $\bar{a} \in [0, \pi/2]$, and $\Delta\phi = \pi/2(M-1)$, then n_{max} satisfies

$$n_{max} \approx 2^n (M-1)^4 \left[\frac{8(Z_{\alpha/2}^2 + Z_{\alpha/2})a_j \sqrt{\bar{a}}\sqrt{1 - a_j^2/2^n\bar{a}}}{\pi^2} + \frac{2\sqrt{\bar{a}}(2Z_{\alpha/2}^4 + Z_{\alpha/2}^2)}{\pi(M-1)} \right]^2$$

$$< 2^n (M-1)^4 \left[2(Z_{\alpha/2}^2 + Z_{\alpha/2}) + \frac{(2Z_{\alpha/2}^4 + Z_{\alpha/2}^2)}{(M-1)} \right]^2.$$

$$(3.96)$$

Through the above analysis, we conclude that a color and coordinate of an image based on NASS can be retrieved by $O(2^n M^4)$ measurements.

THE MODEL OF A NORMAL ARBITRARY SUPERPOSITION STATE WITH THREE COMPONENTS

A normal arbitrary superposition state with three components (NASSTC) was proposed to store color images (Li, Zhu, Zhou, Li, Song, & Ian, 2014). In this section, we describe the representation, storage and retrieval of color images based on NASSTC.

Representation of a Color Image Based on NASSTC

Supposing that y_1, y_2 and y_3 are the grayscale values of three components of the color of the pixel at the coordinate $|j\rangle$, we calculate three angles r_i, g_i and b_i,

$$r_i = \frac{y_1 \pi}{2(256-1)}, g_i = \frac{y_2 \pi}{2(256-1)}, b_i = \frac{y_3 \pi}{2(256-1)}. \tag{3.97}$$

Set

$$\begin{cases} G_{rgb} = \sqrt{\sum_{i=0}^{2^n-1} (r_i^2 + g_i^2 + b_i^2)}, \\ \theta_{ri} = \dfrac{r_i}{G_{rgb}}, \theta_{gi} = \dfrac{g_i}{G_{rgb}}, \theta_{bi} = \dfrac{b_i}{G_{rgb}}, \end{cases} \tag{3.98}$$

then, substituting $\sqrt{3}\theta_{ri}$, $\sqrt{3}\theta_{gi}$, and $\sqrt{3}\theta_{bi}$ for θ_j in (3.58), respectively, we obtain three states

$$\begin{cases} |\psi_r\rangle = \sum_{i=0}^{2^n-1} \sqrt{3}\theta_{ri} |i\rangle = \sum_{i=0}^{2^n-1} \sqrt{3}\theta_{ri} |x_m\rangle |y_k\rangle, \\ |\psi_g\rangle = \sum_{i=0}^{2^n-1} \sqrt{3}\theta_{gi} |i\rangle = \sum_{i=0}^{2^n-1} \sqrt{3}\theta_{gi} |x_m\rangle |y_k\rangle, \\ |\psi_b\rangle = \sum_{i=0}^{2^n-1} \sqrt{3}\theta_{bi} |i\rangle = \sum_{i=0}^{2^n-1} \sqrt{3}\theta_{bi} |x_m\rangle |y_k\rangle. \end{cases} \tag{3.99}$$

To represent quantum color images efficiently, we define

$$\begin{aligned} |\psi_C\rangle &= \frac{1}{\sqrt{3}} |\psi_r\rangle |01\rangle + \frac{1}{\sqrt{3}} |\psi_g\rangle |10\rangle + \frac{1}{\sqrt{3}} |\psi_b\rangle |11\rangle \\ &= \sum_{i=0}^{2^n-1} (\theta_{ri} |i\rangle |01\rangle + \theta_{gi} |i\rangle |10\rangle + \theta_{bi} |i\rangle |11\rangle), \end{aligned} \tag{3.100}$$

where $|\psi_r\rangle$, $|\psi_g\rangle$, and $|\psi_b\rangle$ represent three components of the RGB color image, respectively.

Since

$$\||\psi_C\rangle\| = \sqrt{\sum_{i=0}^{2^n-1} (\theta_{ri}^2 + \theta_{gi}^2 + \theta_{bi}^2)} = 1, \tag{3.101}$$

Figure 11. The implementation circuit of NASSTC

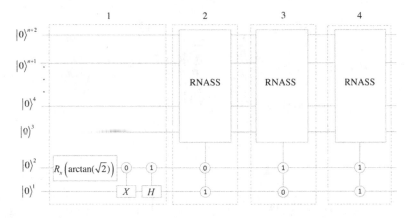

$\left|\psi_C\right\rangle$ is a normal state.

The Implementation Circuit of NASSTC

$\left|\psi_C\right\rangle$ in (3.100) is implemented by the quantum circuit shown in Figure 11. The dashed boxes i (i=2,3,4) are the implementation circuits of $\left|\psi_r\right\rangle$, $\left|\psi_g\right\rangle$ and $\left|\psi_b\right\rangle$ in (3.99), respectively, and their detail circuits are shown in Figure 12. For instance, the dashed box 2 is implemented in Figure 12 when i_1=0 and i_2=1 .

Figure 12. Implementations of The dashed box $i=i_2i_1$ (i=2,3,4) in Figure 11.

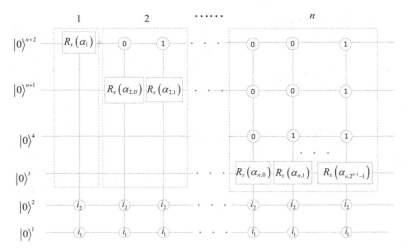

Since

$$[R_x(\arctan 2) \otimes I](|0\rangle \otimes)|0\rangle = \begin{vmatrix} \dfrac{1}{\sqrt{3}} & \dfrac{2}{\sqrt{3}} \\ \dfrac{2}{\sqrt{3}} & -\dfrac{1}{\sqrt{3}} \end{vmatrix}|0\rangle \otimes|0\rangle = \left(\dfrac{1}{\sqrt{3}}|0\rangle + \dfrac{\sqrt{2}}{\sqrt{3}}|1\rangle\right) \otimes|0\rangle,$$

(3.102)

and

$$C_1^1(H)C_1^1(x)\left\{\left[\left(\dfrac{1}{\sqrt{3}}|0\rangle + \dfrac{\sqrt{2}}{\sqrt{3}}|1\rangle\right) \otimes|0\rangle\right]\right\} = \dfrac{1}{\sqrt{3}}|0\rangle|0\rangle + \dfrac{1}{\sqrt{3}}|1\rangle|0\rangle + \dfrac{1}{\sqrt{3}}|1\rangle|1\rangle,$$

(3.103)

applying the circuit in the dashed box 1 to the initial state, we obtain

$$|\psi_C\rangle^1 = \dfrac{1}{\sqrt{3}}|0\rangle^{\otimes n}(|01\rangle + |10\rangle + |11\rangle),$$

(3.104)

Next, applying the circuit in the dashed box 2 to $|\psi_C\rangle^1$, we have

$$|\psi_C\rangle^2 = \dfrac{1}{\sqrt{3}}|\psi_r\rangle|01\rangle + \dfrac{1}{\sqrt{3}}|0\rangle^{\otimes n}(|10\rangle + |11\rangle).$$

(3.105)

Then, applying the circuit in the dashed box 3 to $|\psi_C\rangle^2$, we obtain

$$|\psi_C\rangle^3 = \dfrac{1}{\sqrt{3}}|\psi_r\rangle|01\rangle + \dfrac{1}{\sqrt{3}}|\psi_g\rangle|01\rangle + \dfrac{1}{\sqrt{3}}|0\rangle^{\otimes n}|11\rangle,$$

(3.106)

Finally, after performing the circuit in the dashed box 3 to $|\psi_C\rangle^3$, we obtain the output $|\psi_C\rangle$ in (3.100).

The complexity of the circuit in the dashed box 1 is $O(1)$. Compared the circuits in the dashed boxes i ($i=2,3,4$)in Figure 12 with the circuit in

Figure 8, their complexity is given as $O(n^2 2^n)$. Therefore, the complexity of NASSTC is $O(n^2 2^n)$.

Image Retrieval Based on NASSTC

We define the observable operator M_c,

$$M_c = \sum_{j=0}^{2^n-1} (m_j^i P_j^r + m_j^g P_j^g + m_j^b P_j^b),$$ (3.107)

where $P_j^r = |j\rangle|01\rangle\langle j|\langle 01|$, $P_j^g = |j\rangle|10\rangle\langle j|\langle 10|$ and $P_j^b = |j\rangle|11\rangle\langle j|\langle 11|$.

Applying the observable operator M_c on $|\psi_c\rangle$ obtains m_j^r with probability $p(m_j^r) = \langle \psi_C | P_j^r | \psi_C \rangle = \theta_{rj}^2$, i.e.,

$$\theta_{rj} = \sqrt{p(m_j^r)}.$$ (3.108)

Similarly, we have

$$\theta_{gj} = \sqrt{p(m_j^g)},$$ (3.109)

and

$$\theta_{rj} = \sqrt{p(m_j^r)}.$$ (3.110)

We can calculate $n_{r\theta}$, $n_{g\theta}$, and $n_{b\theta}$ using (3.94) where $n_{r\theta}$, $n_{g\theta}$, and $n_{b\theta}$ are the numbers of identical quantum states required to obtain the accuracy angles θ_{rj}, θ_{gj}, and θ_{bj}, respectively. Therefore, a color and coordinate of an image based on NASSTC can be retrieved by $O(2^n M^4)$ measurements, where $M=256$.

THE MODEL OF A NORMAL ARBITRARY QUANTUM SUPERPOSITION STATE

A normal arbitrary quantum superposition state (NAQSS) consists of $(n+1)$ qubits, where n qubits represent colors and coordinates of 2^n pixels, and the remaining one qubit represents an image segmentation information to improve the accuracy of image segmentation (Li, Zhu, Zhou, Song, & Yang, 2014). In this section, we describe the representation, storage and retrieval of images based on NAQSS.

Representation of a Multidimensional Image Based on NAQSS

We define

$$\left|\chi_i\right\rangle = \cos\gamma_i\left|0\right\rangle + \sin\gamma_i\left|1\right\rangle \tag{3.111}$$

where the angle $\gamma_i \in A_\eta$ in (3.10) an integer.

A normal arbitrary quantum superposition state (NAQSS) is defined as

$$\left|\psi_\chi\right\rangle = \sum_{i=0}^{2^n-1}\theta_i\left|i\right\rangle\left|\chi_i\right\rangle = \sum_{i=0}^{2^n-1}\theta_i\left|x_m\right\rangle\left|y_k\right\rangle\left|\chi_i\right\rangle = \sum_{i=0}^{2^n-1}\theta_i\left|i_n\ldots i_{k+1}\right\rangle\left|i_k\ldots i_1\right\rangle\left|\chi_i\right\rangle, \tag{3.112}$$

where $\left|x_m\right\rangle = \left|i_n\ldots i_{k+1}\right\rangle$ and $\left|y_k\right\rangle = \left|i_k\ldots i_1\right\rangle$ are the X-axis and Y-axis of the image, and $n=m+k$. θ_i encodes the color on the on the coordinate $|i\rangle$. $\left|\psi_\chi\right\rangle$ represents an image of 2^n pixels and its additional information. For instance, suppose that an image is segmented into N sub-images according to the semantic content, and the N sub-images are labeled as $1,2,\ldots,N$, then, the state $\left|\chi_i\right\rangle$ represents the label number of a sub-image which includes the pixel on the coordinate $|i\rangle$.

The Implementation Circuit of NAQSS

We apply the circuit RNASS in Figure 8 on the first n state of the initialized state $\left|0\right\rangle^{\otimes(n+1)}$, and obtain $\left|\psi_t\right\rangle = \sum_{i=0}^{2^n-1}\theta_i\left|i\right\rangle\otimes\left|0\right\rangle$. $C_n^i[R_y(\gamma_i)]\left|\psi_t\right\rangle$ is equal to

$$C_n^i[R_y(\gamma_i)]|\psi_t\rangle = \sum_{i=0}^{2^n-1} \theta_i |i\rangle \otimes (\cos\gamma_i |0\rangle + \sin\gamma_i |1\rangle,$$

where

$$R_y(\gamma_i) = \begin{bmatrix} \cos\gamma_i & -\sin\gamma_i \\ \sin\gamma_i & \cos\gamma_i \end{bmatrix}, \tag{3.113}$$

So applying successively $C_n^i[R_y(\gamma_i)]$ on $|\psi_t\rangle$, we create a NAQSS state,

$$|\psi_\chi\rangle = \left(\prod_{i=0}^{2^n-1} C_n^i[R_y(\gamma_i)]\right)|\psi_t\rangle = \sum_{i=0}^{2^n-1} \theta_i |i\rangle(\cos\gamma_i |0\rangle + \sin\gamma_i |1\rangle). \tag{3.114}$$

$|\psi_\chi\rangle$ is realized by the circuit shown in Figure 13. The circuit in the red box corresponds to $\prod_{i=0}^{2^n-1} C_n^i[R_y(\gamma_i)]$.

The determinant of matrices $R_y(\gamma_i)$ is one, i.e., $R_y(\gamma_i) \in \mathrm{SU}(2)$, so the complexity of $C_n^i(R_y(\gamma_i))$ is $O(n)$ by Corollary 2.8. The circuit in the red box in Figure 13 consists of 2^n gates, so its complexity is $O(n2^n)$. Meanwhile, the complexity of the implementation circuit of NASS is $O(n^2 2^n)$. Therefore, the complexity of the implementation circuit of NAQSS is also $O(n^2 2^n)$.

Image Retrieval Based on NAQSS

Define an observable operator M_1 as

$$M_1 = \sum_{j=0}^{2^n-1} m_j P_j, \tag{3.115}$$

where $P_j = |j\rangle\langle j| \otimes I$. Apply M_1 to measure the NAQSS state $|\psi_\chi\rangle$ in (3.112), and obtain the coordinate $|j\rangle$ with probability $p(m_j) = \langle \psi_\chi | P_j | \psi_\chi \rangle = \theta_j^2$, i.e.,

$$\theta_j = \sqrt{p(m_j)}. \tag{3.116}$$

Figure 13. The realization circuit of NAQSS

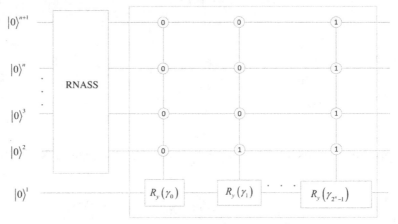

The state after measurement is

$$\frac{P_j \left| \psi_\chi(r) \right\rangle}{\sqrt{p(m_j)}} = \left| j \right\rangle \left| \chi_j \right\rangle, \tag{3.117}$$

where $j=0,1,\ldots,2^n-1$.

We can calculate n_θ using (3.94) where n_θ is the number of identical quantum states required to obtain the accuracy angles θ_j. Therefore, a color and coordinate of an image based on NAQSS can be retrieved by $O(2^n M^4)$ measurements, where M is the size of the color set *Color* in (3.5).

Next, using the method in the model of QSMC and QSNC, we can retrieve the integer from the state $\left| j \right\rangle \left| \chi_j \right\rangle$ after $O(\lambda^4)$ measurements, where λ is the size of the integer set A_η in (3.10).

A coordinate, a color, and an additional information of an image based on NAQSS can be retrieved by $O(2^n M^4 \lambda^4)$ measurements.

FLEXIBLE QUANTUM REPRESENTATION FOR GRAY-LEVEL IMAGES

Flexible quantum representation for gray-level images (FQRGI) was proposed to store a $2^n \times 2^n$ image using phases (Yang, Xia, Jia, & Zhang, 2013). However, the implement circuit and the retrieval method of FQRGI were not given in the reference. In this section, we introduce the representation of image based on FQRGI, and supplement its circuit and retrieval method.

Representation of an Image Based on FQRGI

FQRGI is defined as

$$\left| I(\theta) \right\rangle = \frac{1}{2^n} \sum_{j=0}^{2^{2n}-1} \left| c_j \right\rangle \otimes \left| j \right\rangle,$$
(3.118)

$$\left| c_j \right\rangle = \frac{\sqrt{2}}{2} \left(\left| 0 \right\rangle + e^{i\theta_j} \left| 1 \right\rangle \right),$$
(3.119)

where $|j\rangle$ $(j=0,1,\ldots,2^{2n}-1)$ encodes a coordinate of an $2^n \times 2^n$ gray-level image, and $|c_j\rangle$ represents the color on the coordinate $|j\rangle$.

The Implementation Circuit of FQRGI

The matrixes $E(\theta_j)$ with $j=0,1,\ldots,2^{2n}-1$,

$$E(\theta_j) = \begin{bmatrix} 1 & 0 \\ 0 & e^{i\theta_j} \end{bmatrix},$$
(3.120)

are substituted for U in (2.32) to get

$$V_{2n}^j(E(\theta_j)) = E(\theta_j) \otimes \left(\left| j \right\rangle \left\langle j \right| \right) + \sum_{k=0,k\neq j}^{2^{2n}-1} \left(I \otimes \left(\left| k \right\rangle \left\langle k \right| \right) \right).$$
(3.121)

Applying $V_{2n}^j(E(\theta_j))(I \otimes H^{\otimes 2n})$ on the initial states $\left| 0 \right\rangle^{\otimes 2n+1}$ gives

$$V_{2n}^j(E(\theta_j))H^{\otimes 2n+1}\left|0\right\rangle^{\otimes 2n+1} = V_{2n}^j(E(\theta_j))\frac{1}{2^n}\left[\frac{\sqrt{2}}{2}(\left|0\right\rangle+\left|1\right\rangle)\otimes\sum_{k=0}^{2^{2n}-1}\left|k\right\rangle\right]$$

$$= \frac{1}{2^n}\left[\frac{\sqrt{2}}{2}(\left|0\right\rangle+\left|1\right\rangle)\otimes\sum_{k=0,k\neq ij}^{2^{2n}-1}\left|k\right\rangle+(\left|0\right\rangle+e^{i\theta_j}\left|1\right\rangle)\otimes\left|j\right\rangle\right]. \tag{3.122}$$

Therefore, an image is stored in a quantum system by using

$$\left[\prod_{j=0}^{2^{2n}-1}V_{2n}^j(E(\theta_j))\right]H^{\otimes 2n+1}\left|0\right\rangle^{\otimes 2n+1} = \left|I(\theta)\right\rangle, \tag{3.123}$$

its implementation circuit is as shown in Figure 14. The complexity of $V_{2n}^j(E(\theta_j))$ is $O(n^2)$ by Corollary 2.16, and the implementation circuit of FQRGI consists of 2^{2n} gates for a $2^n \times 2^n$ image, so its complexity is $O(n^2 2^{2n})$.

Figure 14. An implementation circuit of FQRGI.

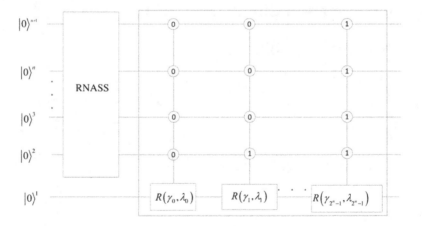

Image Retrieval Based on FQRGI

Using the observable operator M_1 in (3.52) to measure the FQRGI state $\left|I(\theta)\right\rangle$, we obtain the coordinate $\left|j\right\rangle$ with probability $1/2^{2n}$. That is, the coordinate $\left|j\right\rangle$ can be retrieved by 2^{2n} measurements. The state after measurement is

$$\frac{P_j \left| I(\theta) \right\rangle}{2^n} = \frac{\sqrt{2}}{2} \left(\left| 0 \right\rangle + e^{i\theta_j} \left| 1 \right\rangle \right) \left| j \right\rangle = \left| T(\theta_j) \right\rangle \left| j \right\rangle, \tag{3.124}$$

where $\left| T(\theta_j) \right\rangle = \left(\left| 0 \right\rangle + e^{i\theta_j} \left| 1 \right\rangle \right) / \sqrt{2}$.

Applying a Hadanard gate on $|T(\theta_j)\rangle$ gives

$$H \left| T(\theta_j) \right\rangle = \frac{1}{2} [(1 + e^{i\theta_j}) \left| 0 \right\rangle + (1 - e^{i\theta_j}) \left| 1 \right\rangle], \tag{3.125}$$

Suppose the result is $|0\rangle$ with probability p_0. by applying the observable operator $m_0 |0\rangle\langle 0| + m_1 |1\rangle\langle 1|$ in (3.11) to measure

$$[(1 + e^{i\theta_j}) \left| 0 \right\rangle + (1 - e^{i\theta_j}) \left| 1 \right\rangle] / 2,$$

we calculate

$$\theta_j = \arcsin \sqrt{p}, \tag{3.126}$$

where $p = \sqrt{4p_0 - 4p_0^2}$. Thus, using the method in the model of QSMC and QSNC, we can retrieve the angle θ_j after $O(M^4)$ measurements, where M is the size of the color set *Color* in (3.5).

Through the above analysis, we conclude that a color and coordinate of an image based on FQRGI can be retrieved by $O(2^{2n}M^4)$ measurements.

THE MODE OF A NORMAL ARBITRARY SUPERPOSITION STATE WITH RELATIVE PHASES

A normal arbitrary superposition state with relative phases (NASSRP) was proposed to store an image and its additional information (Li, Zhu, Zhou, Li, Song, & Ian, 2014).

Representation of an Image Based on NASSRP

We define

$$\left|\varphi_j\right\rangle = \cos\gamma_j\left|0\right\rangle + e^{i\lambda_j}\sin\gamma_j\left|1\right\rangle, \tag{3.127}$$

where $\gamma_j \in \{A_\eta - \pi/2\}$ and $\lambda_j \in A_\eta$ in (3.10) represent two integers, and the set $\{A_\eta - \pi/2\}$ excludes the element $\pi/2$. Then, a normal arbitrary superposition state with relative phases (NASSRP) for a $2^{n-k} \times 2^k$ image is defined as

$$\left|\psi_{RP}\right\rangle = \sum_{j=0}^{2^n-1}\theta_j\left|j\right\rangle\left|\varphi_j\right\rangle = \sum_{j=0}^{2^n-1}\theta_j\left|x_m\right\rangle\left|y_k\right\rangle\left|\varphi_j\right\rangle = \sum_{j=0}^{2^n-1}\theta_j\left|j_n\cdots j_{k+1}\right\rangle\left|j_k\cdots j_1\right\rangle\left|\varphi_j\right\rangle, \tag{3.128}$$

where $\left|x_m\right\rangle = \left|i_n\cdots i_{k+1}\right\rangle$ and $\left|y_k\right\rangle = \left|i_k\cdots i_1\right\rangle$ are the X-axis and Y-axis of the image, and $n=m+k$. θ_j encodes the color on the on the coordinate $|j\rangle$.

The Implementation Circuit of NASSRP

A unitary matrix is defined as

$$R(\theta,\alpha) = \begin{bmatrix} \cos\theta & -\sin\theta \\ e^{i\alpha}\sin\theta & e^{i\alpha}\cos\theta \end{bmatrix}. \tag{3.129}$$

where $\theta,\alpha \in [0,2\pi]$.

The following state is given by applying the circuit RNASS in Figure 8 on the first n state of the initialized state $\left|0\right\rangle^{\otimes(n+1)}$,

$$\left|\psi_t\right\rangle = \sum_{j=0}^{2^n-1}\theta_j\left|j\right\rangle\otimes\left|0\right\rangle. \tag{3.130}$$

Since the unitary matrix $R(\gamma_j,\lambda_j)$ has the following property

$$R(\gamma_j,\lambda_j)\left|0\right\rangle = \cos\gamma_j\left|0\right\rangle + e^{i\lambda_j}\sin\gamma_j\left|1\right\rangle, \tag{3.131}$$

applying successively $C_n^i[R(\gamma_j,\lambda_j)]$ on $\left|\psi_t\right\rangle$, we obtain a NASSRP state,

$$\left|\psi_{Ap}\right\rangle=\left(\prod_{j=0}^{2^n-1}C_n^j[R(\gamma_j,\lambda_j)]\right)\left|\psi_t\right\rangle=\sum_{j=0}^{2^n-1}\theta_j\left|j\right\rangle(\cos\gamma_j\left|0\right\rangle+e^{i\lambda_j}\sin\gamma_j\left|1\right\rangle).\quad(3.132)$$

Therefore, $\left|\psi_{Ap}\right\rangle$ can be realized by the circuit shown in Figure 15. The circuit in the red box corresponds to $\prod_{j=0}^{2^n-1}C_n^j[R(\gamma_j,\lambda_j)]$.

Figure 15. The realization of NASSRP

$$|I\rangle=\frac{1}{2}(|0\rangle|00\rangle+|100\rangle|01\rangle+|200\rangle|10\rangle+|255\rangle|11\rangle)$$

$$=\frac{1}{2}(|00000000\rangle|00\rangle+|01100100\rangle|01\rangle+|11001000\rangle|10\rangle$$

$$+|11111111\rangle|11\rangle)$$

The complexity of the implementation circuit of NASS is $O(n^2 2^n)$. The complexity of $C_n^i[R(\gamma_j,\lambda_j)]$ is $O(n^2)$ by Corollary 2.16, and the circuit in the red box consists of 2^n gates, so its complexity is $O(n^2 2^n)$. Therefore, the complexity of the implementation circuit of NASSRP for a $2^{n-k}\times 2^k$ image is $O(n^2 2^n)$.

Image Retrieval Based on NASSRP

First applying the observable operator M_1 in (3.115) to measure the NASSRP state $\left|\psi_{RP}\right\rangle$, we obtain the θ_j by $O(2^n M^4)$ measurements. The state after measurement is $|j\rangle|\varphi_j\rangle$ by the observable operator M_j. Next, we use the observable operator $m_0|0\rangle\langle0|+m_1|1\rangle\langle1|$ in (3.11) to measure $|\varphi_j\rangle$, and retrieve γ_j by $O(\lambda^4)$ measurements. Then, a Hadanard gate is applied on $|\varphi_j\rangle$ to give

$$H\left|\varphi_j\right\rangle=\frac{\sqrt{2}}{2}[(\cos\gamma_j+\sin\gamma_j e^{i\lambda_j})\left|0\right\rangle+(\cos\gamma_j-\sin\gamma_j e^{i\lambda_j})\left|1\right\rangle]=\left|\varsigma_j\right\rangle.\quad(3.133)$$

Suppose the result is $|0\rangle$ with probability p by applying the observable operator $m_0|0\rangle\langle0|+m_1|1\rangle\langle1|$ to measure $\left|\varsigma_j\right\rangle$, we calculate

$$\lambda_j = \arcsin \frac{\sqrt{4p - 4p^2 - \cos^2(2\gamma_j)}}{\sin(2\gamma_j)}, \tag{3.134}$$

here, $\sin(2\gamma_j) \neq 0$ because $\gamma_j \in \{A_\eta - \pi/2\}$ (see (3.127)). Thus, using the method in the model of QSMC and QSNC, we can retrieve the angle λ_j after $O(\lambda^4)$ measurements.

Through the above analysis, we conclude that a color, a coordinate, and two integers stored in a NASSRP state can be retrieved by $O(2^n M^4 \lambda^8)$ measurements, where M is the size of the color set *Color* in (3.5), and λ is the size of the integer set *Number* in (3.10).

A NOVEL ENHANCED QUANTUM REPRESENTATION

A novel enhanced quantum representation (NEQR) was proposed to store a color in q-qubit basis states (Zhang, Lu, Gao, & Wang, 2013). In this section, we describe the representation, storage and retrieval of images based on NEQR.

Representation of an Image Based on NEQR

Suppose the gray range of an image is 2^q, the grayscale value $f(Y,X)$ of the corresponding pixel (Y, X) is

$$f(Y, X) = C_{YX}^0 C_{YX}^1 \ldots C_{YX}^{q-2} C_{YX}^{q-1}, \tag{3.135}$$

where $f(Y,X) \in \{0,1,\ldots,2^q - 1\}$, $C_{YX}^k \in \{0,1\}$, and $k = 0,1,\ldots,q - 1$. The representation of a quantum image for a $2^n \times 2^n$ image can be written as

$$|I\rangle = \frac{1}{2^n} \sum_{Y=0}^{2^n-1} \sum_{X=0}^{2^n-1} |f(Y,X)\rangle |YX\rangle, \tag{3.136}$$

where $|Y\rangle = |y_n \ldots y_2 y_1\rangle$ and $|X\rangle = |x_n \ldots x_2 x_1\rangle$ are the Y-axis and X-axis of the image. For instance, a 2×2 grayscale image is shown in Figure 16.

Figure 16. A 2x2 image and its representation of NEQR

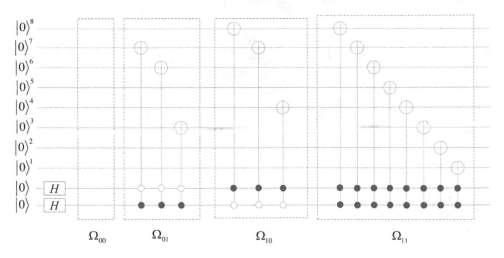

The Implementation Circuit of NEQR

Hadamard gates are used to transform the initial state $|0\rangle^{\otimes 2n+q}$ to the intermediate state $|T\rangle$,

$$(I^{\otimes q} \otimes H^{\otimes 2n})|0\rangle^{\otimes 2n+q} = \frac{1}{2^n} \sum_{Y=0}^{2^n-1} \sum_{X=0}^{2^n-1} |0\rangle^{\otimes q} |YX\rangle = |T\rangle. \qquad (3.137)$$

A quantum operation is defined as

$$\Omega_{YX} = \mathop{\otimes}_{i=0}^{q-1} \Omega_{YX}^i, \qquad (3.138)$$

where Ω_{YX}^i is an identity gate or a NOT gate, i.e.,

$$\Omega_{YX}^i : |0\rangle \to |C_{YX}^i\rangle. \qquad (3.139)$$

Therefore, $|f(Y,X)\rangle$ is given by

$$\Omega_{YX}|0\rangle^{\otimes q} = |f(Y,X)\rangle. \qquad (3.140)$$

Substituting Ω_{YX} for U in (2.32), we have

$$V_{2n}^{YX}(\Omega_{YX}) = \Omega_{YX} \otimes \left(|YX\rangle\langle YX| \right) + \sum_{j=0, j \neq YX}^{2^{2n}-1} \left(I^{\otimes q} \otimes \left(|j\rangle\langle j| \right) \right), \qquad (3.141)$$

which is applied on the intermediate state $|T\rangle$ to give

$$V_{2n}^{YX}(\Omega_{YX})|T\rangle = \frac{1}{2^n}\left[\left| f(Y,X) \right\rangle |YX\rangle + \sum_{j=0, j \neq YX}^{2^{2n}-1} |0\rangle^{\otimes q} |j\rangle \right]. \qquad (3.142)$$

Therefore, an image is stored in a quantum system by using

$$\left[\prod_{Y=0}^{2^n-1} \prod_{X=0}^{2^n-1} V_{2n}^{YX}(\Omega_{YX}) \right] (I^{\otimes q} \otimes H^{\otimes 2n}) |0\rangle^{\otimes 2n+q} = \frac{1}{2^n} \sum_{Y=0}^{2^n-1} \sum_{X=0}^{2^n-1} \left| f(Y,X) \right\rangle |YX\rangle. \quad (3.143)$$

For instance, Figure 17 shows the detailed circuit for NEQR preparation for the image shown in Figure 16.

Let Λ_{2n} be a $(2n+q)$-qubit controlled-NOT gate with n control qubits. Since Ω_{YX}^i is an identity gate or a NOT gate, $V_{2n}^{YX}(\Omega_{YX})$ consists of q identity gates or Λ_{2n} gates. The complexity of $V_{2n}^{YX}(\Omega_{YX})$ is $O(qn)$ by Corollary 2.14. The formula (3.143) shows that the complexity of constructing a $2^n \times 2^n$ image for NEQR is $O(qn2^{2n})$.

Figure 17. Quantum circuit of NEQR for the image in Figure 16

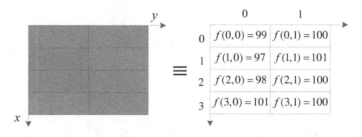

Image Retrieval Based on NEQR

Define an observable operator Γ

$$\Gamma = \sum_{j=0}^{2^{2n}-1} m_j P_j, \tag{3.144}$$

where $P_j = I^{\otimes q} \otimes |j\rangle\langle j|$. Apply Γ to measure the NEQR state $|I\rangle$, and obtain the coordinate $|j\rangle$ by 2^{2n} measurements. The state after measurement is

$$\frac{P_j|I\rangle}{2^n} = |f(Y,Y)\rangle|j\rangle, \tag{3.145}$$

where $|j\rangle = |YX\rangle$.

Since $|f(Y,X)\rangle$ is a basis state with q qubits, after one measurement, the grayscale value $f(Y,X)$ can be retrieved by the following observable operator

$$\left(\sum_{i=0}^{2^q-1} m_i |i\rangle\langle i|\right) \otimes I^{\otimes 2n}. \tag{3.146}$$

Thus, a color and a coordinate of an image based on NEQR can be retrieved by $O(2^{2n})$ measurements.

THE MODEL OF A GENERALIZED NEQR

A generalized NEQR was proposed to store a $2^{n-k} \times 2^k$ image (GNEQR) (Li, Fan, Xia, Peng, & Song, 2019). In this section, we describe the representation of grayscale and color images based on GNEQR, and introduce their implementation circuits and retrieval methods.

Representation and Storage of a Grayscale Image Based on GNEQR

A 2^m-level grayscale set with is defined as

$$\mathcal{C}_m = \{0, 1, \ldots, 2^m - 1\}, \tag{3.147}$$

where m is an integer.

GNEQR for a $2^{n-k} \times 2^k$ grayscale image is defined as

$$\left|\Psi_G^m\right\rangle = \frac{1}{\sqrt{2^n}} \sum_{x=0}^{2^{n-k}-1} \sum_{y=0}^{2^k-1} \left|f(x,y)\right\rangle \left|x\right\rangle \left|y\right\rangle, \tag{3.148}$$

where $\left|x\right\rangle = \left|i_n \ldots i_{k+1}\right\rangle$ and $|y\rangle = |i_k, \ldots, i_1\rangle$ are the X-axis and Y-axis of the image, and $i_1, \ldots i_k, \ldots, i_n \in \{0, 1\}$. Here, $|f(x,y)\rangle$ denotes the color of the pixel on the coordinate (x,y), $f(x,y) \in \mathcal{C}_m$. For instance, the GNEQR state

$$\left|\Psi_1\right\rangle = \frac{1}{\sqrt{2^3}} (\left|99\right\rangle\left|0\right\rangle\left|0\right\rangle + \left|100\right\rangle\left|0\right\rangle\left|1\right\rangle + \left|97\right\rangle\left|1\right\rangle\left|0\right\rangle + \left|101\right\rangle\left|1\right\rangle\left|1\right\rangle$$
$$+ \left|98\right\rangle\left|2\right\rangle\left|0\right\rangle + \left|100\right\rangle\left|2\right\rangle\left|1\right\rangle + \left|101\right\rangle\left|3\right\rangle\left|0\right\rangle + \left|100\right\rangle\left|3\right\rangle\left|1\right\rangle)$$
$$= \frac{1}{\sqrt{2^3}} (\left|1100011\right\rangle\left|00\right\rangle\left|0\right\rangle + \left|1100100\right\rangle\left|00\right\rangle\left|1\right\rangle + \left|1100001\right\rangle\left|01\right\rangle\left|0\right\rangle + \left|1100101\right\rangle\left|01\right\rangle\left|1\right\rangle$$
$$+ \left|1100010\right\rangle\left|10\right\rangle\left|0\right\rangle + \left|1100100\right\rangle\left|10\right\rangle\left|1\right\rangle + \left|1100101\right\rangle\left|11\right\rangle\left|0\right\rangle + \left|1100100\right\rangle\left|11\right\rangle\left|1\right\rangle)$$

$$\tag{3.149}$$

represents a 4×4 grayscale image shown in Figure 18.

Figure 18. A 4x2 image

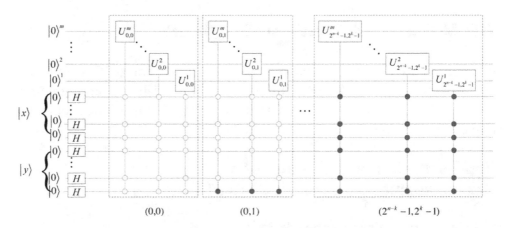

Suppose $f(x,y)$ is expressed as

$$f(x,y) = c_{x,y}^m c_{x,y}^{m-1} \ldots c_{x,y}^1, \tag{3.150}$$

where $c_{x,y}^i \in \{0,1\}$ and $i=1,2,\ldots,m$. Let be

$$U_{x,y}^i = (c_{x,y}^i \oplus 1)I + c_{x,y}^i X, \tag{3.151}$$

where $\oplus$ is an exclusive-or operator, and X is a NOT gate.
Applying

$$V_n^j(\overset{m}{\underset{k=1}{\otimes}} U_{x,y}^k)(I^{\otimes m} \otimes H^{\otimes n})$$

on the initial state $|0\rangle^{\otimes n+m}$ gives

$$V_n^j(\overset{m}{\underset{k=1}{\otimes}} U_{x,y}^k)(I^{\otimes m} \otimes H^{\otimes n}) = \frac{1}{\sqrt{2^n}}\left[\Big| f(x,y)\rangle |x\rangle |y\rangle + \sum_{i=0, i\neq j}^{2^n-1} |0\rangle^{\otimes m} |i\rangle \right]. \tag{3.152}$$

where $|j\rangle = |x\rangle|y\rangle$. Applying the operations $V_n^j(\overset{m}{\underset{k=1}{\otimes}} U_{x,y}^k)$ with $j=0,1,\ldots,2^n-1$ successively on $(I^{\otimes m} \otimes H^{\otimes n})|0\rangle^{\otimes n+m}$, we obtain the circuit of GNEQR for a

Figure 19. The implementation circuit of GNEQR for a $2^{n-k} \times 2^k$ grayscale image.

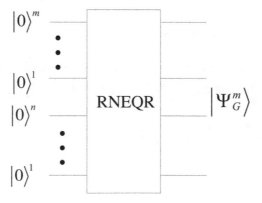

$2^{n-k} \times 2^k$ grayscale image shown in Figure 19. Its abbreviated notation is shown in Figure 20.

Figure 20. The abbreviated notation of the realization circuits of GNEQR.

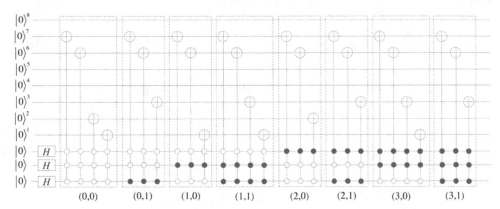

The example of the circuit in Figure 19 is shown in Figure 21. It implements the quantum storage of the 4×2 grayscale image in Figure 18.

Figure 21. The implementation circuit of $\left| \Psi_1 \right\rangle$ in (3.149).

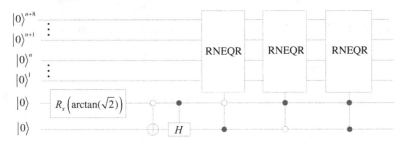

With the analysis similar to the mode of NEQR, we obtain that the complexity of constructing a $2^{n-k} \times 2^k$ grayscale image for GNEQR is $O(mn2^n)$.

Representation and Storage of a RGB Color Image Based on GNEQR

$\left| \Psi^8_G \right\rangle$ can represent the Red, Green, or Blue channel of a $2^{n-k} \times 2^k$ RGB color image, and is renamed by $\left| \Psi^8_{Gr} \right\rangle$, $\left| \Psi^8_{Gg} \right\rangle$, or $\left| \Psi^8_{Gb} \right\rangle$,

$$
\begin{cases}
\left| \Psi^8_{Gr} \right\rangle = \dfrac{1}{\sqrt{2^n}} \sum_{x=0}^{2^{n-k}-1} \sum_{y=0}^{2^k-1} \left| f_r(x,y) \right\rangle \left| x \right\rangle \left| y \right\rangle, \\[2mm]
\left| \Psi^8_{Gg} \right\rangle = \dfrac{1}{\sqrt{2^n}} \sum_{x=0}^{2^{n-k}-1} \sum_{y=0}^{2^k-1} \left| f_g(x,y) \right\rangle \left| x \right\rangle \left| y \right\rangle, \\[2mm]
\left| \Psi^8_{Gg} \right\rangle = \dfrac{1}{\sqrt{2^n}} \sum_{x=0}^{2^{n-k}-1} \sum_{y=0}^{2^k-1} \left| f_b(x,y) \right\rangle \left| x \right\rangle \left| y \right\rangle,
\end{cases}
\tag{3.153}
$$

where $|f_r(x,y)\rangle$, $|f_g(x,y)\rangle$, and $|f_b(x,y)\rangle$ denotes the Red, Green, and Blue components of the color of the pixel on the coordinate (x,y). Then, GNEQR for a $2^{n-k} \times 2^k$ RGB color image is defined as

$$
\left| \Psi_{GC} \right\rangle = \frac{1}{\sqrt{3}} \left(\left| \Psi^8_{Gr} \right\rangle \left| 01 \right\rangle + \left| \Psi^8_{Gg} \right\rangle \left| 10 \right\rangle + \left| \Psi^8_{Gb} \right\rangle \left| 11 \right\rangle \right).
\tag{3.154}
$$

With the analysis similar to the implementation circuit of NASSTC, substituting the circuit RNEQR for the circuit RNASS in Figure 11, we obtain the implementation circuit of GNEQR for a $2^{n-k} \times 2^k$ RGB color image shown in Figure 22.

Figure 22. The implementation circuit of $\left| \Psi_{GC} \right\rangle$.

Since the complexity of the circuit RNEQR is $O(mn2^n)$, the complexity of GNEQR for a $2^{n-k} \times 2^k$ RGB color image is $O(3mn2^n)$, where $m=8$.

Image Retrieval Based on GNEQR

Using the method of NEQR, we retrieve a color and a coordinate of a $2^{n-k} \times 2^k$ grayscale image based on GNEQR after $O(2^n)$ measurements.

Define the observable operator M_c as

$$M_c = \sum_{j=0}^{2} m_j P_j,$$
(3.155)

where $P_j = I^{\otimes n+8} \otimes |j\rangle\langle j|$.

The state $\left|\Psi_{GC}\right\rangle$ for a color image collapses into $\left|\Psi_{Gr}^8\right\rangle$, $\left|\Psi_{Gg}^8\right\rangle$, or $\left|\Psi_{Gb}^8\right\rangle$ with probability 1/3 by the observable operator M_c. Then, we retrieve three grayscale images from $\left|\Psi_{Gr}^8\right\rangle$, $\left|\Psi_{Gg}^8\right\rangle$, and $\left|\Psi_{Gb}^8\right\rangle$ using the method of NEQR. Therefore, a color and a coordinate of a $2^{n-k} \times 2^k$ color image based on GNEQR are retrieved after $O(2^n)$ measurements.

Figure 23. Bitplanes of a grayscale image

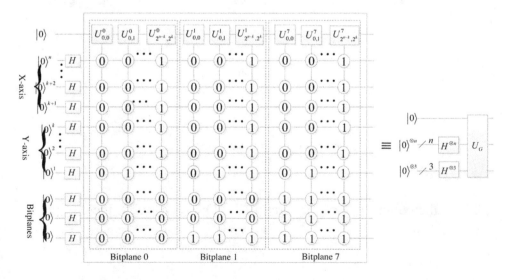

82

A BITPLANE REPRESENTATION OF QUANTUM IMAGES

A bitplane representation of quantum images (BRQI) was proposed to represent grayscale or RGB color images (Li, Chen, Xia, Liang, & Zhou, 2018). In this section, we describe the representation, storage and retrieval of images based on BRQI.

Representation and Storage of a Grayscale Image Based on BRQI

A gray scale consists of 8 binary bits, so a grayscale image can be decomposed into eight binary images (i.e., 8 bitplanes) shown in Figure 23.

Each of bitplanes of a grayscale image can be represented as,

$$\left|\Psi^j\right\rangle = \frac{1}{\sqrt{2^n}} \sum_{x=0}^{2^{n-k}-1} \sum_{y=0}^{2^k-1} \left|g(x,y,j)\right\rangle \left|x\right\rangle \left|y\right\rangle, \tag{3.156}$$

where j denotes the j-th bitplane, $j=0,1,\ldots,7$, and $g(x,y,j)\in\{0,1\}$. For instance, the least significant bit of the image in Figure 18 is represented as

$$\left|\Psi^0\right\rangle = \frac{1}{\sqrt{2^3}} \left(\left|1\right\rangle\left|00\right\rangle\left|0\right\rangle + \left|0\right\rangle\left|00\right\rangle\left|1\right\rangle + \left|1\right\rangle\left|01\right\rangle\left|0\right\rangle + \left|1\right\rangle\left|01\right\rangle\left|1\right\rangle \right.$$
$$\left. + \left|0\right\rangle\left|10\right\rangle\left|0\right\rangle + \left|0\right\rangle\left|10\right\rangle\left|1\right\rangle + \left|1\right\rangle\left|11\right\rangle\left|0\right\rangle + \left|0\right\rangle\left|11\right\rangle\left|1\right\rangle\right). \tag{3.157}$$

To represent the eight bitplanes using a state, we define BRQI for a $2^{n-k} \times 2^k$ grayscale image as follows,

$$\left|\Psi_B^8\right\rangle = \frac{1}{\sqrt{2^3}} \sum_{l=0}^{7} \left|\Psi^i\right\rangle \left|l\right\rangle = \frac{1}{\sqrt{2^{n+3}}} \sum_{l=0}^{7} \sum_{x=0}^{2^{n-k}-1} \sum_{y=0}^{2^k-1} \left|g(x,y,l)\right\rangle \left|x\right\rangle \left|y\right\rangle \left|l\right\rangle. \tag{3.158}$$

Applying Hadamard gates on the initial state $\left|0\right\rangle^{\otimes n+4}$ gives

$$(I \otimes H^{\otimes n+3})\left|0\right\rangle^{\otimes n+4} = \frac{1}{\sqrt{2^{n+3}}} \sum_{x=0}^{2^n-1} \sum_{y=0}^{2^n-1} \left|0\right\rangle \left|x\right\rangle \left|y\right\rangle = \left|T\right\rangle. \tag{3.159}$$

An operator $U_{x,y}^l$ is defined as

$$U_{x,y}^l = (g(x,y,l) \oplus 1)I + g(x,y)X , \qquad (3.160)$$

where $\oplus$ is an exclusive-or operator. If $g(x,y,l)=0$, $U_{x,y}^l = I$, otherwise, $U_{x,y}^l = X$. Then, we obtain the BRQI state for a $2^{n-k} \times 2^k$ grayscale image by applying the operations $V_{n+3}^j(U_{x,y}^l)$ with $j = 0,1,\dots,2^{n+3}-1$ successively on $|T\rangle$,

$$\left[\prod_{j=0}^{2^{n+3}-1} V_{n+3}^j(U_{x,y}^l)\right]|T\rangle = \frac{1}{\sqrt{2^{n+3}}} \sum_{l=0}^{7} \sum_{x=0}^{2^{n-k}-1} \sum_{y=0}^{2^k-1} |g(x,y,l)\rangle|x\rangle|y\rangle|l\rangle = |\Psi_B^8\rangle. \quad (3.161)$$

The implementation circuit of BRQI for a $2^{n-k} \times 2^k$ grayscale image is shown in Figure 24. The circuit in the red box is symbolized as U_G.

Figure 24. The implementation circuit of BRQI for grayscale images.

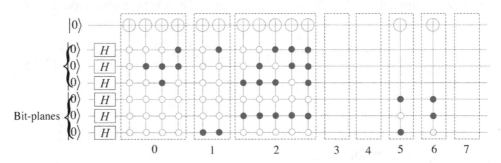

For instance, for a grayscale image shown in Figure 18, the implementation circuit of BRQI is designed in Figure 25.

The circuit in dashed box l is the implementation circuit of the following l-th bitplane $|\Psi^l\rangle$ with $l=0,1,\dots,7$,

Figure 25. The implementation circuit of BRQI for the grayscale image in Figure 18

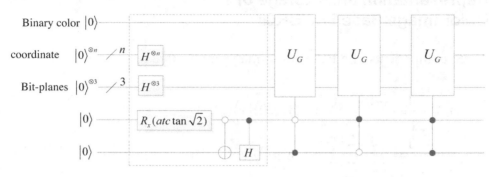

$$\begin{aligned}
\left|\Psi^0\right\rangle &= \frac{1}{\sqrt{2^3}}\left(\left|1\right\rangle\left|00\right\rangle\left|0\right\rangle+\left|0\right\rangle\left|00\right\rangle\left|1\right\rangle+\left|1\right\rangle\left|01\right\rangle\left|0\right\rangle+\left|1\right\rangle\left|01\right\rangle\left|1\right\rangle\right.\\
&\quad\left.+\left|0\right\rangle\left|10\right\rangle\left|0\right\rangle+\left|0\right\rangle\left|10\right\rangle\left|1\right\rangle+\left|1\right\rangle\left|11\right\rangle\left|0\right\rangle+\left|0\right\rangle\left|11\right\rangle\left|1\right\rangle\right),\\
\left|\Psi^1\right\rangle &= \frac{1}{\sqrt{2^3}}\left(\left|1\right\rangle\left|00\right\rangle\left|0\right\rangle+\left|0\right\rangle\left|00\right\rangle\left|1\right\rangle+\left|0\right\rangle\left|01\right\rangle\left|0\right\rangle+\left|0\right\rangle\left|01\right\rangle\left|1\right\rangle\right.\\
&\quad\left.+\left|1\right\rangle\left|10\right\rangle\left|0\right\rangle+\left|0\right\rangle\left|10\right\rangle\left|1\right\rangle+\left|0\right\rangle\left|11\right\rangle\left|0\right\rangle+\left|0\right\rangle\left|11\right\rangle\left|1\right\rangle\right),\\
\left|\Psi^2\right\rangle &= \frac{1}{\sqrt{2^3}}\left(\left|0\right\rangle\left|00\right\rangle\left|0\right\rangle+\left|1\right\rangle\left|00\right\rangle\left|1\right\rangle+\left|0\right\rangle\left|01\right\rangle\left|0\right\rangle+\left|1\right\rangle\left|01\right\rangle\left|1\right\rangle\right.\\
&\quad\left.+\left|0\right\rangle\left|10\right\rangle\left|0\right\rangle+\left|1\right\rangle\left|10\right\rangle\left|1\right\rangle+\left|1\right\rangle\left|11\right\rangle\left|0\right\rangle+\left|1\right\rangle\left|11\right\rangle\left|1\right\rangle\right),\\
\left|\Psi^3\right\rangle &= \left|\Psi^4\right\rangle=\left|\Psi^7\right\rangle=\frac{1}{\sqrt{2^3}}\sum_{x=0}^{3}\sum_{y=0}^{1}\left|0\right\rangle\left|x\right\rangle\left|y\right\rangle,\\
\left|\Psi^5\right\rangle &= \left|\Psi^6\right\rangle=\frac{1}{\sqrt{2^3}}\sum_{x=0}^{3}\sum_{y=0}^{1}\left|1\right\rangle\left|x\right\rangle\left|y\right\rangle.
\end{aligned}$$

$$(3.162)$$

Since the pixel values of the 3rd, 4-th, and 7-th bitplanes are all zero, corresponding circuits do nothing. Values of the pixels in the 5-th and 6-th bitplanes are all one, then, their implementation circuits can be simplified, which are shown in the dashed boxes 5 and 6.

Since the complexity of $V_{n+3}^{j}(U_{x,y}^{l})$ is $O[(n+4)^2]$ by Corollary 2.16, the complexity of the implementation circuit of BRQI for a $2^{n-k}\times 2^{k}$ grayscale image is $O[(n+4)^2 2^{n+3}]$.

Representation and Storage of a Color Image Based on BRQI

Three components of a RGB color image are written as

$$
\begin{cases}
\left|\Psi_B^R\right\rangle = \dfrac{1}{\sqrt{2^{n+3}}} \sum_{l=0}^{2^3-1} \sum_{x=0}^{2^{n-k}-1} \sum_{y=0}^{2^k-1} \left|g_R(x,y,l)\right\rangle\left|x\right\rangle\left|y\right\rangle\left|l\right\rangle, \\
\left|\Psi_B^G\right\rangle = \dfrac{1}{\sqrt{2^{n+3}}} \sum_{l=0}^{2^3-1} \sum_{x=0}^{2^{n-k}-1} \sum_{y=0}^{2^k-1} \left|g_G(x,y,l)\right\rangle\left|x\right\rangle\left|y\right\rangle\left|l\right\rangle, \\
\left|\Psi_B^B\right\rangle = \dfrac{1}{\sqrt{2^{n+3}}} \sum_{l=0}^{2^3-1} \sum_{x=0}^{2^{n-k}-1} \sum_{y=0}^{2^k-1} \left|g_B(x,y,l)\right\rangle\left|x\right\rangle\left|y\right\rangle\left|l\right\rangle,
\end{cases}
\tag{3.163}
$$

where

$$
g_R(x,y,l), g_G(x,y,l), g_B(x,y,l) \in \{0,1\}.
$$

BRQI for a RGB color image is defined as

$$
\left|\Psi_B^{24}\right\rangle = \frac{1}{\sqrt{3}}\left(\left|\Psi_B^R\right\rangle\left|01\right\rangle + \left|\Psi_B^G\right\rangle\left|10\right\rangle + \left|\Psi_B^B\right\rangle\left|11\right\rangle\right),
\tag{3.164}
$$

and is realized by the circuit shown in Figure 26. The circuit in the red dashed box implements

$$
\left|0\right\rangle^{\otimes n+6} \rightarrow \frac{1}{\sqrt{3\times 2^{n+3}}}\left(\sum_{l=0}^{2^3-1}\sum_{x=0}^{2^{n-k}-1}\sum_{y=0}^{2^k-1}\left|0\right\rangle\left|x\right\rangle\left|y\right\rangle\left|l\right\rangle\left|01\right\rangle\right.
$$
$$
\left.+\sum_{l=0}^{2^3-1}\sum_{x=0}^{2^{n-k}-1}\sum_{y=0}^{2^k-1}\left|0\right\rangle\left|x\right\rangle\left|y\right\rangle\left|l\right\rangle\left|10\right\rangle + \sum_{l=0}^{2^3-1}\sum_{x=0}^{2^{n-k}-1}\sum_{y=0}^{2^k-1}\left|0\right\rangle\left|x\right\rangle\left|y\right\rangle\left|l\right\rangle\left|11\right\rangle\right).
\tag{3.165}
$$

Then, BRQI state $\left|\Psi_B^{24}\right\rangle$ for a color image is created by applying successively three controlled-U_G gates, where the detail circuit of U_G is shown in the red box in Figure 24. The complexity of the implementation circuit of BRQI for a $2^{n-k}\times 2^k$ color image is $O[(n+6)^2 2^{n+3}]$.

Figure 26. The implementation circuit of BRQI for RGB color images

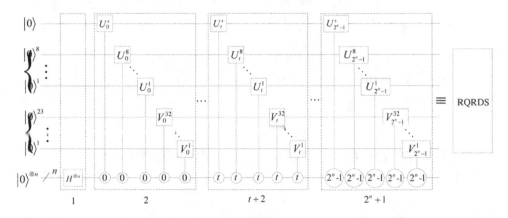

Image Retrieval Based on BRQI

To retrieve a $2^{n-k} \times 2^k$ grayscale image from BRQI $\left| \Psi_B^8 \right\rangle$, we define an observable operator as

$$M = \sum_{i=0}^{2^{n+3}-1} m_i P_i \qquad (3.166)$$

where P_i=$|i\rangle\langle i|$, $|j\rangle$= $|x\rangle|y\rangle|l\rangle$, and $x = 0,1,...,2^{n-k}-1$, $y=0,1,...,2^k-1$, and $l=0,1,...,7$.

Apply M to measure the BRQI state $\left| \Psi_B^8 \right\rangle$, and obtain the coordinate $|x\rangle|y\rangle$ in the l-th bitplane by 2^{n+3} measurements. The state after measurement is $|g(x,y,l)\rangle|x\rangle|y\rangle|l\rangle$. Since $|g(x,y,l)\rangle$ is a basis state with one qubit, $g(x,y,l)$ can be retrieved after one measurement. Therefore, a color and a coordinate of a $2^{n-k} \times 2^k$ grayscale image based on BRQI are retrieved after $O(2^{n+3})$ measurements.

Define the observable operator M_c as

$$M_c = \sum_{j=0}^{2} m_j P_j, \qquad (3.167)$$

where $P_j = I^{\otimes n+4} \otimes |j\rangle\langle j|$. The state $|\Psi_B^{24}\rangle$ for a color image collapses into $|\Psi_B^R\rangle$, $|\Psi_B^G\rangle$, or $|\Psi_B^B\rangle$ with probability 1/3 by the observable operator M_c. Then, we retrieve three grayscale images from $|\Psi_B^R\rangle$, $|\Psi_B^G\rangle$, and $|\Psi_B^B\rangle$ using the observable operator in (3.166). Therefore, a color and a coordinate of a $2^{n-k} \times 2^k$ color image based on BRQI are retrieved after $O(2^{n+3})$ measurements.

THE MODEL OF QUANTUM REPRESENTATION OF REAL-VALUED DIGITAL SIGNALS

Transformed images may have real-valued elements by wavelet transform. Quantum representation of real-valued digital signals (QRDS) was proposed to represent real-valued images (i.e., real-valued digital signals) (Li, Fan, Xia, Peng, & Song, 2019). In this section, we describe the representation, storage and retrieval of real-valued signals based on QRDS.

Representation and Storage of 1D Signals Based on QRDS

For convenience of processing single float numbers, we introduce the model of single float numbers of IEEE754 (Kahan, 1996) as shown in Table 1. In the table, NaN means "Not a Number".

Table 1. A single float number of 32 bits of IEEE 754

Sign bit	8 Bits of Exponent	23 Bits of Mantissa	Float Number
0 or 1	0	0	± 0
0 or 1	0	nonzero	$\pm 0.m \times 2^{-126}$
0 or 1	$k(1 \leq k \leq 254)$	m	$\pm 1.m \times 2^{k-127}$
0 or 1	255	0	$\pm \infty$
0 or 1	255	nonzero	NaN

Similarly with GNEQR, a basis state of 32 qubits can be used to store a single float number. Suppose that $|S_t\rangle$, $|E(t)\rangle$, and $|M(t)\rangle$ store sign bit, Exponent, and Mantissa of a float number (shown in Table 1), respectively.

Then, $|l(t)\rangle = |S_t\rangle |E(t)\rangle |M(t)\rangle$ represents the float number in the position $|t\rangle$. Furthermore, an 1D signal representation QRDS can be defined as

$$\left|\Psi_{QR}^{1}\right\rangle = \frac{1}{\sqrt{2^n}} \sum_{t=0}^{2^n-1} |l(t)\rangle |t\rangle = \frac{1}{\sqrt{2^n}} \sum_{t=0}^{2^n-1} \left| S(t)\right\rangle \left| E(t)\right\rangle \left| M(t)\right\rangle |t\rangle = \frac{1}{\sqrt{2^n}} \sum_{t=0}^{2^n-1} \left| S_t\right\rangle (\overset{8}{\underset{u=1}{\otimes}} \left| E_t^u\right\rangle)(\overset{23}{\underset{v=1}{\otimes}} \left| M_t^v\right\rangle) |t\rangle,$$

(3.168)

where

$$\left| E(t)\right\rangle = \left| E_t^8 E_t^7 \dots E_t^1 \right\rangle = \overset{8}{\underset{u=1}{\otimes}} \left| E_t^u \right\rangle,$$

$$\left| M(t)\right\rangle = \left| M_t^{23} M_t^{22} \dots E_t^1 \right\rangle = \overset{23}{\underset{v=1}{\otimes}} \left| M_t^v \right\rangle,$$

and $S_t, E_t^u, M_t^v \in \{0,1\}$. For instance, a QRDS state

$$\left| S_1 \right\rangle = \frac{1}{\sqrt{2^3}} \sum_{t=0}^{7} \left| S_t\right\rangle \left| E(t)\right\rangle \left| M(t)\right\rangle |t\rangle$$

$$= \frac{1}{\sqrt{2^3}} (\left| 0\right\rangle \left| 10000110\right\rangle \left| 10001101000000000000000\right\rangle \left| 000\right\rangle$$

$$+ \left| 1\right\rangle \left| 10000000\right\rangle \left| 01000000000000000100000\right\rangle \left| 001\right\rangle$$

$$+ \left| 0\right\rangle \left| 10000110\right\rangle \left| 10001111000000000000000\right\rangle \left| 010\right\rangle$$

$$+ \left| 1\right\rangle \left| 01111110\right\rangle \left| 00000000000000000000000\right\rangle \left| 011\right\rangle$$

$$+ \left| 0\right\rangle \left| 01111110\right\rangle \left| 00000000000000000001001\right\rangle \left| 100\right\rangle$$

$$+ \left| 0\right\rangle \left| 01111111\right\rangle \left| 10000000000000000001110\right\rangle \left| 101\right\rangle$$

$$+ \left| 1\right\rangle \left| 01111111\right\rangle \left| 10000000000000000001101\right\rangle \left| 110\right\rangle$$

$$+ \left| 1\right\rangle \left| 01111111\right\rangle \left| 10000000000000000001101\right\rangle \left| 111\right\rangle)$$

(3.169)

stores a 1D signal of single float numbers as shown below,

Figure 27. The realization circuit of QRDS for 1D signals

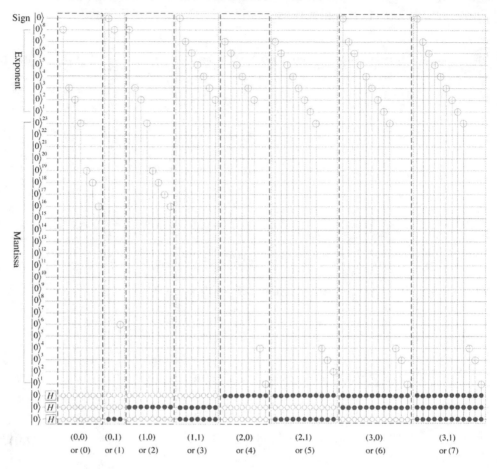

$$
\begin{bmatrix}
198.5 \\
-2.50000762939453125 \\
199.5 \\
-0.5 \\
0.50000053644180297851562 5 \\
1.50000166893005371093 75 \\
-1.50000154972076416015625 \\
-1.50000154972076416015625
\end{bmatrix} .
$$
(3.170)

To implement the storage of ORDS, we first define U_t^s, U_t^u, and V_t^v as follows,

$$\begin{cases} U_t^s = (S_t \oplus 1)I + S_t X, \\ U_t^u = (E_t^u \oplus 1)I + E_t^u X, \\ V_t^v = (S_t \oplus 1)I + M_t^v X, \end{cases} \tag{3.171}$$

where $\oplus$ is an exclusive-or operator, and $t=0,1,\ldots,2^n-1$, $u=1,2,\ldots,8$, and $v=1,2,\ldots,23$ are integers. Applying U_t^s, U_t^u, and V_t^v on $|0\rangle$ gives

$$U_t^s|0\rangle = |S_t\rangle, U_t^u|0\rangle = |E_t^u\rangle, V_t^v|0\rangle = |M_t^v\rangle. \tag{3.172}$$

Using controlled-U_t^s, controlled-U_t^u, and controlled-V_t^v gates, we design the circuit of QRDS for 1D signals in Figure 27, the abbreviated notation of which is denoted as RQRDS.

The first dashed box implements

$$(I^{\otimes 32} \otimes H^{\otimes n})|0\rangle^{\otimes 32+n} = \frac{1}{\sqrt{2^n}}\sum_{t=0}^{2^n-1}|0\rangle^{\otimes 32}|t\rangle = |\Psi\rangle. \tag{3.173}$$

The circuit in the second dashed box is applied on $f(Y,X)$ gives

$$|\Psi\rangle \mapsto \frac{1}{\sqrt{2^n}}\left(|S_0\rangle \overset{8}{\underset{u=1}{\otimes}}|E_0^u\rangle \overset{23}{\underset{v=1}{\otimes}}|M_0^v\rangle + \sum_{t=0}^{2^n-1}|0\rangle^{\otimes 32}|t\rangle + |t\rangle\right). \tag{3.174}$$

Therefore, we successively apply the 2^n+1 dashed boxes in Figure 27 on the state $|0\rangle^{\otimes 32+n}$, and obtain the QRDS state $C_m = \{0,1,\ldots,2^m-1\}$,

$$|\Psi\rangle \mapsto \frac{1}{\sqrt{2^n}}\sum_{t=0}^{2^n-1}|S_t\rangle \overset{8}{\underset{u=1}{\otimes}}|E_t^u\rangle \overset{23}{\underset{v=1}{\otimes}}|M_t^v\rangle \otimes |t\rangle = |\Psi_{QR}^1\rangle. \tag{3.175}$$

Since controlled-U_t^s, controlled-U_t^u, and controlled-V_t^v are $(n+1)$-qubit controlled-NOT gates or $(n+1)$-qubit identity gates, their complexities are

$O(n)$ by Corollary 2.14. The circuit of QRDS for an 1D signal with 2^n elements has 32×2^n controlled gates, so its complexity is $O(n2^n)$.

An example of the circuit of QRDS for the 1D signal in (3.170) is designed in Figure 28.

Figure 28. The implementation circuit of the 1D QRDS $|S_1\rangle$ or the 2D QRDS $|S_2\rangle$

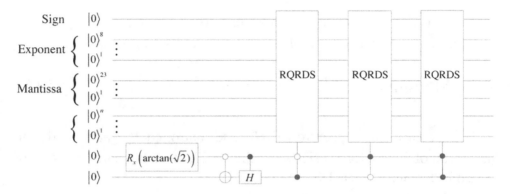

Representation and Storage of 2D Signals Based on QRDS

A basis state $|l(x,y)\rangle$ with 32 qubits can store a single float number, i.e.,

$$\left|l(x,y)\right\rangle = \left|S_{xy}\right\rangle\left|E(x,y)\right\rangle\left|M(x,y)\right\rangle = \left|S_{xy}\right\rangle \left(\overset{8}{\underset{u=1}{\otimes}}\left|E_{xy}^u\right\rangle\right)\left(\overset{23}{\underset{v=1}{\otimes}}\left|M_{xy}^v\right\rangle\right) \tag{3.176}$$

where $|S_{xy}\rangle$, $|E(x,y)\rangle$ and $|M(x,y)\rangle$ store sign bit, Exponent, and Mantissa of a float number, respectively, and $S_{xy}, E_{xy}^u, M_{xy}^v \in \{0,1\}$.

QRDS for a $\oplus$ signal is defined as

$$\left|\Psi_{QR}^2\right\rangle = \frac{1}{\sqrt{2^n}} \sum_{x=0}^{2^{n-k}-1} \sum_{y=0}^{2^k-1} \left|l(x,y)\right\rangle\left|x\right\rangle\left|y\right\rangle, \tag{3.177}$$

where $|l(x,y)\rangle$ denotes the value of the element on the coordinate (x,y). For instance, a QRDS state

$$\left|S_2\right\rangle = \frac{1}{\sqrt{2^3}} \sum_{x=0}^{3} \sum_{y=0}^{1} \left|S_{xy}\right\rangle \left|E(x,y)\right\rangle \left|M(x,y)\right\rangle \left|x\right\rangle \left|y\right\rangle$$

$$
\begin{aligned}
= \frac{1}{\sqrt{2^3}} \big(&\left|0\right\rangle \left|10000110\right\rangle \left|10001101000000000000000\right\rangle \left|00\right\rangle \left|0\right\rangle \\
+ &\left|1\right\rangle \left|10000000\right\rangle \left|01000000000000000100000\right\rangle \left|00\right\rangle \left|1\right\rangle \\
+ &\left|0\right\rangle \left|10000110\right\rangle \left|10001111000000000000000\right\rangle \left|01\right\rangle \left|0\right\rangle \\
+ &\left|1\right\rangle \left|01111110\right\rangle \left|00000000000000000000000\right\rangle \left|01\right\rangle \left|1\right\rangle \\
+ &\left|0\right\rangle \left|01111110\right\rangle \left|00000000000000000001001\right\rangle \left|10\right\rangle \left|0\right\rangle \\
+ &\left|0\right\rangle \left|01111111\right\rangle \left|10000000000000000001110\right\rangle \left|10\right\rangle \left|1\right\rangle \\
+ &\left|1\right\rangle \left|01111111\right\rangle \left|10000000000000000001101\right\rangle \left|11\right\rangle \left|0\right\rangle \\
+ &\left|1\right\rangle \left|01111111\right\rangle \left|10000000000000000001101\right\rangle \left|11\right\rangle \left|1\right\rangle \big)
\end{aligned}
\tag{3.178}
$$

can store a 2D signal of single float numbers as shown below,

$$
\begin{bmatrix}
198.5 & -2.50000762939453125 \\
199.5 & -0.5 \\
0.50000053644180297851562 & 1.5000016689300537109375 \\
-1.5000015497207641601562 & -1.5000015497207641601562
\end{bmatrix}.
\tag{3.179}
$$

Substituting xy for t in (3.171), we obtain

$$
\begin{cases}
U_{xy}^s = (S_{xy} \oplus 1)I + S_{xy}X, \\
U_{xy}^u = (E_{xy}^u \oplus 1)I + E_{xy}^u X, \\
V_{xy}^v = (S_{xy} \oplus 1)I + M_{xy}^v X.
\end{cases}
\tag{3.180}
$$

The realization circuit of QRDS for 2D signals is given by substituting U_{xy}^s, U_{xy}^u, and V_{xy}^v for U_t^s, U_t^u, and V_t^v in Figure 27. Therefore, the realization circuits of QRDS for 1D and 2D signals are the same. The same string can have different meanings for different data types in classical computers. For instance, a binary string 0100001 can express a char 'A' or a number 65. Similarly, using the circuit in Figure 28, we can store a 2D signal in (3.179) or a 1D signal in (3.170). Meanwhile, the prior knowledge $\left|\Psi_G^8\right\rangle$, $2^{n-k} \times 2^k$ or $\left|\Psi_{Gr}^8\right\rangle$ implies a 2D signal or a 1D signal.

Representation and Storage of 2D Signals With Three Channels Based on QRDS

To represent transformed color images by wavelet transform, we define a 2D QRDS state with three channels as below,

$$\left|\Psi_{QC}^{2}\right\rangle=\frac{1}{\sqrt{3}}\left(\left|\Psi_{QR1}^{2}\right\rangle\left|01\right\rangle+\left|\Psi_{QR2}^{2}\right\rangle\left|10\right\rangle+\left|\Psi_{QR3}^{2}\right\rangle\left|11\right\rangle\right),\tag{3.181}$$

where $\left|\Psi_{QR1}^{2}\right\rangle,\left|\Psi_{QR2}^{2}\right\rangle$ and $\left|\Psi_{QR3}^{2}\right\rangle$ are as same as 2D QRDS in (3.177), i.e.,

$$\begin{cases}\left|\Psi_{QR1}^{2}\right\rangle=\frac{1}{\sqrt{2^{n}}}\sum_{x=0}^{2^{n-k}-1}\sum_{y=0}^{2^{k}-1}\left|l_{1}(x,y)\right\rangle\left|x\right\rangle\left|y\right\rangle,\\\left|\Psi_{QR2}^{2}\right\rangle=\frac{1}{\sqrt{2^{n}}}\sum_{x=0}^{2^{n-k}-1}\sum_{y=0}^{2^{k}-1}\left|l_{2}(x,y)\right\rangle\left|x\right\rangle\left|y\right\rangle,\\\left|\Psi_{QR3}^{2}\right\rangle=\frac{1}{\sqrt{2^{n}}}\sum_{x=0}^{2^{n-k}-1}\sum_{y=0}^{2^{k}-1}\left|l_{3}(x,y)\right\rangle\left|x\right\rangle\left|y\right\rangle.\end{cases}\tag{3.182}$$

Next. we design the implementation circuit of $\left|\Psi_{QC}^{2}\right\rangle$ in Figure 29. The detail circuits of RQRDS shown in 3.27 realize $\left|\Psi_{QR1}^{2}\right\rangle,\left|\Psi_{QR2}^{2}\right\rangle$ and $\left|\Psi_{QR3}^{2}\right\rangle$, respectively.

The complexity of a $(n+34)$-qubit controlled-NOT gates with $(n+2)$ control qubits is $O(n)$ by Corollary 2.14. The circuit in Figure 29 consists of 96×2^{n} controlled-NOT gates of $(n+34)$ qubits, so its complexity is $O(n2^{n})$.

Figure 29. The implementation circuit of $\left|\Psi_{QC}^{2}\right\rangle$.

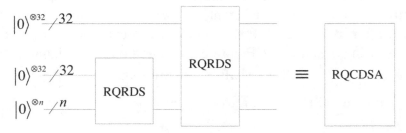

Signal Retrieval Based on QRDS

Using a similar method of grayscale image retrieval based on GNEQR, we obtain the coordinate $|x\rangle\,|y\rangle$ of a 2D signal based on QRDS by 2^n measurements. The state after measurement is $|l(x,y)\rangle\,|x\rangle\,|y\rangle$. Then, the real value $l(x,y)$ can be retrieved after one measurement. Therefore, a element value and a coordinate of a 2D signal based on QRDS after $O(2^n)$ measurements. Similarly, we retrieve a element value and a coordinate of a 2D signal with three channels based on QRDS after $O(2^n)$ measurements.

QUANTUM REPRESENTATION OF COMPLEX-VALUED DIGITAL SIGNALS WITH ALGEBRA FORM

Transformed images may have complex-valued elements by Fourier transform. Quantum representation of complex-valued digital signals with algebra form (QCDSA) was proposed to represent complex-valued signals (Li, Fan, Xia, Peng, & Song, 2019). In this section, we describe the representation, storage and retrieval of complex-valued signals based on QCDSA.

Representation and Storage of 1D Signals Based on QCDSA

A complex number $C(t)$ with algebra form can be expressed into

$$C(t) = iC_I(t) + C_R(t), \tag{3.183}$$

where $C_I(t)$ and $C_R(t)$ are single float numbers of 32 bits.

Suppose that $\left|S_I^t\right\rangle$, $|E_I(t)\rangle$, $|M_I(t)\rangle$, $\left|S_R^t\right\rangle$, $|E_R(t)\rangle$, and $|M_R(t)\rangle$ store the sign bit, Exponent, and Mantissa of single float numbers $C_I(t)$ and $C_R(t)$, respectively, then, a basis state of 64 qubits

$$\left|g(t)\right\rangle = \left|S_I^t\right\rangle\left|E_I(t)\right\rangle\left|M_I(t)\right\rangle\left|S_R^t\right\rangle\left|E_R(t)\right\rangle\left|M_R(t)\right\rangle \tag{3.184}$$

can be used to store the complex number $C(t)$. Then, QCDSA for an 1D signal is defined as

$$\left|\Psi_{QA}^{1}\right\rangle = \frac{1}{\sqrt{2^{n}}}\sum_{t=0}^{2^{n}-1}\left|g(t)\right\rangle\left|t\right\rangle. \tag{3.185}$$

The realization circuit of $\left|\Psi_{QA}^{1}\right\rangle$ is shown in Figure 30, which consists of two RQRDS circuits in Figure 27. The abbreviated notation is denoted as QCDSA.

Figure 30. The realization circuit of QCDSA for an 1D signal or a 2D signal

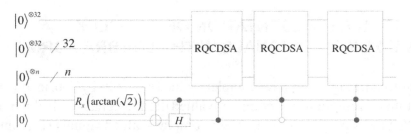

Representation and Storage of 2D Signals Based on QCDSA

Substituting (x, y) for t in (3.184) obtains

$$\left|g(x,y)\right\rangle = \left|S_{I}^{xy}\right\rangle\left|E_{I}(x,y)\right\rangle\left|M_{I}(x,y)\right\rangle\left|S_{R}^{xy}\right\rangle\left|E_{R}(x,y)\right\rangle\left|M_{R}(x,y)\right\rangle, \tag{3.186}$$

which represents the complex number of the element on the coordinate (x, y). Therefore, QCDSA for a $2^{n-k} \times 2^{k}$ signal is defined as follows,

$$\left|\Psi_{QA}^{2}\right\rangle = \frac{1}{\sqrt{2^{n}}}\sum_{x=0}^{2^{n-k}-1}\sum_{y=0}^{2^{k}-1}\left|g(x,y)\right\rangle\left|x\right\rangle\left|y\right\rangle. \tag{3.187}$$

and its implementation circuit is shown in Figure 30.

For instance, a 2D signal of complex numbers

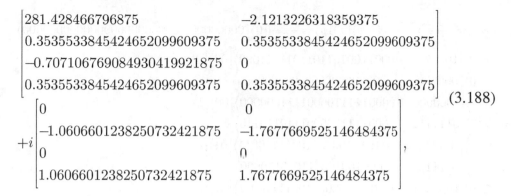

$$\begin{bmatrix} 281.428466796875 & -2.1213226318359375 \\ 0.3535533845424652099609375 & 0.3535533845424652099609375 \\ -0.70710676909084930419921875 & 0 \\ 0.3535533845424652099609375 & 0.3535533845424652099609375 \end{bmatrix}$$

$$+i \begin{bmatrix} 0 & 0 \\ -1.060660123825073242 1875 & -1.7677669525146484375 \\ 0 & 0 \\ 1.060660123825073242 1875 & 1.7677669525146484375 \end{bmatrix},$$

(3.188)

can be stored in the following state

Figure 31. The implementation circuit of the QCDSA state $\left| \Psi^2_{QAC} \right\rangle$.

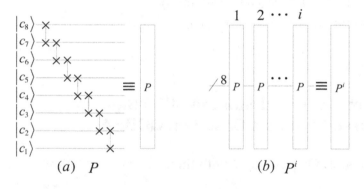

$$|S_3\rangle = \frac{1}{\sqrt{2^3}} \sum_{x=0}^{3} \sum_{y=0}^{1} g(x,y)|x\rangle|y\rangle = \frac{1}{\sqrt{2^3}} (|0\rangle|00000000\rangle|000000000000000000000000\rangle$$

$$\otimes|0\rangle|10000111\rangle|000110010110110110011000\rangle|00\rangle|0\rangle$$
$$+|0\rangle|00000000\rangle|000000000000000000000000\rangle$$
$$\otimes|1\rangle|10000000\rangle|000011111000011111000000\rangle|00\rangle|1\rangle$$
$$+|1\rangle|01111111\rangle|000011111000011110110110\rangle$$
$$\otimes|0\rangle|01111101\rangle|011010100000100111110011\rangle|01\rangle|0\rangle$$
$$+|1\rangle|01111111\rangle|110001001000110000110000\rangle$$
$$\otimes|0\rangle|01111101\rangle|011010100000100111110011\rangle|01\rangle|1\rangle$$
$$+|0\rangle|00000000\rangle|000000000000000000000000\rangle$$
$$\otimes|1\rangle|01111110\rangle|011010100000100111110011\rangle|10\rangle|0\rangle$$
$$+|0\rangle|00000000\rangle|000000000000000000000000\rangle$$
$$\otimes|0\rangle|00000000\rangle|000000000000000000000000\rangle|10\rangle|1\rangle$$
$$+|0\rangle|01111111\rangle|000011111000011110110110\rangle$$
$$\otimes|0\rangle|01111101\rangle|011010100000100111110011\rangle|11\rangle|0\rangle$$
$$+|0\rangle|01111111\rangle|110001001000110000110000\rangle$$
$$\otimes|0\rangle|01111101\rangle|011010100000100111110011\rangle|11\rangle|1\rangle).$$

$$(3.189)$$

Representation and Storage of 2D Signals With Three Channels Based on QCDSA

We define a 2D QCDSA state with three channels as below,

$$\left|\Psi_{QAC}^2\right\rangle = \frac{1}{\sqrt{3}}\left(\left|\Psi_{QA1}^2\right\rangle|01\rangle + \left|\Psi_{QA2}^2\right\rangle|10\rangle + \left|\Psi_{QA3}^2\right\rangle|11\rangle\right), \qquad (3.190)$$

where $\left|\Psi_{QA1}^2\right\rangle$, $\left|\Psi_{QA2}^2\right\rangle$ and $\left|\Psi_{QA3}^2\right\rangle$ are

$$\left\{\begin{aligned}
\left|\Psi_{QA1}^2\right\rangle &= \frac{1}{\sqrt{2^n}} \sum_{x=0}^{2^{n-k}-1} \sum_{y=0}^{2^k-1} \left| g_1(x,y) \right\rangle \left| x \right\rangle \left| y \right\rangle, \\
\left|\Psi_{QA2}^2\right\rangle &= \frac{1}{\sqrt{2^n}} \sum_{x=0}^{2^{n-k}-1} \sum_{y=0}^{2^k-1} \left| g_2(x,y) \right\rangle \left| x \right\rangle \left| y \right\rangle, \\
\left|\Psi_{QA3}^2\right\rangle &= \frac{1}{\sqrt{2^n}} \sum_{x=0}^{2^{n-k}-1} \sum_{y=0}^{2^k-1} \left| g_3(x,y) \right\rangle \left| x \right\rangle \left| y \right\rangle.
\end{aligned}\right. \tag{3.191}$$

The implementation circuit of $\left|\Psi_{QAC}^2\right\rangle$ is shown in Figure 31. The circuits of QCDSA shown in 3.30 realize $\left|\Psi_{QA1}^2\right\rangle$, $\left|\Psi_{QA2}^2\right\rangle$ and $\left|\Psi_{QA3}^2\right\rangle$, respectively. The complexity of a $(n+66)$-qubit controlled-NOT gates with $(n+2)$ control qubits is $O(n)$ by Corollary 2.14. The circuit in Figure 31 consists of 192×2^n controlled-NOT gates of $(n+66)$ qubits, so its complexity is $O(n2^n)$.

Signal Retrieval Based on QCDSA

The coordinate $|x\rangle$ $|y\rangle$ of a 2D signal based on QCDSA by 2^n measurements. The state after measurement is $|g(x,y)\rangle$ $|x\rangle$ $|y\rangle$. Then, the complex value $g(x,y)$ can be retrieved after one measurement. Therefore, a element value and a coordinate of a 2D signal based on QCDSA after $O(2^n)$ measurements. Similarly, we retrieve the coordinate $|x\rangle$ $|y\rangle$ of a 2D signal with three channels based on QRDS after $O(2^n)$ measurements. The state after measurement is

$$\frac{1}{\sqrt{3}} \left(\left| g_1(x,y) \right\rangle \left| x \right\rangle \left| y \right\rangle \left| 01 \right\rangle + \left| g_2(x,y) \right\rangle \left| x \right\rangle \left| y \right\rangle \left| 10 \right\rangle + \left| g_3(x,y) \right\rangle \left| x \right\rangle \left| y \right\rangle \left| 11 \right\rangle \right). \tag{3.192}$$

Then, the three complex values $g_1(x,y)$, $g_2(x,y)$, and $g_3(x,y)$ are retrieved after $O(1)$ measurements. Therefore, a element value and a coordinate of a 2D signal with three channels based on QCDSA after $O(2^n)$ measurements.

QUANTUM REPRESENTATION OF COMPLEX-VALUED DIGITAL SIGNALS WITH EXPONENTIAL FORM

Quantum representation of complex-valued digital signals with exponential form (QCDSE) was proposed to represent complex-valued signals (Li, Fan, Xia, Peng, & Song, 2019). In this section, we describe the model of QCDSA.

A complex number $C(t)$ with exponential form can be expressed into

$$C(t) = r(t)e^{i\theta(t)},\tag{3.193}$$

where the modulus $r(t)$ and the argument $\theta(t)$ are single float numbers of 32 bits, and $\theta(t)\in[0,2\pi)$. We can use a basis state of 64 qubits $|h(t)\rangle$ to store the complex number $C(t)$, i.e.,

$$\left|h(t)\right\rangle = \left|S_\theta(t)\right\rangle\left|E_\theta(t)\right\rangle\left|M_\theta(t)\right\rangle\left|S_r(t)\right\rangle\left|E_r(t)\right\rangle\left|M_r(t)\right\rangle,\tag{3.194}$$

where $\left|S_\theta(t)\right\rangle$, $\left|E_\theta(t)\right\rangle$, $\left|M_\theta(t)\right\rangle$, $|S_r(t)\rangle$, $|E_r(t)\rangle$, and $|M_r(t)\rangle$ store sign bit, Exponent, and Mantissa of the modulus $r(t)$ and the argument $\theta(t)$, respectively.

QCDSE for an 1D signal is defined as

$$\left|\Psi_{QE}^1\right\rangle = \frac{1}{\sqrt{2^n}}\sum_{t=0}^{2^n-1}\left|h(t)\right\rangle\left|t\right\rangle.\tag{3.195}$$

Substituting (x,y) for (t) in (3.194) gives

$$\left|h(x,y)\right\rangle = \left|S_\theta(x,y)\right\rangle\left|E_\theta(x,y)\right\rangle\left|M_\theta(x,y)\right\rangle\left|S_r(x,y)\right\rangle\left|E_r(x,y)\right\rangle\left|M_r(x,y)\right\rangle,\tag{3.196}$$

where $\left|S_\theta(x,y)\right\rangle$, $\left|E_\theta(x,y)\right\rangle$, $\left|M_\theta(x,y)\right\rangle$, $|S_r(x,y)\rangle$, $|E_r(x,y)\rangle$, and $|M_r(x,y)\rangle$ store sign bit, Exponent, and Mantissa of the modulus and argument of a complex number, respectively.

QCDSA for a $2^{n-k}\times 2^k$ signal is defined as,

$$\left|\Psi_{QE}^2\right\rangle = \frac{1}{\sqrt{2^n}}\sum_{x=0}^{2^{n-k}-1}\sum_{y=0}^{2^k-1}\left|h(x,y)\right\rangle\left|x\right\rangle\left|y\right\rangle.\tag{3.197}$$

For instance, a 2D signal

$$
\begin{bmatrix}
281.428466796875e^{i0} & \begin{array}{l} 2.1213226318359375 \\ \times e^{i3.1415927410125732421875} \end{array} \\[2em]
\begin{array}{l} 1.1180338859558105546875 \\ \times e^{-i1.24904572963714599609375} \end{array} & \begin{array}{l} 1.8027756214141845703125 \\ \times e^{-i1.3734008073806762695313125} \end{array} \\[2em]
\begin{array}{l} 0.707106769084930419921875 \\ \times e^{i3.1415927410125732421875} \end{array} & 0e^{i0} \\[2em]
\begin{array}{l} 1.1180338859558105546875 \\ \times e^{i1.24904572963714599609375} \end{array} & \begin{array}{l} 1.8027756214141845703125 \\ \times e^{i1.3734008073806762695313125} \end{array}
\end{bmatrix}, \tag{3.198}
$$

can be stored in the 2D QCDSE state,

Table 2. Type conversion from grayscale to 32 bit single float

Grayscale	32 Bit Single Float			
	Sign	Exponent	Mantissa	Float Number
$1c_7c_6c_5c_4c_3c_2c_1$	0	134	$c_7...c_10...0$	$+1.c_7...c_1\times2^7$
$01c_6c_5c_4c_3c_2c_1$	0	133	$c_6...c_10...0$	$+1.c_6...c_1\times2^6$
$001c_5c_4c_3c_2c_1$	0	132	$c_5...c_10...0$	$+1.c_5...c_1\times2^5$
$0001c_4c_3c_2c_1$	0	131	$c_4...c_10...0$	$+1.c_4...c_1\times2^4$
$00001c_3c_2c_1$	0	130	$c_3c_2c_10...0$	$+1.c_3c_2c_1\times2^3$
$00000c_2c_1$	0	129	$c_2c_10...0$	$+1.c_2c_1\times2^2$
$0000001c_1$	0	128	$c_10...0$	$+1.c_1\times2^1$
00000001	0	127	$0...0$	$+1.0\times2^0$
00000000	0	0	$0...0$	$+0$

Figure 32. The circuits of perfect shuffle permutations P and P^i

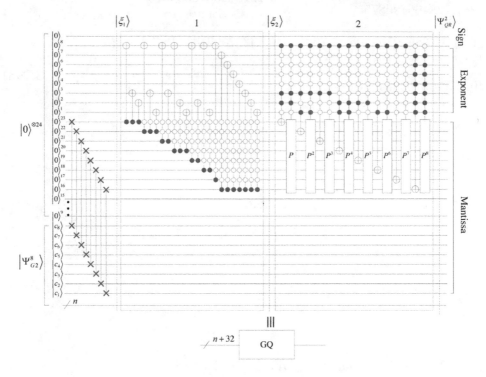

Figure 33. The implementation circuit of type conversion from a grayscale image to a real-value image

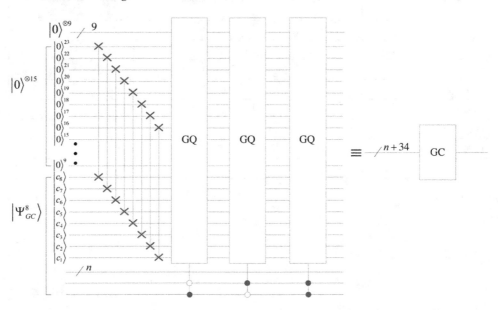

Figure 34. The implementation circuit of type conversion from a color image to a real-value image

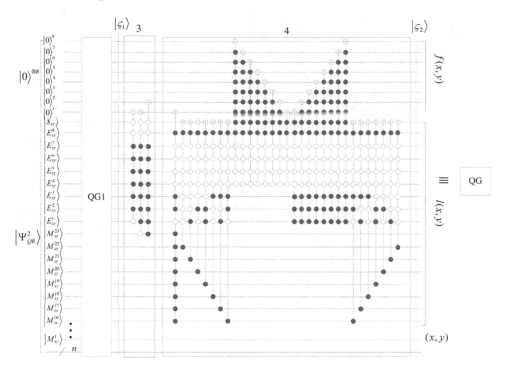

Table 3. Type conversion from 32 bit single float to grayscale

32 Bit Single Float				Grayscale (Rounding Down)
Sign	Exponent	Mantissa	Float Number	
1	*	*	*	0
0	$k(0 \leq k \leq 126)$	*	*	0
0	127	m	$+1.m \times 2^0$	00000001
0	128	m	$+1.m \times 2^1$	$0000001m_{23}$
0	129	m	$+1.m \times 2^2$	$000001m_{23}m_{22}$
0	130	m	$+1.m \times 2^3$	$00001m_{23}m_{22}m_{21}$
0	131	m	$+1.m \times 2^4$	$0001m_{23}...m_{20}$
0	132	m	$+1.m \times 2^5$	$001m_{23}...m_{19}$
0	133	m	$+1.m \times 2^6$	$01m_{23}...m_{18}$
0	134	m	$+1.m \times 2^7$	$1m_{23}...m_{17}$
0	$k(k \geq 135)$	*	*	255

Figure 35. The implementation circuit of type conversion from a real-value image to a grayscale image.

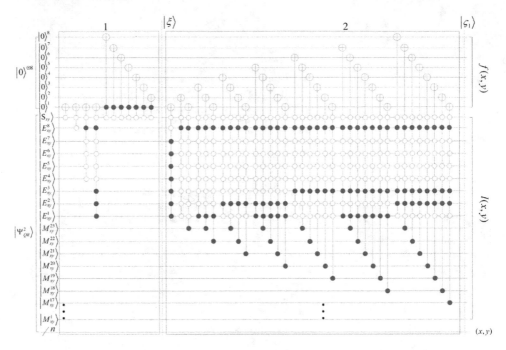

Figure 36. The implementation circuit of QG1.

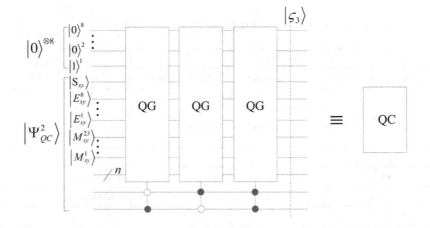

$$\left|S_4\right\rangle = \frac{1}{\sqrt{2^3}} \sum_{x=0}^{3} \sum_{y=0}^{1} h(x,y)\left|x\right\rangle\left|y\right\rangle$$

$$= \frac{1}{\sqrt{2^3}} \left(\left|0\right\rangle\left|00000000\right\rangle\left|00000000000000000000000\right\rangle\right.$$

$$\otimes \left|0\right\rangle\left|10000111\right\rangle\left|00011001011011011011000\right\rangle\left|00\right\rangle\left|0\right\rangle$$

$$+ \left|0\right\rangle\left|10000000\right\rangle\left|10010010000111111011011\right\rangle$$

$$\otimes \left|0\right\rangle\left|10000000\right\rangle\left|00001111100001111000000\right\rangle\left|00\right\rangle\left|1\right\rangle$$

$$+ \left|1\right\rangle\left|01111111\right\rangle\left|00111111110000010111011\right\rangle$$

$$\otimes \left|0\right\rangle\left|01111111\right\rangle\left|00011110001101110111100\right\rangle\left|01\right\rangle\left|0\right\rangle$$

$$+ \left|1\right\rangle\left|01111111\right\rangle\left|01011111100101110011001\right\rangle \tag{3.199}$$

$$\otimes \left|0\right\rangle\left|01111111\right\rangle\left|11001101100000101011010\right\rangle\left|01\right\rangle\left|1\right\rangle$$

$$+ \left|0\right\rangle\left|10000000\right\rangle\left|10010010000111111011011\right\rangle$$

$$\otimes \left|0\right\rangle\left|01111110\right\rangle\left|01101010000010011110011\right\rangle\left|10\right\rangle\left|0\right\rangle$$

$$+ \left|0\right\rangle\left|00000000\right\rangle\left|00000000000000000000000\right\rangle$$

$$\otimes \left|0\right\rangle\left|00000000\right\rangle\left|00000000000000000000000\right\rangle\left|10\right\rangle\left|1\right\rangle$$

$$+ \left|0\right\rangle\left|01111111\right\rangle\left|00111111110000010111011\right\rangle$$

$$\otimes \left|0\right\rangle\left|01111111\right\rangle\left|00011110001101110111100\right\rangle\left|11\right\rangle\left|0\right\rangle$$

$$+ \left|0\right\rangle\left|01111111\right\rangle\left|01011111100101110011001\right\rangle$$

$$\otimes \left|0\right\rangle\left|01111111\right\rangle\left|11001101100000101011010\right\rangle\left|11\right\rangle\left|1\right\rangle\Big).$$

We define a 2D QCDSE state of three channels as below,

$$\left|\Psi_{QEC}^2\right\rangle = \frac{1}{\sqrt{3}}\left(\left|\Psi_{QE1}^2\right\rangle\left|01\right\rangle + \left|\Psi_{QE2}^2\right\rangle\left|10\right\rangle + \left|\Psi_{QE3}^2\right\rangle\left|11\right\rangle\right), \tag{3.200}$$

where $\left|\Psi_{QE1}^2\right\rangle$, $\left|\Psi_{QE2}^2\right\rangle$ and $\left|\Psi_{QE3}^2\right\rangle$ are as same as 2D QCDSE in (3.197), i.e.,

$$\begin{cases} \left|\Psi_{QE1}^2\right\rangle = \dfrac{1}{\sqrt{2^n}} \sum_{x=0}^{2^{n-k}-1} \sum_{y=0}^{2^k-1} \left|h_1(x,y)\right\rangle\left|x\right\rangle\left|y\right\rangle, \\[2mm] \left|\Psi_{QE2}^2\right\rangle = \dfrac{1}{\sqrt{2^n}} \sum_{x=0}^{2^{n-k}-1} \sum_{y=0}^{2^k-1} \left|h_2(x,y)\right\rangle\left|x\right\rangle\left|y\right\rangle, \\[2mm] \left|\Psi_{QE3}^2\right\rangle = \dfrac{1}{\sqrt{2^n}} \sum_{x=0}^{2^{n-k}-1} \sum_{y=0}^{2^k-1} \left|h_3(x,y)\right\rangle\left|x\right\rangle\left|y\right\rangle. \end{cases} \tag{3.201}$$

Compared QSDSE with QSDSA, the circuits of QSDSA are also the circuits of QSDSE. Therefore, a element value and a coordinate of a signal based on QCDSE can be retrieved after $O(2^n)$ measurements.

TYPE CONVERSION OF QUANTUM IMAGE REPRESENTATIONS

A classical image may be changed into a real-value image or a complex-value image by wavelet transform or Fourier transform, so it's necessary to perform type conversion of data for classical image processing. When we use GNEQR, QRDS, QCDSA (or QCDSE) to represent integer images, real-value images and complex-value images, respectively, it's still necessary to perform type conversion. In this section, we describe the implementation of type conversion of these quantum representations.

Type Conversion From GNEQR to QRDS

A grayscale $c=c_8c_7c_6c_5c_4c_3c_2c_1$ is an integer of 8 bits and can be converted into a single float number of 32 bits by the rules in Table 2, where $c_j \in \{0,1\}$, $j=8,\ldots,1$.

A perfect shuffle permutation P *is* defined as

$$P \left| c_8c_7c_6c_5c_4c_3c_2c_1 \right\rangle = \left| c_7c_6c_5c_4c_3c_2c_1c_8 \right\rangle, \tag{3.202}$$

and its implementation circuit is shown in Figure 22 (a). P^i denotes I times of P, the implementation circuit of which is shown in Figure 22 (b).

By analyzing Table 2, we design the implementation circuit of type conversion from a grayscale image $\left| \Psi_G^8 \right\rangle$ in (3.148) to a real-value image $\left| \Psi_{QR}^2 \right\rangle$ in (3.177) as shown in Figure 33. The abbreviated notation of the combination circuit in dashed box 1 and box 2 is denoted as GQ.

The process of type conversion is described as follows. First, applying 8 swap gates on the initial state $\left| 0 \right\rangle^{\otimes 24} \otimes \left| \Psi_G^8 \right\rangle$, we obtain a state $\left| \xi_1 \right\rangle$ as follows,

$$\left| \xi_1 \right\rangle = \frac{1}{\sqrt{2^n}} \sum_{x=0}^{2^{n-k}-1} \sum_{y=0}^{2^k-1} \left| 0 \right\rangle^{\otimes 9} \left| f(x,y) \right\rangle \left| 0 \right\rangle^{\otimes 15} \left| x \right\rangle \left| y \right\rangle. \tag{3.203}$$

Next, applying the circuit in dashed box 1 on $\left| \xi_1 \right\rangle$, we have

$$\left| \xi_2 \right\rangle = \frac{1}{\sqrt{2^n}} \sum_{x=0}^{2^{n-k}-1} \sum_{y=0}^{2^k-1} \left| 0 \right\rangle \left| E(x,y) \right\rangle \left| f(x,y) \right\rangle \left| 0 \right\rangle^{\otimes 15} \left| x \right\rangle \left| y \right\rangle, \qquad (3.204)$$

where $|E(x,y)\rangle$ stores Exponent of a single float number.

Then, the circuit in dashed box 2 transforms $\left| \xi_2 \right\rangle$ into $\left| \Psi_{QR}^2 \right\rangle$.

We design the implementation circuit of type conversion from a grayscale image $\left| \Psi_G^8 \right\rangle$ in (3.148) to a real-value image $\left| \Psi_{QR}^2 \right\rangle$ in (3.177) as shown in Figure 33. The abbreviated notation of the combination circuit in dashed box 1 and box 2 is denoted as GQ.

Using the circuit GQ and Swap gates, we design the circuit in Figure 34 to realize type conversion from a color image $\left| \Psi_{GC} \right\rangle$ in (3.154) to a real-value image with three channels $\left| \Psi_{QC}^2 \right\rangle$ in (3.181). The abbreviated notation of the circuit is denoted as GC.

Figure 33 and Figure 34 show that the circuits of type conversion from GNEQR to QRDS can be implemented by constant basic operations, i.e., their complexities are $O(1)$.

Type Conversion From QRDS to GNEQR

The maximum and minimum in the grayscale set are 0 and 255, therefore, a float number less than 1 or greater than 255 should be converted to grayscale 0 or 255. The rule of type conversion from single float to grayscale is shown in Table 3. In the table, the symbol '*' denotes any numbers, and $m = m_{23} m_{22} \ldots$ m_1, $m_j \in \{0,1\}$, $j = 1, 2, \ldots, 23$.

We design the implementation circuit of type conversion from to a real-value image $\left| \Psi_{QR}^2 \right\rangle$ in (3.177) to a grayscale image $\left| \Psi_G^8 \right\rangle$ in (3.148) as shown in Figure 35. The abbreviated notation of the circuit is denoted as QG. The detail circuit of QG1 is designed in Figure 36 by using Table 3.

The process of type conversion from a real-value image to a grayscale image is described as follows.

First, the circuit in the dashed box 1 in Figure 36 transforms the initial state $\left| 0 \right\rangle^{\otimes 8} \otimes \left| \Psi_{QR}^2 \right\rangle$ into

$$|\xi\rangle = \frac{1}{\sqrt{2^n}} \sum_{x=0}^{2^{n-k}-1} \sum_{y=0}^{2^k-1} \left| f_\xi(x,y) \right\rangle \left| S(x,y) \right\rangle \left| E(x,y) \right\rangle \left| f(x,y) \right\rangle \left| xy \right\rangle, \tag{3.205}$$

where S_{xy} is a sign bit, and $\left| f_\xi(x,y) \right\rangle$ is equal to

$$\begin{cases} \left| 0 \right\rangle^{\otimes 8}, & S_{xy} = 1, \\ \left| 0 \right\rangle^{\otimes 7} \left| 1 \right\rangle, & S_{xy} = 0, \ 0 \le E(x,y) \le 134, \\ \left| 1 \right\rangle^{\otimes 8}, & S_{xy} = 0, \ 135 \le E(x,y). \end{cases} \tag{3.206}$$

Next, applying the circuit in the dashed box 2 on the state $\left| \xi \right\rangle$ obtains

$$\left| \varsigma_1 \right\rangle = \frac{1}{\sqrt{2^n}} \sum_{x=0}^{2^{n-k}-1} \sum_{y=0}^{2^k-1} \left| f_\varsigma(x,y) \right\rangle \left| l(x,y) \right\rangle \left| x \right\rangle \left| y \right\rangle, \tag{3.207}$$

here, $|l(x,y)\rangle$ represents a real value of the element on the coordinate (x,y), and the grayscale $f_\varsigma(x,y)$ on the coordinate (x,y) is given by

$$f_\varsigma(x,y) = \begin{cases} 0, l(x,y) < 1, \\ \left\lfloor l(x,y) \right\rfloor, 1 \le l(x,y) < 255, \\ 255, l(x,y) \ge 255, \end{cases} \tag{3.208}$$

where $\lfloor \ \rfloor$ denotes rounding down, such as $\lfloor 3.9 \rfloor = 3$.

Then, the dashed box 3 in Figure 15 transforms $f_\varsigma(x,y)$ in $\left| \varsigma_1 \right\rangle$ into

$$\lambda(x,y) = \begin{cases} 0, l(x,y) < 0, \\ round(l(x,y)), 0 \le l(x,y) < 2, \\ \left\lfloor l(x,y) \right\rfloor, 2 \le l(x,y) < 255, \\ 255, l(x,y) \ge 255, \end{cases} \tag{3.209}$$

where *round()* denotes the function of rounding off, such as *round*(3.4)=3 and *round*(3.6)=4.

Finally, applying the dashed box 4 in Figure 15, we have

$$\left|\varsigma_2\right\rangle = \frac{1}{\sqrt{2^n}} \sum_{x=0}^{2^{n-k}-1} \sum_{y=0}^{2^k-1} \left|f(x,y)\right\rangle \left|l(x,y)\right\rangle \left|x\right\rangle \left|y\right\rangle, \tag{3.210}$$

where $f(x,y)$ satisfies

$$f(x,y) = \begin{cases} 0, & l(x,y) < 0, \\ round(l(x,y)), & 0 < l(x,y) < 255, \\ 255, & l(x,y) \geq 255. \end{cases} \tag{3.211}$$

Furthermore, using the circuit QG, we design the circuit in Figure 37 to realize type conversion from a real-value image with three channels $\left|\Psi^2_{QC}\right\rangle$ in (3.181) to a color image $\left|\Psi_{GC}\right\rangle$ in (3.154). The abbreviated notation of the circuit is denoted as QC.

Figure 37. The implementation circuit of type conversion from a real-value image to a color image

(a)	(b)	(c)

The circuit QC transforms the initial state $\left|0\right\rangle^{\otimes 8} \otimes \left|\Psi^2_{QC}\right\rangle$ into

$$\left|\varsigma_3\right\rangle = \frac{1}{\sqrt{3 \times 2^n}} \sum_{j=1}^{3} \sum_{x=0}^{2^{n-k}-1} \sum_{y=0}^{2^k-1} \left|f_j(x,y)\right\rangle \left|l_j(x,y)\right\rangle \left|x\right\rangle \left|y\right\rangle, \tag{3.212}$$

where meanings of $|l_j(x,y)\rangle$ for $j=1,2,3$ are seen in (3-182), and $|f_j(x,y)\rangle$ can be given by

$$f_j(x,y) = \begin{cases} 0, & l_j(x,y) < 1, \\ \lfloor l(x,y) \rfloor, & 1 \le l_j(x,y) \le 255, \\ 255, & l_j(x,y) > 255. \end{cases} \tag{3.213}$$

Since the circuits of type conversion from QRDS to GNEQR can be implemented by constant basic operations, their complexities are $O(1)$.

Type Conversions Between GNEQR and QRDS

We discuss type conversions between integer images and real-value using Haar wavelet transform (HWT) and inverse Haar wavelet transform (IHWT). The matrix of HWT on 2^n elements is

$$W_{2^n} = \frac{\sqrt{2}}{2} \begin{bmatrix} 1 & 1 & 0 & 0 & \cdots & 0 & 0 \\ 0 & 0 & 1 & 1 & \cdots & 0 & 0 \\ \vdots & \vdots & \vdots & \vdots & \ddots & \vdots & \vdots \\ 0 & 0 & 0 & 0 & \cdots & 1 & 1 \\ 1 & -1 & 0 & 0 & \cdots & 0 & 0 \\ 0 & 0 & 1 & -1 & \cdots & 0 & 0 \\ \vdots & \vdots & \vdots & \vdots & \ddots & \vdots & \vdots \\ 0 & 0 & 0 & 0 & \cdots & 1 & -1 \end{bmatrix}. \tag{3.214}$$

Suppose the 128×128 grayscale image in Figure 38 (a) corresponds to $I_{2^7,2^7}$, then, the transformed image (i.e., real- value $R_{2^7,2^7}$) in Figure 38 (b) is given by 2D HWT,

$$R_{2^7,2^7} = W_{2^7} I_{2^7,2^7} W_{2^7}^T, \tag{3.215}$$

where $()^T$ is the transpose of a matrix. The transformed image $I_{2^7,2^7}$ in Figure 38 (c) is obtained by 2D IHWT,

$$I_{2^7,2^7} = (W_{2^7})^{-1} R_{2^7,2^7} (W_{2^7}^T)^{-1}, \tag{3.216}$$

where $()^{-1}$ is the inverse operation of a matrix.

Figure 38. The example of type conversions between classical gray images and real-value images. (a) A grayscale image. (b) The transformed image using 2D HWT. (c) The transformed grayscale image using 2D IHWT.

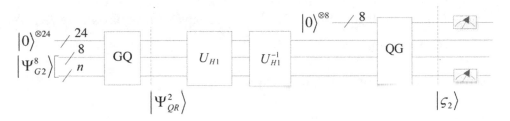

Suppose that the black-box circuits U_{H1} and U_{H1}^{-1} implement 2D Haar quantum wavelet transform (HQWT) and its inverse for grayscale images, respectively. The type conversion circuit between gray images and real-value images for the example in Figure 38 is illustrated in Figure 39.

Figure 39. The type conversion circuit between quantum gray images and real-value images

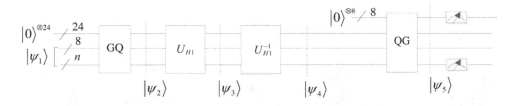

First, a grayscale image is stored in a GNEQR state $\left| \Psi_{G2}^8 \right\rangle$. Next, successively performing type conversion GQ in Figure 33, HQWT and its inverse transform, and type conversion QG in Figure 35, we obtain $\left| \varsigma_2 \right\rangle$ in (3.210). Then, to retrieve images from quantum state $\left| \varsigma_2 \right\rangle$, we perform quantum measurement on the first 8 qubits and last n qubits of the state. The image retrieval process is divided into two steps as below.

Step 1. The observable operator

$$M_1 = \sum_{x=0}^{2^{n-k}-1} \sum_{y=0}^{2^k-1} m_{x,y} |xy\rangle\langle xy|, \tag{3.217}$$

is applied to the last n qubits of $|\varsigma_2\rangle$. $|\varsigma_2\rangle$ collapses into a basis state $|f(x,y)\rangle$ $|l(x,y)\rangle$ $|x\rangle$ $|y\rangle$ with probability of $1/2^n$.

Step 2. We use the observable operator

$$M_2 = \sum_{m=0}^{255} m |m\rangle\langle m|, \tag{3.218}$$

to measure the first 8 qubits of the basis state $|f(x,y)\rangle$ $|l(x,y)\rangle$ $|x\rangle$ $|y\rangle$, and obtain the grayscale $f(x,y)$ on the coordinate (x,y) after one measurement.

For instance, for the grayscale image in Figure 18, the process of the type conversions between quantum grayscale images and quantum real-value images is shown in Figure 40.

Figure 40. An example of the type conversions between GNEQR and QRDS for grayscale images

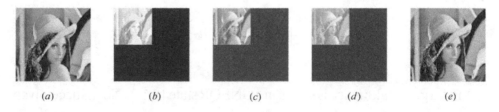

| (a) | (b) | (c) | (d) | (e) |

The input is $|0\rangle^{\otimes 24} |\psi_1\rangle$, *where* $|\psi_1\rangle$ *in* (3.149) stores the grayscale image as follows,

$$\begin{bmatrix} 99 & 100 \\ 97 & 101 \\ 98 & 100 \\ 101 & 100 \end{bmatrix}. \tag{3.219}$$

Applying the circuit GQ on $|0\rangle^{\otimes 24}|\psi_1\rangle$ gives

$$
\begin{aligned}
|\psi_2\rangle = \frac{1}{\sqrt{2^3}}(&|0\rangle|10000101\rangle|100011000000000000000000\rangle|00\rangle|0\rangle \\
+&|0\rangle|10000101\rangle|100100000000000000000000\rangle|00\rangle|1\rangle \\
+&|0\rangle|10000101\rangle|100001000000000000000000\rangle|01\rangle|0\rangle \\
+&|0\rangle|10000101\rangle|100101000000000000000000\rangle|01\rangle|1\rangle \\
+&|0\rangle|10000101\rangle|100010000000000000000000\rangle|10\rangle|0\rangle \\
+&|0\rangle|10000101\rangle|100100000000000000000000\rangle|10\rangle|1\rangle \\
+&|0\rangle|10000101\rangle|100101000000000000000000\rangle|11\rangle|0\rangle \\
+&|0\rangle|10000101\rangle|100100000000000000000000\rangle|11\rangle|1\rangle).
\end{aligned}
\tag{3.220}
$$

The transformed state $|\psi_3\rangle$ is given by

$$
\begin{aligned}
|\psi_3\rangle = \frac{1}{\sqrt{2^3}}(&|0\rangle|10000110\rangle|100011010000000000000000\rangle|00\rangle|0\rangle \\
+&|1\rangle|10000000\rangle|010000000000000000100000\rangle|00\rangle|1\rangle \\
+&|0\rangle|10000110\rangle|100011110000000000000000\rangle|01\rangle|0\rangle \\
+&|1\rangle|01111110\rangle|000000000000000000000000\rangle|01\rangle|1\rangle \\
+&|0\rangle|01111110\rangle|000000000000000000001001\rangle|10\rangle|0\rangle \\
+&|0\rangle|01111111\rangle|100000000000000000001110\rangle|10\rangle|1\rangle \\
+&|1\rangle|01111111\rangle|100000000000000000001101\rangle|11\rangle|0\rangle \\
+&|1\rangle|01111111\rangle|100000000000000000001101\rangle|11\rangle|1\rangle),
\end{aligned}
\tag{3.221}
$$

which stores a following real-value image,

$$
\begin{bmatrix}
198.5 & -2.50000762939453125 \\
199.5 & -0.5 \\
0.50000536441802978515625 & 1.500001668930053710937 \\
-1.5000015497207641601562 & -1.5000015497207641601562
\end{bmatrix}. \tag{3.222}
$$

Performing U_{H1}^{-1}, we obtain

Figure 41. A example of type conversions between classical color images and real-value images. (a) A color image. (b) The red channel of the transformed image using 2D HWT. (c) The green channel of the transformed image using 2D HWT. (d) The blue channel of the transformed image using 2D HQWT. (e) The transformed color image using IHWT.

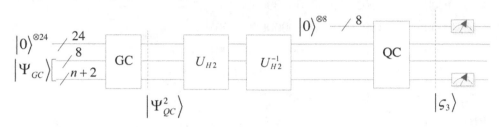

$$|\psi_4\rangle = \frac{1}{\sqrt{2^3}}(|0\rangle|10000101\rangle|10001100000000000000010\rangle|00\rangle|0\rangle$$
$$+|0\rangle|10000101\rangle|10010000000000000000001\rangle|00\rangle|1\rangle$$
$$+|0\rangle|10000101\rangle|01100000111111111111110\rangle|01\rangle|0\rangle$$
$$+|0\rangle|10000101\rangle|01100100111111111111111\rangle|01\rangle|1\rangle \qquad (3.223)$$
$$+|0\rangle|10000101\rangle|10001000000000000000010\rangle|10\rangle|0\rangle$$
$$+|0\rangle|10000101\rangle|10010000000000000000001\rangle|10\rangle|1\rangle$$
$$+|0\rangle|10000101\rangle|10010100000000000000000\rangle|11\rangle|0\rangle$$
$$+|0\rangle|10000101\rangle|10001111111111111111110\rangle|11\rangle|1\rangle),$$

which stores a following real-value image,

$$\begin{bmatrix} 99.0000152587890625 & 100.00000762939453125 \\ 96.9999847412109375 & 100.99999237060546875 \\ 98.0000152587890625 & 100.00000762939453125 \\ 101.0 & 99.9999847412109375 \end{bmatrix}. \qquad (3.224)$$

The type conversion QG transforms $|\psi_4\rangle$ into

Figure 42. The type conversion circuit between quantum color images and quantum real-value images

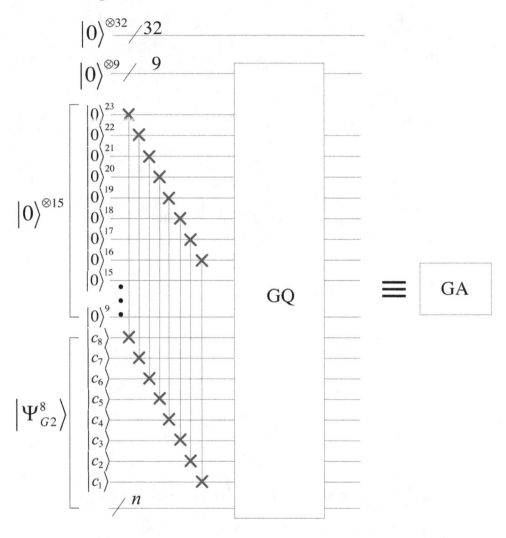

Figure 43. The circuit of type conversion from grayscale images to complex-value images.

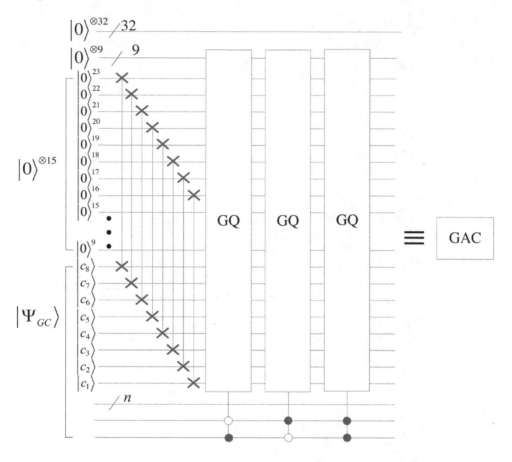

$$|\psi_5\rangle = \frac{1}{\sqrt{2^3}}(|99\rangle|0\rangle|10000101\rangle|100011000000000000000010\rangle|00\rangle|0\rangle$$
$$+|100\rangle|0\rangle|10000101\rangle|100100000000000000000001\rangle|00\rangle|1\rangle$$
$$+|97\rangle|0\rangle|10000101\rangle|011000001111111111111110\rangle|01\rangle|0\rangle$$
$$+|101\rangle|0\rangle|10000101\rangle|011001001111111111111111\rangle|01\rangle|1\rangle \qquad (3.225)$$
$$+|98\rangle|0\rangle|10000101\rangle|100010000000000000000010\rangle|10\rangle|0\rangle$$
$$+|100\rangle|0\rangle|10000101\rangle|100100000000000000000001\rangle|10\rangle|1\rangle$$
$$+|101\rangle|0\rangle|10000101\rangle|100101000000000000000000\rangle|11\rangle|0\rangle$$
$$+|100\rangle|0\rangle|10000101\rangle|100011111111111111111110\rangle|11\rangle|1\rangle).$$

Finally, we retrieve the grayscale image in (3.129) by measuring on the first 8 qubits and last 3 qubits of the state $|\psi_5\rangle$.

The example of type conversions between classical color images and real-value images is shown in Figure 41.

Suppose that the black-box circuits U_{H2} and U_{H2}^{-1} implement 2D HQWT and its inverse for color images, respectively. For the example in Figure 40, the type conversion circuit between color images and real-value images is illustrated in Figure 42.

A color image is stored in a GNEQR state $|\Psi_{GC}\rangle$ in (3.154). Type conversion GC in Figure 34 changes $|0\rangle^{\otimes 24}|\Psi_{GC}\rangle$ into $|\Psi_{QC}^2\rangle$ in (3.181). Successively performing HQWT and its inverse transform, and type conversion QC in Figure 37, we obtain $|\varsigma_3\rangle$ in (3.212). Using a similar measurement method in Figure 39, we retrieve the color image by performing quantum measurement on the first 8 qubits and last n qubits of the state.

Figure 44. The circuit of type conversion from color images to complex-value images

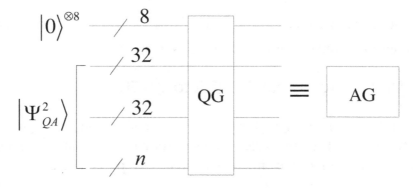

Figure 45. The circuit of type conversion from complex-value images to grayscale images

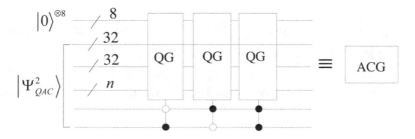

Type Conversion From GNEQR to QCDSA

Using the circuit GQ in Figure 33, we design the implementation circuit of type conversion from a grayscale image to a complex-value image shown in Figure 43. The abbreviated notation of the circuit is denoted as GA, which implements

$$\text{GA} : \left|0\right\rangle^{\otimes 56} \otimes \left|\Psi^8_{G2}\right\rangle \rightarrow \left|\Psi^2_{QA}\right\rangle, \tag{3.226}$$

where $\left|\Psi^8_G\right\rangle$ in (3.148) and $\left|\Psi^2_{QA}\right\rangle$ in (3.187) represent a grayscale image and a complex-value image, respectively.

The implementation circuit of type conversion from a color image to a complex-value image is shown in Figure 44. The abbreviated notation of the circuit is denoted as GAC, which implements

$$\text{GAC} : \left|0\right\rangle^{\otimes 56} \otimes \left|\Psi_{GC}\right\rangle \rightarrow \left|\Psi^2_{QAC}\right\rangle, \tag{3.227}$$

where $\left|\Psi_{GC}\right\rangle$ in (3.154) and $\left|\Psi^2_{QAC}\right\rangle$ in (3.190) represent a color image and a complex-value image with three channels, respectively.

Type Conversion From QCDSA to GNEQR

By using the circuit QG in Figure 35, type conversion from a complex-value image to a grayscale image is realized by the circuit shown in Figure 45. The abbreviated notation of the circuit denoted as AG, implements

$$\text{AG} : \left|0\right\rangle^{\otimes 8} \otimes \left|\Psi^2_{QA}\right\rangle \rightarrow \left|\varsigma_4\right\rangle = \frac{1}{\sqrt{2^n}} \sum_{x=0}^{2^{n-k}-1} \sum_{y=0}^{2^k-1} \left|f(x,y)\right\rangle \left|g(x,y)\right\rangle \left|x\right\rangle \left|y\right\rangle, \tag{3.228}$$

where $\left|\Psi^2_{QA}\right\rangle$ in (3.187) represent a complex-value image, and $|f(x,y)\rangle$ denotes the grayscale of the pixel on the coordinate (x,y).

The implementation circuit of type conversion from a color image to a complex-value image is shown in Figure 46. Its abbreviated notation is denoted as ACG, which implements

Figure 46. The circuit of type conversion from complex-value images to color images

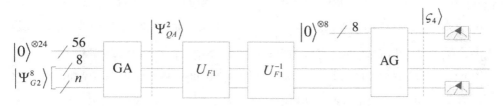

$$\text{ACG}:\left|0\right\rangle^{\otimes 8}\otimes\left|\Psi_{QAC}^{2}\right\rangle\rightarrow\left|\varsigma_{6}\right\rangle=\frac{1}{\sqrt{3\times 2^{n}}}\sum_{j=1}^{3}\sum_{x=0}^{2^{n-k}-1}\sum_{y=0}^{2^{k}-1}\left|f_{j}(x,y)\right\rangle\left|g_{j}(x,y)\right\rangle\left|x\right\rangle\left|y\right\rangle,$$

(3.229)

where $\left|\Psi_{QAC}^{2}\right\rangle$ in (3.190) a complex-value image with three channels, and the meanings of $|f_{j}(x,y)\rangle$ with $j=1,2,3$ are seen in (3.154).

Type Conversions Between GNEQR and QCDSA

Suppose that the black-box circuits U_{F1} and U_{F1}^{-1} implement 2D quantum Fourier transform (QFT) and its inverse for grayscale images, respectively. Using the circuits GA in Figure 43 and AG in Figure 45, we design type conversion circuit between grayscale images and complex-value images shown in Figure 47.

Figure 47. Type conversion circuit between grayscale images and complex-value images.

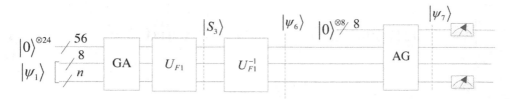

The circuits GA in Figure 43 transforms a grayscale image $|0\rangle^{\otimes 56} \otimes |\Psi_{G2}^8\rangle$ into a complex-value image $|\Psi_{QA}^2\rangle$ in (3.186). Successively performing 2D QFT U_{F1} and its inverse U_{F1}^{-1}, and the type conversion circuit AG in Figure 45, we obtain $|\varsigma_4\rangle$ in (3.228). The grayscale image is retrieved by measuring the first 8 qubits and last n qubits of the state $|\varsigma_4\rangle$. An example of the type conversions between grayscale images and complex-value images is given in Figure 48.

Figure 48. An example of the type conversions between GNEQR and QCDSA for grayscale images

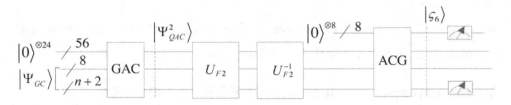

The grayscale image in (3.219) is as the input, and is transformed into an QCDSA state $|S_3\rangle$ by the circuit GA and 2D QFT U_{F1}, where $|S_3\rangle$ is seen in (3.189), and stores a complex-value image as follows,

$$
\begin{bmatrix}
281.428466796875 & -2.1213226318359375 \\
0.353553338454424652099609375 & 0.353553338454424652099609375 \\
-0.70710676909493041992187 5 & 0 \\
0.353553338454424652099609375 & 0.353553338454424652099609375
\end{bmatrix}
$$
$$
+i
\begin{bmatrix}
0 & 0 \\
-1.06066012382507324218 75 & -1.7677669525146484375 \\
0 & 0 \\
1.06066012382507324218 75 & 1.7677669525146484375
\end{bmatrix} . \tag{3.230}
$$

After performing U_{F1}^{-1}, $|\psi_6\rangle$ is given as

$$|\psi_6\rangle = \frac{1}{\sqrt{2^3}} \times (\ |0\rangle^{\otimes 32} |0\rangle |10000101\rangle |10001011111111111111111\rangle |00\rangle |0\rangle$$

$$+|0\rangle^{\otimes 32} |0\rangle |10000101\rangle |10001111111111111111110\rangle |00\rangle |1\rangle$$

$$+|0\rangle^{\otimes 32} |0\rangle |10000101\rangle |10000011111111111111110\rangle |01\rangle |0\rangle$$

$$+|0\rangle^{\otimes 32} |0\rangle |10000101\rangle |10010011111111111111101\rangle |01\rangle |1\rangle$$

$$+|0\rangle^{\otimes 32} |0\rangle |10000101\rangle |10001000000000000000001\rangle |10\rangle |0\rangle$$

$$+|0\rangle^{\otimes 32} |0\rangle |10000101\rangle |10010000000000000000000\rangle |10\rangle |1\rangle$$

$$+|0\rangle^{\otimes 32} |0\rangle |10000101\rangle |10010100000000000000000\rangle |11\rangle |0\rangle$$

$$+|0\rangle^{\otimes 32} |0\rangle |10000101\rangle |10001111111111111111110\rangle |11\rangle |1\rangle),$$

$$(3.231)$$

which stores a complex-value image

$$\begin{bmatrix} 98.99999237060546875+0i & 99.9999847412109375+0i \\ 96.9999847412109375+0i & 100.99997711181640625+0i \\ 98.00000762939453125+0i & 100.0+0i \\ 101.0+0i & 99.9999847412109375+0i \end{bmatrix}. \quad (3.232)$$

$|\psi_7\rangle$ is given by type conversion AG,

$$|\psi_7\rangle = \frac{1}{\sqrt{2^3}} \times (\ |99\rangle|0\rangle^{\otimes 32}|0\rangle|10000101\rangle|100010111111111111111\rangle|00\rangle|0\rangle$$

$$+|100\rangle|0\rangle^{\otimes 32}|0\rangle|10000101\rangle|100011111111111111110\rangle|00\rangle|1\rangle$$

$$+|97\rangle|0\rangle^{\otimes 32}|0\rangle|10000101\rangle|100000111111111111110\rangle|01\rangle|0\rangle$$

$$+|101\rangle|0\rangle^{\otimes 32}|0\rangle|10000101\rangle|100100111111111111101\rangle|01\rangle|1\rangle$$

$$+|98\rangle|0\rangle^{\otimes 32}|0\rangle|10000101\rangle|100010000000000000001\rangle|10\rangle|0\rangle$$

$$+|100\rangle|0\rangle^{\otimes 32}|0\rangle|10000101\rangle|100100000000000000000\rangle|10\rangle|1\rangle$$

$$+|101\rangle|0\rangle^{\otimes 32}|0\rangle|10000101\rangle|100101000000000000000\rangle|11\rangle|0\rangle$$

$$+|100\rangle|0\rangle^{\otimes 32}|0\rangle|10000101\rangle|100011111111111111110\rangle|11\rangle|1\rangle).$$

$$(3.233)$$

Finally, we retrieve the grayscale image in (3.129) by measuring on the first 8 qubits and last 3 qubits of the state $|\psi_7\rangle$.

Suppose that the black-box circuits U_{F2} and U_{F2}^{-1} implement 2D QFT and its inverse for color images, respectively. The type conversion circuit between color images and complex-value images is illustrated in Figure 49.

Figure 49. Type conversion circuit between color images and complex-value images

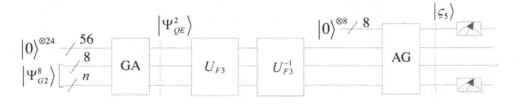

A color image is stored in a GNEQR state $|\Psi_{GC}\rangle$ in (3.154). Type conversion GAC in Figure 44 changes $|0\rangle^{\otimes 24}|\Psi_{GC}\rangle$ into $|\Psi_{QAC}^2\rangle$ in (3.190). Successively performing 2D QWT U_{F2} and its inverse transform U_{F2}^{-1}, and type conversion ACG, we obtain $|\varsigma_6\rangle$ in (3.229). We retrieve the color image by performing quantum measurement on the first 8 qubits and last n qubits of the state $|\varsigma_6\rangle$.

Type Conversions Between GNEQR and QCDSE

Since the implementation circuits of QSDSA and QSDSE are the same, the circuits GA in Figure 43 and GAC in Figure 44 also realize type conversions from GNEQR to QCDSE. Meanwhile, type conversions from QCDSE to GNEQR are implemented by the circuits the circuits AG in Figure 45 and GAC in Figure 46. Therefore, suppose that the black-box circuits U_{F3} and U_{F3}^{-1} implement 2D QFT and its inverse for grayscale images based on QCDSE, type conversion circuit between grayscale images and complex-value images based on QCDSE shown in Figure 50.

Figure 50. Type conversion circuit between GNEQR and QCDSE for grayscale images

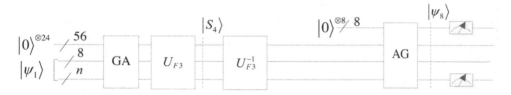

The circuits GA in Figure 43 transforms a grayscale image $|0\rangle^{\otimes 56} \otimes |\Psi_{G2}^8\rangle$ into a complex-value image $|\Psi_{QE}^2\rangle$ in (3.197). Successively performing 2D QFT U_{F3} and its inverse U_{F3}^{-1}, and the type conversion circuit AG, we obtain $|\varsigma_4\rangle$ as follows,

$$|\varsigma_5\rangle = \frac{1}{\sqrt{2^n}} \sum_{x=0}^{2^{n-k}-1} \sum_{y=0}^{2^k-1} |f(x,y)\rangle |h(x,y)\rangle |x\rangle |y\rangle, \tag{3.234}$$

where the meanings of $|f(x,y)\rangle$ and $|h(x,y)\rangle$ are seen in (3.148) and (3.197), respectively. An example of the type conversions between grayscale images and complex-value images based on QCDSE is given in Figure 51.

Figure 51. An example of the type conversions between GNEQR and QCDSE for grayscale images

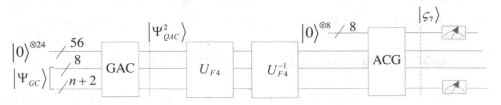

Table 4. The general features concerning the aforementioned QIRs

QIR	Category of QIR	Category of Image	Size of Image	Color Retrieval
Qubit Lattice	First	Grayscale & color	$2^{n_1} \times 2^{n_2}$	Probabilistic
QSMC & QSNC	First	Grayscale & color	$2^{n_1} \times 2^{n_2}$	Probabilistic
FRQI	First	Grayscale & color	$2^{n_1} \times 2^{n_2}$	Probabilistic
NASS	First	Grayscale & color	$2^{n_1} \times 2^{n_2}$	Probabilistic
NASSTC	First	Color	$2^{n_1} \times 2^{n_2}$	Probabilistic
NAQSS	First	Grayscale & color	$2^{n_1} \times 2^{n_2}$	Probabilistic
FQRGI	Second	Grayscale & color	$2^{n} \times 2^{n}$	Probabilistic
NASSRP	First & Second	Grayscale & color	$2^{n_1} \times 2^{n_2}$	Probabilistic
NEQR	Third	Grayscale & color	$2^{n} \times 2^{n}$	Deterministic
GNEQR	Third	Grayscale & color	$2^{n_1} \times 2^{n_2}$	Deterministic
BRQI	Third	Grayscale & color	$2^{n_1} \times 2^{n_2}$	Deterministic
QRDS	Third	Real-value	$2^{n_1} \times 2^{n_2}$	Deterministic
QCDSA	Third	Complex-value	$2^{n_1} \times 2^{n_2}$	Deterministic
QCDSE	Third	Complex-value	$2^{n_1} \times 2^{n_2}$	Deterministic

Table 5. The complexity comparison of the aforementioned QIRs

QIR	Category of Image	Circuit Complexity	Required Qubits	Measurement Number
Qubit Lattice	Grayscale	$O(2^{2n})$	2^{2n}	$O(M_g^4)$
	Color	$O(2^{2n})$	2^{2n}	$O(M_c^4)$
QSMC & QSNC	Grayscale	$O(2^{2n})$	$2^{2n}+m$	$< O(M_g^4)$
	Color	$O(2^{2n})$	$2^{2n}+m$	$< O(M_c^4)$
FRQI	Grayscale	$O(n2^{2n})$	$2n+1$	$O(2^{2n}M_g^4)$
	Color	$O(n2^{2n})$	$2n+1$	$O(2^{2n}M_c^4)$
NASS	Grayscale	$O(n^2 2^{2n})$	$2n$	$O(2^{2n}M_g^4)$
	Color	$O(n^2 2^{2n})$	$2n$	$O(2^{2n}M_c^4)$
NASSTC	Color	$O(n^2 2^{2n})$	$2n+2$	$O(2^{2n}M_g^4)$
NAQSS	Grayscale	$O(n^2 2^{2n})$	$2n+1$	$O(2^{2n}M_g^4\lambda^4)$
	Color	$O(n^2 2^{2n})$	$2n+1$	$O(2^{2n}M_c^4\lambda^4)$
FQRGI	Grayscale	$O(n^2 2^{2n})$	$2n+1$	$O(2^{2n}M_g^4)$
	Color	$O(n^2 2^{2n})$	$2n+1$	$O(2^{2n}M_c^4)$
NASSRP	Grayscale	$O(n^2 2^{2n})$	$2n+1$	$O(2^{2n}M_g^4\lambda^8)$
	Color	$O(n^2 2^{2n})$	$2n+1$	$O(2^{2n}M_c^4\lambda^8)$
NEQR	Grayscale	$O(n2^{2n})$	$2n+8$	$O(2^{2n})$
	Color	$O(n2^{2n})$	$2n+24$	$O(2^{2n})$
GNEQR	Grayscale	$O(n2^{2n})$	$2n+8$	$O(2^{2n})$
	Color	$O(n2^{2n})$	$2n+10$	$O(2^{2n})$
BRQI	Grayscale	$O(n2^{2n})$	$2n+4$	$O(2^{2n})$
	Color	$O(n2^{2n})$	$2n+6$	$O(2^{2n})$
QRDS	Real-value	$O(n2^{2n})$	$2n+32$	$O(2^{2n})$
	Real-value with three channels	$O(n2^{2n})$	$2n+34$	$O(2^{2n})$
QCDSA	Complex-value	$O(n2^{2n})$	$2n+64$	$O(2^{2n})$
	Complex-value with three channels	$O(n2^{2n})$	$2n+66$	$O(2^{2n})$
QCDSE	Complex-value	$O(n2^{2n})$	$2n+64$	$O(2^{2n})$
	Complex-value with three channels	$O(n2^{2n})$	$2n+66$	$O(2^{2n})$

The grayscale image in (3.219) is transformed into an QCDSE state $|S_4\rangle$ by the circuit GA and 2D QFT U_{F3}, where $|S_4\rangle$ is seen in (3.199), and stores a complex-value image as follows,

$$
\begin{bmatrix}
281.428466796875e^{i0} & 2.1213226318359375 \\
 & \times e^{i3.1415927410125732421875} \\
1.1180338859555810546875 & 1.8027756214141845703125 \\
\times e^{-i1.24904572963714599609375} & \times e^{-i1.3734008073806762695312 5} \\
0.70710676908493041992187 5 & \\
\times e^{i3.1415927410125732421875} & 0e^{i0} \\
1.1180338859555810546875 & 1.8027756214141845703125 \\
\times e^{i1.24904572963714599609375} & \times e^{i1.3734008073806762695312 5}
\end{bmatrix}.
\tag{3.235}
$$

Performing U_{F3}^{-1} and type conversion AG obtains $\left| \psi_8 \right\rangle$,

$$
\begin{aligned}
\left| \psi_8 \right\rangle = \frac{1}{\sqrt{2^3}} \times (& \left| 99 \right\rangle \left| 0 \right\rangle^{\otimes 32} \left| 0 \right\rangle \left| 10000101 \right\rangle \left| 100010111111111111111111 \right\rangle \left| 00 \right\rangle \left| 0 \right\rangle \\
+ & \left| 100 \right\rangle \left| 0 \right\rangle^{\otimes 32} \left| 0 \right\rangle \left| 10000101 \right\rangle \left| 100011111111111111111110 \right\rangle \left| 00 \right\rangle \left| 1 \right\rangle \\
+ & \left| 97 \right\rangle \left| 0 \right\rangle^{\otimes 32} \left| 0 \right\rangle \left| 10000101 \right\rangle \left| 100000111111111111111110 \right\rangle \left| 01 \right\rangle \left| 0 \right\rangle \\
+ & \left| 101 \right\rangle \left| 0 \right\rangle^{\otimes 32} \left| 0 \right\rangle \left| 10000101 \right\rangle \left| 100100111111111111111101 \right\rangle \left| 01 \right\rangle \left| 1 \right\rangle \\
+ & \left| 98 \right\rangle \left| 0 \right\rangle^{\otimes 32} \left| 0 \right\rangle \left| 10000101 \right\rangle \left| 100010000000000000000001 \right\rangle \left| 10 \right\rangle \left| 0 \right\rangle \\
+ & \left| 100 \right\rangle \left| 0 \right\rangle^{\otimes 32} \left| 0 \right\rangle \left| 10000101 \right\rangle \left| 100100000000000000000000 \right\rangle \left| 10 \right\rangle \left| 1 \right\rangle \\
+ & \left| 101 \right\rangle \left| 0 \right\rangle^{\otimes 32} \left| 0 \right\rangle \left| 10000101 \right\rangle \left| 100101000000000000000000 \right\rangle \left| 11 \right\rangle \left| 0 \right\rangle \\
+ & \left| 100 \right\rangle \left| 0 \right\rangle^{\otimes 32} \left| 0 \right\rangle \left| 10000101 \right\rangle \left| 100011111111111111111110 \right\rangle \left| 11 \right\rangle \left| 1 \right\rangle),
\end{aligned}
\tag{3.236}
$$

that is, type conversion AG transforms the following complex-value image

$$
\begin{bmatrix}
98.99999237060546875e^{i0} & 99.9999847412109375e^{i0} \\
96.9999847412109375e^{i0} & 100.99997711181640625e^{i0} \\
98.00000762939453125e^{i0} & 100.0e^{i0} \\
101.0e^{i0} & 99.9999847412109375e^{i0}
\end{bmatrix}
\tag{3.237}
$$

into the grayscale image in (3.129)

Table 6. The storage performance comparison of QIRs

QIR	Category of Image	The Amount of Data
FRQI	Grayscale	2^{2n+23}
FRQI	Color	2^{2n+23}
NASS	Grayscale	2^{2n+24}
NASS	Color	2^{2n+24}
NASSTC	Color	2^{2n+22}
NAQSS	Grayscale	2^{2n+24}
NAQSS	Color	2^{2n+24}
FQRGI	Grayscale	2^{2n+23}
FQRGI	Color	2^{2n+23}
NASSRP	Grayscale	$3 \times 2^{2n+23}$
NASSRP	Color	$3 \times 2^{2n+23}$
NEQR	Grayscale	2^{2n+16}
NEQR	Color	2^{2n}
GNEQR	Grayscale	2^{2n+16}
GNEQR	Color	2^{2n+14}
BRQI	Grayscale	2^{2n+20}
BRQI	Color	2^{2n+18}

Suppose that the black-box circuits U_{F4} and U_{F4}^{-1} implement 2D QFT and its inverse for color images based on QCDSE, respectively. The type conversion circuit between color images and complex-value images is illustrated in Figure 52.

Figure 52. Type conversion circuit between GNEQR and QCDSE for color images

Type conversion GAC in Figure 44 changes $\left|0\right\rangle^{\otimes 24}\left|\Psi_{GC}\right\rangle$ into $\left|\Psi_{QAC}^{2}\right\rangle$ in (3.190). Successively performing 2D QWT U_{F4} and its inverse transform U_{F4}^{-1}, and type conversion ACG, we obtain $\left|\varsigma_{7}\right\rangle$ as follows,

$$\left|\varsigma_{7}\right\rangle = \frac{1}{\sqrt{3\times 2^{n}}}\sum_{j=1}^{3}\sum_{x=0}^{2^{n-k}-1}\sum_{y=0}^{2^{k}-1}\left|f_{j}(x,y)\right\rangle\left|h_{j}(x,y)\right\rangle\left|x\right\rangle\left|y\right\rangle, \tag{3.238}$$

where the meanings of $|f_j(x,y)\rangle$ and $|h_j(x,y)\rangle$ with $j=1,2,3$ are seen in (3.154) and (3.201), respectively. The color image is retrieved by measuring the first 8 qubits and last n qubits of the state $\left|\varsigma_{7}\right\rangle$.

COMPARISONS OF QUANTUM IMAGE REPRESENTATIONS

Comparisons of parts of quantum image representations in this chapter were discussed (Yan, Iliyasu, & Venegas-Andraca, 2016; Li, Song, Fan, Peng, Xia, & Liang 2019). In this section, we discuss circuit complexities, retrieval technologies, and storage performances of the aforementioned QIRs in this chapter.

The general features concerning the aforementioned QIRs are shown in Table 4. Compared the third category of QIR with other two categories, the most noticeable difference is color retrieval. The third category of QIR has an advantage, that is, its color retrieval is deterministic.

For a $2^{n}\times 2^{n}$ image, complexity of the implementation circuits, required qubits, and measurement number for retrieving the color and the coordinate of a pixel are shown in Table 5. Here, $M_{c}=2^{24}$ and $M_{g}=2^{8}$ are the sizes of a grayscale set and a RGB color set, respectively. m is the number of deferent colors in an image. λ is the sizes of a integer set.

Table 5 shows that required qubits of Qubit Lattice and QSMC & QSNC are maximum, and their Measurement numbers are minimum. Except for Qubit Lattice and QSMC & QSNC, the third category of QIRs needs more qubits and less measurement number than other two categories.

For a more detailed comparison of storage performances of QIRs except for Qubit Lattice, QSMC & QSNC, QRDS, QCDSA and QCDSE, Table 6 lists the amount of data for $2n+24$ qubits.

Table 6 shows that the storage performance of NASSRP is best than other QIRs in the table. A NASSRP state with *2n+24* qubits can store $3 \times 2^{2n+23}$ Data for color images, which is 3×2^{23} times of the amount of data stored in NEQR using the same qubits.

CONCLUSION

This chapter described some typical examples of quantum image representations of three categories, which solve how to store an image in a quantum system, and to retrieve the image from the quantum system. The chapter provides the necessary foundation for quantum image processing in the following chapters.

REFERENCES

Cohen, N., & Weiss, S. (2012). Complex floating point—A novel data word representation for DSP processors. *IEEE Transactions on Circuits and Systems. I, Regular Papers*, *59*(10), 2252–2262.

Feynman, R. P. (1982). Simulating physics with computers. *International Journal of Theoretical Physics*, *21*, 467–488.

Jiang, N., & Wang, L. (2015). Quantum image scaling using nearest neighbor interpolation. *Quantum Information Processing*, *14*(5), 1559–1571.

Kahan, W. (1996). IEEE Standard 754 for Binary Floating-Point Arithmetic, IEEE Standard 754.94720-1776. *Lecture Notes on the Status*, 11.

Le, P. Q., Dong, F., & Hirota, K. (2011). A flexible representation of quantum images for polynomial preparation, image compression, and processing operations. *Quantum Information Processing*, *10*, 63–84.

Li, H. S., Chen, X., Xia, H., Liang, Y., & Zhou, Z. (2018). A quantum image representation based on bitplanes. *IEEE Access: Practical Innovations, Open Solutions*, *6*(1), 62396–62404.

Li, H. S., Fan, P., Xia, H. Y., Peng, H., & Song, S. (2019). Quantum implementation circuits of quantum signal representation and type conversion. *IEEE Transactions on Circuits and Systems. I, Regular Papers*, *66*(1), 341–354.

Li, H. S., Song, S., Fan, P., Peng, H., Xia, H. Y., & Liang, Y. (2019). Quantum vision representations and multi-dimensional quantum transforms. *Information Sciences*, *502*, 42–58.

Li, H. S., Zhu, Q., Song, L., Shen, C. Y., Zhou, R., & Mo, J. (2013). Image storage, retrieval, compression and segmentation in a quantum system. *Quantum Information Processing*, *12*(6), 2269–2290.

Li, H. S., Zhu, Q., Zhou, R. G., Li, M. C., Song, L., & Ian, H. (2014). Multidimensional color image storage, retrieval, and compression based on quantum amplitudes and phases. *Information Sciences*, *273*, 212–232.

Li, H. S., Zhu, Q., Zhou, R. G., Song, L., & Yang, X. J. (2014). Multidimensional color image storage and retrieval for a normal arbitrary quantum superposition state. *Quantum Information Processing*, *13*(4), 991–1011.

Long, G. L., & Sun, Y. (2001). Efficient Scheme for Initializing a quantum register with an arbitrary superposed state. *Physical Review A.*, *64*, 014303.

Nielsen, M. A., & Chuang, I. L. (2000). *Quantum Computation and Quantum Information*. Cambridge University Press.

Sang, J., Wang, S., & Li, Q. (2017). A novel quantum representation of color digital images. *Quantum Information Processing*, *16*(2), 42.

Sun, B., Iliyasu, A. M., Yan, F., Dong, F., & Hirota, K. (2013). An RGB multi-channel representation for images on quantum computers. *Journal of Advanced Computational Intelligence and Intelligent Informatics*, *17*(3), 404–417.

Venegas-Andraca, S. E., & Ball, J. L. (2010). Processing images in entangled quantum systems. *Quantum Information Processing*, *9*(1), 1–11.

Venegas-Andraca, S. E., & Bose, S. (2003). Storing, processing and retrieving an image using quantum mechanics. *Proceeding of SPIE Conference Quantum Information and Computation*, *5105*, 137–147.

Yan, F., Iliyasu, A. M., & Guo, Y. (2018). Flexible representation and manipulation of audio signals on quantum computers. *Theoretical Computer Science*, *752*, 71–85.

Yan, F., Iliyasu, A. M., & Venegas-Andraca, S. E. (2016). A survey of quantum image representations. *Quantum Information Processing*, *15*(1), 1–35.

Yang, Y. G., Xia, J., Jia, X., & Zhang, H. (2013). Novel image encryption/ decryption based on quantum fourier transform and double phase encoding. *Quantum Information Processing*, *12*(11), 3477–3493.

Yuan, S., Mao, X., Xue, Y., Chen, L., Xiong, Q., & Compare, A. (2014). SQR: A simple quantum representation of infrared images. *Quantum Information Processing*, *13*(6), 1353–1379.

Zhang, Y., Lu, K., Gao, Y., & Wang, M. (2013). NEQR: A novel enhanced quantum representation of digital images. *Quantum Information Processing*, *12*(8), 2833–2860.

Zhang, Y., Lu, K., Gao, Y., & Xu, K. (2013). A novel quantum representation for log-polar images. *Quantum Information Processing*, *12*(9), 3103–3126.

Chapter 3
Quantum Geometric Transformations

ABSTRACT

Geometric transformations are basic operations in image processing. This chapter describes geometric transformations of images and videos. These geometric transformations include two-point swapping, symmetric flip, local flip, orthogonal rotation, and translation.

INTRODUCTION

Many applications in both 2D and 3D biomedical imaging require efficient techniques for geometric transformations of images (Arce-Santana & Alba, 2009; Dooley, Stewart, Durrani, Setarehdan, & Soraghan, 2004). Quantum geometric transformations provides a feasible method to implement efficient geometric transformation. Geometric transformations, such as two-point swapping, flip, orthogonal rotation, and restricted geometric transformation, are applied to images based on FRQI (Iliyasu, Le, Dong, & Hirota, 2012; Le, Iliyasu, Dong, & Hirota, 2010, 2011). Next, quantum geometric transformations of images and videos based on NASS were proposed (Fan, Zhou, Jing, & Li, 2016). This chapter introduces quantum geometric transformations of images and videos based on NASS, which include two-point swapping, symmetric flip, local flip, orthogonal rotation, and translation.

DOI: 10.4018/978-1-7998-3799-2.ch003

TWO-POINT SWAPPING

Definition 4.1. A two-point swapping operator G_s^t for images and videos is defined as

$$G_s^t = |s\rangle\langle t| + |t\rangle\langle s| + \sum_{i=0, i\neq s,t}^{2^n-1} |i\rangle\langle i|, \tag{4.1}$$

where $|s\rangle$ and $|t\rangle$ encode the coordinates of the two swapped pixels. The binary expansions of the integers s, t, and i are $s=s_1,\ldots,s_n$, $t=t_1,\ldots,t_n$, and $i=i_1,\ldots,i_n$, respectively.

The NASS state $|\psi\rangle$ represents a multi-dimensional image (i.e., a 2D image or a 3D video) with 2^n pixels,

$$|\psi\rangle = \sum_{j=0}^{2^n-1} \theta_j |j\rangle. \tag{4.2}$$

Applying G_s^t on the NASS state $|\psi\rangle$ implements the two-point swapping of a multi-dimensional image,

$$G_s^t|\psi\rangle = \sum_{i=0}^{2^n-1} \theta_i G_s^t|i\rangle = \theta_s|t\rangle + \theta_t|s\rangle + \sum_{i=0, i\neq s,t}^{2^n-1} \theta_i|i\rangle. \tag{4.3}$$

To design the quantum circuit of the two-point swapping operator G_s^t, we first introduce Gray code (Nielsen & Chuang, 2000). Suppose that s and t are two distinct binary numbers, then a Gray code that connects s and t is a sequence of binary numbers, which starts with s and ends with t, where adjacent members in the list differ by exactly one bit. For example, when n bit binary numbers $s=0\ldots0\ldots0$ and $t=1\ldots1\ldots1$ are the binary expansions of the integers 0 and 2^n-1, respectively, the Gray code is as follows,

$$
\begin{matrix}
0 & \cdots & 0 & \cdots & 0 \\
0 & \cdots & 0 & \cdots & 1 \\
\vdots & & \vdots & & \vdots \\
0 & \cdots & 1 & \cdots & 1 \\
\vdots & & \vdots & & \vdots \\
1 & \cdots & 1 & \cdots & 1
\end{matrix} .
\tag{4.4}
$$

Let $g_1,g_2,\ldots,g_m$ be the elements of a Gray code that connects s and t, where $g_1=s$ and $g_m=t$. s and t differ in at most n locations, thus we can find a Gray code such that $m \leq n+1$. Since the elements g_i and g_{i+1} ($1 \leq i \leq m-1$) differ at only one location, we can implement the transformation $\left|g_i\right\rangle \rightarrow \left|g_{i+1}\right\rangle$ by using the $C^n(X_k)$ gate shown in Figure 8. For example, when $|g_2\rangle=|0\ldots01\rangle$ and $|g_3\rangle=|0\ldots11\rangle$, where $|g_2\rangle$ and $|g_3\rangle$ are two elements of the Gray codes in (4.4), the $C^n(X_{n-1})$ gate can achieve the transformation $|g_2\rangle \rightarrow |g_3\rangle$.

Let the matrix W *and* its conjugate transpose $W^\dagger$, *two sets* $\mathbb{W}$ *and* $\mathbb{X}$ be

$$
\left\{
\begin{aligned}
W &= \begin{bmatrix} 0 & 1 \\ -1 & 0 \end{bmatrix}, W^\dagger = \begin{bmatrix} 0 & -1 \\ 1 & 0 \end{bmatrix}, \\
\mathbb{W} &= \{S_k^n(W), S_k^n(W^\dagger) \,|\, k=1,2,\ldots n\}, . \\
\mathbb{X} &= \{S_k^n(X) \,|\, k=1,2,\ldots n\},
\end{aligned}
\right.
\tag{4.5}
$$

where these gates $S_k^n(U)$ with $U=W$, $U=W^\dagger$, or $U=X$ are shown in Figure 8.

Theorem 4.1. Let $g_1,g_2,\ldots,g_m$ be the elements of a Gray code that connects s and t, where $|g_1\rangle=|s\rangle$ and $|g_m\rangle=|t\rangle$ encode the coordinates of the two swapped pixels in G_s^t. The operator G_s^t can be implemented by $2m-4$ gates in the set $\mathbb{W}$ and one gate in the set $\mathbb{X}$, whose complexity is $O(n^2)$.

Proof. Suppose that a quantum circuit C_i implements

$$
C_i\left|g_i\right\rangle = \left|g_{i+1}\right\rangle,
\tag{4.6}
$$

where $1 \leq i \leq m-1$. Since g_i and g_{i+1} in a Gay code differ by exactly one bit, C_i is an element of the set $\mathbb{X}$. For instance, when g_i and g_{i+1} differ by the j-th bit, i.e.,

$$\begin{cases} g_i = i_1 \cdots i_j \cdots i_n, \\ g_{i+1} = i_1 \cdots \bar{i}_j \cdots i_n, \end{cases} \tag{4.7}$$

then $C_i = S_j^n(X)$ realizes

$$\begin{cases} C_i \left| g_i \right\rangle = S_j^n(X) \left| g_i \right\rangle = \left| g_{i+1} \right\rangle, \\ C_i \left| g_{i+1} \right\rangle = S_j^n(X) \left| g_{i+1} \right\rangle = \left| g_i \right\rangle. \end{cases} \tag{4.8}$$

When $|x\rangle \neq |g_i\rangle$ and $\left| x \right\rangle \neq \left| g_{i+1} \right\rangle$,

$$C_i \left| x \right\rangle = S_j^n(X) \left| x \right\rangle = \left| x \right\rangle. \tag{4.9}$$

Therefore,

$$C_T = C_1 C_2 \cdots C_{m-2} C_{m-1} C_{m-2} \cdots C_1$$

implement the transformations $|g_1\rangle \to |g_2\rangle \to \ldots |g_m\rangle$ and $\left| g_{m-1} \right\rangle \to \left| g_{m-2} \right\rangle \to \cdots \left| g_1 \right\rangle$. From equations (4.8) and (4.9), we obtain

$$\begin{cases} C_T \left| s \right\rangle = C_T \left| g_1 \right\rangle = \left| g_m \right\rangle = \left| t \right\rangle, \\ C_T \left| t \right\rangle = C_T \left| g_m \right\rangle = \left| g_1 \right\rangle = \left| s \right\rangle, \\ C_T \left| x \right\rangle = \left| x \right\rangle, \end{cases} \tag{4.10}$$

where $|x\rangle \neq |s\rangle$ and $|x\rangle \neq |t\rangle$. Thus, applying C_T on the NASS state $\left| \psi \right\rangle$ gives

$$C_T \left| \psi \right\rangle = \sum_{i=0}^{2^n-1} \theta_i C_T \left| i \right\rangle = \theta_s \left| t \right\rangle + \theta_t \left| s \right\rangle + \sum_{i=0,i\neq s,t}^{2^n-1} \theta_i \left| i \right\rangle. \tag{4.11}$$

Comparing (4.11) with (4.3), we conclude that $C_T = G_s^t$. Substituting W and $W^\dagger$ for X in C_i gives V_i and $V_i^\dagger$. For instance, if $C_i = S_j^n(X)$, the $V_i = S_j^n(W)$ and $V_i^\dagger = S_j^n(W^\dagger)$. Since $W|0\rangle = -|1\rangle$, $W|1\rangle = |0\rangle$, and $W^\dagger W = I$,

$$V_T = V_1^\dagger V_2^\dagger \cdots V_{m-2}^\dagger C_{m-1} V_{m-2} \cdots V_2 V_1$$

is equal to C_T, i.e., $V_T = G_s^t$. We conclude that G_s^t can be implemented by $2m - 4$ gates in the set $\mathbb{W}$ and one gate in the set $\mathbb{X}$.

Since $W, W^\dagger \in SU(2)$, the complexity of any gate in the set $\mathbb{W}$ is $O(n)$ by Corollary 2.18. Meanwhile, the complexity of any gate in the set $\mathbb{X}$ is $O(n^2)$ by Corollary 2.16. Since s and t can differ in at most n locations, we obtain $m \le n+1$. Therefore, the complexity of G_s^t is $O(n^2)$.

To understand the quantum circuit implementation of two-point swapping more clearly, let us consider the 2D image in Figure 6 and the video in Figure 7 as examples. When $n=5$, the Gray code in (44) is changed into

$$
\begin{array}{ccccc}
0 & 0 & 0 & 0 & 0 \\
0 & 0 & 0 & 0 & 1 \\
0 & 0 & 0 & 1 & 1 \\
0 & 0 & 1 & 1 & 1 \\
0 & 1 & 1 & 1 & 1 \\
1 & 1 & 1 & 1 & 1
\end{array}
\text{'} \qquad (4.12)
$$

and its elements are successively denoted as $g_1, g_2, \ldots, g_6$, such as $|g_1\rangle = |s\rangle = |00000\rangle$ and $|g_6\rangle = |t\rangle = |11111\rangle$. According to Theorem 4.1, the two-point swapping is realized by 8 gates in the set $\mathbb{W}$ and one gate in the set $\mathbb{X}$, the quantum circuit of which is shown in Figure 1.

For clarity, the state $\left|\psi_2^{3,2}\right\rangle$ in (3.59) is rewritten as

$$\left|\psi_2^{3,2}\right\rangle = \sum_{i=0}^{2^5-1} \theta_i \left|i_5 i_4 i_3\right\rangle \left|i_2 i_1\right\rangle = \theta_0 \left|000\right\rangle\left|00\right\rangle + \theta_1 \left|000\right\rangle\left|01\right\rangle + \cdots + \theta_{30}\left|111\right\rangle\left|10\right\rangle + \theta_{31}\left|111\right\rangle\left|11\right\rangle,$$

$$(4.13)$$

Figure 1. The implementation of the two-point swapping for the Gray code in (4.12).

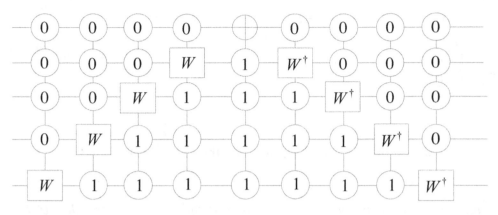

which represents the image in Figure 2 (a). Applying the circuit on $\left|\psi_2^{3,2}\right\rangle$, we implement the two-point swapping between the first coordinate and the last coordinate. The result is shown in Figure 2 (b).

Figure 2. The example of a two-point swapping for a 8x4 image.

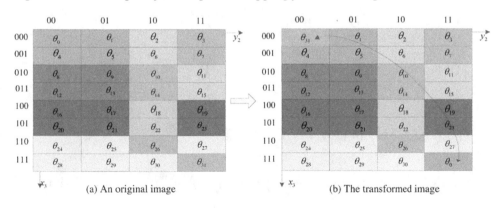

(a) An original image   (b) The transformed image

More than one Gray code often connects s and t, so we can implement the two-point swapping of s and t using more than one quantum circuit. For example, when $s=00000$ and $t=11111$, another Gray code is as follows,

$$
\begin{matrix}
0 & 0 & 0 & 0 & 0 \\
1 & 0 & 0 & 0 & 0 \\
1 & 1 & 0 & 0 & 0 \\
1 & 1 & 1 & 0 & 0 \\
1 & 1 & 1 & 1 & 0 \\
1 & 1 & 1 & 1 & 1
\end{matrix}, \tag{4.14}
$$

and the two-point swapping is realized by the circuit in Figure 3.

Figure 3. The implementation of the two-point swapping for the Gray code in (4.14).

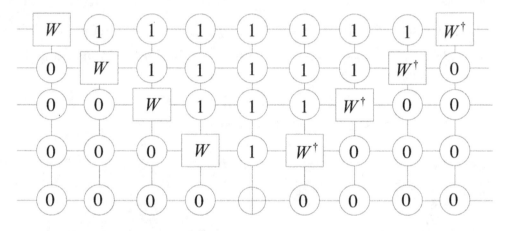

The state $\left|\psi_3^{2,1,2}\right\rangle$ in (3.61) is rewritten as

$$
\left|\psi_3^{2,1,2}\right\rangle = \sum_{i=0}^{2^5-1} \theta_i \left|i_5 i_4\right\rangle \left|i_3\right\rangle \left|i_2 i_1\right\rangle = \theta_0 \left|00\right\rangle\left|0\right\rangle\left|00\right\rangle + \theta_1 \left|00\right\rangle\left|0\right\rangle\left|01\right\rangle + \cdots + \theta_{31}\left|11\right\rangle\left|1\right\rangle\left|11\right\rangle, \tag{4.15}
$$

which represents the video in Figure 4 (a). The two-point swapping between the first coordinate $|s\rangle = |00\rangle\,|0\rangle\,|00\rangle$ and the last coordinate $|t\rangle = |11\rangle\,|1\rangle\,|11\rangle$ is realized by performing the circuit on the state $\left|\psi_3^{2,1,2}\right\rangle$, and the result is shown in Figure 4.

Figure 4. The example of a two-point swapping for a 4x2x4 video

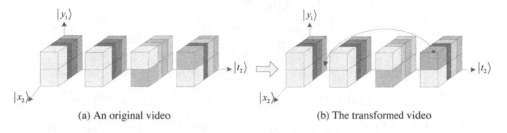

(a) An original video   (b) The transformed video

SYMMETRIC FLIP TRANSFORMATION

Definition 4.2. Two symmetric flip operators G_{F2}^x and G_{F2}^y for $2^{n-k} \times 2^k$ images are defined as

$$
\begin{cases}
G_{F2}^x = I^{\otimes n-k} \otimes X^{\otimes k}, \\
G_{F2}^y = X^{\otimes n-k} \otimes I^{\otimes k},
\end{cases}
\tag{4.16}
$$

where I and X are identity gate and NOT gate, respectively.

The symmetric flip transformations of the image $\left| \psi_2 \right\rangle$ in (3.58) are realized by

Figure 5. The example of the symmetric flip transformation G_{F2}^x.

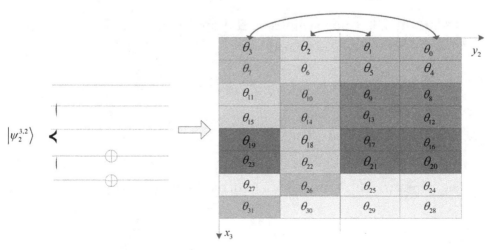

$$\begin{cases} G_{F2}^{x}\left|\psi_{2}\right\rangle = \sum_{i=0}^{2^{n}-1} \theta_{i}\left|i_{n}\dots i_{k+1}\right\rangle\left|\overline{i_{k}}\dots\overline{i_{1}}\right\rangle, \\ G_{F2}^{y}\left|\psi_{2}\right\rangle = \sum_{i=0}^{2^{n}-1} \theta_{i}\left|\overline{i_{n}}\dots\overline{i_{k+1}}\right\rangle\left|i_{k}\dots i_{1}\right\rangle, \end{cases} \qquad (4.17)$$

where $\overline{j_{h}} = 1 - j_{h}$, and $h=1,2,\dots,n$. For instance, applying G_{F2}^{x} on $\left|\psi_{2}^{3,2}\right\rangle$ in (4.13), we implement the symmetric flip transformation of the image in Figure 2 (a), the result of which is shown in Figure 5.

Another symmetric flip transformation of the image in Figure 2 (a) is realized by applying G_{F2}^{y} on $\left|\psi_{2}^{3,2}\right\rangle$, and its result is shown in Figure 6.

Figure 6. The example of the symmetric flip transformation G_{F2}^{y}.

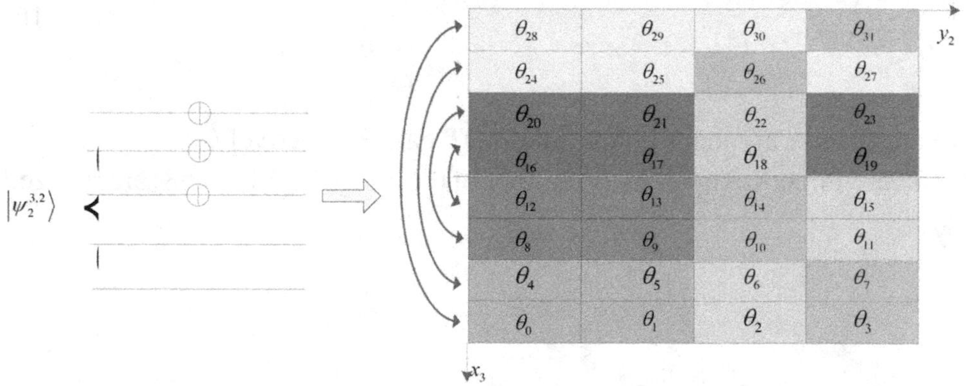

Definition 4.3. Three symmetric flip operators G_{F3}^{x}, G_{F3}^{y} and G_{F3}^{t} for $2^{n-k-h} \times 2^{k} \times 2^{h}$ videos are defined as

$$\begin{cases} G_{F3}^{x} = I^{\otimes n-k-h} \otimes X^{\otimes k} \otimes X^{\otimes h}, \\ G_{F3}^{y} = X^{\otimes n-k-h} \otimes I^{\otimes k} \otimes X^{\otimes h}, \\ G_{F3}^{t} = X^{\otimes n-k-h} \otimes X^{\otimes k} \otimes I^{\otimes h}. \end{cases} \qquad (4.18)$$

The symmetric flip transformations of the video $\left|\psi_{3}\right\rangle$ in (3.60) are realized by

$$\begin{cases} G_{F3}^{x}\left|\psi_{3}\right\rangle = \displaystyle\sum_{i=0}^{2^{n}-1}\theta_{i}\left|i_{n}...i_{h+k+1}\right\rangle\left|\overline{i_{h+k}...i_{h+1}}\right\rangle\left|\overline{i_{h}...i_{1}}\right\rangle, \\[2mm] G_{F3}^{y}\left|\psi_{3}\right\rangle = \displaystyle\sum_{i=0}^{2^{n}-1}\theta_{i}\left|\overline{i_{n}...i_{h+k+1}}\right\rangle\left|i_{h+k}...i_{h+1}\right\rangle\left|\overline{i_{h}...i_{1}}\right\rangle, \\[2mm] G_{F3}^{t}\left|\psi_{3}\right\rangle = \displaystyle\sum_{i=0}^{2^{n}-1}\theta_{i}\left|\overline{i_{n}...i_{h+k+1}}\right\rangle\left|\overline{i_{h+k}...i_{h+1}}\right\rangle\left|i_{h}...i_{1}\right\rangle, \end{cases} \quad (4.19)$$

where $\overline{j}_{m} = 1 - j_{m}$, and $m=1,2,...,n$. For instance, applying G_{F3}^{x}, G_{F3}^{y} and G_{F3}^{t} on $\left|\psi_{3}^{2,1,2}\right\rangle$ in (4.15), we implement the symmetric flip transformations of the video in Figure 4 (a), the results of which are shown in Figure 7, Figure 8, and Figure 9, respectively.

Figure 7. The example of the symmetric flip transformation G_{F3}^{x}.

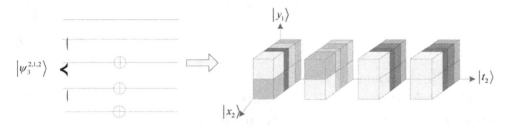

Figure 8. The example of the symmetric flip transformation G_{F3}^{y}.

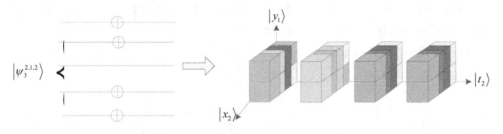

From Definition 4.2 and Definition 4.3, every symmetric flip operator consists of n NOT gates at most, so its complexity is $O(n)$.

Figure 9. The example of the symmetric flip transformation G^t_{F3}.

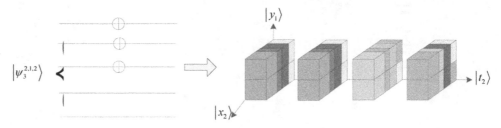

LOCAL FLIP TRANSFORMATION

Definition 4.4. A local flip operator $G^{x,j,m}_{LF2}$ along the x axis for $2^{n-k} \times 2^k$ images is defined as

$$G^{x,j,m}_{LF2}\left|\psi_2\right\rangle = \sum_{i=0,i_j \neq m}^{2^n-1} \theta_i \left|i_n \cdots i_{k+1}\right\rangle\left|i_k \cdots i_1\right\rangle + \sum_{i=0,i_j=m}^{2^n-1} \theta_i \left|i_n \cdots i_{k+1}\right\rangle\left|\overline{i_k} \cdots \overline{i_{j+1}}\,\overline{i_j}\,\overline{i_{j-1}} \cdots \overline{i_1}\right\rangle \ ,$$

(4.20)

where $1 \leq j \leq k$, and $m \in \{0,1\}$.

The local flip operator $G^{x,j,m}_{LF2}$ is realized by the circuit shown in Figure 10 (a), and its complexity is $O(n)$. For example, when $j=2$ and $m=1$, the circuit of $G^{x,2,1}_{LF2}$ for a 8x4 image is shown in Figure 10 (b).

Applying $G^{x,2,1}_{F2}$ on $\left|\psi_2^{3,2}\right\rangle$ in (4.13), we implement the local flip transformation of the image shown in Figure 11. The result shows that pixels in the dashed are transformed by the local flip transformation $G^{x,2,1}_{F2}$.

Definition 4.5. A local flip operator $G^{t,y,j,m}_{LF3}$ along the t axis for $2^{n-k-h} \times 2^k \times 2^h$ videos is defined as

$$G^{t,y,j,m}_{LF3}\left|\psi_3\right\rangle = \sum_{i=0,i_j \neq m}^{2^n-1} \theta_i \left|i\right\rangle + \sum_{i=0,i_j=m}^{2^n-1} \theta_i \left|\overline{i_n \cdots i_{h+k+1}}\right\rangle\left|\overline{i_{h+k}} \cdots \overline{i_{j+1}}\,\overline{i_j}\,\overline{i_{j-1}} \cdots \overline{i_{h+1}}\right\rangle\left|i_h \cdots i_1\right\rangle \ ,$$

(4.21)

where $h+1 \leq j \leq h+k$, and $m \in \{0,1\}$.

The circuit of the local flip operator $G^{t,y,j,m}_{LF3}$ is designed in Figure 12 (a), and its complexity is $O(n)$. For instance, when $j=3$ and $m=1$, the circuit of $G^{t,y,3,1}_{LF3}$ for a 4×2×4 video is designed in Figure 12 (b), and the result in Figure

Figure 10. The Implementation circuits of local flip operators for images

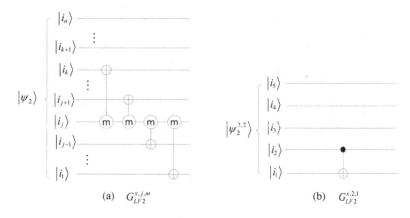

(a) $G_{LF2}^{x,j,m}$ (b) $G_{LF2}^{x,2,1}$

Figure 11. The example of the local flip transformation $G_{LF2}^{x,2,1}$.

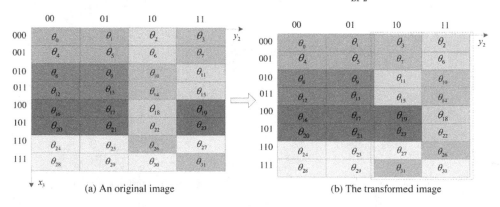

(a) An original image (b) The transformed image

13 shows that $G_{LF3}^{t,y,3,1}$ keeps these pixels in the right part in the image frames unchanged.

ORTHOGONAL ROTATION

Definition 4.6. The orthogonal rotation operators $R_2^{\alpha}(\left|x_m\right\rangle \otimes \left|y_k\right\rangle)$ and $R_3^{\alpha}(\left|x_m\right\rangle \otimes \left|y_k\right\rangle)$ for images and videos along the plane spanned by $\left|x_m\right\rangle \otimes \left|y_k\right\rangle$ are defined as

Figure 12. The implementation circuits of local flip operators for videos.

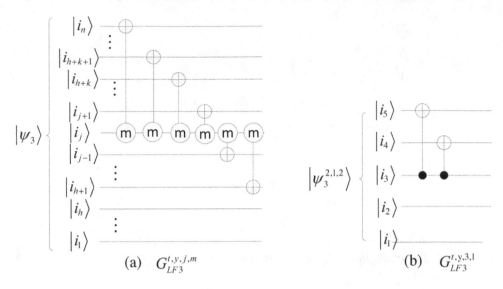

(a) $G_{LF3}^{t,y,j,m}$ (b) $G_{LF3}^{t,y,3,1}$

Figure 13. The example of the local flip transformation $G_{LF3}^{t,y,3,1}$.

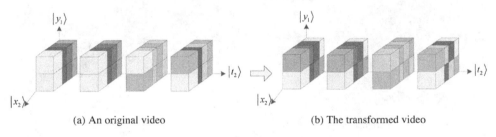

(a) An original video (b) The transformed video

$$\begin{cases} R_2^\alpha(|x_m\rangle \otimes |y_k\rangle)|\psi_2\rangle = \sum_{i=0}^{2^n-1} \theta_i |x'\rangle|y'\rangle, \\ R_3^\alpha(|x_m\rangle \otimes |y_k\rangle)|\psi_3\rangle = \sum_{i=0}^{2^n-1} \theta_i |x'\rangle|y'\rangle|t_h\rangle, \end{cases} \tag{4.22}$$

here, $\alpha \in \{\pi/2, \pi, 3\pi/2\}$, $m=k$ (i.e. the sizes of $|x_m\rangle$ and $|y_k\rangle$ are the same), and

$$\begin{cases} \left|x'\right\rangle\left|y'\right\rangle = \left|y_k\right\rangle\overline{\left|x_m\right\rangle} & \text{for } \alpha = \dfrac{\pi}{2}, \\[2mm] \left|x'\right\rangle\left|y'\right\rangle = \overline{\left|x_m\right\rangle}\left|y_k\right\rangle & \text{for } \alpha = \pi, \\[2mm] \left|x'\right\rangle\left|y'\right\rangle = \overline{\left|y_k\right\rangle}\left|x_m\right\rangle & \text{for } \alpha = \dfrac{3\pi}{2}. \end{cases} \tag{4.23}$$

where $\overline{\left|x_m\right\rangle}$ and $\overline{\left|y_k\right\rangle}$ implement the NOT operation for every qubit in $\left|x_m\right\rangle$ and $\left|y_k\right\rangle$, respectively.

The implementation circuits of $R_2^\alpha(\left|x_m\right\rangle\otimes\left|y_k\right\rangle)$ and $R_3^\alpha(\left|x_m\right\rangle\otimes\left|y_k\right\rangle)$ are shown in Figure 14, and Figure 15, respectively. Since $R_2^\alpha(\left|x_m\right\rangle\otimes\left|y_k\right\rangle)$ and $R_3^\alpha(\left|x_m\right\rangle\otimes\left|y_k\right\rangle)$ can be realized by n NOT gates and n Swap gates at most, their complexities are both $O(n)$.

Figure 14. The circuits of the orthogonal rotation operators $R_2^\alpha(\left|x_m\right\rangle\otimes\left|y_k\right\rangle)$ for images.

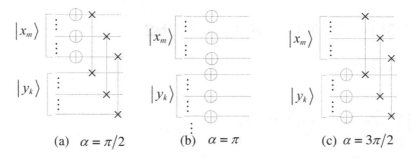

(a) $\alpha = \pi/2$ (b) $\alpha = \pi$ (c) $\alpha = 3\pi/2$

Applying $R_2^\alpha(\left|x_m\right\rangle\otimes\left|y_k\right\rangle)$ on $\left|\psi_2^{3,2}\right\rangle$ in (4.13), we implement the orthogonal rotations of the image in Figure 16 (a), results of which are shown in Figure 16 (b), (c) and (d).

Suppose the state $\left|\psi_3^{1,1,2}\right\rangle$,

$$\left|\psi_3^{1,1,2}\right\rangle = \sum_{i=0}^{2^4-1}\theta_i\left|i_4\right\rangle\left|i_3\right\rangle\left|i_2 i_1\right\rangle \tag{4.24}$$

Figure 15. The circuits of the orthogonal rotation operators $R_3^\alpha(|x_m\rangle \otimes |y_k\rangle)$ *for videos.*

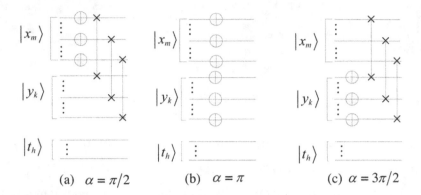

(a) $\alpha = \pi/2$ (b) $\alpha = \pi$ (c) $\alpha = 3\pi/2$

represents the video in Figure 17 (a), applying $R_3^\alpha(|x_m\rangle \otimes |y_k\rangle)$ on $|\psi_3^{1,1,2}\rangle$, we implement the orthogonal rotations of the video, results of which are shown in Figure 17 (b), (c) and (d).

TRANSLATION TRANSFORMATIONS

An operator T_k is

$$T_k = \left(\sum_{i=0}^{2^k-2}|i+1\rangle\langle i|\right) + |0\rangle\langle 2^k - 1|, \tag{4.25}$$

then $T_k|j\rangle$ is equal to

$$T_k|j\rangle = \begin{cases} |j+1\rangle, & 0 \le j \le 2^k - 2, \\ |0\rangle, & j = 2^k - 1. \end{cases} \tag{4.26}$$

The circuit of the operator T_k is designed in Figure 18 (a), and its example for $k=7$ is shown in Figure 18 (b). From Corollary 2.14 and Corollary 2.16, we conclude that the complexity of the operator T_k is $O(k^2)$.

Definition 4.7. Two translation transformation operators $T_{|x_m\rangle}^2$ and $T_{|y_k\rangle}^2$ for $2^{n-k} \times 2^k$ images are defined as

Figure 16. The examples of the orthogonal rotation transformation $R_2^{\alpha}\left(\left|x_m\right\rangle \otimes \left|y_k\right\rangle\right)$.

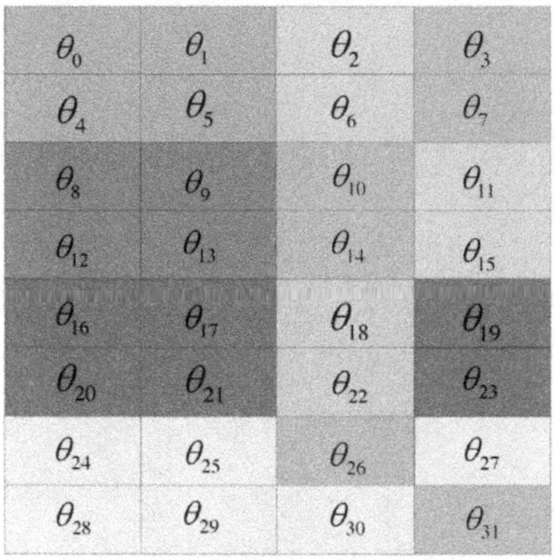

(a) An original image

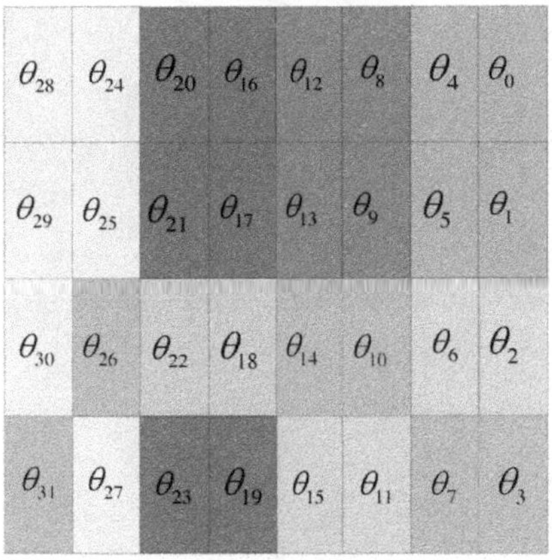

(b) $\alpha = \pi/2$

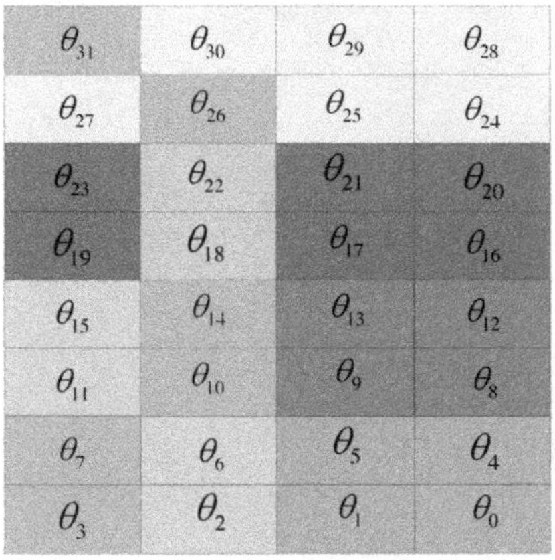

(c) $\alpha = \pi$

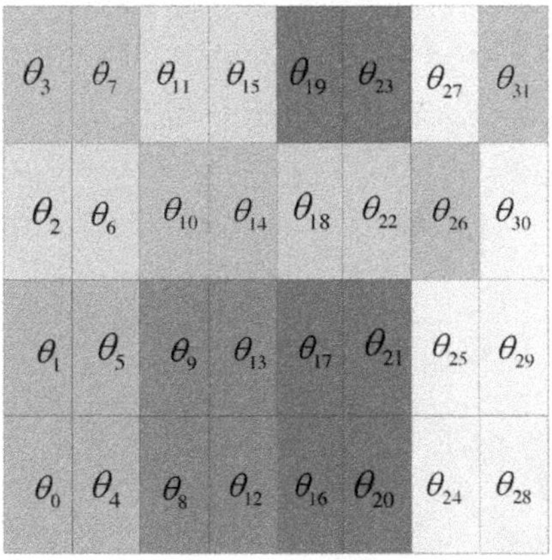

(d) $\alpha = 3\pi/2$

$$\begin{cases} T_{\left|x_m\right\rangle}^2 = T_{n-k} \otimes I^{\otimes k}, \\ T_{\left|y_k\right\rangle}^2 = I^{\otimes n-k} \otimes T_k. \end{cases} \tag{4.27}$$

Applying $T_{\left|x_m\right\rangle}^2$ and $T_{\left|y_k\right\rangle}^2$ on $\left|\psi_2^{3,2}\right\rangle$ in (4.13), we implement the translations of the image in Figure 19 (a), results of which are shown in Figure 16 (b) and (c).

Figure 17. The examples of the orthogonal rotation transformation $R_3^\alpha\left(\left|x_m\right\rangle \otimes \left|y_k\right\rangle\right)$.

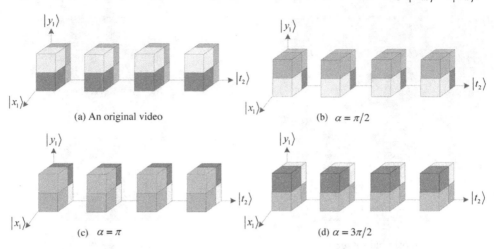

(a) An original video

(b) $\alpha = \pi/2$

(c) $\alpha = \pi$

(d) $\alpha = 3\pi/2$

Figure 18. The circuits of the operator T_k.

(a) T_k

(b) T_7

Figure 19. The examples of the translation transforms for 8x4 images.

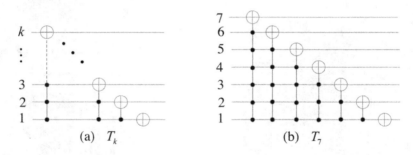

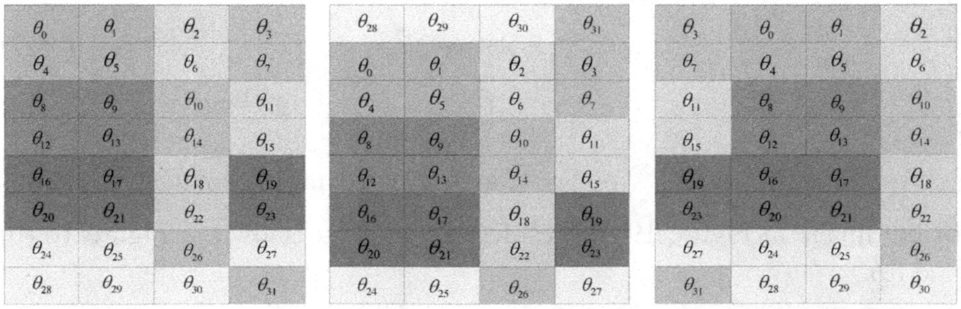

(a) An original image

(b) The transformed image by $T_{\left|x_m\right\rangle}^2$

(c) The transformed image by $T_{\left|y_k\right\rangle}^2$

Definition 4.8. The translation transformation operator $T^3_{|t_h\rangle}$ for $2^{n-k-h} \times 2^k \times 2^h$ videos is defined as

$$T^3_{|t_h\rangle} = I^{\otimes n-k-h} \otimes I^{\otimes k} \otimes T_h . \tag{4.28}$$

Applying $T^3_{|t_1\rangle}$ on $\left| \psi_3^{2,1,2} \right\rangle$ in (4.15), we implement the translation of the video in Figure 20 (a), results of which is shown in Figure 20 (b).

Figure 20. The example of the translation transform

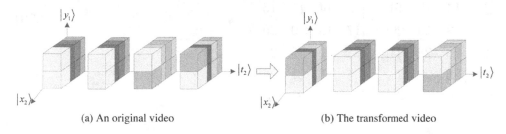

(a) An original video   (b) The transformed video

The complexity of the operator T_k is $O(k^2)$, then complexities of translation transformation operators $T^2_{|x_m\rangle}$, $T^2_{|y_k\rangle}$ and $T^3_{|t_h\rangle}$ are $O(k^2)$, $O((n-k)^2)$ and $O(h^2)$, respectively. Meanwhile, $n-k <n$, $k<n$, and $h<n$, so the complexities of the above translation transformations are all $O(n^2)$.

SIMULATIONS OF GEOMETRIC TRANSFORMATIONS

Now, we describe the experiments of two-point swapping, symmetric flip, local flip, orthogonal rotation, and translation, their codes are seen in Appendix B.

The Simulation of Two-Point Swapping

Let us consider the following image as an example for two-point swapping,

Figure 21. The experiment of a two-point swapping for a 4x2x4 video

$$\begin{bmatrix} 1 & 5 \\ 9 & 13 \\ 17 & 21 \\ 25 & 29 \end{bmatrix}\begin{bmatrix} 2 & 6 \\ 10 & 14 \\ 18 & 22 \\ 26 & 30 \end{bmatrix}\begin{bmatrix} 3 & 7 \\ 11 & 15 \\ 19 & 23 \\ 27 & 31 \end{bmatrix}\begin{bmatrix} 4 & 8 \\ 12 & 16 \\ 20 & 24 \\ 28 & 32 \end{bmatrix}_{\!|t_2\rangle} \Longrightarrow \begin{bmatrix} \mathbf{32} & 5 \\ 9 & 13 \\ 17 & 21 \\ 25 & 29 \end{bmatrix}\begin{bmatrix} 2 & 6 \\ 10 & 14 \\ 18 & 22 \\ 26 & 30 \end{bmatrix}\begin{bmatrix} 3 & 7 \\ 11 & 15 \\ 19 & 23 \\ 27 & 31 \end{bmatrix}\begin{bmatrix} 4 & 8 \\ 12 & 16 \\ 20 & 24 \\ 28 & \mathbf{1} \end{bmatrix}_{\!|t_2\rangle}$$

(a) An original video   (b) The transformed video

$$\begin{bmatrix} 1 & 2 & 3 & 4 \\ 5 & 6 & 7 & 8 \\ 9 & 10 & 11 & 12 \\ 13 & 14 & 15 & 16 \\ 17 & 18 & 19 & 20 \\ 21 & 22 & 23 & 24 \\ 25 & 26 & 27 & 28 \\ 29 & 30 & 31 & 32 \end{bmatrix} \Rightarrow \begin{bmatrix} \mathbf{32} & 2 & 3 & 4 \\ 5 & 6 & 7 & 8 \\ 9 & 10 & 11 & 12 \\ 13 & 14 & 15 & 16 \\ 17 & 18 & 19 & 20 \\ 21 & 22 & 23 & 24 \\ 25 & 26 & 27 & 28 \\ 29 & 30 & 31 & \mathbf{1} \end{bmatrix}. \tag{4.29}$$

the Gray code of which is shown in (4.14). Therefore, we calculate the matrix of the circuit in Figure 1 using Code B.13, and the result of the two-point swapping is in the right of (4.29).

We use Code B.14 to calculate the matrix of the circuit in Figure 1. The result of the two-point swapping for the video on the left of Figure 21 is shown on the right.

Figure 22. Experiments of symmetric flip transformations for a 128x128 image.

(a) An original image   (b) Flip along x axis   (c) Flip along y axis

The Simulation of Symmetric Flip Transformations

The 128×128 color image is regarded as the input image shown in Figure 22 (a). Results of symmetric flip experiments are shown in Figure 22 (b) and (c) using Code B.15. The flip operators are $G_{F2}^x = I^{\otimes 7} \otimes X^{\otimes 7}$ and $G_{F2}^y = X^{\otimes 7} \otimes I^{\otimes 7}$ for Figure 22 (b) and (c), respectively.

Code B.16 realizes symmetric flip transformations for the video in Figure 23 (a). The results of G_{F3}^x, G_{F3}^y and G_{F3}^t are shown in Figure 23 (b), (c) and (d), respectively. These results show that all image frames in the video are transformed by G_{F3}^x, G_{F3}^y and G_{F3}^t.

Figure 23. Experiments of symmetric flip transformations for a 128x128x2 video

(a) An original video   (b) The transformed video by G_{F3}^x

(c) The transformed video by G_{F3}^y (d) The transformed video by G_{F3}^t

Figure 24. Experiments of local flip transformations for an image

(a) An original image   (b) Local flip for the left part   (c) Local flip for the right part

The Simulation of Local Flip Transformations

From the circuit in Figure 10 (a) for $n=14$ and $j=7$, we obtain that the local flip operator $G_{LF2}^{x,7,m}$ is as follows,

$$G_{LF2}^{x,7,m} = I^{\otimes 7} \otimes C_1^m(X^{\otimes 6}),\tag{4.30}$$

where $m=0,1$. That is, $G_{LF2}^{x,7,0}$ and $G_{LF2}^{x,7,1}$ realize local flip transformations for the left part and the right part of the image in Figure 24 (a), and results are shown in Figure 24 by Code B.17.

Similarly, the circuit in Figure 12 (a) for a $2^7 \times 2^7 \times 2$ video gives the local flip operator $G_{LF3}^{t,y,9,m}$ as follows,

$$G_{LF3}^{t,y,9,m} = [I^{\otimes 7} \otimes C_1^m(X^{\otimes 6}) \otimes I][V_1^m(X^{\otimes 7}) \otimes I^{\otimes 7}],\tag{4.31}$$

where $m=0,1$.

Figure 25. Experiments of local flip transformations for a video

(a) An original video   (b) Local flip for the left part   (c) Local flip for the right part

Figure 26. An with n-qubit Swap gate

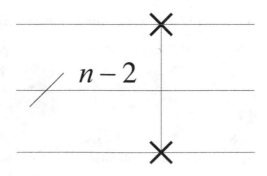

$G_{LF3}^{t,y,9,0}$ and $G_{LF3}^{t,y,9,1}$ realize local flip transformations for the left part and the right part of image frames in the video in Figure 25 (a), and results are shown in Figure 25 (b) and (c) by Code B.18.

The Simulation of Orthogonal Rotation Transformations

The matrix of an n-qubit Swap gate shown in Figure 26, denoted as Swa(n), is calculated by Code B.19.

For a $2^7 \times 2^7$ image, $R_2^{\pi/2}(|x_m\rangle \otimes |y_k\rangle)$, $R_2^{\pi}(|x_m\rangle \otimes |y_k\rangle)$ and $R_2^{3\pi/2}(|x_m\rangle \otimes |y_k\rangle)$ in Figure 14 are

$$
\begin{vmatrix}
R_2^{\pi/2}(|x_m\rangle \otimes |y_k\rangle) = (I^{\otimes 6} \otimes Swa(8)) \left(\prod_{i=1}^{5} I^{\otimes 6-i} \otimes Swa(8) \otimes I^{\otimes i} \right) (Swa(8) \otimes I^{\otimes 6})(X^{\otimes 7} \otimes I^{\otimes 7}), \\
R_2^{\pi}(|x_m\rangle \otimes |y_k\rangle) = X^{\otimes 14}, \\
R_2^{3\pi/2}(|x_m\rangle \otimes |y_k\rangle) = (I^{\otimes 6} \otimes Swa(8)) \left(\prod_{i=1}^{5} I^{\otimes 6-i} \otimes Swa(8) \otimes I^{\otimes i} \right) (Swa(8) \otimes I^{\otimes 6})(I^{\otimes 7} \otimes X^{\otimes 7}),
\end{vmatrix}
$$

$$(4.32)$$

which is realized by Code B.20, and results are shown in Figure 27.

Figure 27. Experiments of orthogonal rotation transformations for an image

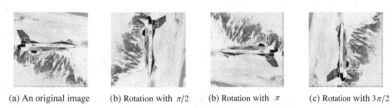

(a) An original image   (b) Rotation with $\pi/2$ (b) Rotation with π (c) Rotation with $3\pi/2$

For a $2^7 \times 2^7 \times 2$ video, the circuits in Figure 15 correspond to the operators as follows,

Figure 28. Experiments of orthogonal rotation transformations for a video

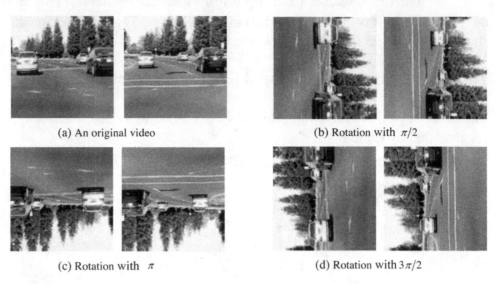

(a) An original video

(b) Rotation with $\pi/2$

(c) Rotation with π

(d) Rotation with $3\pi/2$

$$
\begin{cases}
R_3^{\pi/2}(\left|x_m\right\rangle \otimes \left|y_k\right\rangle) = \left(\prod_{i=0}^{5} I^{\otimes 6-i} \otimes Swa(8) \otimes I^{\otimes i+1}\right)(Swa(8) \otimes I^{\otimes 7})(X^{\otimes 7} \otimes I^{\otimes 8}), \\
R_3^{\pi}(\left|x_m\right\rangle \otimes \left|y_k\right\rangle) = X^{\otimes 14} \otimes I, \\
R_3^{3\pi/2}(\left|x_m\right\rangle \otimes \left|y_k\right\rangle) = \left(\prod_{i=0}^{5} I^{\otimes 6-i} \otimes Swa(8) \otimes I^{\otimes i+1}\right)(Swa(8) \otimes I^{\otimes 7})(I^{\otimes 7} \otimes X^{\otimes 7} \otimes I),
\end{cases}
$$

$$(4.33)$$

which is realized by Code B.21, and results are shown in Figure 28.

Figure 29. Experiments of translation transformations for an image

(a) An original image

(b) Translate 10 pixels along x axis

(c) Translate 10 pixels along y axis

The Simulation of Translation Transformations

We first calculate the matrix of the circuit of the operator T_k in Figure 18 (a) using Code B.22. Then, for a $2^7 \times 2^7$ image, two translation transformation operators $T^2_{|x_m\rangle} = T_7 \otimes I^{\otimes 7}$ and $T^2_{|y_k\rangle} = I^{\otimes 7} \otimes T_7$ are applied repeatedly 10 times on the original image in Figure 29 (a), and results are given in Figure 29 (b) and (c) by Code B.23.

Code B.24 realizes the translation transformation $T^3_{|t_h\rangle}$ in (4.28) for the video in Figure 30 (a). The result in Figure 30 (b) shows that $T^3_{|t_h\rangle}$ implements the translation of two image frames of the video.

Figure 30. The experiment of a translation transformation for a video.

(a) An original video   (b) The transformed video

CONCLUSION

This chapter described quantum geometric transformations of images and videos. Complexities of the global operators (symmetric flips, local flips, orthogonal rotations and translations) are $O(n^2)$ at most. Since complexities of classical global operators are $O(n^2)$, quantum global geometric transformations offer exponential speedup over their classical counterparts. The disadvantage of quantum geometric transformations is that two-point swapping requires $O(n^2)$ basis operations, and its classical counterpart only requires $O(1)$ basis operations.

REFERENCES

Arce-Santana, E. R., & Alba, A. (2009). Image registration using Markov random coefficient and geometric transformation fields. *Pattern Recognition*, *42*(8), 1660–1671. doi:10.1016/j.patcog.2008.11.033

Fan, P., Zhou, R. G., Jing, N., & Li, H. S. (2016). Geometric transformations of multidimensional color images based on NASS. *Information Sciences*, *340*, 191–208. doi:10.1016/j.ins.2015.12.024

Iliyasu, A. M., Le, P. Q., Dong, F., & Hirota, K. (2012). Watermarking and authentication of quantum images based on restricted geometric transformations. *Information Sciences*, *186*(1), 126–149. doi:10.1016/j.ins.2011.09.028

Le, P. Q., Iliyasu, A. M., Dong, F., & Hirota, K. (2010). Fast Geometric Transformations on Quantum Images. *International Journal of Applied Mathematics*, *40*(3), 113–123.

Le, P. Q., Iliyasu, A. M., Dong, F., & Hirota, K. (2011). Strategies for designing geometric transformations on quantum images. *Theoretical Computer Science*, *412*(15), 1406–1418. doi:10.1016/j.tcs.2010.11.029

Nielsen, M. A., & Chuang, I. L. (2000). *Quantum Computation and Quantum Information*. Cambridge University Press.

Chapter 4
Quantum Fourier Transforms

ABSTRACT

Quantum Fourier transform (QFT) plays a key role in many quantum algorithms, but the existing circuits of QFT are incomplete and lacking the proof of correctness. Furthermore, it is difficult to apply QFT to the concrete field of information processing. Thus, this chapter firstly investigates quantum vision representation (QVR) and develops a model of QVR (MQVR). Then, four complete circuits of QFT and inverse QFT (IQFT) are designed. Meanwhile, this chapter proves the correctness of the four complete circuits using formula derivation. Next, 2D QFT and 3D QFT based on QVR are proposed. Experimental results with simulation show the proposed QFTs are valid and useful in processing quantum images and videos. In conclusion, this chapter develops a complete framework of QFT based on QVR and provides a feasible scheme for QFT to be applied in quantum vision information processing.

INTRODUCTION

Quantum Fourier transform (QFT) plays the key role in Shor's prime factorization and discrete logarithms (Shor, 1994). In the aspect of information processing, quantum image algorithms based on QFT are research hotspots, and their examples include the watermarking algorithms of quantum images (Zhang, Gao, Liu, Wen, & Chen, 2013; Zhang, Gao, Liu, Wen, & Chen, 2013), and the encryption and decryption algorithm (Yang, Xia, Jia, & Zhang, 2013; Li, Li, Chen, & Xia, 2018).

DOI: 10.4018/978-1-7998-3799-2.ch004

QFT can be classified with 1-dimensional or multi-dimensional according to the types of data it acts on are 1-dimension or multi-dimension. Some quantum circuits of 1D QFT have been designed (Nielsen, & Chuang, 2000; Barenco, Ekert, Suominen, & Törmä, 1996; Karafyllidis, 2003; Wang, Zhu, Zhang, & Yeon, 2011; Heo, Kang, Hong, Yang, & Choi, 2016). In addition, the semi-classical Fourier transform (Coppersmith, 2002) and the approximate Fourier transform (Griffiths, & Niu, 1996) have been proposed. The complexity of 1D QFT implementation on elements is (Nielsen, & Chuang, 2000). In contrast, fast Fourier Transform (Cooley, & Tukey, 1965), one of the best classical algorithms, computes the discrete Fourier transform with the complexity. Thus, QFT achieves exponentially speed up in comparison with its classical counterpart. The classical 2D and 3D discrete Fourier transforms were applied directly to image processing (Park, 2015; He, Zhou, & Cui, 2012), and their quantum counterparts were proposed for quantum image processing (Li, Fan, Xia, Song, & He, 2018).

This chapter describes perfect shuffle permutations, generalized tensor products and their implementation circuits (Li, Fan, Xia, Song, & He, 2018). Next, the implementation circuits of 1D, 2D and 3D QFTs by using perfect shuffle permutations and generalized tensor products (Li, Fan, Xia, Song, & He, 2018).

PERFECT SHUFFLE PERMUTATIONS

The perfect shuffle permutation $P_{n,m}$ is an $mn \times mn$ matrix, which shuffles n packs of m cards into m packs of n cards, and satisfies

$$(P_{n,m})_{k,l} = \delta_{v,z'}\delta_{z,v'}, \tag{5.1}$$

where

$$k = vn + z, l = v'm + z',$$

$$0 \le v, z' < m, 0 \le v', z < n.$$

$\delta_{x,y}$ is the Kronecker delta function, i.e., $\delta_{x,y}=0$ if $x \ne y$, otherwise $\delta_{x,y}=1$ (Fino & Algazi, 1977).

Two perfect shuffle permutations $P_{2^{n-1},2}$ and $P_{2,2^{n-1}}$ are defined as (Hoyer, 1997),

$$\begin{cases} P_{2^{n-1},2} = (P_{2^{n-2},2} \otimes I_2)(I_{2^{n-2}} \otimes P_{2,2}), \\ P_{2,2^{n-1}} = (I_2 \otimes P_{2,2^{n-2}})(P_{2,2} \otimes I_{2^{n-2}}), \end{cases} \tag{5.2}$$

where $P_{2,2}$ is a Swap gate, i.e.,

$$P_{2,2} = \begin{bmatrix} 1 & 0 & 0 & 0 \\ 0 & 0 & 1 & 0 \\ 0 & 1 & 0 & 0 \\ 0 & 0 & 0 & 1 \end{bmatrix}. \tag{5.3}$$

Since

$$P_{2^{n-1},2}P_{2,2^{n-1}} = P_{2,2^{n-1}}P_{2^{n-1},2} = I_{2^n},$$

$P_{2^{n-1},2}$ is the inverse of $P_{2,2^{n-1}}$, where I_{2^n} is a $2^n \times 2^n$ identity matrix. $P_{2^{n-1},2}$ and $P_{2,2^{n-1}}$ are applied on the quantum state $|j_n,\ldots,j_2 j_1\rangle$ to give

$$\begin{cases} P_{2^{n-1},2}\big|j_n \cdots j_2 j_1\big\rangle = \big|j_1 j_n \cdots j_2\big\rangle, \\ P_{2,2^{n-1}}\big|j_n j_{n-1} \cdots j_1\big\rangle = \big|j_{n-1} \cdots j_1 j_n\big\rangle, \end{cases} \tag{5.4}$$

and their implementation circuits are shown in Figure 1.

The operator Γ_{2^n} is defined as

$$\Gamma_{2^n} = P_{2^{n-1},2}(P_{2^{n-2},2} \otimes I_2)\ldots(P_{2^2,2} \otimes I_{2^{n-3}})(P_{2,2} \otimes I_{2^{n-2}}), \tag{5.5}$$

and its inverse is

$$\Gamma_{2^n}^{-1} = (P_{2,2} \otimes I_{2^{n-2}})(P_{2,2^2} \otimes I_{2^{n-3}})\ldots(P_{2,2^{n-2}} \otimes I_2)P_{2,2^{n-1}}. \tag{5.6}$$

Since

Figure 1. The implementation circuits of $P_{2^{n-1},2}$ *and* $P_{2,2^{n-1}}$

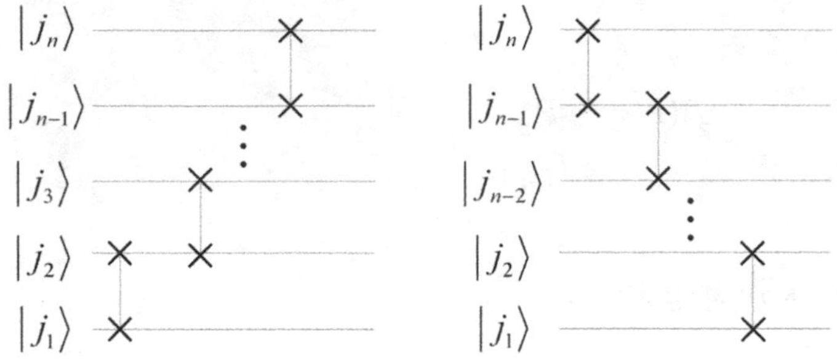

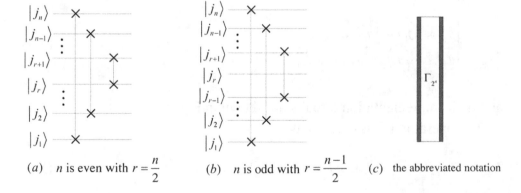

(a) $P_{2^{n-1},2}$ (b) $P_{2,2^{n-1}}$

$$\Gamma_{2^n}\left|j_n j_{n-1} j_{n-2} \cdots j_2 j_1\right\rangle = \left|j_1 j_2 \cdots j_{n-2} j_{n-1} j_n\right\rangle = \Gamma_{2^n}^{-1}\left|j_n j_{n-1} j_{n-2} \cdots j_2 j_1\right\rangle,$$

we conclude $\Gamma_{2^n} = \Gamma_{2^n}^{-1}$ and design quantum circuits shown in Figure 2. The circuit of Γ_{2^n} consists of $n/2$ Swap gates at most, so its complexity is $O(n)$. Its implementation code is seen in Code B.25.

Figure 2. The quantum circuits of Γ_{2^n} *and* $\Gamma_{2^n}^{-1}$.

(a) n is even with $r = \dfrac{n}{2}$ (b) n is odd with $r = \dfrac{n-1}{2}$ (c)   the abbreviated notation

The iterations of Γ_{2^n} and $\Gamma_{2^n}^{-1}$ are given by

$$\begin{cases} \Gamma_{2^n} = P_{2^{n-1},2}(\Gamma_{2^{n-1}} \otimes I_2), \\ \Gamma_{2^n}^{-1} = (\Gamma_{2^{n-1}}^{-1} \otimes I_2)P_{2,2^{n-1}}, \end{cases} \tag{5.7}$$

then, we obtain

$$\begin{cases} P_{2^{n-1},2} = \Gamma_{2^n}(\Gamma_{2^{n-1}} \otimes I_2), \\ P_{2,2^{n-1}} = (\Gamma_{2^{n-1}} \otimes I_2)\Gamma_{2^n}. \end{cases} \tag{5.8}$$

Therefore, we design the simplified circuits of $P_{2^{n-1},2}$ and $P_{2,2^{n-1}}$ as shown in Figure 3. Their implementation codes are seen in Code B.26 and Code B.27.

Figure 3. The simplified circuits of $P_{2^{n-1},2}$ and $P_{2,2^{n-1}}$.

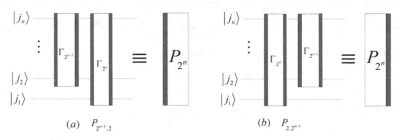

Quantum gates are the same in Figure 3 (a) and (b), but these quantum gates are in reverse order. Therefore, the results are the same by running circuits in the direction of the black box. We also adopt similar abbreviated notations to denote the circuits which consist of the same quantum gates with reverse order in the following sections.

Compared the circuits in Figure 3 with ones in Figure 1, the circuits of $P_{2^{n-1},2}$ and $P_{2,2^{n-1}}$ both consists of $(n-1)$ Swap gates, so their complexities are $O(n)$. But, the circuits in Figure 3 have less time delay than ones in Figure 1, because these Swap gates of Γ_{2^n} can run in parallel (see Figure 4).

In addition, the iterations of $P_{2^n,2^{m-1}}$ and $P_{2^{m-1},2^n}$ are given by

$$\begin{cases} P_{2^n,2^{m-1}} = (P_{2,2^{m-1}} \otimes I_{2^{n-1}})\left(I_2 \otimes P_{2^{n-1},2^{m-1}}\right), \\ P_{2^{m-1},2^n} = \left(I_2 \otimes P_{2^{m-1},2^{n-1}}\right)(P_{2^{m-1},2} \otimes I_{2^{n-1}}), \end{cases} \tag{5.9}$$

Figure 4. The parallel circuits of Γ_{2^n}

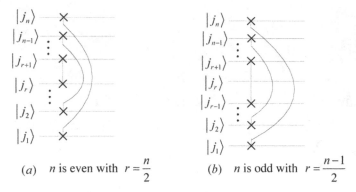

(a) n is even with $r = \dfrac{n}{2}$ (b) n is odd with $r = \dfrac{n-1}{2}$

and their implementation circuits are shown in Figure 5. The dotted boxes in (a) and (b) are the circuits of $P_{2^{m-1},2^n}$ and $P_{2^n,2^{m-1}}$, respectively. From Figure 5, we conclude that the complexities of $P_{2^n,2^{m-1}}$ and $P_{2^{m-1},2^n}$ are both $O(nm)$.

Figure 5. The circuits of $P_{2^{m-1},2^n}$ and $P_{2^n,2^{m-1}}$.

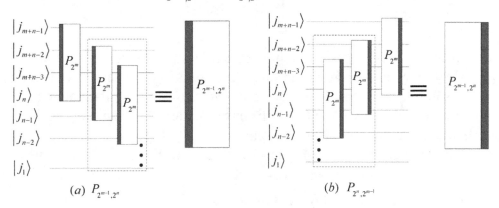

$(a)\ P_{2^{m-1},2^n}$ $(b)\ P_{2^n,2^{m-1}}$

GENERALIZED TENSOR PRODUCTS AND THEIR QUANTUM CIRCUITS

In this section, we describe generalized tensor product (GTP) (Fino & Algazi, 1977; Hoyer, 1997), and design quantum circuits of some special generalized tensor products (Li, Fan, Xia, Song, & He, 2018); Li, Fan, Xia, & Song, 2019).

Generalized Tensor Product

In quantum computing, the tensor product, denoted by $\otimes$, is a way of putting vector spaces together to form larger vector spaces. The tensor product is defined as follows.

Let A be an $n \times n$ matrix and B be an $m \times m$ matrix, then the tensor product

$$A \otimes B = \begin{bmatrix} A_{0,0}B & \cdots & A_{0,n-1}B \\ \vdots & \ddots & \vdots \\ A_{n-1,0}B & \cdots & A_{n-1,n-1}B \end{bmatrix} \tag{5.10}$$

is an $mn \times mn$ block matrix.

Suppose that $\mathbb{A} = \left\{ A_0, A_1, ..., A_{m-1} \right\}$ and $\mathbb{B} = \left\{ B_0, B_1, ..., B_{n-1} \right\}$ are two sets of matrices, where A_i is an $n \times n$ matrix, $0 \leq i < m$, and B_j is an $m \times m$ matrix, $0 \leq j < n$. Then, the generalized tensor product $C = \mathbb{A} \otimes \mathbb{B}$ is an $mn \times mn$ matrix and can be calculated by

$$C_{um+w,vm+z} = \left(a_w \right)_{u,v} \left(b_v \right)_{w,z} \tag{5.11}$$

with

$$0 \leq u, v < n,\ 0 \leq w, z < m\ ,$$

where $C_{um+w,vm+z}$, $\left(a_w \right)_{u,v}$ and $\left(b_v \right)_{w,z}$ are the elements of matrices C, A_w and B_v, respectively.

If A_i and B_j are unitary matrices, then the generalized tensor product $\mathbb{A} \otimes \mathbb{B}$ is a unitary matrix and is factorized into

$$\mathbb{A} \otimes \mathbb{B} = P_{m,n} Diag(\mathbb{A}) P_{n,m} Diag(\mathbb{B})\ , \tag{5.12}$$

where

$$Diag(\mathbb{A}) = Diag(A_0, A_1, ..., A_{m-1})$$

and

$$Diag(\mathbb{B}) = Diag(B_0, B_1, \ldots, B_{n-1})$$

are block diagonal matrices, i.e.,

$$Diag(\mathbb{A}) = \begin{bmatrix} A_0 & 0 & \cdots & 0 \\ 0 & A_1 & \cdots & 0 \\ \vdots & \vdots & \ddots & \vdots \\ 0 & 0 & \cdots & A_{m-1} \end{bmatrix}, Diag(\mathbb{B}) = \begin{bmatrix} B_0 & 0 & \cdots & 0 \\ 0 & B_1 & \cdots & 0 \\ \vdots & \vdots & \ddots & \vdots \\ 0 & 0 & \cdots & B_{n-1} \end{bmatrix}. \qquad (5.13)$$

When

$$A_0 = A_1 = \ldots = A_{m-1} = A,$$

the generalized tensor product $\mathbb{A} \otimes \mathbb{B}$ is denoted as $A \otimes \mathbb{B}$. If

$$B_0 = B_1 = \ldots = B_{n-1} = B$$

also holds, the generalized tensor product $\mathbb{A} \otimes \mathbb{B}$ degenerates into the tensor product $A \otimes B$.

To build the relatively complete system of a generalized tensor product, we define some new concepts of generalized tensor product as follows.

Definition 5.1 Let $\mathbb{A} = \left\{ A_0, A_1, \ldots, A_{m-1} \right\}$ and $\mathbb{D} = \left\{ D_0, D_1, \ldots, D_{m-1} \right\}$ be two sets of matrices where A_i and D_i are $n \times n$ matrices. Then, the generalized product of two sets is defined as

$$\mathbb{A} \times \mathbb{D} = \mathbb{A}\mathbb{D} = \left\{ A_0 D_0, A_1 D_1, \ldots, A_{m-1} D_{m-1} \right\}. \qquad (5.14)$$

Definition 5.2 The transpose, conjugate transpose and inverse of the matrix set $\mathbb{A}$ are defined as follows,

$$\begin{bmatrix} \mathbb{A}^T = \left\{ A_0^T, A_1^T, \ldots, A_{m-1}^T \right\}, \\ \mathbb{A}^\dagger = \left\{ A_0^\dagger, A_1^\dagger, \ldots, A_{m-1}^\dagger \right\}, \\ \mathbb{A}^{-1} = \left\{ A_0^{-1}, A_1^{-1}, \ldots, A_{m-1}^{-1} \right\}, \end{bmatrix} \qquad (5.15)$$

where A_i^T, $A_i^\dagger$ and A_i^{-1} denote the transpose, conjugate transpose and inverse of the matrix A_i, respectively.

Let $\mathbb{A}$ and $\mathbb{C}$ be two sets of matrices containing m matrices with size $n \times n$, $\mathbb{B}$ and $\mathbb{D}$ be two sets of matrices containing n matrices with size $m \times m$, I_m and I_n be $m \times m$ and $n \times n$ identity matrices, respectively. Then, we give the following equations by

$$\begin{cases} (\mathbb{A} \otimes \mathbb{D})^T = P_{m,n}(\mathbb{B}^T \otimes \mathbb{A}^T)P_{n,m}, \\ (\mathbb{A} \otimes \mathbb{B})^\dagger = P_{m,n}(\mathbb{B}^\dagger \otimes \mathbb{A}^\dagger)P_{n,m}, \\ (\mathbb{A} \otimes \mathbb{B})^{-1} = P_{m,n}(\mathbb{B}^{-1} \otimes \mathbb{A}^{-1})P_{n,m}, \end{cases} \tag{5.16}$$

and

$$(\mathbb{A} \times \mathbb{C}) \otimes (\mathbb{B} \times \mathbb{D}) = (\mathbb{A} \otimes I_m) \times (\mathbb{C} \otimes \mathbb{B}) \times (I_n \otimes \mathbb{D}). \tag{5.17}$$

Quantum Circuits of Some Special Generalized Tensor Products

Let U_{2^n} be a $2^n \times 2^n$ unitary matrix, and I_{2^n} be $2^n \times 2^n$ identity matrices. These special generalized tensor products $I \otimes \{I_{2^n}, U_{2^n}\}$, $I \otimes \{U_{2^n}, I_{2^n}\}$, $\{I_{2^n}, U_{2^n}\} \otimes I$, and $\{U_{2^n}, I_{2^n}\} \otimes I$ are calculated by (5.12), and are equal to

$$\begin{cases} I \otimes \{I_{2^n}, U_{2^n}\} = (|0\rangle\langle 0|) \otimes I_{2^n} + (|1\rangle\langle 1|) \otimes U_{2^n} = C_1^1(U_{2^n}), \\ I \otimes \{U_{2^n}, I_{2^n}\} = (|0\rangle\langle 0|) \otimes U_{2^n} + (|1\rangle\langle 1|) \otimes I_{2^n} = C_1^0(U_{2^n}), \\ \{I_{2^n}, U_{2^n}\} \otimes I = I_{2^n} \otimes (|0\rangle\langle 0|) + U_{2^n} \otimes (|1\rangle\langle 1|) = V_1^1(U_{2^n}), \\ \{U_{2^n}, I_{2^n}\} \otimes I = U_{2^n} \otimes (|0\rangle\langle 0|) + I_{2^n} \otimes (|1\rangle\langle 1|) = V_1^0(U_{2^n}), \end{cases} \tag{5.18}$$

where I is an 2×2 identity matrix. Therefore, the above GTPs can be implemented by the circuits in Figure 6.

Suppose that $\mathbb{A} = \{A_0, A_1, ..., A_{2^{n-1}}\}$, and $A_i = I_{2^m}$ for $i \neq j$, i.e.,

$$\mathbb{A} = \{I_{2^m}, ..., I_{2^m}, A_j, I_{2^m}, ..., I_{2^m}\},$$

Figure 6. The implementation circuits of four GTPs in (5.18)

GTP   Quantum Circuit

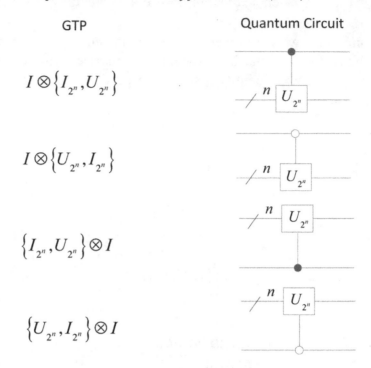

$$I \otimes \left\{ I_{2^n}, U_{2^n} \right\}$$

$$I \otimes \left\{ U_{2^n}, I_{2^n} \right\}$$

$$\left\{ I_{2^n}, U_{2^n} \right\} \otimes I$$

$$\left\{ U_{2^n}, I_{2^n} \right\} \otimes I$$

then we have

$$
\begin{cases}
I_{2^n} \otimes \left\{ I_{2^m}, \ldots, I_{2^m}, A_j, I_{2^m}, \ldots, I_{2^m} \right\} = \left(|j\rangle \langle j| \right) \otimes A_j + \sum_{i=0, i \neq j}^{2^n - 1} \left(|i\rangle \langle i| \right) \otimes I_{2^m} = C_n^j(A_j), \\
\left\{ I_{2^m}, \ldots, I_{2^m}, A_j, I_{2^m}, \ldots, I_{2^m} \right\} \otimes I_{2^n} = A_j \otimes \left(|j\rangle \langle j| \right) + \sum_{i=0, i \neq j}^{2^n - 1} I_{2^m} \otimes \left(|i\rangle \langle i| \right) = V_n^j(A_j).
\end{cases}
$$

$$(5.19)$$

The two GTPs above can be implemented by the circuits in Figure 7.

Lemma 5.1 Suppose that $\mathbb{A} = \left\{ A_0, A_1, \ldots, A_{2^{n-1}-1} \right\}$, and $A_{2i} = I_{2^m}$ and $A_{2i+1} = U_{2^m}$ for $i = 0, 1, \ldots, 2^{n-2} - 1$, i.e.,

$$\mathbb{A} = \left\{ I_{2^m}, U_{2^m}, I_{2^m}, U_{2^m}, \ldots, I_{2^m}, U_{2^m} \right\},$$

then

Figure 7. The implementation circuits of two GTPs in (5.19)

GTP   Quantum Circuit

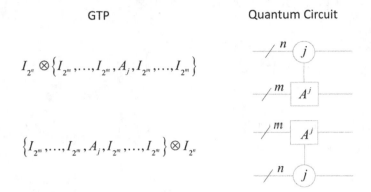

$$I_{2^n} \otimes \left\{ I_{2^m}, \ldots, I_{2^m}, A_j, I_{2^m}, \ldots, I_{2^m} \right\}$$

$$\left\{ I_{2^m}, \ldots, I_{2^m}, A_j, I_{2^m}, \ldots, I_{2^m} \right\} \otimes I_{2^n}$$

$$\mathbb{A} \otimes I_{2^{n-1}} = V_1^1 (U_{2^m} \otimes I_{2^{n-2}})$$

and

$$I_{2^{n-1}} \otimes \mathbb{A} = I_{2^{n-2}} \otimes C_1^1 (U_{2^m})$$

hold.

Proof. From (5.14), we have

$$
\begin{aligned}
\mathbb{A} &= \left\{ I_{2^m}, A_1, I_{2^m}, A_3, \ldots, I_{2^m}, A_{2^{n-1}-1} \right\} = \left\{ I_{2^m}, A_1, I_{2^m}, I_{2^m}, \ldots, I_{2^m}, I_{2^m} \right\} \\
&\times \left\{ I_{2^m}, I_{2^m}, I_{2^m}, A_3, \ldots, I_{2^m}, A_{2^{n-1}-1} \right\} = \prod_{j \text{ is odd}} \left\{ I_{2^m}, \ldots, I_{2^m}, A_j, I_{2^m}, \ldots, I_{2^m} \right\}.
\end{aligned}
\tag{5.20}
$$

We infer the following equation using (5.17),

$$\left(\mathbb{A} \times \mathbb{C} \right) \otimes I_m = (\mathbb{A} \otimes I_m)(\mathbb{C} \otimes I_m). \tag{5.21}$$

Combining (5.19) with (5.21), we obtain

$$\mathbb{A} \otimes I_{2^{n-1}} = \left[\prod_{j \text{ is odd}} \left\{ I_{2^m}, \ldots, I_{2^m}, A_j, I_{2^m}, \ldots, I_{2^m} \right\} \right] \otimes I_{2^{n-1}}$$

$$= \prod_{j \text{ is odd}} \left[\left\{ I_{2^m}, \ldots, I_{2^m}, A_j, I_{2^m}, \ldots, I_{2^m} \right\} \otimes I_{2^{n-1}} \right] \tag{5.22}$$

$$= \prod_{j \text{ is odd}} V_{n-1}^j(A_j) = \prod_{j \text{ is odd}} V_{n-1}^j(U_{2^m}),$$

Since the integer j is odd for $j = i_{n-1} \cdots i_2 1$, the circuit of $\mathbb{A} \otimes I_{2^{n-1}}$ is shown in Figure 8.

Figure 8. The circuit of $\mathbb{A} \otimes I_{2^{n-1}}$

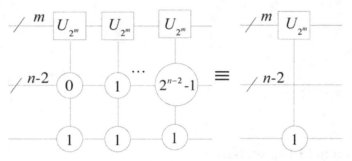

Simplifying the circuit in Figure 8, we obtain $\mathbb{A} \otimes I_{2^{n-1}} = V_1^1(U_2 \otimes I_{2^{n-2}})$. From (5.17), we infer

$$I_m \otimes \left(\mathbb{A} \times \mathbb{C} \right) = (I_m \otimes \mathbb{A})(I_m \otimes \mathbb{C}). \tag{5.23}$$

Then, $I_{2^{n-1}} \otimes \mathbb{A}$ is given by

$$I_{2^{n-1}} \otimes \mathbb{A} = I_{2^{n-1}} \otimes \left[\prod_{j \text{ is odd}} \left\{ I_{2^m}, \ldots, I_{2^m}, A_j, I_{2^m}, \ldots, I_{2^m} \right\} \right]$$

$$= \prod_{j \text{ is odd}} \left[I_{2^{n-1}} \otimes \left\{ I_{2^m}, \ldots, I_{2^m}, A_j, I_{2^m}, \ldots, I_{2^m} \right\} \right] \tag{5.24}$$

$$= \prod_{j \text{ is odd}} C_{n-1}^j(A_j) = \prod_{j \text{ is odd}} C_{n-1}^j(U_{2^m}) = I_{2^{n-2}} \otimes C_1^1(U_{2^m})$$

In conclusion,

$$\mathbb{A} \otimes I_{2^{n-1}} = V_1^1 (U_{2^m} \otimes I_{2^{n-2}})$$

and

$$I_{2^{n-1}} \otimes \mathbb{A} = I_{2^{n-2}} \otimes C_1^1 (U_{2^m})$$

hold,

Lemma 5.2 Suppose $\mathbb{A} = \left\{ A_0, A_1, \ldots, A_{2^{n-1}-1} \right\}$ and $\mathbb{B} = \left\{ B_0, B_1, \ldots, B_{2^{n-2}-1} \right\}$ where these $2^n \times 2^n$ matrices in $\mathbb{A}$ and $\mathbb{B}$ satisfy that $A_{2i} = A_{2i+1} = B_i$ with $i = 0, 1, \ldots, 2^{n-2} - 1$, then

$$\mathbb{A} \otimes I_{2^{n-1}} = (\mathbb{B} \otimes I_{2^{n-2}}) \otimes I$$

holds.

Proof. The set $\mathbb{A}$ is changed into

$$\mathbb{A} = \prod_{i=0}^{2^{n-2}-1} \left\{ I_{2^m}, \ldots, I_{2^m}, A_{2i}, A_{2i+1}, I_{2^m}, \ldots, I_{2^m} \right\}. \tag{5.25}$$

Using (5.19) and (5.21), we have

$$
\begin{aligned}
\mathbb{A} \otimes I_{2^{n-1}} &= \left[\prod_{i=0}^{2^{n-2}-1} \left\{ I_{2^m}, \ldots, I_{2^m}, A_{2i}, A_{2i+1}, I_{2^m}, \ldots, I_{2^m} \right\} \right] \otimes I_{2^{n-1}} \\
&= \prod_{i=0}^{2^{n-2}-1} \left[\left\{ I_{2^m}, \ldots, I_{2^m}, A_{2i}, A_{2i+1}, I_{2^m}, \ldots, I_{2^m} \right\} \otimes I_{2^{n-1}} \right], \\
&= \prod_{i=0}^{2^{n-2}-1} \left[\left(\left\{ I_{2^m}, \ldots, I_{2^m}, A_{2i+1}, I_{2^m}, \ldots, I_{2^m} \right\} \otimes I_{2^{n-1}} \right) \left(\left\{ I_{2^m}, \ldots, I_{2^m}, A_{2i}, I_{2^m}, \ldots, I_{2^m} \right\} \otimes I_{2^{n-1}} \right) \right] \\
&= \prod_{i=0}^{2^{n-2}-1} \left[V_{n-1}^{2i+1} (A_{2i+1}) V_{n-1}^{2i} (A_{2i}) \right].
\end{aligned}
$$

$$\tag{5.26}$$

Suppose that the binary expansion of integer i is $i = i_{n-2} \ldots i_2 i_1$, then $2i = i_{n-2} \ldots i_2 i_1 0$ and $2i + 1 = i_{n-2} \ldots i_2 i_1 1$ hold. Since $A_{2i} = A_{2i+1} = B_i$, the left circuit in Figure 9 can be simplified into the right circuit, i.e.,

Figure 9. The circuit of $V_{n-1}^{2i+1}(A_{2i+1})V_{n-1}^{2i}(A_{2i})$.

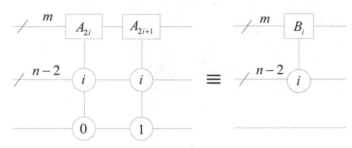

$$V_{n-1}^{2i+1}(A_{2i+1})V_{n-1}^{2i}(A_{2i}) = V_{n-2}^{i}(B_i) \otimes I. \tag{5.27}$$

Therefore, the equation

$$
\mathbb{A} \otimes I_{2^{n-1}} = \prod_{i=0}^{2^{n-2}-1} \left[V_{n-2}^{i}(B_i) \otimes I \right] = \left[\prod_{i=0}^{2^{n-2}-1} V_{n-2}^{i}(B_i) \right] \otimes I
$$

$$
= \left[\prod_{i=0}^{2^{n-2}-1} \left(\left\{ I_{2^m}, \ldots, I_{2^m}, B_i, I_{2^m}, \ldots, I_{2^m} \right\} \otimes I_{2^{n-2}} \right) \right] \otimes I = \left[\mathbb{B} \otimes I_{2^{n-2}} \right] \otimes I \tag{5.28}
$$

holds.

Lemma 5.3 Suppose $\mathbb{A} = \left\{ A_0, A_1, \ldots, A_{2^{n-1}-1} \right\}$ and

$$\mathbb{B} = \left\{ I \otimes B_0, I \otimes B_1, \ldots, I \otimes B_{2^{n-2}-1} \right\}$$

where these $2^n \times 2^n$ matrices in $\mathbb{A}$ and $\mathbb{B}$ satisfy that $A_{2i} = A_{2i+1} = B_i$ with $i = 0, 1, \ldots, 2^{n-2} - 1$, then $I_{2^{n-1}} \otimes \mathbb{A} = I_{2^{n-2}} \otimes \mathbb{B}$ holds.

Proof. From (5.19) and (5.23), $I_{2^{n-1}} \otimes \mathbb{A}$ is given by

$$I_{2^{n-1}} \otimes \mathbb{A} = I_{2^{n-1}} \otimes \left[\prod_{i=0}^{2^{n-2}-1} \left\{ I_{2^m}, \ldots, I_{2^m}, A_{2i}, A_{2i+1}, I_{2^m}, \ldots, I_{2^m} \right\} \right]$$

$$= \prod_{i=0}^{2^{n-2}-1} \left[I_{2^{n-1}} \otimes \left\{ I_{2^m}, \ldots, I_{2^m}, A_{2i}, A_{2i+1}, I_{2^m}, \ldots, I_{2^m} \right\} \right],$$

$$= \prod_{i=0}^{2^{n-2}-1} \left[\left(I_{2^{n-1}} \otimes \left\{ I_{2^m}, \ldots, I_{2^m}, A_{2i+1}, I_{2^m}, \ldots, I_{2^m} \right\} \right) \left(I_{2^{n-1}} \otimes \left\{ I_{2^m}, \ldots, I_{2^m}, A_{2i}, I_{2^m}, \ldots, I_{2^m} \right\} \right) \right]$$

$$= \prod_{i=0}^{2^{n-2}-1} \left[C_{n-1}^{2i+1}(A_{2i+1}) C_{n-1}^{2i}(A_{2i}) \right],$$

$$(5.29)$$

Since $A_{2i} = A_{2i+1} = B_i$, $C_{n-1}^{2i+1}(A_{2i+1}) C_{n-1}^{2i}(A_{2i})$ shown in Figure 10 can be simplified into $C_{n-2}^{i}(I \otimes B_i)$.

Figure 10. The circuit of $C_{n-1}^{2i+1}(A_{2i+1}) C_{n-1}^{2i}(A_{2i})$

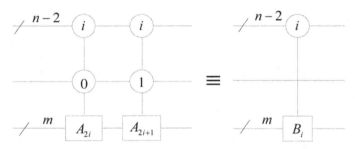

Next, we give $I_{2^{n-2}} \otimes \mathbb{B}$ as follows,

$$I_{2^{n-2}} \otimes \mathbb{B} = I_{2^{n-2}} \otimes \left[\prod_{i=0}^{2^{n-2}-1} \left\{ I \otimes I_{2^m}, \ldots, I \otimes I_{2^m}, I \otimes B_i, I \otimes I_{2^m}, \ldots, I \otimes I_{2^m} \right\} \right]$$

$$= \prod_{i=0}^{2^{n-2}-1} \left[I_{2^{n-2}} \otimes \left\{ I \otimes I_{2^m}, \ldots, I \otimes I_{2^m}, I \otimes B_i, I \otimes I_{2^m}, \ldots, I \otimes I_{2^m} \right\} \right]$$

$$= \prod_{i=0}^{2^{n-2}-1} C_{n-2}^{i}(I \otimes B_i).$$

$$(5.30)$$

Therefore, we conclude $I_{2^{n-1}} \otimes \mathbb{A} = I_{2^{n-2}} \otimes \mathbb{B}$.
Set

$$\begin{cases} S_{2^n}(U_{2^m}) = \left\{ I_{2^m}, U_{2^m}, U_{2^m}^2, \ldots, U_{2^m}^{2^{n-1}-1} \right\} \otimes I_{2^{n-1}}, \\ T_{2^n}(U_{2^m}) = I_{2^{n-1}} \otimes \left\{ I_{2^m}, U_{2^m}, U_{2^m}^2, \ldots, U_{2^m}^{2^{n-1}-1} \right\}, \end{cases}$$

(5.31)

where $U_{2^m}^i$ is the *i*-th power of the $2^m \times 2^m$ matrix U_{2^m}.

A 2×2 matrix R_n is defined as

$$R_n = \begin{bmatrix} 1 & 0 \\ 0 & e^{2\pi i/2^n} \end{bmatrix}.$$

(5.32)

Corollary 5.4 The iteration formula of $S_{2^n}(R_n)$ is

$$S_{2^n}(R_n) = \left[S_{2^{n-1}}(R_{n-1}) \otimes I \right] V_1^1 (R_n \otimes I_{2^{n-2}}),$$

(5.33)

and its circuit is as shown in Figure 11.

Figure 11. The circuit of $S_{2^n}(R_n)$

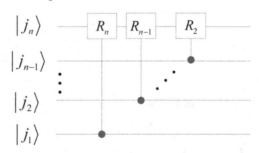

Proof. From (5.14), $S_{2^n}(R_n)$ is equal to

$$S_{2^n}(R_n) = [\{I, I, R_n^2, R_n^2, \ldots, R_n^{2^{n-1}-2}, R_n^{2^{n-1}-2}\} \otimes I_{2^{n-1}}][\{I, R_n, I, R_n, \ldots, I, R_n\} \otimes I_{2^{n-1}}].$$

(5.34)

Lemma 5.1 gives

$$\{I, R_n, I, R_n, \ldots, I, R_n\} \otimes I_{2^{n-1}} = V_1^1(R_n \otimes I_{2^{n-2}}).$$

(5.35)

172

Since $R_n^2 = R_{n-1}$, by Lemma 5.2, we have

$$\{I, I, R_n^2, R_n^2, \ldots, R_n^{2^{n-1}-2}, R_n^{2^{n-1}-2}\} \otimes I_{2^{n-1}} = \{I, I, R_{n-1}, R_{n-1}, \ldots, R_{n-1}^{2^{n-2}-1}, R_{n-1}^{2^{n-2}-1}\} \otimes I_{2^{n-1}}$$

$$= [\{I, R_{n-1}, \ldots, R_{n-1}^{2^{n-2}-1}\} \otimes I_{2^{n-2}}] \otimes I = S_{2^{n-1}}(R_{n-1}) \otimes I.$$

$$(5.36)$$

From (5.35) and (5.36),

$$S_{2^n}(R_n) = \left[S_{2^{n-1}}(R_{n-1}) \otimes I\right] V_1^1(R_n \otimes I_{2^{n-2}})$$

holds. From (5.31), we obtain

$$S_{2^2}(R_2) = \{I, R_n\} \otimes I = V_1^1(R_2).$$

Therefore, the circuit of $S_{2^n}(R_n)$ is as shown in Figure 11.

Corollary 5.5 $T_{2^n}(U_{2^m})$ is equal to

$$T_{2^n}(U_{2^m}) = \left[I_{2^{n-2}} \otimes C_1^1(U_{2^m})\right] T_{2^{n-1}}(I \otimes U_{2^m}^2).$$

$$(5.37)$$

Figure 12. The circuit of $T_{2^n}(R_n)$

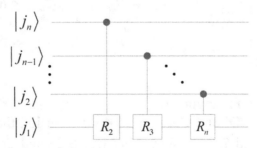

When $U_{2^m} = R_n$, the circuit of $T_{2^n}(R_n)$ is as shown in Figure 12.

Proof. $T_{2^n}(U_{2^m})$ is rewritten as

$$T_{2^n}(U_{2^m}) = [I_{2^{n-1}} \otimes \{I_{2^m}, U_{2^m}, I_{2^m}, U_{2^m}, \ldots, I_{2^m}, U_{2^m}\}][I_{2^{n-1}} \otimes \{I_{2^m}, I_{2^m}, U_{2^m}^2, U_{2^m}^2, \ldots, U_{2^m}^{2^{n-1}-2}, U_{2^m}^{2^{n-1}-2}\}].$$

$$(5.38)$$

Lemma 5.1 gives

$$I_{2^{n-1}} \otimes \{I_{2^m}, U_{2^m}, I_{2^m}, U_{2^m}, \ldots, I_{2^m}, U_{2^m}\} = I_{2^{n-2}} \otimes C_1^1(U_{2^m}). \qquad (5.39)$$

By Lemma 5.3, we have

$$I_{2^{n-1}} \otimes \{I_{2^m}, I_{2^m}, U_{2^m}^2, U_{2^m}^2, \ldots, U_{2^m}^{2^{n-1}-2}, U_{2^m}^{2^{n-1}-2}\}$$
$$= I_{2^{n-2}} \otimes \{I \otimes I_{2^m}, I \otimes U_{2^m}^2, \ldots, I \otimes U_{2^m}^{2^{n-1}-2}\} = T_{2^{n-1}}(I \otimes U_{2^m}^2). \qquad (5.40)$$

Combining (5.39) with (5.40) gives

$$T_{2^n}(U_{2^m}) = \left[I_{2^{n-2}} \otimes C_1^1(U_{2^m})\right] T_{2^{n-1}}(I \otimes U_{2^m}^2). \qquad (5.41)$$

For $U_{2^m} = R_n$, repeatedly using (5.41), we obtain

$$T_{2^n}(R_n) = \left[I_{2^{n-2}} \otimes C_1^1(R_n)\right] T_{2^{n-1}}(I \otimes R_{n-1})$$
$$= \left[I_{2^{n-2}} \otimes C_1^1(R_n)\right]\left[I_{2^{n-3}} \otimes C_1^1(I \otimes R_{n-1})\right] T_{2^{n-2}}(I_{2^2} \otimes R_{n-2})$$
$$= \ldots \qquad (5.42)$$
$$= \left[I_{2^{n-2}} \otimes C_1^1(R_n)\right]\left[\prod_{i=3}^{n-1}\left(I_{2^{n-i}} \otimes C_1^1(I_{2^{i-2}} \otimes R_{n-i+2})\right)\right] T_{2^2}(I_{2^{n-2}} \otimes R_2)$$
$$= \left[I_{2^{n-2}} \otimes C_1^1(R_n)\right]\left[\prod_{i=3}^{n-1}\left(I_{2^{n-i}} \otimes C_1^1(I_{2^{i-2}} \otimes R_{n-i+2})\right)\right] C_1^1(I_{2^{n-2}} \otimes R_2).$$

and its circuit shown in Figure 12.

From Corollary 5.4 and Corollary 5.45, we design the implementation codes of $S_{2^n}(R_n)$ and $T_{2^n}(R_n)$ shown in Code B.28 and Code B.29.

1D QUANTUM FOURIER TRANSFORM

In this section, we firstly give the iteration formulas of 1D quantum Fourier transform (1D-QFT). Next, we design the four implementation circuits of 1D-QFT, the implementation codes of which are seen in Code B.30 - Code B.33.

The Iteration Formulas of 1D-QFT

Quantum Fourier transform F_{2^n} on 2^n elements is defined by (Nielsen, & Chuang, 2000)

$$F_{2^n} : |k\rangle \rightarrow \frac{1}{\sqrt{2^n}} \sum_{j=0}^{2^n-1} e^{2\pi ijk/2^n} |j\rangle, \qquad (5.43)$$

where i is the imaginary unit, and $k,j \in [0, 2^n - 1]$.

Applying F_{2^n} on the quantum state $|\psi\rangle = \sum_{i=0}^{2^n-1} \theta_i |i\rangle$ gives

$$F_{2^n} |\psi\rangle = \sum_{k=0}^{2^n-1} \alpha_k |k\rangle, \qquad (5.44)$$

where

$$\alpha_k = \frac{1}{\sqrt{2^n}} \sum_{j=0}^{2^n-1} \theta_j e^{2\pi ijk/2^n} .$$

Its corresponding matrix form is

$$F_{2^n} \begin{bmatrix} \theta_0 & \cdots & \theta_{2^n-1} \end{bmatrix}^T = \begin{bmatrix} \alpha_0 & \cdots & \alpha_{2^n-1} \end{bmatrix}^T . \qquad (5.45)$$

Using Fourier transform based on generalized tensor product (Fino & Algazi,1977) and (5.31), we give the iteration formulas of 1D-QFT and its inverse,

$$\begin{cases} F_{2^n} = (H \otimes I_{2^{n-1}}) S_{2^n}(R_n)(I_2 \otimes F_{2^{n-1}}) P_{2^{n-1},2}, \\ F_{2^n}^{-1} = (H \otimes I_{2^{n-1}}) S_{2^n}(R_n^{-1}) \times \left(I_2 \otimes F_{2^{n-1}}^{-1}\right) P_{2^{n-1},2}, \end{cases} \tag{5.46}$$

with initial values of the iteration $P_{2,2} = Swap$, $F_2 = H$ and $S_4(R_2) = \{I_2, R_2\} \otimes I_2$.

Next, we describe the four circuits of 1D-QFT in detail.

Figure 13. The first circuit of 1D-QFT

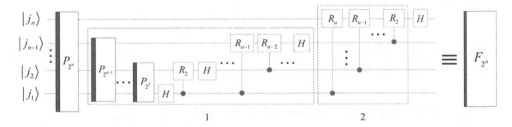

The First Circuit of 1D-QFT

The quantum circuit of 1D-QFT is given in Figure 13 by using the iteration formula (5.46) and Corollary 5.4. The circuits in the dashed box 1 and box 2 implement the 1D-QFT $F_{2^{n-1}}$ and $S_{2^n}(R_n)$, respectively. Since $S_{2^n}(R_n)$ consists of n controlled-R_n, its complexity is $O(n)$. Meanwhile, the complexity of $P_{2^{n-1},2}$ is also $O(n)$, so the complexity of the circuit in Figure 13 is $O(n^2)$.

Substitute R_n^{-1} for R_n in (5.33), we obtain

$$S_{2^n}(R_n^{-1}) = \left[S_{2^{n-1}}(R_n^{-1}) \otimes I\right] V_1^1(R_n^{-1} \otimes I_{2^{n-2}}). \tag{5.47}$$

Therefore, the quantum circuit of the inverse of 1D-QFT $F_{2^n}^{-1}$ can be designed in Figure 14 with complexity $O(n^2)$. The circuits in the dashed box 1 and box 2 implement $F_{2^{n-1}}^{-1}$ and $S_{2^n}(R_n^{-1})$, respectively.

The Second Circuit of 1D-QFT

For convenience of designs of other circuits of 1D-QFT, we define

Figure 14. The first circuit of the inverse of 1D-QFT

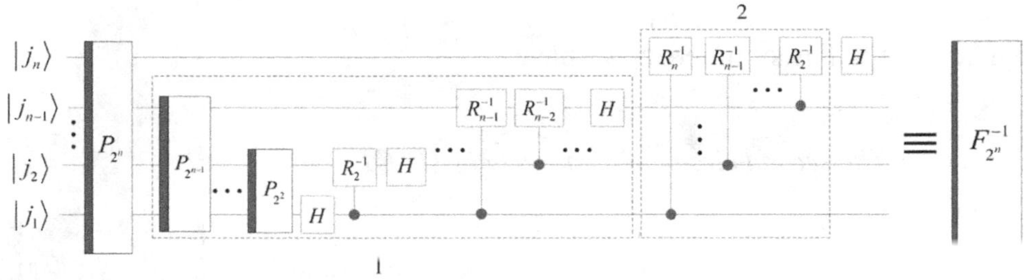

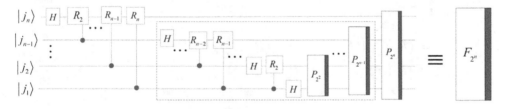

$$F^2_{2^m} = F^3_{2^m} = F^4_{2^m} = F_{2^m},\tag{5.48}$$

where $F^i_{2^m}$ corresponds to the *i*-th circuit of 1D-QFT, $i\in\{2,3,4\}$ and $m\in\{2,3,..,n\}$.

$F^2_{2^n}$ is given by

$$F^2_{2^n} = F_{2^n} = (F^{-1}_{2^n})^{-1} = \{(H \otimes I_{2^{n-1}})S_{2^n}(R^{-1}_n) \times \left(I_2 \otimes F^{-1}_{2^{n-1}}\right) P_{2^{n-1},2}\}^{-1}$$
$$= P_{2,2^{n-1}}(I_2 \otimes F_{2^{n-1}})S_{2^n}(R_n)(H \otimes I_{2^{n-1}}) = P_{2,2^{n-1}}(I_2 \otimes F^2_{2^{n-1}})S_{2^n}(R_n)(H \otimes I_{2^{n-1}}),$$
$$\tag{5.49}$$

Figure 15. The second circuit of 1D-QFT.

and its implementation circuit is shown in Figure 15. The circuits in the dashed box implements the 1D-QFT $F^2_{2^{n-1}}$. Compared with circuit of F_{2^n}, the circuit of $F^2_{2^n}$ consists of the same gates with reverse order, so its complexity is also $O(n^2)$.

Substituting R^{-1}_n for R_n in Figure 15, we obtain the circuit of $(F^2_{2^n})^{-1}$ shown in Figure 16.

The Third Circuit of 1D-QFT

Since 1D-QFT is symmetric, we have

Figure 16. The second circuit of the inverse of 1D-QFT

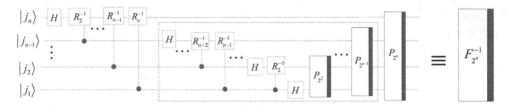

Figure 17. The third circuit of 1D-QFT

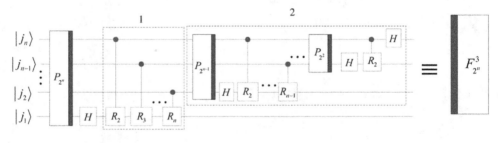

$$F_{2^n}^3 = F_{2^n} = (F_{2^n})^T = \left((F_{2^{n-1}}) \otimes I_2\right) T_{2^n}(R_n)(I_{2^{n-1}} \otimes H) P_{2,2^{n-1}}$$
$$= (F_{2^{n-1}}^3 \otimes I_2) T_{2^n}(R_n)(I_{2^{n-1}} \otimes H) P_{2,2^{n-1}}, \tag{5.50}$$

where $T_{2^n}(R_n)$ is seen in (5.31).

Figure 18. The third circuit of the inverse of 1D-QFT

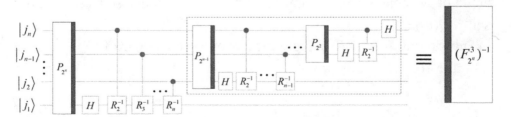

According to Corollary 5.5, the third circuit of 1D-QFT with the complexity of $O(n^2)$ is shown in Figure 17. The circuits in the dashed box 2 and box 1 implement the 1D-QFT $F^3_{2^{n-1}}$ and $T_{2^n}(R_n)$, respectively.

The circuit of $(F^3_{2^n})^{-1}$ is given in Figure 18 by substituting R_n^{-1} for R_n in Figure 17.

The Fourth Circuit of 1D-QFT

$F^4_{2^n}$ is given by

Figure 19. The fourth circuit of 1D-QFT

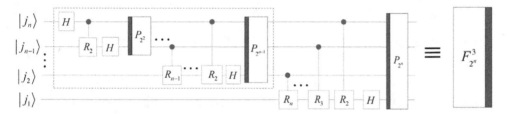

$$F^4_{2^n} = F^2_{2^n} = (F^2_{2^n})^T$$
$$= P_{2^{n-1},2}(I_{2^{n-1}} \otimes H)T_{2^n}(R_n)(F^2_{2^{n-1}} \otimes I_2) = P_{2^{n-1},2}(I_{2^{n-1}} \otimes H)T_{2^n}(R_n)(F^4_{2^{n-1}} \otimes I_2).$$

Figure 20. The fourth circuit of the inverse of 1D-QFT

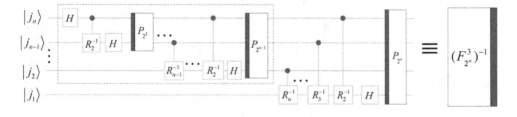

$$(5.51)$$

By using Corollary 5.5, the fourth circuit of 1D-QFT with the complexity of $O(n^2)$ is shown in Figure 19.

The circuit of $(F_{2^n}^4)^{-1}$ is given in Figure 20 by substituting R_n^{-1} for R_n in Figure 19.

Figure 21. The circuit of 1D-QFT in the reference
(Nielsen, & Chuang, 2000).

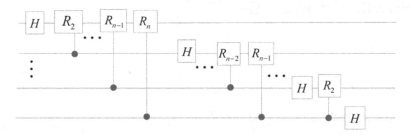

The Comparison of Circuits of 1D-QFT

In this section, we analyze and compare the circuits in references (Nielsen, & Chuang, 2000; Barenco, Ekert, Suominen, & Törmä, 1996; Karafyllidis, 2003) with our proposed ones.

Firstly, the circuit of 1D-QFT in references (Nielsen, & Chuang, 2000) is shown in Figure 21. We find that it is the second circuit of QFT without perfect shuffle permutations, which implement the bit reversal.

Next, the circuit in the reference (Barenco, Ekert, Suominen, & Törmä, 1996) is shown in Figure 22 and Figure 23, respectively, where $A=H$ and

$$\theta_{jk} = \frac{\pi}{2^{j-k}} \, .$$

The gate Figure 22 (b) is

Figure 22. The circuit of 1D- QFT
(Barenco, Ekert, Suominen, & Törmä, 1996).

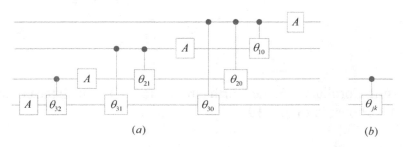

(a)   (b)

Figure 23. The first circuit of 1D-QFT for $n = 4$

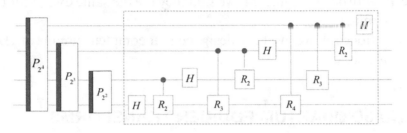

Figure 24. The circuit of 1D-QFT
(Karafyllidis, 2003).

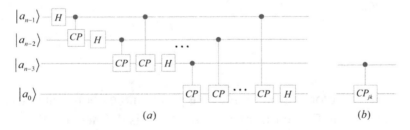

$$
\begin{bmatrix}
1 & 0 & 0 & 0 \\
0 & 1 & 0 & 0 \\
0 & 0 & 1 & 0 \\
0 & 0 & 0 & e^{i\theta_{jk}}
\end{bmatrix},
\tag{5.52}
$$

and is equal to $C_1^1(R_{j-k+1})$.

Since $C_1^1(R_{j-k+1}) = V_1^1(R_{j-k+1})$, thus, the first circuit of the QFT for $n=4$ is redesigned and shown in Figure 13, and the circuit of the dashed box is exactly same with one in Figure 22.

The circuit in the reference (Karafyllidis, 2003) is shown in Figure 24. The matrix of the gate is also equal to $C_1^1(R_{j-k+1})$. Compared the circuit in Figure 19 with one in Figure 24, we find they are the same except for perfect shuffle permutations.

As mentioned above, we have designed four complete circuits of 1D-QFT and its inverse.

2D AND 3D QUANTUM FOURIER TRANSFORMS

In this section. we describe 2D quantum Fourier transform (2D-QFT) and 3D quantum Fourier transform (3D-QFT) for images and videos.

2D-QFT for Images

A $2^m \times 2^k$ image can be expressed as a matrix,

$$
\Lambda_{2^m,2^k} = \begin{bmatrix} \theta_{0,0} & \theta_{0,1} & \cdots & \theta_{0,2^k-1} \\ \theta_{1,0} & \theta_{1,1} & \cdots & \theta_{1,2^k-1} \\ \vdots & \vdots & \cdots & \vdots \\ \theta_{2^m-1,0} & \theta_{2^m-1,1} & \cdots & \theta_{2^m-1,2^k-1} \end{bmatrix},
\tag{5.53}
$$

where $\theta_{x,y}$ is the color information of the pixel on the coordinate (x,y).

The 2D discrete Fourier transform for $\Lambda_{2^m,2^k}$ is defined as

$$
ft2(\Lambda_{2^m,2^k}) = F_{2^m} \Lambda_{2^m,2^k} (F_{2^k})^T = F_{2^m} \Lambda_{2^m,2^k} F_{2^k}.
\tag{5.54}
$$

An image can be stored in the state NASS $|\psi_2\rangle$ in (3.58). Suppose that the function $f(\bullet)$ is equivalent to the quantum circuit in Figure 3.8, i.e., the function $f(\bullet)$ implements

$$f(\Lambda_{2^m,2^k}) = |\psi_2\rangle = \begin{bmatrix} B_1^T \\ \vdots \\ B_{2^m}^T \end{bmatrix}, \tag{5.55}$$

where $B_j = \begin{bmatrix} \theta_{j,0} & \theta_{j,1} & \cdots & \theta_{j,2^k-1} \end{bmatrix}$ is the row vector of $\Lambda_{2^n,2^m}$.

Applying the function $f(\bullet)$ on $\Lambda_{2^m,2^k} \times F_{2^k}$, the result is

$$f(\Lambda_{2^m,2^k}F_{2^k}) = \begin{bmatrix} F_{2^k}B_1^T \\ \vdots \\ F_{2^k}B_{2^n}^T \end{bmatrix} = \left(I_{2^m} \otimes F_{2^k} \right) f(\Lambda_{2^m,2^k}). \tag{5.56}$$

Since

Figure 25. The circuits of 2D-QFT and its inverse.

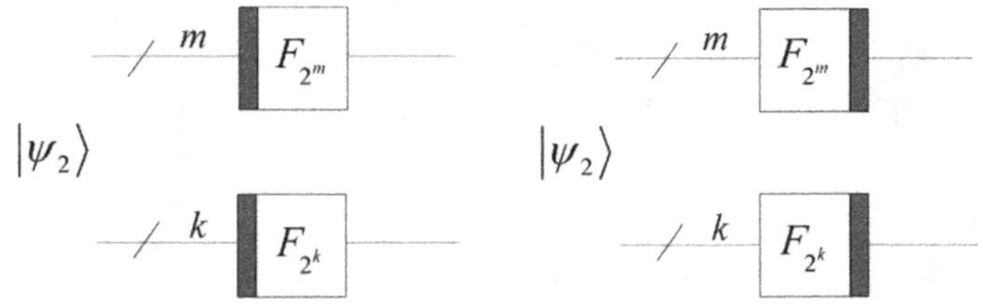

(a) 2D-QFT   (b) The inverse of 2D-QFT

$$f(\Lambda_{2^m,2^k}) = P_{2^k,2^m} f\left((\Lambda_{2^m,2^k})^T \right), \tag{5.57}$$

we have

$$f(F_{2^m}\Lambda_{2^m,2^k}) = P_{2^k,2^m} f\left((\Lambda_{2^m,2^k})^T F_{2^m} \right)$$
$$= P_{2^k,2^m} \left(I_{2^k} \otimes F_{2^m} \right) P_{2^m,2^k} f(\Lambda_{2^m,2^k}) = \left(F_{2^m} \otimes I_{2^k} \right) f(\Lambda_{2^m,2^k}). \tag{5.58}$$

From (5.54), (5.56) and (5.58), 2D-QFT is given by

$$ft2(\Lambda_{2^m,2^k}) = f(F_{2^m}\Lambda_{2^m,2^k}F_{2^k}) = \left(F_{2^m} \otimes F_{2^k} \right) |\psi_2\rangle \tag{5.59}$$

and its circuit is designed in Figure 25 (a) with the complexity $O(m^2+k^2)$ for a $2^m \times 2^k$ image. $\left(F_{2^m} \otimes F_{2^k} \right)\left(F_{2^m}^{-1} \otimes F_{2^k}^{-1} \right) = I_{2^{k+m}}$, so the circuit of the inverse of 2D-QFT is designed in Figure 25 (b). The implementation code of 2D-QFT and its inverse is seen in Code B.35.

3D-QFT for Videos

A $2^m \times 2^k \times 2^h$ video corresponds to the following matrix,

$$A_{2^m,2^k,2^h} = \left(\Lambda^1_{2^m,2^k}, \Lambda^2_{2^m,2^k}, \cdots, \Lambda^{2^h}_{2^m,2^k} \right), \tag{5.60}$$

where the matrix $\Lambda^j_{2^m,2^k}$ is the j-th image frame.

We firstly define the following discrete Fourier transforms: $F^x(\bullet)$, $F^y(\bullet)$ and $F^t(\bullet)$ as below.

$$\begin{cases} F^x(A_{2^m,2^k,2^h}) = \left(F_{2^m}\Lambda^1_{2^m,2^k}, \cdots, F_{2^m}\Lambda^{2^h}_{2^m,2^k} \right), \\ F^y(A_{2^m,2^k,2^h}) = \left(\Lambda^1_{2^m,2^k}F_{2^k}, \cdots, \Lambda^{2^h}_{2^m,2^k}F_{2^k} \right), \\ F^t(A_{2^m,2^k,2^h}) = \left(C^1_{2^m,2^k}, \cdots, C^{2^h}_{2^m,2^k} \right). \end{cases} \tag{5.61}$$

Let a column vector $u_{x,y}$ be

$$u_{x,y} = \begin{bmatrix} \theta^1_{x,y} & \theta^2_{x,y} & \cdots & \theta^{2^h}_{x,y} \end{bmatrix}^T, \tag{5.62}$$

where $\theta^j_{x,y}$ is the element of the matrix $\Lambda^j_{2^m,2^k}$ on the position (x,y). Then elements of $F^t(A_{2^m,2^k,2^h})$ can be calculated by

$$\begin{bmatrix} C^1_{x,y} & C^2_{x,y} & \cdots & C^{2^h}_{x,y} \end{bmatrix} = u^T_{x,y} F_{2^h} \tag{5.63}$$

where $C^j_{x,y}$ is the elements of the matrix $C^j_{2^n,2^m}$ on the position (x,y).

The 3D discrete Fourier transform for the video $A_{2^m,2^k,2^h}$ is defined as

$$ft3(A_{2^m,2^k,2^h}) = F^t(F^y(F^x(A_{2^m,2^k,2^h}))).$$

(5.64)

Similarly, suppose that the video $A_{2^m,2^k,2^h}$ is stored in the state NASS $\left| \psi_3 \right\rangle$ in (3.60), and the function $f(\bullet)$ implements

$$\left| \psi_3 \right\rangle = f(A_{2^m,2^k,2^h}) = \begin{bmatrix} u_{0,0} \\ \vdots \\ u_{0,2^k-1} \\ u_{1,0} \\ \vdots \\ u_{1,2^k-1} \\ \vdots \\ u_{2^m-1,0} \\ \vdots \\ u_{2^m-1,2^k-1} \end{bmatrix},$$

(5.65)

Figure 26. The circuits of 3D-QFT and its inverse

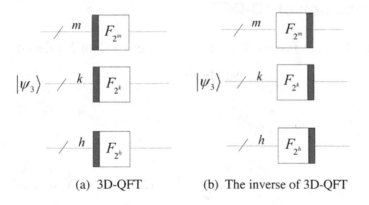

(a) 3D-QFT   (b) The inverse of 3D-QFT

where the column vector $u_{x,y}$ is shown in (5.62).

Applying the function $f(\bullet)$ on $F^t(A_{2^n,2^m,2^p})$, $F^y(A_{2^n,2^m,2^p})$ and $F^x(A_{2^n,2^m,2^p})$, we obtain

$$\begin{cases} f(F^x(A_{2^m,2^k,2^h})) = \left(F_{2^m} \otimes I_{2^k} \otimes I_{2^h}\right)\big|\psi_3\big\rangle, \\ f(F^y(A_{2^m,2^k,2^h})) = \left(I_{2^m} \otimes F_{2^k} \otimes I_{2^h}\right)\big|\psi_3\big\rangle, \\ f(F^t(A_{2^m,2^k,2^h})) = \left(I_{2^m} \otimes I_{2^k} \otimes F_{2^h}\right)\big|\psi_3\big\rangle. \end{cases} \tag{5.66}$$

From (5.64) and (5.66), 3D-QFT is given by

$$f(ft3(A_{2^m,2^k,2^h})) = (F_{2^m} \otimes F_{2^k} \otimes F_{2^h})\big|\psi_3\big\rangle, \tag{5.67}$$

and its implementation circuit is as shown in Figure 26 (a). Meanwhile, the circuit of the inverse of 3D-QFT is designed in Figure 26 (b). Their complexities are both $O(m^2+k^2+h^2)$. The implementation code of 3D-QFT and its inverse is seen in Code B.37.

SIMULATION S

In this section, we describe the simulation experiments of 1D-QFT, 2D-QFT and 3D-QFT. Their codes are seen in Appendix B.

The Simulation of 1D-QFT

Applying classical inverse Fourier transform *ifft*() in Matlab on a column vector $X = \begin{bmatrix} \theta_0 & \cdots & \theta_{2^n-1} \end{bmatrix}^T$, we obtain

$$ifft(\mathrm{X}) = \begin{bmatrix} y_0 & \cdots & y_{2^n-1} \end{bmatrix}^T, \tag{5.68}$$

where $y_k = \dfrac{1}{2^n}\displaystyle\sum_{j=0}^{2^n-1}\theta_j e^{2\pi ijk/2^n}$. Compared *ifft*(X) with $F_{2^n}X$ in (5.45), we have

$$\sqrt{2^n} \times ifft(X) = F_{2^n}X . \tag{5.69}$$

We consider the column vector

$X = [1, 2, 3, 4, 5, 6, 7, 8, 9, 10, 11, 12, 13, 14, 15, 16]^T$

as an example. The results are (see Code B.34)

$$4 \times ifft(X) = \begin{bmatrix} 34.0000 + 0.0000i \\ -2.0000 - 10.0547i \\ -2.0000 - 4.8284i \\ -2.0000 - 2.9932i \\ -2.0000 - 2.0000i \\ -2.0000 - 1.3364i \\ -2.0000 - 0.8284i \\ -2.0000 - 0.3978i \\ -2.0000 + 0.0000i \\ -2.0000 + 0.3978i \\ -2.0000 + 0.8284i \\ -2.0000 + 1.3364i \\ -2.0000 + 2.0000i \\ -2.0000 + 2.9932i \\ -2.0000 + 4.8284i \\ -2.0000 + 10.0547i \end{bmatrix}, F_{2^n} X = \begin{bmatrix} 34.0000 + 0.0000i \\ -2.0000 - 10.0547i \\ -2.0000 - 4.8284i \\ -2.0000 - 2.9932i \\ -2.0000 - 2.0000i \\ -2.0000 - 1.3364i \\ -2.0000 - 0.8284i \\ -2.0000 - 0.3978i \\ -2.0000 + 0.0000i \\ -2.0000 + 0.3978i \\ -2.0000 + 0.8284i \\ -2.0000 + 1.3364i \\ -2.0000 + 2.0000i \\ -2.0000 + 2.9932i \\ -2.0000 + 4.8284i \\ -2.0000 + 10.0547i \end{bmatrix} . \quad (5.70)$$

Table 1. Comparisons between classical inverse Fourier transform and 1D-QFTs

	First Circuit	Second Circuit	Third Circuit	Fourth Circuit
$norm(abs(4 \times ifft(X) - F_{2^n}X))$	9.3549×10^{-15}	9.7270×10^{-15}	9.7270×10^{-15}	9.3549×10^{-15}
$norm(abs(F_{2^n}^{-1}F_{2^n}X - X))$	1.8359×10^{-14}	1.9193×10^{-14}	1.9193×10^{-14}	1.8359×10^{-14}

where only four decimal places are displayed. To compare the above data precisely, we define the function $norm(abs(X))$ as

$$norm(\mathrm{abs}(X)) = \sqrt{\sum_{j=0}^{2^n-1} abs(\theta_j)^2} , \quad (5.71)$$

where $abs(\theta_j)$ returns the magnitude of the complex θ_j. Since

$$norm(abs(\sqrt{8} \times ifft(X) - F_{2^n}X))$$

Figure 27. An example of 2D-QFT for a 128×128 image

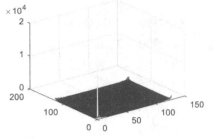

(a) An *original image*   (b) The amplitude spectrum of the transformed image

is equal to 9.3549×10^{-15}, we conclude that the results of $4 \times ifft(X)$ and $F_{2^n} X$ are the same without consideration of truncation error on machine computing. Comparisons between classical inverse Fourier transform and 1D-QFTs are shown in Table 1, and illustrate the four circuits of 1D-QFT are correct for the column vector X.

The Simulation of 2D-QFT

Let A_g be the matrix of the 128×128 image in Figure 27 (a), and be stored in the NASS state $|\psi_2\rangle$, i.e.,

$$|\psi_2\rangle = f(A_g),$$
(5.72)

where the function $f(\bullet)$ is equivalent to the quantum circuit in Figure 3.9.

Applying 2D-QFT $F_{2^7} \otimes F_{2^7}$ on $|\psi_2\rangle$, we use the inverse of the function $f(\bullet)$ to retrieve the transformed image, i.e., the transformed image is $f^{-1}\left[(F_{2^7} \otimes F_{2^7})|\psi_2\rangle\right]$. Its amplitude spectrum is shown in Figure 27 (b).

The classical 2D inverse Fourier transform *ifft2()* in Matlab consists of two 1D inverse Fourier transform *ifft()*, from (5.69) and (5.72), so we obtain

$$2^7 \times ifft2(A_g) = f^{-1}\left[(F_{2^7} \otimes F_{2^7})|\psi_2\rangle\right].$$
(5.73)

Let the two differences $r1$ and $r2$ be

Figure 28. An example of 3D-QFT for a $128 \times 128 \times 2$ *video*

(a) An *original video*

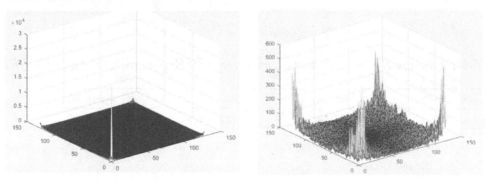

(b) The amplitude spectrums of the image frames of the transformed video

$$
\begin{cases}
r_1 = 2^7 \times ifft2(A_g) - f^{-1}\left[(F_{2^7} \otimes F_{2^7})\big|\psi_2\rangle\right], \\
r_2 = A_g - f^{-1}\left[(F_{2^7}^{-1} \otimes F_{2^7}^{-1})(F_{2^7} \otimes F_{2^7})\big|\psi_2\rangle\right].
\end{cases}
\tag{5.74}
$$

Code B.36 shows that $norm(abs(r_1))$ and $norm(abs(r_2))$ are 8.5991×10⁻¹¹ and 1.7937×10⁻¹⁰, respectively. It illustrates the circuits of 2D-QFT and its inverse are correct for the image in Figure 27 (a).

The Simulation of 3D-QFT

Let V_g be the matrix of the 128×128×2 video in Figure 28 (a), and be stored in the NASS state $\big|\psi_3\rangle$, i.e.,

$$
\big|\psi_3\rangle = f(V_g). \tag{5.75}
$$

Applying 3D-QFT $F_{2^7} \otimes F_{2^7} \otimes F_2$ on $|\psi_3\rangle$, we obtain the transformed video $f^{-1}\left[(F_{2^7} \otimes F_{2^7} \otimes F_2)|\psi_3\rangle\right]$. the amplitude spectrums of which are shown in Figure 28 (b) .

The classical 3D inverse Fourier transform *ifftn*() in Matlab consists of three 1D inverse Fourier transform *ifft*(), so we obtain

$$\sqrt{2^{15}} \times ifftn(V_g) = f^{-1}\left[(F_{2^7} \otimes F_{2^7} \otimes F_2)|\psi_3\rangle\right]. \tag{5.76}$$

Table 2. Comparisons between classical inverse 3D Fourier transform and 3D-QFT

norm(abs(v_1))	norm(abs(v_2))	norm(abs(v_3))	norm(abs(v_4))
1.1679×10^{-9}	2.9563×10^{-9}	1.1296×10^{-9}	1.1310×10^{-9}

We define

$$\begin{cases} FT3 = \sqrt{2^{15}} \times ifftn(V_g), \\ QFT3 = f^{-1}\left[(F_{2^7} \otimes F_{2^7} \otimes F_2)|\psi_3\rangle\right], \\ IQFT3 = f^{-1}\left[(F_{2^7}^{-1} \otimes F_{2^7}^{-1} \otimes F_2^{-1})(F_{2^7} \otimes F_{2^7} \otimes F_2)|\psi_3\rangle\right], \end{cases} \tag{5.77}$$

and

$$\begin{cases} v_1 = FT3(:,:,1) - QFT3(:,:,1), \\ v_2 = FT3(:,:,2) - QFT3(:,:,2), \\ v_3 = V_g(:,:,1) - IQFT3(:,:,1), \\ v_4 = V_g(:,:,2) - IQFT3(:,:,2), \end{cases} \tag{5.78}$$

where $(:,:,j)$ denotes the j-th image frame of a video. Comparisons between classical 3D inverse Fourier transform and 3D-QFT are shown in Table 2, and illustrate the circuits of 3D-QFT and its inverse are correct for the video in Figure 28 (a) (see Code B.38).

CONCLUSION

This chapter described perfect shuffle permutations and generalized tensor products, quantum circuits of which are designed. The complete circuits of 1D-QFT, 2D-QFT, 3D-QFT and their inverses are realized. Since complexities of these quantum Fourier transforms are all $O(n^2)$ for 2^n data, quantum Fourier transforms offer exponential speedup over their classical counterparts.

REFERENCES

Barenco, A., Ekert, A., Suominen, K. A., & Törmä, P. (1996). Approximate quantum Fourier transform and decoherence. *Physical Review A.*, *54*(1), 139–146. doi:10.1103/PhysRevA.54.139 PMID:9913466

Cooley, J. W., & Tukey, J. W. (1965). An algorithm for the machine calculation of complex Fourier series. *Mathematics of Computation*, *19*(90), 297–301. doi:10.1090/S0025-5718-1965-0178586-1

Coppersmith, D. (2002). *An approximate Fourier transform useful in quantum factoring*. arXiv preprint quant-ph/0201067

Fino, B. J., & Algazi, V. R. (1977). A unified treatment of discrete fast unitary transforms. *SIAM Journal on Computing*, *6*(4), 700–717. doi:10.1137/0206051

Griffiths, R. B., & Niu, C. S. (1996). Semiclassical Fourier transform for quantum computation. *Physical Review Letters*, *76*(17), 3228–3231. doi:10.1103/PhysRevLett.76.3228 PMID:10060907

He, X. Y., Zhou, X. Y., & Cui, T. J. (2012). Fast 3D-ISAR image simulation of targets at arbitrary aspect angles through nonuniform fast Fourier transform (NUFFT). *IEEE Transactions on Antennas and Propagation*, *60*(5), 2597–2602. doi:10.1109/TAP.2012.2189717

Heo, J., Kang, M. S., Hong, C. H., Yang, H., & Choi, S. G. (2016). Discrete quantum Fourier transform using weak cross-Kerr nonlinearity and displacement operator and photon-number-resolving measurement under the decoherence effect. *Quantum Information Processing*, *15*(12), 4955–4971. doi:10.100711128-016-1439-0

Hoyer, P. (1997). *Efficient quantum transforms*. arXiv preprint quant-ph/9702028

Karafyllidis, I. G. (2003). Visualization of the quantum Fourier transform using a quantum computer simulator. *Quantum Information Processing, 2*(4), 271–288. doi:10.1023/B:QINP.0000020076.36114.13

Li, H. S., Fan, P., Xia, H. Y., Song, S., & He, X. (2018). The quantum Fourier transform based on quantum vision representation. *Quantum Information Processing, 17*(12), 333. doi:10.100711128-018-2096-2

Li, H. S., Fan, P., Xia, H. Y., & Song, S. X. (2019). Quantum multi-level wavelet transforms. *Information Sciences, 504*, 113–115. doi:10.1016/j.ins.2019.07.057

Li, H. S., Li, C., Chen, X., & Xia, H. Y. (2018). Quantum image encryption algorithm based on NASS. *International Journal of Theoretical Physics, 57*(12), 3745–3760. doi:10.100710773-018-3887-z

Nielsen, M. A., & Chuang, I. L. (2000). *Quantum Computation and Quantum Information*. Cambridge University Press.

Park, C. S. (2015). 2D discrete Fourier transform on sliding windows. *IEEE Transactions on Image Processing, 24*(3), 901–907. doi:10.1109/TIP.2015.2389627 PMID:25585421

Shor, P. W. (1994). Algorithms for quantum computation: discrete logarithms and factoring. *Proceedings of 35th Annual Symposium on Foundations of Computer Science*, 124–134. 10.1109/SFCS.1994.365700

Wang, H. F., Zhu, A. D., Zhang, S., & Yeon, K. H. (2011). Simple implementation of discrete quantum Fourier transform via cavity quantum electrodynamics. *New Journal of Physics, 13*(1), 013021. doi:10.1088/1367-2630/13/1/013021

Yang, Y. G., Xia, J., Jia, X., & Zhang, H. (2013). Novel image encryption/decryption based on quantum Fourier transform and double phase encoding. *Quantum Information Processing, 12*(11), 3477–3493. doi:10.100711128-013-0612-y

Zhang, W. W., Gao, F., Liu, B., Wen, Q. Y., & Chen, H. (2013). A watermark strategy for quantum images based on quantum Fourier transform. *Quantum Information Processing, 12*(2), 793–803. doi:10.100711128-012-0423-6

Chapter 5
Quantum Wavelet Transforms

ABSTRACT

The classical wavelet transform has been widely applied in the information processing field. It implies that quantum wavelet transform (QWT) may play an important role in quantum information processing. This chapter firstly describes the iteration equations of the general QWT using generalized tensor product. Then, Haar QWT (HQWT), Daubechies D4 QWT (DQWT), and their inverse transforms are proposed respectively. Meanwhile, the circuits of the two kinds of multi-level HQWT are designed. What's more, the multi-level DQWT based on the periodization extension is implemented. The complexity analysis shows that the proposed multi-level QWTs on 2n elements can be implemented by O(n3) basic operations. Simulation experiments demonstrate that the proposed QWTs are correct and effective.

INTRODUCTION

The classical wavelet transform has been widely spread to the information processing field (Mallat, 1989), such as image encryption (Belazi, El-Latif, Diaconu, Rhouma, & Belghith, 2017), image watermarking (Makbol, Khoo, Rassem, & Loukhaoukha, 2017). Its quantum versions, such as Haar quantum wavelet transform (HQWT) and Daubechies D4 quantum wavelet transform (D4QWT), have been proposed (Hoyer, 1997; Fijan & Williams, 1998; Terraneo & Shepelyansky, 2003; Li, Fan, Xia, & Song, 2019). Complexities of HQWT and D4QWT on 2^n elements are $O(n^2)$ and $O(n^3)$, respectively. In contrast, the classical fast wavelet transform needs $O(2^n)$ basic operations

DOI: 10.4018/978-1-7998-3799-2.ch005

to implement the discrete wavelet transform (Beylkin, Coifman, & Rokhlin, 1991). Therefore, quantum wavelet transform achieves exponentially speed up in comparison with its classical counterpart.

This chapter introduces the general quantum wavelet transform, multi-level HQWT and multi-level D4QWT (Li, Fan, Xia, Song, & He, 2018).

GENERAL QUANTUM WAVELET TRANSFORM

Suppose that $W_{2^n}^0 = W_{2^n}$ is a kernel matrix of the general wavelet, then, the (k+1)-level iteration of discrete wavelet transform is defined by (Ruch & Van Fleet, 2011),

$$Y_{2^n}^k = W_{2^n}^k W_{2^n}^{k-1} \ldots W_{2^n}^1 W_{2^n}^0, \tag{6.1}$$

where the iteration matrix $W_{2^n}^j$ is

$$W_{2^n}^j = Diag(W_{2^{n-j}}, I_{2^{n-j}}, I_{2^{n-j+1}}, \ldots, I_{2^{n-1}}), \tag{6.2}$$

and

$$Diag(W_{2^{n-j}}, I_{2^{n-j}}, I_{2^{n-j+1}}, \ldots, I_{2^{n-1}})$$

is a matrix with blocks $W_{2^{n-j}}$, $I_{2^{n-j}}, I_{2^{n-j+1}}, \ldots, I_{2^{n-1}}$ on the main diagonal and zeros elsewhere. I_{2^m} is a $2^m \times 2^m$ identity matrix

The iteration equations of $W_{2^n}^j$ and $Y_{2^n}^k$ can be written as

$$W_{2^n}^j = Diag(W_{2^{n-1}}^{j-1}, I_{2^{n-1}}), \tag{6.3}$$

and

$$Y_{2^n}^k = Diag(Y_{2^{n-1}}^{k-1}, I_{2^{n-1}})W_{2^n}. \tag{6.4}$$

From (5.12), we have

$$\begin{cases} I \otimes \left\{ Y^{k-1}_{2^{n-1}}, I_{2^{n-1}} \right\} = P_{2^{n-1},2} I_{2^n} P_{2,2^{n-1}} Diag(Y^{k-1}_{2^{n-1}}, I_{2^{n-1}}) = Diag(Y^{k-1}_{2^{n-1}}, I_{2^{n-1}}), \\ \left\{ Y^{k-1}_{2^{n-1}}, I_{2^{n-1}} \right\} \otimes I = P_{2,2^{n-1}} Diag(Y^{k-1}_{2^{n-1}}, I_{2^{n-1}}) P_{2^{n-1},2} I_{2^n} = P_{2,2^{n-1}} Diag(Y^{k-1}_{2^{n-1}}, I_{2^{n-1}}) P_{2^{n-1},2}. \end{cases}$$

$$(6.5)$$

Combining (6.4) with (6.5), we give the $(k+1)$-level iteration of general quantum wavelet transform

$$Y^k_{2^n} = \left(I \otimes \left\{ Y^{k-1}_{2^{n-1}}, I_{2^{n-1}} \right\} \right) W_{2^n}, \tag{6.6}$$

or

$$Y^k_{2^n} = P_{2^{n-1},2} \left(\left\{ Y^{k-1}_{2^{n-1}}, I_{2^{n-1}} \right\} \otimes I \right) P_{2,2^{n-1}} W_{2^n}, \tag{6.7}$$

where the initial value is $Y^0_{2^{n-k}} = W_{2^{n-k}}$.

Since

$$I \otimes \left\{ Y^{k-1}_{2^{n-1}}, I_{2^{n-1}} \right\} = C^0_{n-1}(Y^{k-1}_{2^{n-1}})$$

and

$$\left\{ Y^{k-1}_{2^{n-1}}, I_{2^{n-1}} \right\} \otimes I = V^0_{n-1}(Y^{k-1}_{2^{n-1}})$$

(see (5.18)), we design the quantum circuits of $Y^k_{2^n}$ shown in Figure 1. The detail circuits of perfect shuffle permutations $P_{2^{n-1},2}$ and $P_{2,2^{n-1}}$ are seen in Figure 3.

The inverse of $Y^k_{2^n}$ is

$$\left(Y^k_{2^n} \right)^{-1} = \left(W_{2^n} \right)^{-1} \left[I_2 \otimes \left\{ \left(Y^{k-1}_{2^{n-1}} \right)^{-1}, I_{2^{n-1}} \right\} \right], \tag{6.8}$$

or

Figure 1. The implement circuits of $Y_{2^n}^k$.

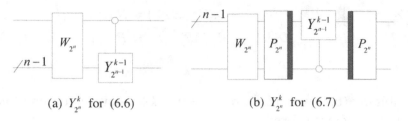

(a) $Y_{2^n}^k$ for (6.6) (b) $Y_{2^n}^k$ for (6.7)

$$\left(Y_{2^n}^k\right)^{-1} = \left(W_{2^n}\right)^{-1} P_{2^{n-1},2} \left[\left\{\left(Y_{2^{n-1}}^{k-1}\right)^{-1}, I_{2^{n-1}}\right\} \otimes I_2\right] P_{2,2^{n-1}}, \tag{6.9}$$

where the initial value is $\left(Y_{2^{n-k}}^0\right)^{-1} = \left(W_{2^{n-k}}\right)^{-1}$. The quantum circuits of $\left(Y_{2^n}^k\right)^{-1}$ are shown in Figure 2.

Figure 2. The implement circuits of $\left(Y_{2^n}^k\right)^{-1}$.

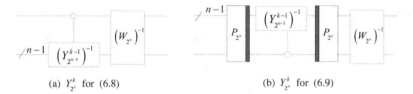

(a) $Y_{2^n}^k$ for (6.8) (b) $Y_{2^n}^k$ for (6.9)

HAAR QUANTUM WAVELET TRANSFORM

The kernel matrix of Haar quantum wavelet transform (HQWT) can be rewritten as

$$\begin{cases} W_{2^n} = P_{2^{n-1},2}\left(I_{2^{n-1}} \otimes H\right), n > 1, \\ W_2 = H, \end{cases} \tag{6.10}$$

where H is a Hadamard matrix.

Substituting the kernel matrix $W_{2^n} = P_{2^{n-1},2}\left(I_{2^{n-1}} \otimes H\right)$ into (6.6) or (6.7), we obtain that the k-level iteration of HQWT is

$$H_{2^n}^k = \left(I_2 \otimes \left\{ H_{2^{n-1}}^{k-1}, I_{2^{n-1}} \right\} \right) P_{2^{n-1},2} \left(I_{2^{n-1}} \otimes H \right), \tag{6.11}$$

or

$$H_{2^n}^k = P_{2^{n-1},2} \left(\left\{ H_{2^{n-1}}^{k-1}, I_{2^{n-1}} \right\} \otimes I_2 \right) \left(I_{2^{n-1}} \otimes H \right), \tag{6.12}$$

where the initial value is

$$\begin{cases} H_{2^{n-k}}^0 = P_{2^{n-k-1},2} \left(I_{2^{n-k-1}} \otimes H \right), & 1 \le k < n-1, \\ H_2^0 = H, & k = n-1. \end{cases} \tag{6.13}$$

When $1 \le k < n-1$, the implementation circuits of $H_{2^n}^k$ in (6.11) and (6.12) are shown in Figure 3 and Figure 4, marked by $FH_{2^n}^k$ and $SH_{2^n}^k$, respectively. Similarly, $k = n-1$, the circuits for $H_{2^n}^{n-1}$, denoted as $FH_{2^n}^{n-1}$ and $SH_{2^n}^{n-1}$, are shown in Figure 5 and Figure 6, respectively.

Another n-level Haar wavelet transform is defined by (Fino & Algazi, 1977)

$$H_{2^n}^{n-1} = Zb_{2^n} \times N_{2^n}, \tag{6.14}$$

where N_{2^n} is Haar wavelet transform in "natural" order, and the permutation Zb_{2^n} performs a "zonal bit reversal" ordering.

Figure 3. The quantum circuit of $H_{2^n}^k$ in (6.11). The circuit in the dashed box implements $H_{2^{n-1}}^{k-1}$.

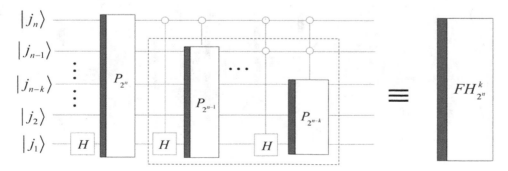

Figure 4. The quantum circuit of $H_{2^n}^k$ in (6.12). The circuit in the dashed box implements $H_{2^{n-1}}^{k-1}$.

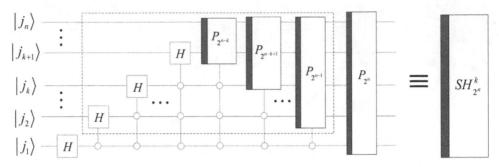

Figure 5. The quantum circuit of $H_{2^n}^{n-1}$ in (6.11). The circuit in the dashed box implements $H_{2^{n-1}}^{n-2}$.

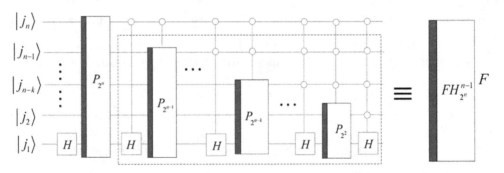

Figure 6. The quantum circuit of $H_{2^n}^{n-1}$ in (6.12). The circuit in the dashed box 1 implements $H_{2^{n-1}}^{n-2}$.

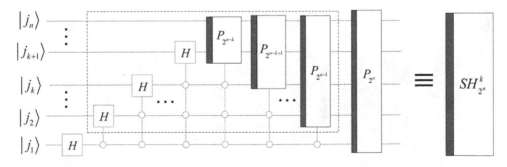

N_{2^n} is given by

$$N_{2^n} = \{H, I_2, \ldots, I_2\} \otimes N_{2^{n-1}} = \left(\{H, I_2, \ldots, I_2\} \otimes I_{2^{n-1}}\right)\left(I_2 \otimes N_{2^{n-1}}\right), \qquad (6.15)$$

where the initial value is $N_2 = H$. Since

$$\left[H, I_2, \ldots, I_2\right] \otimes I_{2^{n-1}} = V_{n-1}^0(II)$$

(see (5.18)), whose implementation circuit is shown in Figure 6, we obtain that the circuit in the dashed box 2 in Figure 6 implements N_{2^n}.

The permutation Zb_{2^n} plays an important role in wavelet transforms (Fino & Algazi, 1977). A zone is a set of indexes between two successive powers of 2, that is, the zone 0 is the set $\{0\}$, and the zone $(i+1)$ is the set $[2^i, 2^{i+1})$ where $i \geq 0$. The "zonal bit reversal" ordering is a bit reversal followed by a reordering in the original order inside each zone. For instance, when $n=3$, the permutation Zb_{2^3} performs the "zonal bit reversal" ordering in Table 1. It implements the following permutation: $|i\rangle \rightarrow |j\rangle$ where $i \in FinalOrder$ and $j \in Index$. "Final order" is the decimal form of "Reordering inside zones".

Table 1. Zonal bit reversal.

Index	Zone	Binary Form of Index	Bit Reversal	Reordering Inside Zones	Final Order
0	0	000	000	000	0
1	1	001	100	100	4
2	2	010	010	010	2
3	3	011	110	110	6
4	4	100	001	001	1
5	5	101	101	011	3
6	6	110	011	101	5
7	7	111	111	111	7

The circuit of the permutation Zb_{2^3} shown in Figure 8 is the same as the one in the box 3 in Figure 6 for $n=3$. Since the circuit of $H_{2^n}^{n-1}$ consists of

Figure 7. The quantum circuit of the permutation Zb_{2^3}

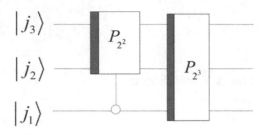

the dashed box 2 and the dashed box 3, combining (6.14) and Figure 6, we conclude that the circuit in the dashed box 3 implement the permutation Zb_{2^n}.

The inverse transform of $H_{2^n}^k$ is

$$\left(H_{2^n}^k\right)^{-1} = \left(I_{2^{n-1}} \otimes H\right) P_{2,2^{n-1}} \left[I_2 \otimes \left\{\left(H_{2^{n-1}}^{k-1}\right)^{-1}, I_{2^{n-1}}\right\}\right], \tag{6.16}$$

or

$$\left(H_{2^n}^k\right)^{-1} = \left(I_{2^{n-1}} \otimes H\right) \left(\left\{\left(H_{2^{n-1}}^{k-1}\right)^{-1}, I_{2^{n-1}}\right\} \otimes I_2\right) P_{2,2^{n-1}}, \tag{6.17}$$

where the initial value is

$$\begin{cases} \left(H_{2^{n-k}}^0\right)^{-1} = \left(I_{2^{n-k-1}} \otimes H\right) P_{2,2^{n-k-1}}, & 1 \le k < n-1, \\ \left(H_2^0\right)^{-1} = H, & k = n-1. \end{cases} \tag{6.18}$$

From (6.11), (6.12), (6.16) and (6.17), we conclude that the quantum circuits of $\left(H_{2^n}^k\right)^{-1}$ and $H_{2^n}^k$ consist of the same quantum gates with the reverse order, and the implementation circuits of $\left(H_{2^n}^k\right)^{-1}$ are shown in Figure 8. The integer k in Figure 8 (a) and (b) is the element in the set $\{1,2,\ldots,n-2\}$.

The implementation codes of HQWTs and their inverse are designed in Code B.40 - Code B.43.

Figure 8. The quantum circuits of the inverse of HQWT

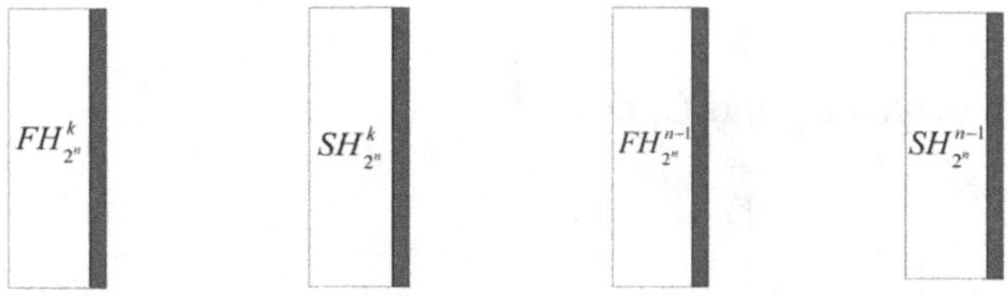

(a) $\left(H_{2^n}^k\right)^{-1}$ *in (6.16)*   (b) $\left(H_{2^n}^k\right)^{-1}$ *in (6.17)*   (c) $\left(H_{2^n}^{n-1}\right)^{-1}$ *in (6.16)*   (d) $\left(H_{2^n}^{n-1}\right)^{-1}$ *in (6.17)*

DAUBECHIES D4 QUANTUM WAVELET TRANSFORM

Let h_0, h_1, h_2, and h_3 be equal to

$$h_0 = \frac{1+\sqrt{3}}{4\sqrt{2}}, \quad h_1 = \frac{3+\sqrt{3}}{4\sqrt{2}}, \quad h_2 = \frac{3-\sqrt{3}}{4\sqrt{2}} \text{ and } h_3 = \frac{1-\sqrt{3}}{4\sqrt{2}},$$

respectively, then, the kernel matrix of the D4 wavelet transform is defined by (Ruch & Van Fleet, 2011)

$$T_{2^n} = \begin{bmatrix} h_0 & h_1 & h_2 & h_3 & 0 & 0 & \cdots & 0 & 0 & 0 & 0 \\ 0 & 0 & h_0 & h_1 & h_2 & h_3 & \cdots & 0 & 0 & 0 & 0 \\ \vdots & \vdots & \vdots & \vdots & \vdots & \vdots & \ddots & \vdots & \vdots & \vdots & \vdots \\ 0 & 0 & 0 & 0 & 0 & 0 & \cdots & h_0 & h_1 & h_2 & h_3 \\ h_2 & h_3 & 0 & 0 & 0 & 0 & \cdots & 0 & 0 & h_0 & h_1 \\ h_3 & -h_2 & h_1 & -h_0 & 0 & 0 & \cdots & 0 & 0 & 0 & 0 \\ 0 & 0 & h_3 & -h_2 & h_1 & -h_0 & \cdots & 0 & 0 & 0 & 0 \\ \vdots & \vdots & \vdots & \vdots & \vdots & \vdots & \ddots & \vdots & \vdots & \vdots & 0 \\ 0 & 0 & 0 & 0 & 0 & 0 & \cdots & h_3 & -h_2 & h_1 & -h_0 \\ h_1 & -h_0 & 0 & 0 & 0 & 0 & \cdots & 0 & 0 & h_3 & -h_2 \end{bmatrix}. \quad (6.19)$$

Next, we introduce Daubechies D4 quantum wavelet transform (D4QWT).

The Implementation of the Single-Level D4QWT

$D_{2^n} = P_{2,2^{n-1}} T_{2^n}$ is rewritten as (Fijany & Williams, 1998)

$$D_{2^n} = \left(I_{2^{n-1}} \otimes C_1\right)Q_{2^n}\left(I_{2^{n-1}} \otimes X\right)\left(I_{2^{n-1}} \otimes C_0\right), \tag{6.20}$$

where two matrices C_0 and C_1 are

$$C_0 = 2\begin{bmatrix} h_3 & -h_2 \\ h_2 & h_3 \end{bmatrix}, C_1 = \frac{1}{2}\begin{bmatrix} \dfrac{h_0}{h_3} & 1 \\ & \dfrac{h_1}{1} \\ 1 & \dfrac{h_1}{h_2} \end{bmatrix}, \tag{6.21}$$

and the downshift matrix Q_{2^n} is given by

$$Q_{2^n} = \begin{bmatrix} 0 & 1 & 0 & \cdots & 0 \\ 0 & 0 & 1 & \cdots & 0 \\ \vdots & \vdots & \vdots & \ddots & \vdots \\ 0 & 0 & 0 & \cdots & 1 \\ 1 & 0 & 0 & 0 & 0 \end{bmatrix}. \tag{6.22}$$

The iteration of the downshift matrix Q_{2^n} can be expressed as

$$Q_{2^n} = \left(I_{2^{n-1}} \otimes X\right)\left(\{Q_{2^{n-1}}, I_{2^{n-1}}\} \otimes I_2\right) = \left(I_{2^{n-1}} \otimes X\right)V_1^0(Q_{2^{n-1}}), \tag{6.23}$$

where the initial value is $Q_2=X$, and the implementation circuit is shown in Figure 9 (a).

Figure 9. The quantum circuits of Q_{2^n}, D_{2^n} and T_{2^n} with $n \geq 2$

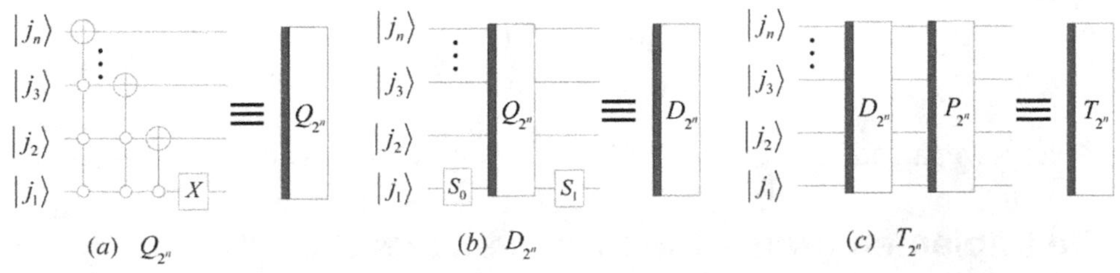

202

Two rotation matrices are defined by

$$S_0 = \begin{bmatrix} \sin\dfrac{2\pi}{3} & \cos\dfrac{2\pi}{3} \\ \cos\dfrac{2\pi}{3} & -\sin\dfrac{2\pi}{3} \end{bmatrix}, S_1 = \begin{bmatrix} -\sin\dfrac{5\pi}{12} & \cos\dfrac{5\pi}{12} \\ \cos\dfrac{5\pi}{12} & \sin\dfrac{5\pi}{12} \end{bmatrix}. \tag{6.24}$$

Since $C_0 = \sqrt{2-\sqrt{3}} \times X \times S_0$ and $C_1 = \sqrt{2+\sqrt{3}} \times S_1$, D_{2^n} and T_{2^n} are rewritten by

$$D_{2^n} = \left(I_{2^{n-1}} \otimes S_1\right) Q_{2^n} \left(I_{2^{n-1}} \otimes S_0\right), \tag{6.25}$$

and

$$T_{2^n} = P_{2^{n-1},2} D_{2^n}, \tag{6.26}$$

where $n \geq 2$. Their implementation circuits are shown in Figure 9 (b) and (c).
The inverse of Q_{2^n} is calculated by

$$\left(Q_{2^n}\right)^{-1} = \left[\left\{\left(Q_{2^{n-1}}\right)^{-1}, I_{2^{n-1}}\right\} \otimes I_2\right]\left(I_{2^{n-1}} \otimes X\right) = V_1^0\left(\left(Q_{2^{n-1}}\right)^{-1}\right)\left(I_{2^{n-1}} \otimes X\right), \tag{6.27}$$

where the initial value is $(Q_2)^{-1}=X$, and its implementation circuit is shown in Figure 10 (a).
Since $(S_1)^{-1}=S_1$ and $(S_0)^{-1}=S_0$, we get

Figure 10. The quantum circuits of $\left(Q_{2^n}\right)^{-1}, \left(D_{2^n}\right)^{-1}$ and $\left(T_{2^n}\right)^{-1}$ with $n \geq 2$

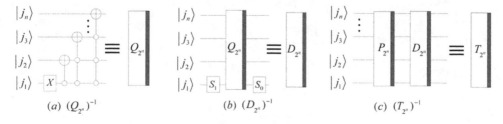

$$\left(D_{2^n}\right)^{-1} = \left(I_{2^{n-1}} \otimes S_0\right)\left(Q_{2^n}\right)^{-1}\left(I_{2^{n-1}} \otimes S_1\right), \tag{6.28}$$

$$\left(T_{2^n}\right)^{-1} = \left(D_{2^n}\right)^{-1} P_{2,2^{n-1}}, \tag{6.29}$$

where $n \geq 2$. Their implementation circuits are designed in Figure 10 (b) and (c). The implementation codes of Q_{2^n}, D_{2^n}, and their inverses are seen in Code B.47 - Code B.50.

The Circuit of the Single-Level D4QWT Based on Periodization Extension

Since the size of the single-level D4QWT defined in (6.19) is finite, its input should be extended by extension methods, such as zero-padding extension and circular extension (Karlsson & Vetterli, 1989).

Suppose that the input is a column vector $V = \begin{bmatrix} v_1 & v_2 & \cdots & v_{2^n} \end{bmatrix}^T$, then the extended vectors are

$$V_e = \begin{cases} \begin{bmatrix} 0 & 0 & v_1 & v_2 & \cdots & v_{2^n} \end{bmatrix}^T, \text{Zero-padding extension,} \\ \begin{bmatrix} v_{2^n} & v_1 & v_2 & \cdots & v_{2^n} & v_1 \end{bmatrix}^T, \text{Circular extension,} \end{cases} \tag{6.30}$$

where the extension length is 2 for the D4 wavelet scaling filter (Ruch & Van Fleet, 2011).

Quantum circuits require that the lengths of the input and the output are equal, so the two extension methods in (6.30) are not suitable for D4QWT.

By the periodization extension method, the vector $V = \begin{bmatrix} v_1 & v_2 & \cdots & v_{2^n} \end{bmatrix}^T$ is changed into

$$V_p = \begin{bmatrix} v_{2^n} & v_1 & v_2 & \cdots & v_{2^n-1} \end{bmatrix}^T. \tag{6.31}$$

Suppose

$$T_{2^n} v_p = \begin{bmatrix} A \\ B \end{bmatrix}, \tag{6.32}$$

where A and B are two $2^{n-1} \times 1$ vectors, then, applying T_{2^n+2} on the vector V_e with circular extension gives

$$T_{2^n+2} V_e = \begin{bmatrix} A \\ h_2 v_{2^n} + h_3 v_1 + h_0 v_{2^n} + h_1 v_1 \\ B \\ h_1 v_{2^n} - h_0 v_1 + h_3 v_{2^n} - h_2 v_1 \end{bmatrix}. \tag{6.33}$$

Comparing (6.32) with (6.33), the elements in $T_{2^n+2} V_e$ are equal to the ones in $T_{2^n} V_p$ except for the $(2^{n-1}+1)$-th and (2^n+2)-the elements. Furthermore, the $(2^{n-1}+1)$-th and (2^n+2)-th rows of $T_{2^n+2} V_e$ are just the wrapping rows of D4 wavelet transform when the input vector isn't infinite (Ruch & Van Fleet, 2011). Hence, the circular extension can be changed to periodization extension by transforming the input vector V into V_p.

Since $(Q_{2^n})^{-1} V = V_p$, the single-level D4QWT based on periodization extension can be defined as

$$F_{2^n} = T_{2^n} (Q_{2^n})^{-1} = P_{2^{n-1},2} D_{2^n} \left(Q_{2^n} \right)^{-1}, \tag{6.34}$$

and its inverse is

$$\left(F_{2^n} \right)^{-1} = Q_{2^n} \left(T_{2^n} \right)^{-1} = Q_{2^n} \left(D_{2^n} \right)^{-1} P_{2,2^{n-1}}. \tag{6.35}$$

Let $D_{2^n}^p = D_{2^n} \left(Q_{2^n} \right)^{-1}$ and $\left(D_{2^n}^p \right)^{-1} = Q_{2^n} \left(D_{2^n} \right)^{-1}$, then, we have

$$\begin{cases} F_{2^n} = P_{2^{n-1},2} D_{2^n}^p, \\ \left(F_{2^n} \right)^{-1} = \left(D_{2^n}^p \right)^{-1} P_{2,2^{n-1}}. \end{cases} \tag{6.36}$$

The circuits of F_{2^n}, $D_{2^n}^p$ and their inverses are designed in Figure 11.

Figure 11. The circuits of F_{2^n}, $D_{2^n}^p$ and their inverses

(a) $D_{2^n}^p$ (b) $(D_{2^n}^p)^{-1}$ (c) F_{2^n} (d) $(F_{2^n})^{-1}$

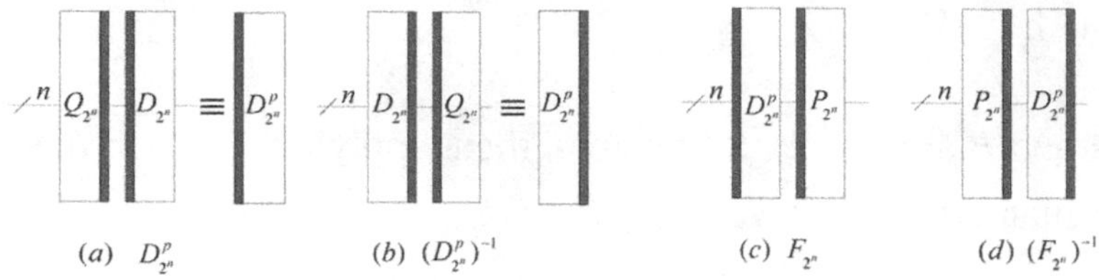

The Multi-Level D4QWT Based on Periodization Extension

Substituting the kernel matrix W_{2^n} with $F_{2^n} = P_{2^{n-1},2} D_{2^n}^p$ in (6.7), the $(k+1)$-level D4QWT based on periodization extension is given by

$$F_{2^n}^k = P_{2^{n-1},2}\left(\left\{F_{2^{n-1}}^{k-1}, I_{2^{n-1}}\right\} \otimes I_2\right) D_{2^n}^p, \tag{6.37}$$

where the initial value is

$$F_{2^{n-k}}^0 = F_{2^{n-k}} = P_{2^{n-k-1},2} D_{2^{n-k}}^p$$

with $1 \leq k \leq n-2$, and its implementation circuit is shown in Figure 12. The circuit in the dashed box implements $F_{2^{n-1}}^{k-1}$.

Substituting $\left(W_{2^n}\right)^{-1}$ with $\left(F_{2^n}\right)^{-1}$ in (6.9), The inverse of the $(k+1)$-level D4QWT is

Figure 12. The circuit of $F_{2^n}^k$.

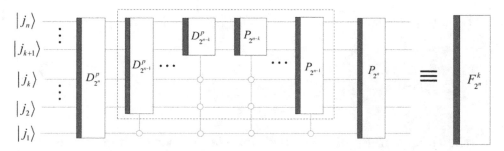

$$\left(F_{2^n}^k\right)^{-1} = \left(D_{2^n}^p\right)^{-1}\left(\left\{\left(F_{2^{n-1}}^{k-1}\right)^{-1}, I_{2^{n-1}}\right\} \otimes I_2\right)P_{2,2^{n-1}}, \tag{6.38}$$

where the initial value is

$$\left(F_{2^{n-k}}^0\right)^{-1} = \left(D_{2^{n-k}}^p\right)^{-1} P_{2,2^{n-k-1}}$$

with $1 \leq k \leq n-2$, and its implementation circuit is shown in Figure 13. The circuit in the dashed box implements $\left(F_{2^{n-1}}^{k-1}\right)^{-1}$.

Figure 13. The quantum circuits of $\left(F_{2^n}\right)^{-1}$.

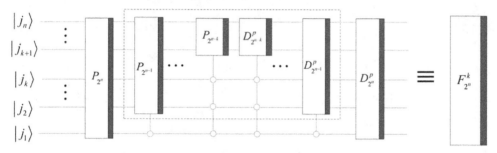

The implementation codes of $D_{2^n}^p$, $F_{2^n}^k$, and their inverses are seen in Code B.51 - Code B.54.

THE COMPLEXITY ANALYSIS

In this section, we use lemmas and corollaries in Chapter 2 to analyze complexities of quantum wavelet transforms.

The Complexity of HQWT

Single-level HQWT $H_{2^n}^0$ consists of $P_{2^{n-1},2}$ and $I_{2^{n-1}} \otimes H$, so the complexity of $H_{2^n}^0$ is $O(n)$. For multi-level HQWT, we firstly analyze the complexity of $SH_{2^n}^{n-1}$ in Figure 6. We adopt the notation $\Lambda_m(Swap)$ to denote an n-qubit controlled-*Swap* gate with m control qubits. $\Lambda_m(Swap)$ can be simulated by one $\Lambda_{m+1}(\sigma_x)$ gate and two 1-quit controlled-NOT gates. For instance, $V_m^0(Swap \otimes I_{2^{n-m-2}})$ and $C_m^0(I_{2^{n-m}} \otimes Swap)$ can be simulated by the circuits in Figure 14. By Corollary 2.14 and Corollary 2.16, we give the following two corollaries.

Figure 14. Simulated networks of $V_m^0(Swap \otimes I_{2^{n-m-2}})$ and $C_m^0(I_{2^{n-m}} \otimes Swap)$ gates.

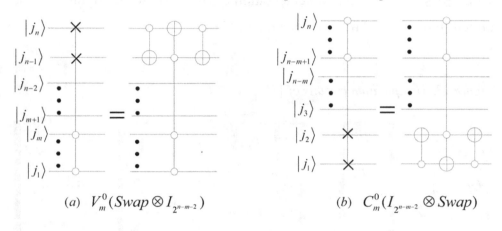

(a) $V_m^0(Swap \otimes I_{2^{n-m-2}})$ (b) $C_m^0(I_{2^{n-m-2}} \otimes Swap)$

Corollary 6.1. When $m<n-2$, the complexity of a $\Lambda_m(Swap)$ gate is $O(n)$.

Corollary 6.2. The complexity of a $\Lambda_{n-2}(Swap)$ gate is $O(n^2)$.

Corollary 6.3. When $1\leq m<n-2$, complexities of $V_m^0(P_{2^{n-m-1},2})$ and $C_m^0(P_{2^{n-m-1},2})$ are both $O(n^2)$.

Proof. Since $P_{2^{n-1},2}|j_n \cdots j_2 j_1\rangle = |j_1 j_n \cdots j_2\rangle$ (see (5.4)), and

$$\left[Swa(n)(P_{2^{n-2},2} \otimes I)\right]|j_n \cdots j_3 j_2 j_1\rangle = Swa(n)|j_2 j_n \cdots j_3 j_1\rangle = |j_1 j_n \cdots j_3 j_2\rangle,$$

$$(6.39)$$

Since

$$P_{2^{n-1},2} = Swa(n)(P_{2^{n-2},2} \otimes I),$$

where $Swa(n)$ is an n-qubit Swap gate, we have

$$V_m^0(P_{2^{n-m-1},2}) = V_m^0\left[Swa(n-m)(P_{2^{n-m-2},2} \otimes I)\right] = V_m^0\left[Swa(n-m)\right]V_m^0\left[(P_{2^{n-m-2},2} \otimes I)\right].$$

$$(6.40)$$

$V_m^0\left[(P_{2^{n-m-2},2} \otimes I)\right]$ can be simulated by the circuit in the dashed box in Figure 15 (a), so the simulated network of $V_m^0(P_{2^{n-m-1},2})$ is shown in Figure 15 (a). Similarly, the simulated network *of* $C_m^0(P_{2^{n-m-1},2})$ is designed in Figure 15 (b). From Figure 2 and Figure 3, we obtain that the $P_{2^{n-m-1},2}$ gate consists of $(n-m-1)$ $Swa(n-m)$ gates, so $V_1^0(P_{2^{n-m-1},2})$ and $C_1^0(P_{2^{n-m-1},2})$ consist of $(n-m-1)$ controlled $Swa(n-m)$ gates, and their complexities are both $O(n)$. By Corollary 2.14 and Corollary 6.1, complexities of $V_m^0(P_{2^{n-m-1},2})$ and $C_m^0(P_{2^{n-m-1},2})$ are both $O(n^2)$.

Figure 15. Simulated networks of $V_m^0(P_{2^{n-m-1},2})$ *and* $C_m^0(P_{2^{n-m-1},2})$ *with* $1 \le m < n-2$.

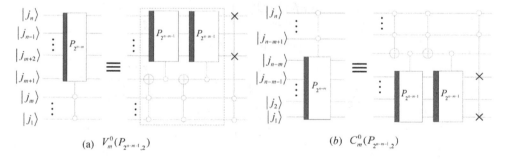

(a) $V_m^0(P_{2^{n-m-1},2})$ (b) $C_m^0(P_{2^{n-m-1},2})$

The circuit in the dashed box 2 in Figure 6 consists of one H gate, $(n-2)$ $\Lambda_m(H)$ gates with $m < n-1$, and one $\Lambda_{n-1}(H)$ gate, so its complexity is $O(n^2)$ by Corollary 2.14 and Corollary 2.16. The circuit in the dashed box 3 in Figure 6 consists of one $\Lambda_{n-2}(Swap)$ gate, $(n-3)$ $V_m^0(P_{2^{n-m-1},2})$ gates with $1 \le m < n-1$, and one $P_{2^{n-1},2}$ gate, thus, its complexity is $O(n^2)$ by Corollary 6.2 and Corollary 6.3. In conclusion, the complexity of $H_{2^n}^{n-1}$ in Figure 6 is $O(n^2)$. Similarly, the complexity of $H_{2^n}^{n-1}$ in Figure 5 is also $O(n^2)$.

Comparing between the circuit in Figure 4 and the one in Figure 6, $SH_{2^n}^k$ has only a $V_{n-1}^0(H)$ gate less than $SH_{2^n}^{n-1}$ when $k=n-2$, so the complexity of $SH_{2^n}^k$ is $O(n^2)$. Similarly, the complexity of $FH_{2^n}^k$ in Figure 3 is also $O(n^2)$.

Since The inverse of HQWT consists of the same gates with HQWT, $\left(H_{2^n}^k\right)^{-1}$ and $\left(H_{2^n}^{n-1}\right)^{-1}$ can be both simulated by $O(n^2)$ basic operations, respectively.

The Complexity of D4QWT

By Corollary 2.14 and Corollary 2.16, complexities of Q_{2^n} and $\left(Q_{2^n}\right)^{-1}$ are both v. In addition, complexities of D_{2^n}, T_{2^n}, $D_{2^n}^p$, F_{2^n} and their inverse transforms are all $O(n^2)$, i.e., the complexity of single-level D4QWT is $O(n^2)$.

The detail circuit of $V_m^0(D_{2^{n-m}}^p)$ is shown in Figure 16, and the quantum circuit in the dashed box implements $D_{2^{n-m}}^p$.

Figure 16. The quantum circuit of $V_m^0(D_{2^{n-m}}^p)$ with $1 \leq m \leq n-2$.

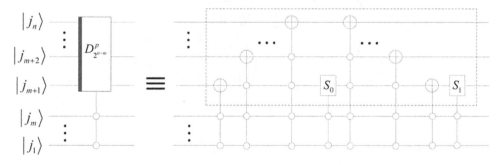

By Corollary 2.14 and Corollary 2.16, the gate $V_m^0(D_{2^{n-m}}^p)$ can be simulated by $O(n^2)$ basic operations where $1 \leq m \leq n-2$. Observing the circuits in Figure 12 and Figure 13, we conclude that complexities of $F_{2^n}^k$ and $\left(F_{2^n}^k\right)^{-1}$ are $O(n^3)$.

THE COMPARISON OF CIRCUITS OF HQWT AND D4QWT

In this section, we analyze and compare the circuits of HQWT and D4QWT in (Hoyer, 1997; Fijany & Williams, 1998; Terraneo & Shepelyansky, 2003) with the proposed ones (Li, Fan, Xia, Song, & He, 2018).

The Comparison of Circuits of HQWT

The circuit of HQWT (Hoyer, 1997) is designed with 3 qubits as an example, and is not implemented with n qubits, therefore we only introduce the circuit of HQWT with n qubits (Fijany & Williams, 1998) as follows.

A factorization of HQWT is defined as

$$
\begin{aligned}
H_{2^n} &= (I_{2^{n-1}} \otimes W) \cdots (I_{2^{n-1}} \otimes W \oplus I_{2^n - 2^{n-i+1}}) \cdots (W \oplus I_{2^n - 2}) \\
&\times (\Pi_4 \oplus I_{2^n - 4}) \cdots (\Pi_{2^i} \oplus I_{2^n - 2^i}) \cdots (\Pi_{2^{n-1}} \oplus I_{2^{n-1}}) \Pi_{2^n},
\end{aligned}
\tag{6.41}
$$

where $W = H$, $\Pi_{2^i} = P_{2^{i-1},2}$, and the symbol $\oplus$ is a conditional operator. Its circuit is shown in Figure 17. The gate in the dashed box is lacking in (Fijany & Williams, 1998).

Figure 17. A circuit for multi-level HQWT

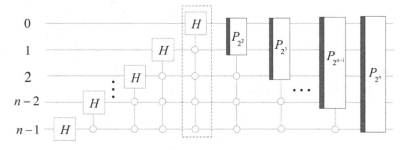

We find that the circuit without the gate in the dashed box in Figure 17 can't implement (6.41). Furthermore, the circuit in Figure 17 is the same with the one in Figure 6. I.e., it is the implementation circuit of the n-level HQWT.

The Comparison of Circuits of D4QWT

The circuit of D4QWT (Terraneo & Shepelyansky, 2003) is designed by optimizing ones of D4QWT in (Hoyer, 1997; Fijany & Williams, 1998), therefore, we only introduce the circuit of D4QWT in (Terraneo & Shepelyansky, 2003) as follows.

The kernel matrix of the D4 wavelet transform is defined by

$$
D_{2^n} = \begin{bmatrix}
c_0 & c_1 & c_2 & c_3 & 0 & 0 & \cdots & 0 & 0 & 0 & 0 \\
c_3 & -c_2 & c_1 & -c_0 & 0 & 0 & \cdots & 0 & 0 & 0 & 0 \\
0 & 0 & c_0 & c_1 & c_2 & c_3 & \cdots & 0 & 0 & 0 & 0 \\
0 & 0 & c_3 & -c_2 & c_1 & -c_0 & \cdots & 0 & 0 & 0 & 0 \\
\vdots & \vdots & \vdots & \vdots & \vdots & \vdots & \ddots & \vdots & \vdots & \vdots & \vdots \\
0 & 0 & 0 & 0 & 0 & 0 & \cdots & c_0 & c_1 & c_2 & c_3 \\
0 & 0 & 0 & 0 & 0 & 0 & \cdots & c_3 & -c_2 & c_1 & -c_0 \\
c_2 & c_3 & 0 & 0 & 0 & 0 & \cdots & 0 & 0 & c_0 & c_1 \\
c_1 & -c_0 & 0 & 0 & 0 & 0 & \cdots & 0 & 0 & c_3 & -c_2
\end{bmatrix}, \tag{6.42}
$$

where $c_0 = \dfrac{1+\sqrt{3}}{4\sqrt{2}}$, $c_1 = \dfrac{3+\sqrt{3}}{4\sqrt{2}}$, $c_2 = \dfrac{3-\sqrt{3}}{4\sqrt{2}}$ and $c_3 = \dfrac{1-\sqrt{3}}{4\sqrt{2}}$.

A factorization of D4QWT is defined as

$$
D_{2^n} = (I_{2^{n-1}} \otimes S_4)\Gamma_{2^n}(X \otimes I_{2^{n-1}})(X \otimes I_{2^{n-2}} \oplus I_{2^{n-2}})\cdots(X \otimes I_2 \oplus I_{2^{n-4}}) \times (X \oplus I_{2^{n}-2})\Gamma_{2^n}(I_{2^{n-1}} \otimes S_3), \tag{6.43}
$$

where the symbol $\oplus$ is a conditional operator, and

$$
\begin{cases}
S_3 = \begin{bmatrix} \sin\dfrac{\pi}{3} & \cos\dfrac{\pi}{3} \\ \cos\dfrac{\pi}{3} & -\sin\dfrac{\pi}{3} \end{bmatrix}, S_4 = \begin{bmatrix} \sin\dfrac{5\pi}{12} & \cos\dfrac{5\pi}{12} \\ \cos\dfrac{5\pi}{12} & -\sin\dfrac{5\pi}{12} \end{bmatrix}, \\
\Gamma_{2^n} = P_{2^{n-1},2}(P_{2^{n-2},2} \otimes I_2)\cdots(P_{2^2,2} \otimes I_{2^{n-3}})(P_{2,2} \otimes I_{2^{n-2}}).
\end{cases} \tag{6.44}
$$

The implementation circuit of (6.43) is shown in Figure 18.

Figure 18. Quantum circuit for the wavelet kernel

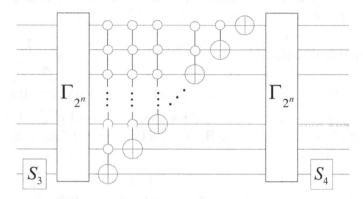

Comparing between two circuits in Figure 9 (b) and Figure 18, we use less gates to implement D_{2^n}. That is, we do not need to use the two circuits of Γ_{2^n} for the implementation of D_{2^n}.

SIMULATIONS OF QUANTUM WAVELET TRANSFORMS

Consider a quantum state

$$|v\rangle = \frac{1}{\sqrt{\sum_{i=0}^{2047}(v_i)^2}}\begin{bmatrix} v_0 & v_1 & \cdots & v_{2047} \end{bmatrix}^T \tag{6.45}$$

as an input of quantum wavelet transforms where $v_k = d(k/2048), k=0,\ldots,2047$, and

$$d(t) = \sqrt{t(1-t)}\,\sin(\frac{2\pi * 1.05}{t + 0.05})$$

is Doppler function (Ruch & Van Fleet, 2011).

For simplicity, we can take a vector

$$V = \begin{bmatrix} v_0 & v_1 & \cdots & v_{2047} \end{bmatrix}^T \tag{6.46}$$

as the input of simulation programs, which is in accord with the state $|v\rangle$ without the normalized item.

Simulations of HQWT

Applying $FH_{2^{11}}^{k}$ with $k=0,1,\ldots,10$ in Figure 3 and Figure 5 on the input V in (6.46) gives the simulation results of the first 3 levels of HQWT with multi-windows in Figure 19 (see Code B.44), and the results of all levels in Figure 20 (see Code B.45).

Figure 19. The simulation results of the first 3 levels of HQWT.

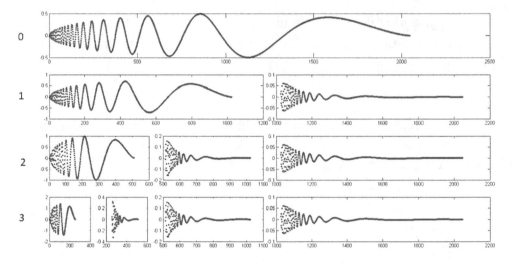

Table 2 shows the comparisons of simulation results of HQWTs, their inverses, and classical Haar wavelet transform using the 2-norm function *norm( )* (see Code B.46). The symbols in this table are listed as follows,

$$
\begin{cases}
F_1 = FH_{2^{11}}^{j} \times V, \\
F_2 = \left(FH_{2^{11}}^{j}\right)^{-1} \times F_1, \\
S_1 = SH_{2^{11}}^{j} \times V, \\
S_2 = \left(SH_{2^{11}}^{j}\right)^{-1} \times S_1, \\
M = wavedec(V, j+1,' haar'),
\end{cases}
\tag{6.47}
$$

Figure 20. Simulation results of HQWT. The left number i refers to i -level QWT with 1≤i≤11, and i = 0 refers to the input signal.

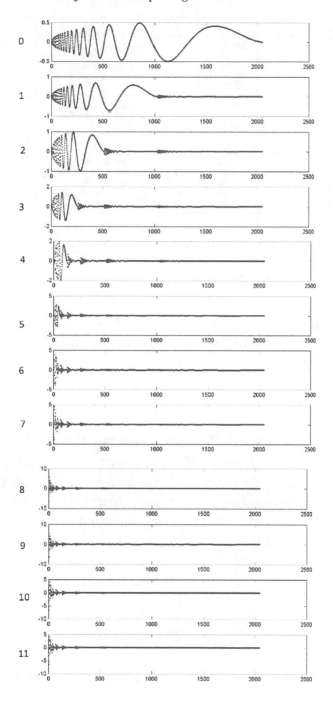

Table 2. The comparisons of HQWTs, their inverse and classical Haar wavelet transform

Level	$norm(F_1 - M)$	$norm(S_1 - M)$	$norm(V - F_2)$	$norm(V - S_2)$
1	0.0123×10^{-13}	0.0123×10^{-13}	0.0218×10^{-13}	0.0218×10^{-13}
2	0.0189×10^{-13}	0.0189×10^{-13}	0.0608×10^{-13}	0.0608×10^{-13}
3	0.0217×10^{-13}	0.0217×10^{-13}	0.0617×10^{-13}	0.0617×10^{-13}
4	0.0297×10^{-13}	0.0297×10^{-13}	0.0607×10^{-13}	0.0601×10^{-13}
5	0.0344×10^{-13}	0.0344×10^{-13}	0.0642×10^{-13}	0.0642×10^{-13}
6	0.0460×10^{-13}	0.0460×10^{-13}	0.0683×10^{-13}	0.0683×10^{-13}
7	0.0743×10^{-13}	0.0743×10^{-13}	0.0820×10^{-13}	0.0820×10^{-13}
8	0.1021×10^{-13}	0.1021×10^{-13}	0.0875×10^{-13}	0.0875×10^{-13}
9	0.1420×10^{-13}	0.1420×10^{-13}	0.1335×10^{-13}	0.1335×10^{-13}
10	0.1619×10^{-13}	0.1619×10^{-13}	0.1399×10^{-13}	0.1399×10^{-13}
11	0.1697×10^{-13}	0.1697×10^{-13}	0.1413×10^{-13}	0.1413×10^{-13}

where the function $wavedec(V, j{+}1, 'haar')$ in Matlab performs a $(j{+}1)$-level one-dimensional wavelet analysis using the Haar wavelet.

Table 2 illustrates that HQWTs and their inverse are correct for the column vector V in (6.46).

Simulations of D4QWT

Applying $F_{2^n}^j$ to the input V in (6.46), the simulation results of the first 3 levels of D4QWT are shown in Figure 21 with multi-windows (see Code B.55), and the results of all levels are shown in Figure 22 (see Code B.56).

Table 3 shows the comparisons of simulation results of D4QWT, its inverse, and classical D4 wavelet transform using the 2-norm function *norm()* (see Code B.57). The symbols in this table are listed as follows,

$$\begin{cases} D_{per} = F_{2^{11}}^j \times V, \\ R_{per} = (F_{2^{11}}^j)^{-1} \times D_{per}, \\ M_{per} = wavedec(V, j{+}1, 'db2'), \end{cases} \qquad (6.48)$$

where the function $wavedec(V, j{+}1, 'db2')$ in Matlab performs a $(j{+}1)$-level D4 wavelet analysis using periodization extension.

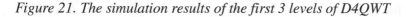

Figure 21. The simulation results of the first 3 levels of D4QWT

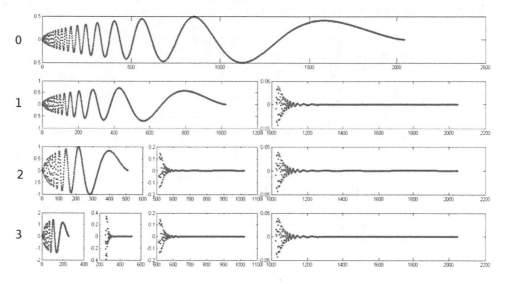

Figure 21, Figure 22, and Table 3 illustrate that D4QWT and its inverse are correct, and can perform the decomposition and reconstruction of D4 wavelet transform for the column vector V in (6.46).

CONCLUSION

In this chapter, multi-level Haar quantum wavelet transforms, multi-level Daubechies D4 quantum wavelet transform and their inverse are described. The implementation circuits of these quantum wavelet transforms are designed. For 2^n data, complexities of Haar quantum wavelet transforms and Daubechies D4 quantum wavelet transform are $O(n^2)$ and $O(n^3)$, so quantum wavelet transforms offer exponential speedup over their classical counterparts.

Figure 22. The simulation results of D4QWT. The left number i refers to i-level QWT with 1≤i≤10, and i=0 refers to the input.

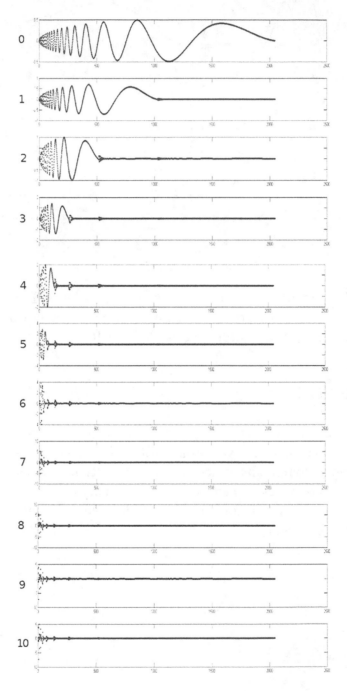

Table 3. The comparisons of D4QWT, its inverse, and classical D4 wavelet transform

Level	$norm(D_{per} - M_{per})$	$norm(D_{per} - M_{per})$
1	0.0057×10^{-10}	0.0246×10^{-13}
2	0.0125×10^{-10}	0.0472×10^{-13}
3	0.0222×10^{-10}	0.0729×10^{-13}
4	0.0352×10^{-10}	0.0927×10^{-13}
5	0.0525×10^{-10}	0.1245×10^{-13}
6	0.0734×10^{-10}	0.1541×10^{-13}
7	0.0973×10^{-10}	0.2044×10^{-13}
8	0.1213×10^{-10}	0.1846×10^{-13}
9	0.1372×10^{-10}	0.1557×10^{-13}
10	0.1435×10^{-10}	0.1702×10^{-13}

REFERENCES

Belazi, A., El-Latif, A. A. A., Diaconu, A. V., Rhouma, R., & Belghith, S. (2017). Chaos-based partial image encryption scheme based on linear fractional and lifting wavelet transforms. *Optics and Lasers in Engineering*, *88*, 37–50. doi:10.1016/j.optlaseng.2016.07.010

Beylkin, G., Coifman, R., & Rokhlin, V. (1991). Fast wavelet transforms and numerical algorithms I. *Communications on Pure and Applied Mathematics*, *44*(2), 141–183. doi:10.1002/cpa.3160440202

Fijany, A., & Williams, C. P. (1998). Quantum wavelet transforms: Fast algorithms and complete circuits. *NASA International Conference on Quantum Computing and Quantum Communications*, 10-33.

Fino, B. J., & Algazi, V. R. (1977). A unified treatment of discrete fast unitary transforms. *SIAM Journal on Computing*, *6*(4), 700–717. doi:10.1137/0206051

Hoyer, P. (1997). *Efficient quantum transforms*. arXiv preprint quant-ph/9702028

Karlsson, G., & Vetterli, M. (1989). Extension of finite length signals for sub-band coding. *Signal Processing*, *17*(2), 161–168. doi:10.1016/0165-1684(89)90019-4

Li, H. S., Fan, P., Xia, H. Y., & Song, S. X. (2019). Quantum multi-level wavelet transforms. *Information Sciences*, *504*, 113–115. doi:10.1016/j. ins.2019.07.057

Makbol, N. M., Khoo, B. E., Rassem, T. H., & Loukhaoukha, K. (2017). A new reliable optimized image watermarking scheme based on the integer wavelet transform and singular value decomposition for copyright protection. *Information Sciences*, *417*, 381–400. doi:10.1016/j.ins.2017.07.026

Mallat, S. G. (1989). A theory for multiresolution signal decomposition: The wavelet representation. *IEEE Transactions on Pattern Analysis and Machine Intelligence*, *11*(7), 674–693. doi:10.1109/34.192463

Ruch, D. K., & Van Fleet, P. J. (2011). *Wavelet theory: an elementary approach with applications*. John Wiley & Sons.

Terraneo, M., & Shepelyansky, D. L. (2003). *Imperfection effects for multiple applications of the quantum wavelet transform*. ArXiv preprint arXiv: quant-ph/ 0303043

Chapter 6
Quantum Wavelet
Packet Transforms

ABSTRACT

Quantum wavelet packet transform (QWPT) may play an important role in quantum information processing. In this chapter, the authors design quantum circuits of a generalized tensor product (GTP) and a perfect shuffle permutation (PSP). Next, they propose multi-level and multi-dimensional (1D, 2D and 3D) QWPTs, including Haar QWPT (HQWPT), D4 QWPT (DQWPT) based on the periodization extension and their inverse transforms for the first time, and prove the correctness based on the GTP and PSP. Furthermore, they analyze the quantum costs and the time complexities of the proposed QWPTs and obtain precise results. The time complexities of HQWPTs is at most six basic operations on 2n elements, which illustrates high efficiency of the proposed QWPTs.

INTRODUCTION

Quantum wavelet packet transform (QWPT) can be classified with one-dimensional or multi-dimensional according to the types of data it acts on are 1-dimension or multi-dimension. The QWPT can be used repeatedly. The level of QWPT describes the number of times QWPT acts on data. Two 1-dimensional QWPTs have been developed, which are the single-level 1-dimensional Haar QWPT, and the single-level 1-dimensional Daubechies D4 QWPT, respectively (Hoyer, 1997; Fijany & Williams, 1998; Terraneo

DOI: 10.4018/978-1-7998-3799-2.ch006

& Shepelyansky, 2003; Klappenecker, 1999). In addition, multi-level and multi-dimensional QWPTs were proposed (Li, Fan, Xia, Song, & He, 2018).

This chapter introduces multi-level and multi-dimensional QWPTs (Li, Fan, Xia, Song, & He, 2018), and uses 2-dimensional quantum wavelet packet transforms to implement quantum image compression (Li, Zhu, Zhou, Li, Song, & Ian, 2014). Meanwhile, simulations of multi-level and multi-dimensional QWPTs are given.

1-DIMENSIONAL QUANTUM WAVELET PACKET TRANSFORMS

In this section, multi-level 1-dimensional quantum wavelet packet transforms (1D-QWPTs) are introduced. These 1D-QWPTs include 1-dimensional general quantum wavelet packet transform, 1-dimensional Haar quantum wavelet packet transform (1D-HQWPT), and 1-dimensional Daubechies D4 quantum wavelet packet transform (1D-D4QWPT).

1-Dimensional General Quantum Wavelet Packet Transform

Let $W_{2^n}^0 = W_{2^n}$ be a wavelet kernel matrix. Then, the $(k+1)$-level iteration of a discrete wavelet packet transform is defined by (Ruch, & Van Fleet, 2011)

$$\begin{cases} Z_{2^n}^k = W_{2^n}^k W_{2^n}^{k-1} \ldots W_{2^n}^1 W_{2^n}^0, \\ W_{2^n}^j = Diag(W_{2^{n-j}}, W_{2^{n-j}}, \ldots, W_{2^{n-j}}), \end{cases} \tag{7.1}$$

where $Diag(W_{2^{n-j}}, W_{2^{n-j}}, \ldots, W_{2^{n-j}})$ with $j=1,\ldots,k$ is a matrix with 2^j blocks of $W_{2^{n-j}}$ on the main diagonal and zeros elsewhere. We infer the following equations,

$$\begin{cases} W_{2^n}^j = Diag(W_{2^n}^{j-1}, W_{2^n}^{j-1}), \\ Z_{2^n}^k = Diag(Z_{2^{n-1}}^{k-1}, Z_{2^{n-1}}^{k-1})W_{2^n}. \end{cases} \tag{7.2}$$

According to the generalized tensor product in (5.12), we have

$$Z_{2^{n-1}}^{k-1} \otimes I_2 = P_{2,2^{n-1}} Diag(Z_{2^{n-1}}^{k-1}, Z_{2^{n-1}}^{k-1}) P_{2^{n-1},2}.$$ (7.3)

The iteration of QWPT is given by

$$Z_{2^n}^k = P_{2^{n-1},2}\left(Z_{2^{n-1}}^{k-1} \otimes I_2\right) P_{2,2^n} W_{2^n}$$ (7.4)

with the initial value $Z_{2^{n-k}}^0 = W_{2^{n-k}}$. Its implemented circuit is shown in Figure 1 (a). The inverse of $Z_{2^n}^k$ is calculated by

$$(Z_{2^n}^k)^{-1} = (W_{2^n})^{-1} P_{2^{n-1},2} ((Z_{2^{n-1}}^{k-1})^{-1} \otimes I_2) P_{2,2^{n-1}}$$ (7.5)

with the initial value $\left(Z_{2^{n-k}}^0\right)^{-1} = \left(W_{2^{n-k}}\right)^{-1}$. The implemented circuit of $\left(Z_{2^n}^k\right)^{-1}$ is shown in Figure 1 (b).

Figure 1. The implemented circuits of $Z_{2^n}^k$ and $\left(Z_{2^n}^k\right)^{-1}$.

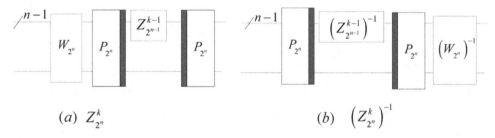

(a) $Z_{2^n}^k$ (b) $\left(Z_{2^n}^k\right)^{-1}$

1D-HQWPT and Its Inverse

Substituting the kernel matrix $W_{2^n} = P_{2^{n-1},2}\left(I_{2^{n-1}} \otimes H\right)$ into (7.4) and (7.5), the $(k+1)$-level iteration of Haar quantum wavelet packet transform (HQWPT) and its inverse are

$$\begin{cases} R_{2^n}^k = P_{2^{n-1},2}\left(R_{2^{n-1}}^{k-1} \otimes I_2\right)\left(I_{2^{n-1}} \otimes H\right), \\ \left(R_{2^n}^k\right)^{-1} = \left(I_{2^{n-1}} \otimes H\right)\left[\left(R_{2^{n-1}}^{k-1}\right)^{-1} \otimes I_2\right] P_{2,2^{n-1}} \end{cases}$$ (7.6)

with the initial values

$$\begin{cases} R^0_{2^{n-k}} = P_{2^{n-k-1},2}\left(I_{2^{n-k-1}} \otimes H\right), & 1 \le k < n-1, \\ \left(R^0_{2^{n-k}}\right)^{-1} = \left(H \otimes I_{2^{n-k-1}}\right)P_{2,2^{n-k-1}}, & 1 \le k < n-1, \\ R^0_2 = \left(R^0_2\right)^{-1} = H, & k = n-1. \end{cases} \quad (7.7)$$

The circuits of $R^{n-1}_{2^n}$ and $R^k_{2^n}$ $(1 \le k < n-1)$ are designed in Figure 2. The dashed boxes 1 and boxes 2 are the circuits of $R^{n-2}_{2^{n-1}}$ and $R^{k-1}_{2^{n-1}}$, respectively.

Figure 2. The circuits of $R^{n-1}_{2^n}$ and $R^k_{2^n}$.

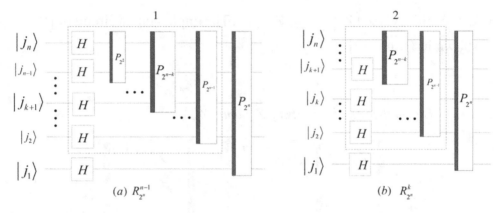

(a) $R^{n-1}_{2^n}$ (b) $R^k_{2^n}$

From (5.5) and (5.6), we obtain

$$\begin{cases} P_{2^{n-1},2}(P_{2^{n-2},2} \otimes I_2)\dots(P_{2,2} \otimes I_{2^{n-2}}) = \Gamma_{2^n}, \\ P_{2^{n-1},2}(P_{2^{n-2},2} \otimes I_2)\dots(P_{2^{n-k-1},2} \otimes I_{2^k}) = \Gamma_{2^n}(\Gamma^{-1}_{2^{n-k-1}} \otimes I_{2^{k+1}}), \end{cases} \quad (7.8)$$

therefore, quantum circuits of $R^k_{2^n}$ with $0 \le k < n-2$, $R^{n-2}_{2^n}$ and $R^{n-1}_{2^n}$ can be simplified into the ones in Figure 3. Their implementation codes are seen in Code B.58 and Code B.59.

Similarly, the circuits of the inverses of $R^k_{2^n}$, $R^{n-2}_{2^n}$ and $R^{n-1}_{2^n}$ can be designed as shown in Figure 4.

Figure 3 and Figure 4 show that complexities of multi-level HQWPT and its inverse are $O(n)$.

Figure 3. The simplified circuits of $R_{2^n}^k$ with $0 \leq k < n - 2$, $R_{2^n}^{n-2}$ and $R_{2^n}^{n-1}$

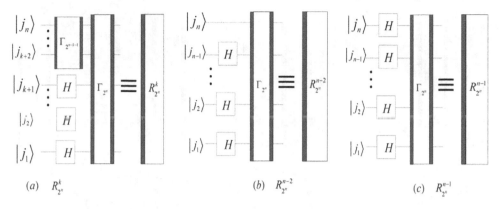

(a) $R_{2^n}^k$

(b) $R_{2^n}^{n-2}$

(c) $R_{2^n}^{n-1}$

1D-D4QWPT and Its Inverse

Since a single-level quantum wavelet packet transform is also a single-level quantum wavelet transform, the single-level Daubechies D4 quantum wavelet packet transform (D4QWPT) based on periodization extension and its inverse can be defined as F_{2^n} and $(F_{2^n})^{-1}$ in (6.36), i.e.,

$$\begin{cases} F_{2^n} = P_{2^{n-1},2} D_{2^n}^p, \\ (F_{2^n})^{-1} = (D_{2^n}^p)^{-1} P_{2,2^{n-1}}, \end{cases} \tag{7.9}$$

Figure 4. The circuits of $(R_{2^n}^k)^{-1}$ with $0 \leq k < n - 2$, $(R_{2^n}^{n-2})^{-1}$ and $(R_{2^n}^{n-1})^{-1}$.

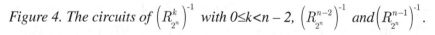

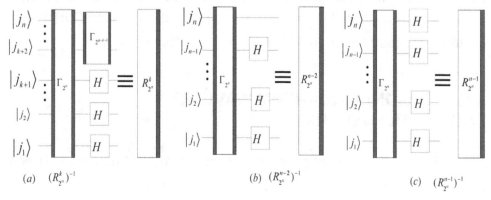

(a) $(R_{2^n}^k)^{-1}$

(b) $(R_{2^n}^{n-2})^{-1}$

(c) $(R_{2^n}^{n-1})^{-1}$

Figure 5. The circuits of $A_{2^n}^k$ and $(A_{2^n}^k)^{-1}$ with $1 \le k < n - 1$.

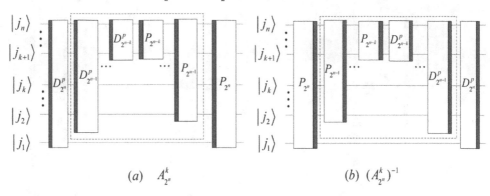

(a) $\quad A_{2^n}^k$ $\qquad\qquad\qquad\qquad$ (b) $\quad (A_{2^n}^k)^{-1}$

where the circuits of F_{2^n}, $D_{2^n}^p$, and their inverse are shown in Figure 6.11.

Substituting the kernel matrix $W_{2^n} = F_{2^n}$ into (7.4) and (7.5), we obtain the $(k+1)$-level iterations of D4QWPT based on periodization extension and its inverse as follows,

$$\begin{cases} A_{2^n}^k = P_{2^{n-1},2}\left(A_{2^{n-1}}^{k-1} \otimes I_2\right) D_{2^n}^p, \\ (A_{2^n}^k)^{-1} = (D_{2^n}^p)^{-1}\left[(A_{2^{n-1}}^{k-1})^{-1} \otimes I_2\right] P_{2,2^{n-1}}, \end{cases} \qquad (7.10)$$

with the initial values $A_{2^{n-k}}^0 = F_{2^{n-k}}$, and $(A_{2^{n-k}}^0)^{-1} = (F_{2^{n-k}})^{-1}$. When $1 \le k < n-1$, the circuits of $A_{2^n}^k$ and $(A_{2^n}^k)^{-1}$ are designed in Figure 5. The dotted boxes in (a) and (b) are the circuits of $A_{2^{n-1}}^{k-1}$ and $\left(A_{2^{n-1}}^{k-1}\right)^{-1}$, respectively.

By (7.8), the circuits of $A_{2^n}^k$ and $(A_{2^n}^k)^{-1}$ can be simplified into the ones in Figure 6. Their implementation codes are seen in Code B.60 band Code B.61.

Since complexities of $D_{2^n}^p$ and Γ_{2^n} are respectively $O(n^2)$ and $O(n)$, Figure 6 shows that complexities of $A_{2^n}^k$ and $(A_{2^n}^k)^{-1}$ are both $O(n^3)$.

2-DIMENSIONAL QUANTUM WAVELET PACKET TRANSFORMS

The 2-dimensional wavelet packet transform on $\Lambda_{2^m,2^k}$ is defined as (Ruch, & Van Fleet, 2011)

Figure 6. The simplified circuits of $A_{2^n}^k$ and $(A_{2^n}^k)^{-1}$ with $0 \leq k < n-1$

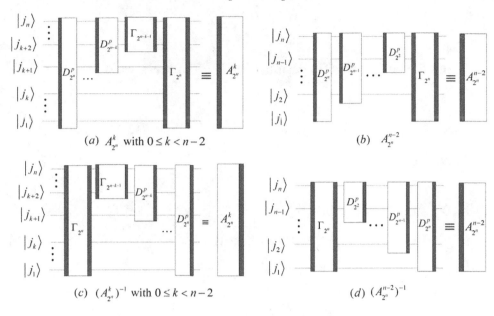

(a) $A_{2^n}^k$ with $0 \leq k < n-2$

(b) $A_{2^n}^{n-2}$

(c) $(A_{2^n}^k)^{-1}$ with $0 \leq k < n-2$

(d) $(A_{2^n}^{n-2})^{-1}$

$$wt2(\Lambda_{2^m,2^k}) = W_{2^m} \times \Lambda_{2^m,2^k} \times (W_{2^k})^T, \tag{7.11}$$

where $\Lambda_{2^n,2^m}$ is a $2^m \times 2^k$ image in (5.53), and W_{2^m} and W_{2^k} are $2^m \times 2^m$ and $2^k \times 2^k$ wavelet packet transforms, respectively

An image can be stored in the state NASS $|\psi_2\rangle$ in (3.58) by using the function $f(\bullet)$, which is equivalent to the quantum circuit in Figure 3.9, i.e.,

$$f(\Lambda_{2^m,2^k}) = |\psi_2\rangle = \begin{bmatrix} B_1^T \\ \vdots \\ B_{2^m}^T \end{bmatrix}, \tag{7.12}$$

where B_j with $j=1,\ldots,2^m$ are the row vectors of $\Lambda_{2^n,2^m}$.

Applying the function $f(\bullet)$ on $\Lambda_{2^m,2^k} \times (W_{2^k})^T$ and $(\Lambda_{2^m,2^k})^T \times (W_{2^m})^T$, we have

$$\begin{cases} f(\Lambda_{2^m,2^k} \times (W_{2^k})^T) = \left(I_{2^m} \otimes W_{2^k}\right) f(\Lambda_{2^m,2^k}), \\ f\left((\Lambda_{2^m,2^k})^T \times (W_{2^m})^T\right) = \left(I_{2^k} \otimes W_{2^m}\right) f((\Lambda_{2^m,2^k})^T). \end{cases} \tag{7.13}$$

Using the perfect shuffle permutation $P_{2^k,2^m}$ in (5.9), we obtain

$$f\left((\Lambda_{2^m,2^k})^T\right) = P_{2^m,2^k} f(\Lambda_{2^m,2^k}). \tag{7.14}$$

Then, we calculate

$$\begin{aligned} f(W_{2^m}\Lambda_{2^m,2^k}) &= f\left(\left[(\Lambda_{2^m,2^k})^T \times (W_{2^m})^T\right]^T\right) \\ &= P_{2^k,2^m} f\left((\Lambda_{2^m,2^k})^T \times (W_{2^m})^T\right) = P_{2^k,2^m}\left(I_{2^k} \otimes W_{2^m}\right) f((\Lambda_{2^m,2^k})^T) \\ &= P_{2^k,2^m}\left(I_{2^k} \otimes W_{2^m}\right) P_{2^m,2^k} f(\Lambda_{2^m,2^k}) = \left(W_{2^m} \otimes I_{2^k}\right) f(\Lambda_{2^m,2^k}). \end{aligned} \tag{7.15}$$

Combining (7.13) and (7.15), we infer

$$f(W_{2^m}\Lambda_{2^m,2^k}(W_{2^m})^T) = \left(W_{2^m} \otimes W_{2^k}\right) f(\Lambda_{2^m,2^k}). \tag{7.16}$$

Therefore, the 2-dimensional quantum wavelet packet transform (2D-QWPT) of $\Lambda_{2^m,2^k}$ is given by

$$f\left(wt2(\Lambda_{2^m,2^k})\right) = \left(W_{2^m} \otimes W_{2^k}\right)\left|\psi_2\right\rangle. \tag{7.17}$$

Since the equation

$$(W_{2^m} \otimes W_{2^k})\left[(W_{2^m})^{-1} \otimes (W_{2^k})^{-1}\right] = I_{2^m} \otimes I_{2^k} = I_{2^{m+k}}$$

holds, the inverse of 2D-QWPT of $\Lambda_{2^m,2^k}$ is

$$\left[(W_{2^m})^{-1} \otimes (W_{2^k})^{-1}\right]\left|\psi_2\right\rangle. \tag{7.18}$$

Substituting 1D-HQWPT and 1D-D4QWPT into (7.17), we obtain $(h+1)$-level 2D-HQWPT and $(l+1)$-level 2D-D4QWPT of $\Lambda_{2^m,2^k}$ as follows,

$$\left[\begin{matrix} \left(R^h_{2^m} \otimes R^h_{2^k}\right)|\psi_2\rangle, \\ \left(A^l_{2^m} \otimes A^l_{2^k}\right)|\psi_2\rangle, \end{matrix}\right. \tag{7.19}$$

where $0 \leq h \leq \min(m,k) - 1$ and $0 \leq l \leq \min(m,k) - 2$. Similarly, the inverses of $(h+1)$-level 2D-HQWPT and $(l+1)$-level 2D-D4QWPT of $\Lambda_{2^m,2^k}$ are given by

$$\left[\begin{matrix} \left[(R^h_{2^m})^{-1} \otimes (R^h_{2^k})^{-1}\right]|\psi_2\rangle, \\ \left[(A^l_{2^m})^{-1} \otimes (A^l_{2^k})^{-1}\right]|\psi_2\rangle. \end{matrix}\right. \tag{7.20}$$

When $h=0$ and $l=0$, by (7.19) and (7.20), we design the circuits of single-level 2D-HQWPT, single-level 2D-D4QWPT and their inverses in Figure 7.

Figure 7. The circuits of single-level 2D-HQWPT, single-level 2D-D4QWPT and their inverses

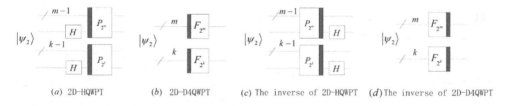

(a) 2D–HQWPT　　　(b) 2D–D4QWPT　　　(c) The inverse of 2D–HQWPT　　(d) The inverse of 2D–D4QWPT

When $h>0$ and $l>0$, the circuits of multi-level 2D-HQWPT, multi-level 2D-D4QWPT and their inverses are given in Figure 8. The implementation codes of 1D-HQWPT, 2D-D4QWPT and their inverse are designed in Code B.66 - Code B.69.

Since the complexity of 1D-HQWPT is $O(n)$, from Figure 7 and Figure 8, we obtain the complexity of 2D-HQWPT is also $O(n)$.

Figure 7 shows that the complexity of single-level 2D-D4QWPT is $O(n^2)$. Since the complexity of 1D-D4QWPT is $O(n^3)$, from Figure 8, we conclude that the complexity of multi-level 2D-D4QWPT is also $O(n^3)$.

Figure 8. The circuits of multi-level 2D-HQWPT, multi-level 2D-D4QWPT and their inverses

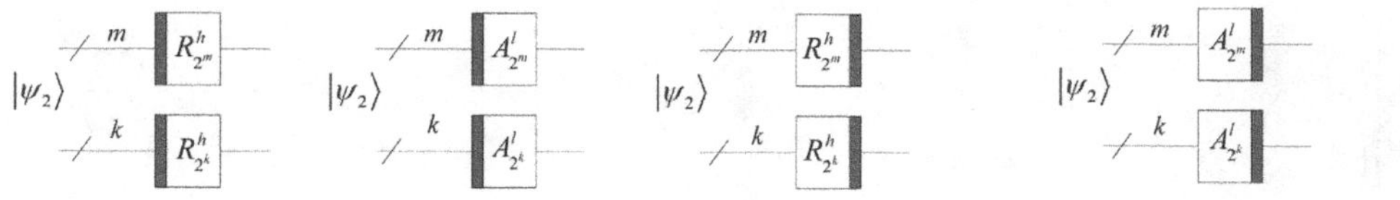

(a) 2D–HQWPT   (b) 2D–D4QWPT   (c) The inverse of 2D–HQWPT   (d) The inverse of 2D–D4QWPT

3-DIMENSIONAL QUANTUM WAVELET PACKET TRANSFORMS

We firstly define the following discrete wavelet packet transforms: $W^x(\bullet)$, $W^y(\bullet)$ and $W^t(\bullet)$ as below.

$$
\begin{cases}
W^x(A_{2^m,2^k,2^h}) = \left(W_{2^m}\Lambda^1_{2^m,2^k}, \cdots, W_{2^m}\Lambda^{2^h}_{2^m,2^k} \right), \\
W^y(A_{2^m,2^k,2^h}) = \left(\Lambda^1_{2^m,2^k}(W_{2^k})^T, \cdots, \Lambda^{2^h}_{2^m,2^k}(W_{2^k})^T \right), \\
W^t(A_{2^m,2^k,2^h}) = \left(C^1_{2^m,2^k}, \cdots, C^{2^h}_{2^m,2^k} \right).
\end{cases}
\tag{7.21}
$$

where the matrix $\Lambda^j_{2^m,2^k}$ is the j-th image frame of the $2^m \times 2^k \times 2^h$ video $A_{2^m,2^k,2^h}$ in (5.60).

Let a column vector $u_{x,y}$ be

$$
u_{x,y} = \begin{bmatrix} \theta^1_{x,y} & \theta^2_{x,y} & \cdots & \theta^{2^h}_{x,y} \end{bmatrix}^T,
\tag{7.22}
$$

where $\theta^j_{x,y}$ is the element of the matrix $\Lambda^j_{2^m,2^k}$ on the position (x,y). Then elements of $W^t(A_{2^m,2^k,2^h})$ can be calculated by

$$
\begin{bmatrix} C^1_{x,y} & C^2_{x,y} & \cdots & C^{2^h}_{x,y} \end{bmatrix} = u^T_{x,y}(W_{2^h})^T
\tag{7.23}
$$

where $C^j_{x,y}$ is the elements of the matrix $C^j_{2^h,2^m}$ on the position (x,y).

The 3D discrete wavelet packet transform of the video $A_{2^m,2^k,2^h}$ is defined as

$$WPT3(A_{2^m,2^k,2^h}) = W^t(W^y(W^x(A_{2^m,2^k,2^h}))).$$ (7.24)

Suppose the function $f(\bullet)$ implements the quantum storage of the video $A_{2^m,2^k,2^h}$, i.e., $|\psi_3\rangle = f(A_{2^m,2^k,2^h})$ shown in (5.65). Applying the function $f(\bullet)$ on $W^t(A_{2^m,2^k,2^h})$, $W^y(A_{2^m,2^k,2^h})$ and $W^x(A_{2^m,2^k,2^h})$ respectively, we have the following three equations,

$$\begin{cases} f(W^t(A_{2^m,2^k,2^h})) = \left(I_{2^{m+k}} \otimes W_{2^h}\right)|\psi_3\rangle, \\ f(W^y(A_{2^m,2^k,2^h})) = \left(I_{2^m} \otimes W_{2^k} \otimes I_{2^h}\right)|\psi_3\rangle, \\ f(W^x(A_{2^m,2^k,2^h})) = \left(W_{2^m} \otimes I_{2^k} \otimes I_{2^h}\right)|\psi_3\rangle. \end{cases}$$ (7.25)

Therefore, we infer the 3D QWPT of $A_{2^m,2^k,2^h}$

$$f\left(WPT3(A_{2^m,2^k,2^h})\right) = \left(W_{2^m} \otimes W_{2^k} \otimes W_{2^h}\right)|\psi_3\rangle.$$ (7.26)

Substituting 1D-HQWPT and 1D-D4QWPT into (7.26), we obtain $(i+1)$-level 3D-HQWPT and $(j+1)$-level 3D-D4QWPT of $\Lambda_{2^m,2^k}$ as follows,

$$\begin{cases} \left(R^i_{2^m} \otimes R^i_{2^k} \otimes R^i_{2^h}\right)|\psi_3\rangle, \\ \left(A^j_{2^m} \otimes A^j_{2^k} \otimes A^j_{2^h}\right)|\psi_3\rangle, \end{cases}$$ (7.27)

where $0 \leq i \leq \min(m,k,h)-1$ and $0 \leq j \leq \min(m,k,h)-2$. Their inverses are given by

$$\begin{cases} \left[(R^i_{2^m})^{-1} \otimes (R^i_{2^k})^{-1} \otimes (R^i_{2^h})^{-1}\right]|\psi_3\rangle, \\ \left[(A^j_{2^m})^{-1} \otimes (A^j_{2^k})^{-1} \otimes (A^j_{2^h})^{-1}\right]|\psi_3\rangle, \end{cases}$$ (7.28)

Using (7.27) and (7.28), we design the circuits of single-level 3D-HQWPT, single-level 3D-D4QWPT and their inverses in Figure 9, and the circuits of multi-level 3D-HQWPT, multi-level 3D-D4QWPT and their inverses in Figure 10, respectively. Their implementation codes are designed in Code B.75 and Code B.76.

Figure 9 shows the complexities of single-level 3D-HQWPT and single-level 3D-D4QWPT are $O(n)$ and $O(n^2)$, respectively. From Figure 10, we

Figure 9. The circuits of single-level 3D-HQWPT, single-level 3D-D4QWPT and their inverses.

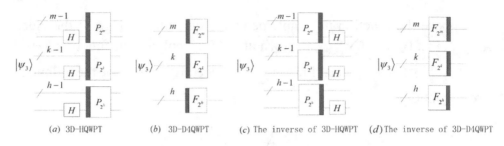

(a) 3D–HQWPT   (b) 3D–D4QWPT   (c) The inverse of 3D–HQWPT   (d) The inverse of 3D–D4QWPT

Figure 10. The circuits of multi-level 3D-HQWPT, multi-level 3D-D4QWPT and their inverses.

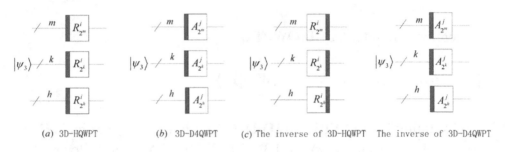

(a) 3D–HQWPT   (b) 3D–D4QWPT   (c) The inverse of 3D–HQWPT   The inverse of 3D–D4QWPT

obtain that the complexities of multi-level 3D-HQWPT and multi-level 3D-D4QWPT are $O(n)$ and $O(n^3)$.

QUANTUM IMAGE COMPRESSION FOR 2D-QWPT

Image compression solves the problem of reducing the amount of computational resources required to store or reconstruct digital images. The classical wavelet packet transform compression can be used to realize image compression (Marpe, Blattermann, & Ricke, 2000). Chapter 3 shows that a lot of quantum measurements are needed to read out an image in quantum systems. Quantum image compression is used to reduce the number of quantum measurements (Li, Zhu, Zhou, Li, Song, & Ian, 2014). Suppose that m_1 amplitudes of the original state and m_2 amplitudes of the compressed state are needed to be retrieved from quantum systems, then, quantum compression ratio (QCR) is defined as

$$Q_r = \frac{m_1}{m_2}. \tag{7.29}$$

Applying multi-level 2D-HQWPT $R_{2^m}^h \otimes R_{2^k}^h$ on the NASS state $|\psi_2\rangle$ gives the transformed state as follows,

$$
\begin{aligned}
\left(R_{2^m}^h \otimes R_{2^k}^h \right) |\psi_2\rangle &= \left(R_{2^m}^h \otimes R_{2^k}^h \right) \sum_{i=0}^{2^n-1} \theta_i |x_m\rangle |y_k\rangle \\
&= \sum_{i=0}^{2^n-1} \theta_i^c |x_m\rangle |y_k\rangle = |\psi_2^c\rangle,
\end{aligned} \tag{7.30}
$$

where $|\psi_2\rangle$ encodes a $2^m \times 2^k$ gray scale image $\Lambda_{2^m,2^k}$ with $n=m+k$.

The image is retrieved by using quantum measurement method in Chapter 3. From (3.96), when $M=256$, the amplitude θ_i on the position $|x_m\rangle |y_k\rangle$ can be retrieved with $O(2^n)$ measurements. Therefore, the image $\Lambda_{2^m,2^k}$ is retrieved from $|\psi_2\rangle$ with $O(2^{2n})$ measurements. Suppose that the results of ξ measurements are ξ_i times of $|i\rangle = |x_m\rangle |y_k\rangle$, we make $\xi_i = 0$ if $\xi_i/\xi < \zeta$ where ζ is a threshold. Therefore, we don't need to acquire the accurate value of θ_i^c for $\theta_i^c < \zeta$. If there are m_1 amplitudes greater than the threshold, we only obtain accurate values of the m_2 amplitudes to retrieve the compressed image. Therefore, the compressed image is retrieved from $|\psi_2^c\rangle$ with $O(m_1 2^n)$ measurements. Quantum compression ratio is given by $Q_r = 2^n/m_2$.

The process of quantum image compression for multi-level 2D-HQWPT is shown in Figure 11 (a). Similarly, its process for multi-level 2D-D4QWPT is shown in Figure 11 (b).

SIMULATIONS OF QUANTUM WAVELET PACKET TRANSFORMS

In this section, we describe simulations of 1D, 2D and 3D quantum wavelet packet transforms, and introduce simulations of quantum image compression for 2D quantum wavelet packet transforms.

Figure 11. The process of quantum image compression.

(a) Quantum image compression for 2D–HQWPT (b) Quantum image compression for 2D–D4QWPT

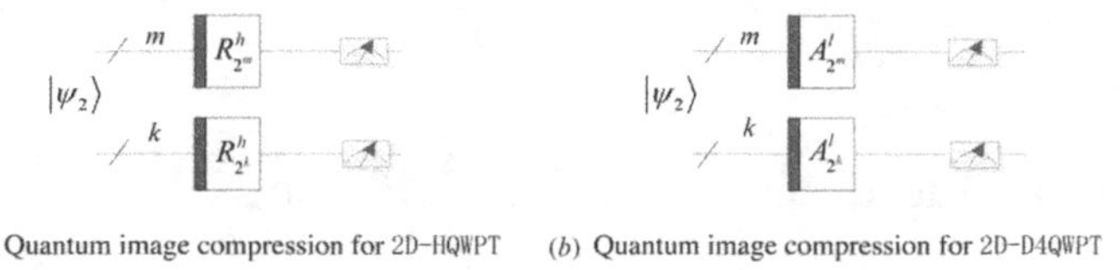

Simulations of 1D-QWPTs

Applying 1D-HQWPT $R^k_{2^{11}}, k = 0, 1, \ldots 10$ on the input vector V in (6.46), we obtain the simulation results of the first 3 levels shown in Figure 12 with multi-windows (see Code B.62). The left number i refers to QWT with i-level QWT with $1 \leq i \leq 10$, and $i=0$ refers to the input vector V.

Table 1 shows the comparisons of simulations of 1D-HQWPT, its inverse, and classical Haar wavelet packet transform using the 2-norm function *norm( )* (see Code B.63). The symbols in this table are listed as follows,

$$
\begin{cases}
M^k_1 = R^k_{2^{11}} \times V, & 0 \leq k \leq 10, \\
M^k_2 = (R^k_{2^{11}})^{-1} \times M^k_1, & 0 \leq k \leq 10, \\
M^k_3, & 0 \leq k \leq 10
\end{cases}
\tag{7.31}
$$

Figure 12. The simulation results of the first 3 levels of 1D-HQWPT.

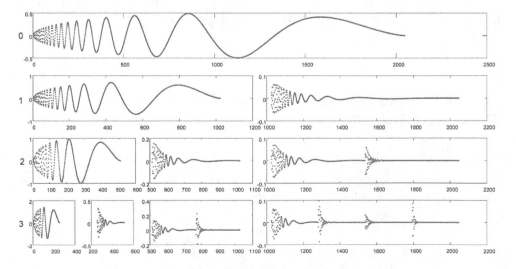

where the vector M_3^k is given by classical Haar wavelet packet functions $wpdec(V, k+1,'db1')$ and $wpcoef()$.

Figure 11 and Table 1 illustrate that 1D-HQWPT and its inverse are correct, and can perform the decomposition and reconstruction of Haar wavelet packet transform for the column vector V in (6.46).

Table 1. The comparisons of 1D-HQWPT, its inverse and classical Haar wavelet packet transform

Level	$norm\left(M_1^k - M_3^k\right)$	$norm\left(V - M_2^k\right)$
1	0.0123×10⁻¹³	0.0218×10⁻¹³
2	0.0193×10⁻¹³	0.0610×10⁻¹³
3	0.0223×10⁻¹³	0.0627×10⁻¹³
4	0.0298×10⁻¹³	0.0630×10⁻¹³
5	0.0351×10⁻¹³	0.0704×10⁻¹³
6	0.0478×10⁻¹³	0.0809×10⁻¹³
7	0.0757×10⁻¹³	0.1021×10⁻¹³
8	0.1020×10⁻¹³	0.1212×10⁻¹³
9	0.1387×10⁻¹³	0.1914×10⁻¹³
10	0.1712×10⁻¹³	0.2262×10⁻¹³
11	0.1825×10⁻¹³	0.3149×10⁻¹³

Similarly, applying 1D-D4QWPT $A_{2^{11}}^k, k = 0, 1, \ldots 9$ on the input vector V in (6.46) gives the simulation results of the first 3 levels in Figure 13 with multi-windows (see Code B.64).

Table 2 shows the comparison of simulations of 1D-D4QWPT, its inverse, and classical D4 wavelet packet transform (see Code B.65). The symbols in this table are listed as follows,

$$\begin{cases} M_4^k = A_{2^{11}}^k \times V, & 0 \le k \le 9, \\ M_5^k = (A_{2^{11}}^k)^{-1} \times M_4^k, & 0 \le k \le 9, \\ M_6^k, & 0 \le k \le 9 \end{cases} \qquad (7.32)$$

Figure 13. The simulation results of the first 3 levels of 1D-D4QWPT.

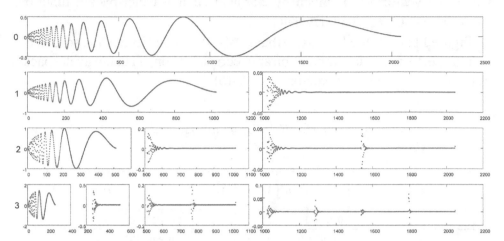

where the vector M_6^k is given by classical D4 wavelet packet functions $wpdec(V, k + 1,' db2')$ and $wpcoef()$.

Figure 13 illustrates that 1D-D4QWPT can perform the decomposition and reconstruction of D4 wavelet packet transform for the column vector V in (6.46). Table 2 shows that 1D-D4QWPT and its inverse are correct for the column vector V.

Table 2. The comparisons of 1D-D4QWPT, its inverse and classical D4 wavelet packet transform

Level	$norm\left(M_4^k - M_6^k\right)$	$norm\left(V - M_5^k\right)$
1	0.0057×10^{-10}	0.0246×10^{-13}
2	0.0128×10^{-10}	0.0482×10^{-13}
3	0.0230×10^{-10}	0.0768×10^{-13}
4	0.0374×10^{-10}	0.1017×10^{-13}
5	0.0574×10^{-10}	0.1347×10^{-13}
6	0.0842×10^{-10}	0.1658×10^{-13}
7	0.1168×10^{-10}	0.2390×10^{-13}
8	0.1564×10^{-10}	0.2565×10^{-13}
9	0.1963×10^{-10}	0.30401×10^{-13}
10	0.2369×10^{-10}	0.3590×10^{-13}

Figure 14. The simulation results of the first 2 levels of 2D-HQWPT for a 256x256 image

(a) An original image   (b) 1-level 2D-HQWPT   (c) 2-level 2D-HQWPT

Simulations of 2D-QWPTs

Let A_g be the matrix of the 256×256 image in Figure 14 (a), and be stored in the NASS state $\left|\psi_2\right\rangle$, i.e., $\left|\psi_2\right\rangle = f(A_g)$, where the function $f(\bullet)$ is equivalent to the quantum circuit in Figure 9.

Applying 2D-HQWPT $R_{2^8}^h \otimes R_{2^8}^h$ on $\left|\psi_2\right\rangle$, we obtain the transformed image $f^{-1}\left[(R_{2^8}^h \otimes R_{2^8}^h)\left|\psi_2\right\rangle\right]$. The simulation results of the first 2 levels of 2D-HQWPT are shown in Figure 14 (b) and (c) (see Code B.70). The comparisons of simulations of 2D-HQWPT, its inverse, and classical 2D Haar wavelet packet transform are shown in Table 3 (see Code B.72). The symbols in Table 3 are listed as follows,

$$
\begin{cases}
M_{21}^h = f^{-1}\left[(R_{2^8}^h \otimes R_{2^8}^h)\left|\psi_2\right\rangle\right], & 0 \le h \le 7, \\
M_{22}^h = f^{-1}\left[\left((R_{2^8}^h)^{-1} \otimes (R_{2^8}^h)^{-1}\right)(R_{2^8}^h \otimes R_{2^8}^h)\left|\psi_2\right\rangle\right], & 0 \le h \le 7, \\
M_{23}^h, & 0 \le h \le 7,
\end{cases} \tag{7.33}
$$

where the matrix M_{23}^h is given by classical 2D Haar wavelet packet functions $wpdec2(Ag, j, \text{'}db1\text{'})$ and $wpcoef()$. The code of M_{23}^h is designed in Code B.71.

Applying 2D-D4QWPT $A_{2^8}^h \otimes A_{2^8}^h$ on $\left|\psi_2\right\rangle$ gives the transformed image $f^{-1}\left[(A_{2^8}^h \otimes A_{2^8}^h)\left|\psi_2\right\rangle\right]$. Figure 15 shows the simulation results of the first 2 levels of 2D-D4QWPT (see Code B.73). The comparisons of simulations of 2D-D4QWPT, its inverse, and classical 2D D4 wavelet packet transform are shown in Table 4 (see Code B.74). The symbols in Table 4 are listed as follows,

Table 3. The comparisons of 2D-HQWPT, its inverse and classical 2D Haar wavelet packet transform

Level	$norm\left(M_{21}^{h} - M_{23}^{h}\right)$	$norm\left(Ag - M_{22}^{h}\right)$
1	0.0022×10^{-9}	0.0142×10^{-9}
2	0.0045×10^{-9}	0.0285×10^{-9}
3	0.0046×10^{-9}	0.0280×10^{-9}
4	0.0141×10^{-9}	0.0350×10^{-9}
5	0.0419×10^{-9}	0.0388×10^{-9}
6	0.1639×10^{-9}	0.1715×10^{-9}
7	0.2786×10^{-9}	0.2577×10^{-9}
8	0.5888×10^{-9}	0.6085×10^{-9}

$$\begin{cases} M_{24}^{h} = f^{-1}\left[\left(A_{2^8}^{h} \otimes A_{2^8}^{h}\right)\big|\psi_2\rangle\right], & 0 \leq h \leq 6, \\ M_{25}^{h} = f^{-1}\left[\left((A_{2^8}^{h})^{-1} \otimes (A_{2^8}^{h})^{-1}\right)\left(A_{2^8}^{h} \otimes A_{2^8}^{h}\right)\big|\psi_2\rangle\right], & 0 \leq h \leq 6, \\ M_{26}^{h}, & 0 \leq h \leq 6, \end{cases}$$

$$(7.34)$$

where the matrix M_{26}^{h} is given by classical 2D Haar wavelet packet functions $wpdec2(Ag, j, 'db2')$ and $wpcoef()$.

Figure 14 and Figure 15 illustrate that 2D-HQWPT and 2D-D4QWPT can perform the decomposition and reconstruction of images.

Figure 15. The simulation results of the first 2 levels of 2D-D4QWPT for a 256x256 image.

(a) An original image   (b) 1-level 2D-D4QWPT   (c) 2-level 2D-D4QWPT

Table 4. The comparisons of 2D-D4QWPT, its inverse and classical 2D D4 wavelet packet transform

Level	$norm\left(M_{24}^h - M_{26}^h\right)$	$norm\left(Ag - M_{25}^h\right)$
1	0.0102×10^{-7}	0.0113×10^{-9}
2	0.0211×10^{-7}	0.0228×10^{-9}
3	0.0342×10^{-7}	0.0353×10^{-9}
4	0.0562×10^{-7}	0.0540×10^{-9}
5	0.0818×10^{-7}	0.0884×10^{-9}
6	0.1199×10^{-7}	0.2078×10^{-9}
7	0.1832×10^{-7}	0.3943×10^{-9}

Simulations of 3D-QWPTs

Let V_g be the matrix of the $64\times32\times8$ video in Figure 16 (a), and be stored in the NASS state $\left|\psi_3\right\rangle$, i.e., $\left|\psi_3\right\rangle = f(V_g)$. We apply 3D-HQWPT $R_{2^m}^i \otimes R_{2^k}^i \otimes R_{2^h}^i$ on $\left|\psi_3\right\rangle$ and obtain the transformed image $f^{-1}\left[(R_{2^m}^i \otimes R_{2^k}^i \otimes R_{2^h}^i)\left|\psi_3\right\rangle\right]$. We give the simulation results of the first 2 levels of 3D-HQWPT in Figure 16 (b) and (c) (see Code B.77). The comparisons of simulations of 3D-HQWPT, its inverse, and classical 3D Haar wavelet packet transform are shown in Table 5 (see Code B.79).

The function $norm3(V_g)$ is defined as

$$norm3(\text{Vg}) = \sqrt{\sum_i \sum_j \sum_k Vg(i,j,k)^2}\ . \tag{7.35}$$

The other symbols in Table 5 are listed as follows,

$$\begin{cases} M_{31}^j = f^{-1}\left[(R_{2^6}^j \otimes R_{2^5}^j \otimes R_{2^3}^j)\left|\psi_2\right\rangle\right], & 0 \le j \le 2, \\ M_{32}^j = f^{-1}\left[\left((R_{2^6}^j)^{-1} \otimes (R_{2^5}^j)^{-1} \otimes (R_{2^3}^j)^{-1}\right)(R_{2^6}^j \otimes R_{2^5}^j \otimes R_{2^3}^j)\left|\psi_2\right\rangle\right], & 0 \le j \le 2, \\ M_{33}^j, & 0 \le j \le 2, \end{cases} \tag{7.36}$$

where the matrix M_{33}^j is given by classical 3D Haar wavelet packet function $WPT3(Ag, j, 'db1')$. The classical 3D Haar wavelet packet functions $WPT3()$

Figure 16. The simulation results of the first 2 levels of 3D-HQWPT for a 64x32x8 video.

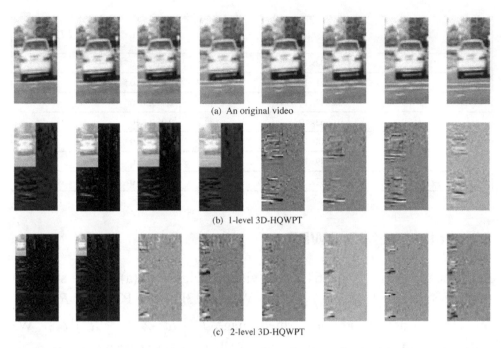

(a) An original video

(b) 1-level 3D-HQWPT

(c) 2-level 3D-HQWPT

in (7-24) are implemented by using the functions *wpdec2*() and *wpdec*() (see Code B.78).

The 3D-D4QWPT $A_{2^6}^j \otimes A_{2^5}^j \otimes A_{2^3}^j$ is applied on $\left| \psi_3 \right\rangle$, and the transformed image is given by $f^{-1}\left[(A_{2^8}^h \otimes A_{2^8}^h) \left| \psi_2 \right\rangle \right]$. Figure 17 shows the simulation results of the first 2 levels of 3D-D4QWPT (see Code B.80).

The comparisons of simulations of 3D-D4QWPT, its inverse, and classical 3D D4 wavelet packet transform are shown in Table 6 (see Code B.81). The symbols in Table 5 are listed as follows,

Table 5. The comparisons of 3D-HQWPT, its inverse and classical 3D Haar wavelet packet transform

Level	$norm3\left(M_{31}^j - M_{33}^j \right)$	$norm3\left(Vg - M_{33}^j \right)$
1	0.0162×10⁻¹⁰	0.0908×10⁻¹⁰
2	0.0592×10⁻¹⁰	0.2706×10⁻¹⁰
3	0.2058×10⁻¹⁰	0.4199×10⁻¹⁰

Figure 17. The simulation results of the first 2 levels of 3D-D4QWPT for a 64x32x8 video

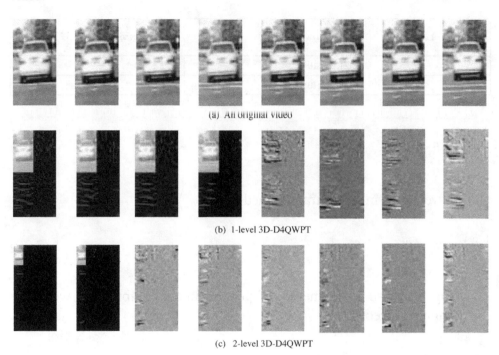

(a) An original video

(b) 1-level 3D-D4QWPT

(c) 2-level 3D-D4QWPT

$$
\begin{cases}
M_{34}^{j} = f^{-1}\left[\left(A_{2^6}^{j} \otimes A_{2^5}^{j} \otimes A_{2^3}^{j}\right)\left|\psi_2\right\rangle\right], & 0 \leq j \leq 1, \\
M_{35}^{j} = f^{-1}\left[\left((A_{2^6}^{j})^{-1} \otimes (A_{2^5}^{j})^{-1} \otimes (A_{2^3}^{j})^{-1}\right)\left(A_{2^6}^{j} \otimes A_{2^5}^{j} \otimes A_{2^3}^{j}\right)\left|\psi_2\right\rangle\right], & 0 \leq j \leq 1, \\
M_{36}^{j}, & 0 \leq j \leq 1,
\end{cases}
$$

$$(7.37)$$

where the matrix M_{33}^{j} is given by classical 3D Haar wavelet packet function $WPT3(Ag, j, 'db2')$.

Figure 16 and Figure 17 illustrate that 3D-HQWPT and 3D-D4QWPT can perform the decomposition and reconstruction of videos.

Simulations of Quantum Image Compression for 2D-QWPTs

The vector form of the NASS state $\left|\psi_2\right\rangle$ is

Table 6. The comparisons of 3D-D4QWPT, its inverse and classical 3D D4 wavelet packet transform

Level	$norm3\left(M_{34}^{j} - M_{36}^{j}\right)$	$norm3\left(Vg - M_{35}^{j}\right)$
1	0.1787×10^{-8}	0.1046×10^{-10}
2	0.3328×10^{-8}	0.2196×10^{-10}

$$\left|\psi_2\right\rangle = \begin{bmatrix} \theta_0 & \theta_1 & \cdots & \theta_{2^n-1} \end{bmatrix}^T, \tag{7.38}$$

and the vector form of the transformed state $\left|\psi_2^c\right\rangle$ is

$$\left|\psi_2^c\right\rangle = \begin{bmatrix} \theta_0^c & \theta_1^c & \cdots & \theta_{2^n-1}^c \end{bmatrix}^T. \tag{7.39}$$

Using the measurement method of quantum image compression, we obtain the compressed vector

$$\vec{\zeta} = \begin{bmatrix} \theta_0^\zeta & \theta_1^\zeta & \cdots & \theta_{2^n-1}^\zeta \end{bmatrix}^T, \tag{7.40}$$

where ζ is a threshold, and $\theta_i^\zeta = \theta_i^c$ for $\theta_i^c \geq \zeta$, and $\theta_i^\zeta = 0$ for $\theta_i^c < \zeta$. The compressed image is required by applying the inverse of 2D-QWPT on the vector $\vec{\zeta}$.

To evaluate the performance of quantum image compression, we define the mean squared error (MSE) and the peak signal-to-noise ratio (PSNR) as follows (Ruch, & Van Fleet, 2011),

$$\begin{cases} MSE(\Lambda_{2^m,2^k}, \Lambda_{2^m,2^k}^c) = \dfrac{1}{2^{m+k}} \displaystyle\sum_{i=0}^{2^m-1} \sum_{j=1}^{2^k-1} \left[\Lambda_{2^m,2^k}(i,j) - \Lambda_{2^m,2^k}^c(i,j)\right]^2, \\[2mm] PSNR(\Lambda_{2^m,2^k}, \Lambda_{2^m,2^k}^c) = 10 \log_{10} \dfrac{\max(\Lambda_{2^m,2^k})^2}{MSE(\Lambda_{2^m,2^k}, \Lambda_{2^m,2^k}^c)}, \end{cases} \tag{7.41}$$

where $\Lambda_{2^m,2^k}$ and $\Lambda_{2^m,2^k}^c$ are the original image and the compressed image, respectively. The maximum value of the image $\Lambda_{2^m,2^k}$ is given by $\max(\Lambda_{2^m,2^k})$.

Through the above analysis, we design the implementation code of quantum image compression in Code B.82.

let us consider the 256x256 image shown in Figure 18 (a) as examples of quantum image compression for 3-level 2D-HQWPT and 3-level 2D-D4QWPT. The simulation results are summarized in Table 7, and the compressed images are shown in Figure 18 (b) and 18 (c) (see Code B.83).

Table 7. The performances of quantum image compression for 3-level 2D-QWPTs

	3-Level 2D-HQWPT		3-Level 2D-D4QWPT	
	QCR	PSNR	QCR	PSNR
The first image	10.57	30.26	11.07	30.46
The second image	11.71	30.42	13.39	31.42
The third image	10.94	24.97	11.25	25.52
The fourth image	12.15	27.04	13.42	27.48
Mean value	11.34	28.17	12.28	28.72

CONCLUSION

In this chapter, multi-dimensional Haar quantum wavelet packet transforms, multi-dimensional Daubechies D4 quantum wavelet packet transform and their inverse are described. For 2^n data, the complexities of multi-dimensional Haar quantum wavelet packet transforms are all $O(n)$. The complexities of multi-dimensional Daubechies D4 quantum wavelet packet transforms are all $O(n^3)$. Therefore, quantum wavelet packet transforms are efficient. 2D quantum wavelet packet transforms have been used to realize quantum image compression. The simulation results show that quantum image compression can reduce the number of quantum measurements by about 90 percent.

Figure 18. The simulation results of quantum image compression for 3-level 2D-QWPTs.

(a) Four original images

(b) Four compressed images for 3-level 2D-HQWPT

(c) Four compressed image for 3-level 2D-D4QWPT

REFERENCES

Fijany, A., & Williams, C. P. (1998). Quantum wavelet transforms: Fast algorithms and complete circuits. *NASA International Conference on Quantum Computing and Quantum Communications*, 10-33.

Hoyer, P. (1997). *Efficient quantum transforms*. arXiv preprint quant-ph/9702028

Klappenecker, A. (1999). *Wavelets and wavelet packets on quantum computers*. arXiv preprint quant-ph/9909014

Li, H. S., Fan, P., Xia, H. Y., Song, S., & He, X. (2018). The multi-level and multi-dimensional quantum wavelet packet transforms. *Scientific Reports*, *8*(1), 13884. doi:10.103841598-018-32348-8 PMID:30224678

Li, H. S., Zhu, Q., Zhou, R. G., Li, M. C., Song, L., & Ian, H. (2014). Multidimensional color image storage, retrieval, and compression based on quantum amplitudes and phases. *Information Sciences, 273*, 212–232. doi:10.1016/j.ins.2014.03.035

Marpe, D., Blattermann, G., Ricke, J., & Maass. (2000). A two-layered wavelet-based algorithm for efficient lossless and lossy image compression. *IEEE Transactions on Circuits and Systems for Video Technology, 10*(7), 1094–1102. doi:10.1109/76.875514

Ruch, D. K., & Van Fleet, P. J. (2011). *Wavelet theory: an elementary approach with applications*. John Wiley & Sons.

Terraneo, M., & Shepelyansky, D. L. (2003). *Imperfection effects for multiple applications of the quantum wavelet transform*. ArXiv preprint quant-ph/0303043

Chapter 7
Quantum Image Segmentation Algorithms

ABSTRACT

Quantum image segmentation has always been one of the difficult tasks in quantum image processing. This chapter introduce two quantum image segmentation algorithms. One is quantum edge detection algorithm; the other one is quantum image segmentation based on generalized Grover search algorithm.

INTRODUCTION

A typical image processing task is the recognition of boundaries (intensity changes) between two adjacent regions. Classically, edge detection methods rely on the computation of image gradients by different types of filtering masks. Therefore, all classical algorithms require a computational complexity of at least $O(2^n)$ because each pixel needs to be processed (Yao, Wang, Liao, Chen, & Suter, 2017). A quantum algorithm has been proposed that is supposed to provide an exponential speedup compared with existing edge extraction algorithms (Zhang, Lu, & Gao. 2015). However, this algorithm includes a COPY operation and a quantum black box for calculating the gradients of all the pixels simultaneously. For both steps, no efficient implementations are currently available. A highly efficient quantum algorithm, named as quantum Hadamard edge detection, was proposed to find the boundaries (Yao, Wang,

DOI: 10.4018/978-1-7998-3799-2.ch007

Liao, Chen, & Suter, 2017), which is the first algorithm of quantum image segmentation in this chapter.

The accuracy or efficiency of image segmentation isn't high enough for some special images by employing classical segmentation algorithms. The special images, such as overlapping target objects (Venegas-Andraca & Ball, 2010), and the target object and the background with similar colors (Zhang, Fritts, & Goldman, 2008) are difficult to be segmented by classical algorithms.

For the above special image, segmentation information of target objects from the image is given by human-computer interaction. For instance, for the image in Figure 1 (a), its edge information is shown in Figure 1 (b) by using Photoshop software.

Figure 1. The target object and the background with similar colors.

(a)   (b)

The colors, coordinates and segmentation information of an image can be stored in a quantum system by using NAQSS (see Chapter 3). A generalized Grover search algorithm with arbitrary rotation phases was used to efficiently retrieve a target for the special images (Li, Zhu, Zhou, Song, & Yang, 2014). It is the second algorithm of quantum image segmentation in this chapter.

QUANTUM HADAMARD EDGE DETECTION

Given a 2D image $F = (F_{i,j})_{M \times L}$, where $F_{i,j}$ represents the pixel value at position (i,j) with $i=1,2,\ldots,M$ and $j=1,2,\ldots,L$, a vector $\vec{f}$ with ML elements can be formed by

$$\vec{f} = (F_{1,1}, F_{2,1}, \ldots, F_{M,1}, F_{1,2}, F_{2,2}, \ldots, F_{M,L})^T. \tag{8.1}$$

Suppose $2^n = ML$, then, the image $\vec{f}$ can be mapped onto a pure quantum state $|\psi_f\rangle$ as follows,

$$|\psi_f\rangle = \sum_{k=0}^{2^n-1} c_k |k\rangle, \tag{8.2}$$

where the computational basis $|k\rangle$ encodes the position (i,j) of each pixel, and the coefficient c_k encodes the pixel value at the position (i,j), i.e., $c_k = F_{i,j} / \sqrt{\sum F_{i,j}^2}$.

The 2D image $F = (F_{i,j})_{M \times L}$ can be stored in a quantum system using the initialization method (Long, & Sun, 2001) or the quantum random access memory (Giovannetti, Lloyd, & Maccone, 2008).

Applying the operator $I_{2^n} \otimes H$ on the state $|\psi_f\rangle \otimes |0\rangle$ gives

$$(I_{2^n} \otimes H)(|\psi_f\rangle \otimes |0\rangle) = \frac{1}{\sqrt{2}}\left[c_0, c_0, c_1, c_1, c_2, c_2, \ldots, c_{2^n-2}, c_{2^n-2}, c_{2^n-1}, c_{2^n-1}\right]^T = |\psi_{f0}\rangle. \tag{8.3}$$

The downshift matrix $Q_{2^{n+1}}$ in (6.22) is preformed to yield

$$Q_{2^{n+1}}(I_{2^n} \otimes H)(|\psi_f\rangle \otimes |0\rangle) = \frac{1}{\sqrt{2}}\left[c_0, c_1, c_1, c_2, c_2, \ldots, c_{2^n-2}, c_{2^n-2}, c_{2^n-1}, c_{2^n-1}, c_0\right]^T = |\psi_{f1}\rangle, \tag{8.4}$$

After applying $I_{2^n} \otimes H$ on the state $|\psi_{f1}\rangle$, the result is

$$(I_{2^n} \otimes H)\left|\psi_{f1}\right\rangle$$
$$= \frac{1}{2}\left[c_0 + c_1, c_0 - c_1, c_1 + c_2, c_1 - c_2, \ldots, c_{2^n-2} + c_{2^n-1}, c_{2^n-2} - c_{2^n-1}, c_{2^n-1} + c_0, c_{2^n-1} - c_0\right]^T$$
$$= \left|\psi_{f2}\right\rangle.$$

$$(8.5)$$

By measuring the last qubit, conditioned on obtaining $|1\rangle$, the output state $|g\rangle$ is given by

$$\left|g\right\rangle = \frac{1}{2}\left[c_0 - c_1, c_1 - c_2, c_2 - c_3, \ldots, c_{2^n-2} - c_{2^n-1}, c_{2^n-1} - c_0\right]^T, \qquad (8.6)$$

which contains the full boundary information of the image F.

Through the above analysis, the quantum Hadamard edge detection (QHED) algorithm is described as follows.

Step1. Encode a $2^m \otimes 2^l$ input image into a quantum state $\left|\psi_f\right\rangle$ with $n=m+l$ qubits.

Step2. Create the input state $\left|\psi_f\right\rangle \otimes |0\rangle$, which consists of $\left|\psi_f\right\rangle$ and the 1-qubit auxiliary state $|0\rangle$.

Step3. Obtain the state $\left|\psi_{f0}\right\rangle$ in (8.3) by applying a Hadamard gate on the auxiliary state $|0\rangle$.

Step4. Perform the operator $Q_{2^{n+1}}$ on the state $\left|\psi_{f0}\right\rangle$, and give a transformed state $\left|\psi_{f1}\right\rangle$ in (8.4).

Figure 2. The implemented circuit of the QHED algorithm.

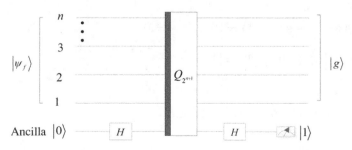

Step5. Yield a new state $\left| \psi_{f2} \right\rangle$ in (8.5) by applying the operator $I_{2^n} \otimes H$ on the state $\left| \psi_{f1} \right\rangle$.

Step6. Give the output state $|g\rangle$ in (8.6) by measuring the last qubit with the

Figure 3. The simulation result of the QHED algorithm.

(a) A 128×128 binary image   (b) The output image encoding the edge information

result $|1\rangle$.

The implemented circuit of the QHED algorithm is shown in Figure 2, and its implementation code is seen in Code B.84.

The detail circuit of $Q_{2^{n+1}}$ is shown in Figure 10 (a), and its complexity is $O(n^2)$. Therefore, the complexity of the circuit of the QHED algorithm in Figure 2 is also $O(n^2)$.

As an example, Figure 3 (b) shows the result of the QHED algorithm simulated on a classical computer for a 128×128 binary image in Figure 3 (a) (see Code B.85). It demonstrates that the QHED algorithm can successfully detect the boundaries in the image.

QUANTUM IMAGE SEGMENTATION BASED ON GENERALIZED GROVER SEARCH ALGORITHM

Suppose that an image is only divided into two sub-images (i.e., target and background), in the case, we define

$$
\left| \chi_i \right\rangle = \begin{cases} \cos \gamma_i \left| 0 \right\rangle + \sin \gamma_i \left| 1 \right\rangle = \left| 0 \right\rangle, & \gamma_i = 0, \\ \cos \gamma_i \left| 0 \right\rangle + \sin \gamma_i \left| 1 \right\rangle = \left| 1 \right\rangle, & \gamma_i = \frac{\pi}{2}, \end{cases}
\tag{8.7}
$$

where $\gamma_i=0$ for $i \in B$, and $\gamma_i=\pi/2$ for $i \in B$.

Figure 4. The retrieval of the target sub-image

$$|\psi_\chi(r)\rangle \left[\begin{array}{c} \overset{n}{/} \quad\quad\quad\quad |\psi_g\rangle \\ \quad\quad\quad\quad \boxed{\,} |1\rangle \end{array}\right.$$

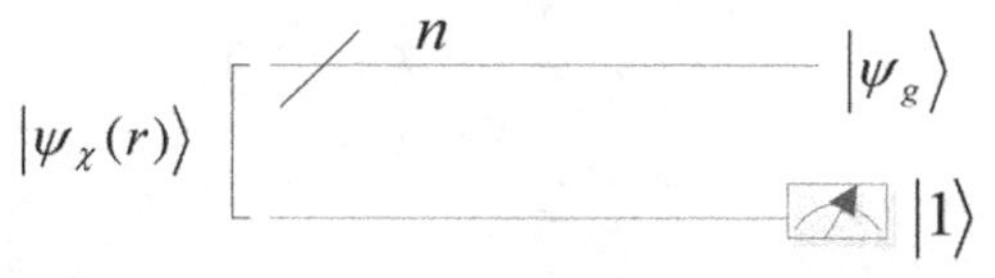

Then, to store the image, the NAQSS state $|\psi_\chi\rangle$ in (3.112) in Chapter 3 is rewritten

$$|\psi_\chi(r)\rangle = \sum_{i=0}^{2^n-1}\theta_i|i\rangle|\chi_i\rangle = \sum_{i\in B}\theta_i|i\rangle|0\rangle + \sum_{i\in A}\theta_i|i\rangle|1\rangle, \tag{8.8}$$

where A and B are defined as sets contain coordinates of the target and background in an image, respectively.

By measuring the last qubit of $|\psi_\chi(r)\rangle$ with the result $|1\rangle$, the output state $|\psi_g\rangle$ is given by

$$|\psi_g\rangle = \left(\sum_{i\in A}\theta_i|i\rangle|1\rangle\right)\Big/\sqrt{\sum_{i\in A}(\theta_i)^2}. \tag{8.9}$$

The retrieval of the target sub-image is shown in Figure 4. Form (8.8), the state $|\psi_g\rangle$ is obtained with probability

$$\Pr(\psi_g) = \sum_{i\in A}(\theta_i)^2. \tag{8.10}$$

To increase the probability of obtaining the state $|\psi_g\rangle$, we consider Grover search algorithm. Grover search algorithm (Grover, 1996) is one of the most important quantum algorithms. Grover algorithm is generalized to deal with an arbitrary initial amplitude distribution, and a bound of the success probability of searching a marked state was derived (Biron, Biham, Biham, Grassl, & Lidar, 1998). In this section, we first introduce Grover search algorithm. Next, we describe a generalized Grover search algorithm with arbitrary rotation phases and an arbitrary initial state, which is used to efficiently retrieve a target sub-image of an image (Li, Zhu, Zhou, Song, & Yang, 2014).

Figure 5. The schematic circuit of Grover search algorithm

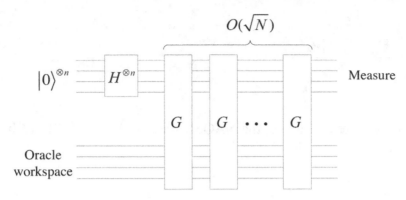

Grover Search Algorithm

Let us begin by setting the definition: A quantum oracle, i.e., a black box, is a unitary operator O, defined by its action on the computational basis (Berthiaume & Brassard, 1994; Nielsen, & Chuang, 2000),

$$\left|x\right\rangle\left|q\right\rangle\xrightarrow{\quad O \quad}\left|x\right\rangle\left|q\oplus f(x)\right\rangle, \tag{8.11}$$

where $|x\rangle$ is the index register, $\oplus$ denotes addition modulo 2, and the oracle qubit $|q\rangle$ is a single qubit which is flipped if $f(x)=1$, and is unchanged otherwise.

The circuit of Grover search algorithm is illustrated in Figure 5.

The goal of the algorithm is to find a solution to the search problem, using the smallest possible number of applications of the oracle.

Figure 6. The circuit of the Grover iteration G

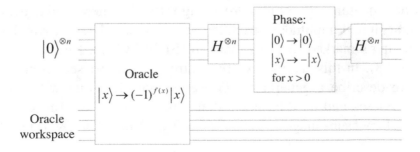

The algorithm begins with the state $\left| 0 \right\rangle^{\otimes n}$. The Hadamard transform is applied on the state $\left| 0 \right\rangle^{\otimes n}$, i.e.,

$$\left| \psi \right\rangle = H^{\otimes n} \left| 0 \right\rangle^{\otimes n} = \frac{1}{\sqrt{N}} \sum_{x=0}^{N-1} \left| x \right\rangle. \tag{8.12}$$

Then, the quantum search algorithm consists of $O(\sqrt{N})$ Grover iterations. The Grover iteration is denoted as G, the circuit of which is shown in Figure 6. It may be broken up into four steps:

Step1. Apply the oracle to obtain

$$\left| x \right\rangle \xrightarrow{\quad O \quad} (-1)^{f(x)} \left| x \right\rangle, \tag{8.13}$$

where $f(x)=1$ if x is a solution to the search problem, and $f(x)=0$ if x is not a solution to the search problem.

Step2. Apply Hadamard transform.
Step 3. Perform a conditional phase shift to obtain

$$\left| x \right\rangle \rightarrow -(-1)^{\delta_{x,0}} \left| x \right\rangle, \tag{8.14}$$

where $\delta_{x,0}=0$ for $x \neq 0$, and $\delta_{x,0}=1$ for $x=0$.

Step4. Apply Hadamard transform.

It is useful to note that the combined effect of steps 2, 3, and 4 is

$$H^{\otimes n} I_0 H^{\otimes n} = H^{\otimes n} (I_{2^n} - 2 \left| 0 \right\rangle \left\langle 0 \right|) H^{\otimes n}, \tag{8.15}$$

where $I_0 = 2 \left| 0 \right\rangle \left\langle 0 \right| - I_{2^n}$. Therefore, the Grover iteration G can be written as

$$G = H^{\otimes n} I_0 H^{\otimes n} O. \tag{8.16}$$

Define normalized states

$$\begin{cases} \left| \alpha \right\rangle = \dfrac{1}{\sqrt{N-M}} \sum_x {}^2 \left| x \right\rangle, \\[3mm] \left| \beta \right\rangle = \dfrac{1}{\sqrt{M}} \sum_x {}^1 \left| x \right\rangle, \end{cases} \tag{8.17}$$

where $\sum_x {}^1$ indicates a sum over all x which are solutions to the search problem, and indicates a sum over all x which are not solutions to the search problem. Thus, the initial state $\left| \psi \right\rangle$ may be rewritten as

$$\left| \psi \right\rangle = \sqrt{\frac{N-M}{N}} \left| \alpha \right\rangle + \sqrt{\frac{M}{N}} \left| \beta \right\rangle = \cos\frac{\theta}{2} \left| \alpha \right\rangle + \sin\frac{\theta}{2} \left| \beta \right\rangle. \tag{8.18}$$

So $\left| \psi \right\rangle$ is in the space spanned by |α⟩ and |β⟩, and $\cos\theta/2 = \sqrt{(N-M)/N}$, $\sin\theta/2 = \sqrt{M/N}$. Furthermore, the Grover iteration in the |α⟩ and |β⟩ basis may be rewritten as

$$G = \begin{bmatrix} \cos\theta & -\sin\theta \\ \sin\theta & \cos\theta \end{bmatrix}, \tag{8.19}$$

where θ is a real number in the range 0 to 2π, and

$$\sin\theta = \frac{2\sqrt{M(N-M)}}{N}. \tag{8.20}$$

Applying G to $\left| \psi \right\rangle$, we obtain

$$G\left| \psi \right\rangle = \cos\frac{3\theta}{2} \left| \alpha \right\rangle + \sin\frac{3\theta}{2} \left| \beta \right\rangle, \tag{8.21}$$

which is illustrated in Figure 7.

Figure 7. The action of a single Grover iteration

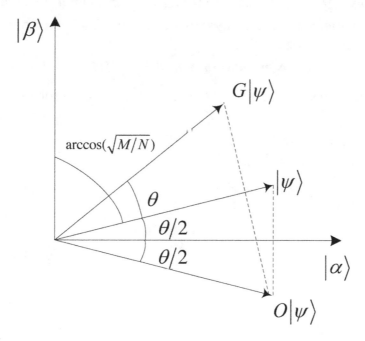

In this figure, an oracle operation O reflects the state about the state $|\alpha\rangle$, then the operation $2|\psi\rangle\langle\psi| - I$ reflects it about $|\psi\rangle$. Therefore, continued application of G takes the state to

$$G^k|\psi\rangle = \cos(\frac{2k+1}{2}\theta)|\alpha\rangle + \sin(\frac{2k+1}{2}\theta)|\beta\rangle. \qquad (8.22)$$

How many times must the Grover iteration be repeated in order to obtain a solution to the search problem with high probability? Figure 7 shows that rotating through $\arccos\sqrt{M/N}$ radians takes the initial state of the system $|\psi\rangle$ to I$\beta\rangle$. Let *fix(x)* round the elements of x to the nearest integers towards zero.

Therefore, repeating G

$$R = fix(\frac{\arccos\sqrt{M/N}}{\theta}) \qquad (8.23)$$

times rotates $|\psi\rangle$ to within an angle $\theta/2 \leq \pi/4$ of $|\beta\rangle$. Observation of the state in the computational basis then yields a solution to the search problem with probability at least one-half.

Indeed, when $M \ll N$, we have $\theta \approx \sin\theta \approx 2\sqrt{M/N}$, and thus the angular error in the final state is at most $\theta/2 \approx \sqrt{M/N}$, giving a probability of error of at most M/N.

Suppose that $M \leq N/2$, we have

$$\frac{\theta}{2} \leq \sin\frac{\theta}{2} = \sqrt{\frac{M}{N}},$$

(8.24)

and obtain

$$R \leq \left\lceil \frac{\pi}{4}\sqrt{\frac{N}{M}} \right\rceil,$$

(8.25)

i.e., $R = O(\sqrt{N/M})$. Grover iterations must be performed in order to obtain a solution to the search problem with high probability, a quadratic improvement over the $O(N/M)$ oracle calls required classically.

For the case $M=1$, Grover search algorithm is summarized below.

Algorithm: Grover search
Inputs: (1) a black box oracle O which performs the transformation $O|x\rangle|q\rangle = |x\rangle|q \oplus f(x)\rangle$, where $f(x)=0$ for all $0 \leq x < 2^n$ except x_0, and $f(x_0)=1$; (2) the initial state $|0\rangle^{\otimes n+1}$ with $(n+1)$ qubits.
Output: x_0.
Runtime: $O(\sqrt{2^n})$ operations. Succeeds with probability O(1).
Procedure:

(1) The initial state $|0\rangle^{\otimes n+1}$;
(2) Apply $H^{\otimes n}$ to the first n qubits, and HX to the last qubit,

$$|0\rangle^{\otimes n+1} \to \frac{1}{\sqrt{2^n}} \sum_{x=0}^{2^n-1} |x\rangle \left(\frac{|0\rangle - |1\rangle}{\sqrt{2}} \right); \tag{8.26}$$

(3) Apply the Grover iteration $R \approx \left\lceil \pi \sqrt{2^n}/4 \right\rceil$ times, and obtain

$$\left[(2|\psi\rangle\langle\psi| \quad I_{2^n})O \right]^R \frac{1}{\sqrt{2^n}} \sum_{x=0}^{2^n-1} |x\rangle \left(\frac{|0\rangle - |1\rangle}{\sqrt{2}} \right) \approx |x_0\rangle \left(\frac{|0\rangle - |1\rangle}{\sqrt{2}} \right); \tag{8.27}$$

(4) Measure the first n qubits to obtain x_0.

Generalized Grover Search Algorithm

For $|\psi_\chi(r)\rangle$ in (8.8), A is a set of marked states and B is a set of unmarked states. Then, a quantum oracle R_1 and a rotation operator of the initial state R_0 are defined as

$$\begin{cases} R_1 = I^{\otimes n+1} - 2\sum_{\tau \in A} |\tau\rangle\langle\tau|, \\ R_0 = 2|0\rangle\langle0| - I^{\otimes n}, \end{cases} \tag{8.28}$$

where α is the rotation angle of marked states and initial states.

Let a unitary operator U satisfy

$$U|0\rangle^{\otimes n+1} = \frac{1}{\sqrt{N}} \sum_{i \in B} |i\rangle|0\rangle + \frac{1}{\sqrt{N}} \sum_{i \in A} |i\rangle|1\rangle = |\psi_1\rangle, \tag{8.29}$$

where $N = 2^n$ is a total of states.

Substituting U, $R_0 \otimes I$ and R_1 for $H^{\otimes n}$, I_0, and O in (8.16), we obtain the generalized Grover search operator as follows,

$$G_\psi = U(R_0 \otimes I)U^{-1}R_1, \tag{8.30}$$

where U^{-1} is the inverse of the operator U.

Now, we analyze the performance of the generalized Grover search algorithm.

Applying Grover search operator G_ψ to $\left|\psi_\chi(r)\right\rangle$, we have

$$G_\psi\left|\psi_\chi(r)\right\rangle = \sum_{i=0,i\in B}^{N} G_\psi(\theta_i\left|i\right\rangle\left|0\right\rangle) + \sum_{i=0,i\in A}^{N} G_\psi(\theta_i\left|i\right\rangle\left|1\right\rangle). \tag{8.31}$$

After t iterations of G_ψ, the initial state is changed into

$$\left|\psi_\chi(t)\right\rangle = \sum_{i\in B} l_i(t)\left|i\right\rangle\left|0\right\rangle + \sum_{i\in A} k_i(t)\left|i\right\rangle\left|1\right\rangle \tag{8.32}$$

The averages of the amplitudes as follows are denoted as

$$\begin{cases} \overline{l}(t) = \dfrac{1}{N-r}\sum_{i\in B} l_i(t), \\ \overline{k}(t) = \dfrac{1}{r}\sum_{i\in A} k_i(t), \end{cases} \tag{8.33}$$

where r is a number of marked states.

The recursion equations of the amplitudes take

$$\begin{cases} k_i(t+1) = C(t) + k_i(t), \\ l_i(t+1) = C(t) - l_i(t), \end{cases} \tag{8.34}$$

where

$$C(t) = \frac{2(N-r)}{N}\overline{l}(t) - \frac{2r}{N}\overline{k}(t). \tag{8.35}$$

Accumulating respectively (8.34) from $i=0$ to $i=N-1$, we gain another recursion equations

$$\begin{cases} \overline{k}(t+1) = C(t) + \overline{k}(t), \\ \overline{l}(t+1) = C(t) - \overline{l}(t). \end{cases} \tag{8.36}$$

From (8.34) and (8.36), we find

$$\begin{cases} k_i(t) - \overline{k}(t) = k_i(t-1) - \overline{k}(t-1) = \cdots = k_i(0) - \overline{k}(0), \\ l_i(t) - \overline{l}(t) = -\left[l_i(t-1) - \overline{l}(t-1) \right] = \cdots = (-1)^t \left[l_i(0) - \overline{l}(0) \right], \end{cases} \tag{8.37}$$

and obtain

$$\begin{cases} k_i(t) = \overline{k}(t) + k_i(0) - \overline{k}(0), \\ l_i(t) = \overline{l}(t) + (-1)^t \left[l_i(0) - \overline{l}(0) \right]. \end{cases} \tag{8.38}$$

Let

$$\begin{cases} \sigma_k^2(t) = \dfrac{1}{r} \sum_{i \in A} \left| k_i(t) - \overline{k}(t) \right|^2 \\ \sigma_l^2(t) = \dfrac{1}{N-r} \sum_{i \in B} \left| l_i(t) - \overline{l}(t) \right|^2 \end{cases} \tag{8.39}$$

be the variances of the amplitudes of $\left| \psi_\chi(t) \right\rangle$ in (8.32), then, we obtain

$$\begin{cases} \sigma_k^2(t) = \sigma_k^2(0), \\ \sigma_l^2(t) = \sigma_l^2(0). \end{cases} \tag{8.40}$$

Solving (8.36) gives

$$\begin{cases} \overline{k}(t) = \alpha \sin(\omega t + \phi), \\ \overline{l}(t) = \beta \cos(\omega t + \phi), \end{cases} \tag{8.41}$$

where

$$
\begin{cases}
\phi = \arctan \dfrac{\overline{k}(0)}{\overline{l}(0)} \sqrt{\dfrac{r}{N-r}}, \\[2mm]
\omega = \arccos(1 - \dfrac{2r}{N}) \\[2mm]
\alpha^2 = \overline{k}(0)^2 + \overline{l}(0)^2 \dfrac{N-r}{r}, \\[2mm]
\beta^2 = \overline{l}(0)^2 + \overline{k}(0)^2 \dfrac{r}{N-r}.
\end{cases}
\tag{8.42}
$$

Suppose that P_t is the probability of success after t iterations to search out marked states, then

$$
\begin{aligned}
P_t &= \sum_{i \in A} \left| k_i(t) \right|^2 \\
&= 1 - \sum_{i \in B} \left| l_i(t) \right|^2 \\
&= 1 - (N-r)\sigma_l^2(t) - (N-r)\left| \overline{l}(t) \right|^2 \\
&= 1 - (N-r)\sigma_l^2(0) - (N-r)\left| \overline{l}(t) \right|^2 .
\end{aligned}
\tag{8.43}
$$

When $\overline{l}(t) = 0$, i.e.,

$$
\omega t + \phi = \frac{\pi}{2},
\tag{8.44}
$$

we obtain the maximal probability of success $P_{\max}$ as follows,

$$
P_{\max} = 1 - (N-r)\sigma_l^2(0).
\tag{8.45}
$$

Form (8.44), the optimal iterations of Grover is

$$
t = round \left(\frac{\dfrac{\pi}{2} - \arctan \left[\dfrac{\overline{k}(0)}{\overline{l}(0)} \sqrt{\dfrac{r}{N-r}} \right]}{\arccos(1 - \dfrac{2r}{N})} \right),
\tag{8.46}
$$

Figure 8. The circuits of U and its inverse

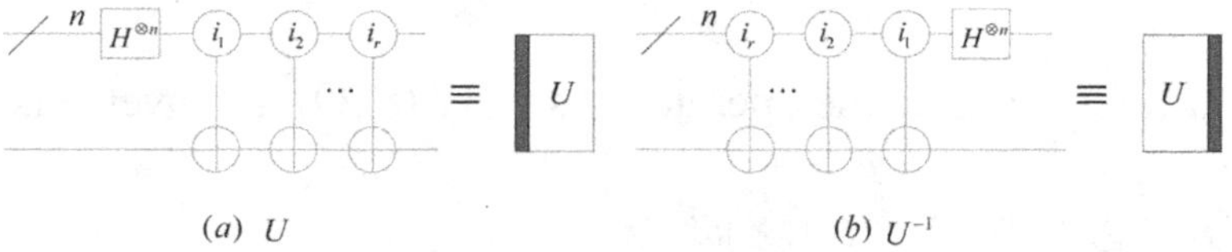

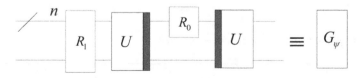

(a) U

(b) U^{-1}

where the function *round()* rounds a number to the nearest integer.
When $r \ll N$, we infer

$$t < \frac{\pi}{2} \frac{1}{\arccos(1 - 2\frac{r}{N})} < \frac{\frac{\pi}{4}\sqrt{N/r}}{\sqrt{1 - \frac{r}{N}}} \approx \frac{\pi}{4}\sqrt{N/r}. \tag{8.47}$$

Therefore, the minimum number of iterations t is $O(\sqrt{N/r})$.

Figure 9. The circuits of R_0 and $R_{0'}$.

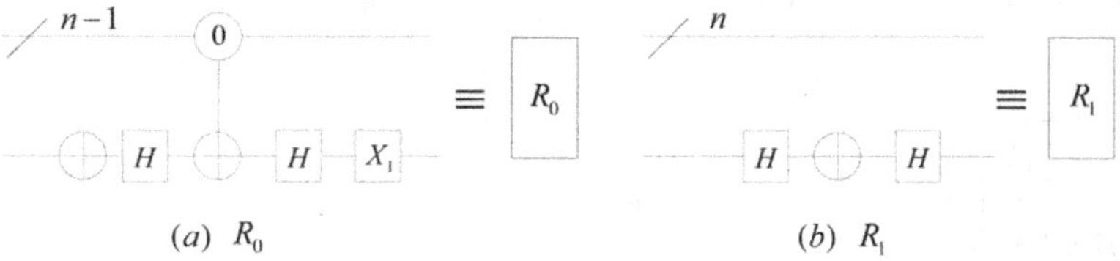

(a) R_0

(b) R_1

The Implementation of Quantum Image Segmentation

Figure 10. The circuit of G_ψ.

Let *U* be

$$U = C_n^{i_1}(X)C_n^{i_2}(X)...C_n^{i_r}(X)(H^{\otimes n} \otimes I),\tag{8.48}$$

where $i_1,i_2,...,i_r \in A$, then the operator U satisfy (8.29). Its inverse is

$$U^{-1} = (H^{\otimes n} \otimes I)C_n^{i_r}(X)...C_n^{i_2}(X)C_n^{i_1}(X).\tag{8.49}$$

The circuits of U and its inverse are designed in Figure 8.

Let the operator X_1 be equal to $-X$, then the operators HXH and X_1HXHX

Figure 11. The t iterations of the operator G_ψ

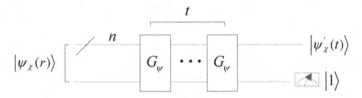

have the following properties

$$\begin{cases} HXH|0\rangle = |0\rangle, \\ HXH|1\rangle = -|1\rangle, \\ X_1HXHX|0\rangle = |0\rangle, \\ X_1HXHX|1\rangle = -|1\rangle, \\ X_1 HHX = -I, \end{cases}\tag{8.50}$$

where X and H are NOT gate and Hadamard gate, respectively. Therefore, we design the circuits of R_0 and R_1 in Figure 9.

Table 1. Some priori data of the first example

N	R	$\bar{k}(0)$	$\bar{l}(0)$	$\sigma_l^2(0)$
4096	135	0.0156	0.0152	2.0064×10^{-5}

Figure 12. The first example of quantum image segmentation

(*a*) An original image   (*b*)   The target sub-image

From (8.30), we design the implemented circuit of the generalized Grover search operator G_ψ in Figure 10.

Applying the t iterations of the operator G_ψ on the state $\left|\psi_\chi(r)\right\rangle$, and measuring the last qubit, we obtain

$$\left|\psi'_\chi(t)\right\rangle = \left[\sum_{i\in A} k_i(t)\left|i\right\rangle\right]\bigg/ \sqrt{\sum_{i\in A} k_i(t)^2} \tag{8.51}$$

with the probability $P_t \approx 1-(N-r)\sigma_l^2(0)$ and the circuit shown in Figure 11

Using $\bar{k}(t)$, $\bar{k}(0)$ and $\bar{k}_i(t)$, we calculate

$$k_i(0) = k_i(t) - \bar{k}(t) + \bar{k}(0), \tag{8.52}$$

i.e., we retrieve the target sub-image.

In order to make the above description explicit, let us consider a 64×64 grayscale image shown in Figure 12 (a) as the first example. The original image is segmented into two sub-images, one of which is marked '0' as a background sub-image and the other one is marked '1' as a target sub-image.

Some priori data are shown in Table 1. N and r are number of pixels of the original image and the target sub-image, respectively.

The set A of marked states of the first example is

$A = [$ 964,965,966,967,968,1028,1033,1034,1092,1099,1156,1164,1221,1229,1286,
1294,1350,1359,1414,1424,1478,1489,1543,1554,1607,1619,1620,1640,1641,
1642,1643,1644,1645,1646,1647,1648,1649,1671,1685,1686,1687,1688,1691,
1692,1693,1695,1696,1697,1698,1699,1700,1701,1702,1703,1714,1715,1735,
1753,1754,1758,1780,1781,1798,1846,1847,1848,1849,1860,1861,1914,1915,
1916,1924,1981,1982,1983,1984,1988,2031,2032,2033,2034,2035,**2036**,2037,
2038,2039,2040,2041,2042,2043,2044,2053,2054,2055,2094,2120,2158,2185,
2186,2187,2188,2189,2190,2191,2199,2215,2216,2217,2218,2219,2220,2221,
2256,2257,2262,2264,2265,2267,2268,2269,2270,2271,2272,**2273**,2274,2275,
2276,2277,2278,2322,2323,2324,2325,2330$]^T$.

Table 2. Other priori data of the second example

N	r	$\bar{k}(0)$	$\bar{l}(0)$	$\sigma_l^2(0)$
16384	2058	0.0065	0.0077	1.1466×10^{-5}

$$(8.53)$$

Using the set A and the circuit in Figure 10, we design the simulated program of the generalized Grover search operator G_ψ (see Code B. 86).

Figure 13. The second example of quantum image segmentation.

(*a*) An original image   (*b*) The binary image   (*c*) The target sub-image

From (8.46) and Table 1, we calculate $t=4$. Applying 4 iterations of the operator G_ψ on the state $\left|\psi_\chi(r)\right\rangle$, we obtain the target sub-image with the probability $P_t=0.9462$ (see Code B. 87). The retrieved target sub-image is shown in Figure 12 (b).

Applying the operator U in (8.48) on the state $\left|0\right\rangle^{\otimes n}\left|1\right\rangle$, we have

$$U\left|0\right\rangle^{\otimes n}\left|1\right\rangle = \frac{1}{\sqrt{N}}\sum_{i\in A}\left|i\right\rangle\left|0\right\rangle + \frac{1}{\sqrt{N}}\sum_{i\in B}\left|i\right\rangle\left|1\right\rangle = \left|\psi_2\right\rangle. \qquad (8.54)$$

We calculate $U(R_0 \otimes I)U^{-1}$ by

$$\begin{aligned}
U(R_0 \otimes I)U^{-1} &= U[(2\left|0\right\rangle\left\langle 0\right| - I^{\otimes n}) \otimes I]U^{-1}\\
&= U(2\left|0\right\rangle^{\otimes n+1}\left\langle 0\right|^{\otimes n+1} + 2\left|0\right\rangle^{\otimes n}\left|1\right\rangle\left\langle 0\right|^{\otimes n}\left\langle 1\right| - I^{\otimes n+1})U^{-1}\\
&= 2\left|\psi_1\right\rangle\left\langle\psi_1\right| + 2\left|\psi_2\right\rangle\left\langle\psi_2\right| - I^{\otimes n+1},
\end{aligned} \qquad (8.55)$$

where $\left|\psi_1\right\rangle$ and $\left|\psi_2\right\rangle$ are seen (8.29) and (8.54), respectively. Therefore, the generalized Grover search operator G_ψ is rewritten as

$$G_\psi = (2\left|\psi_1\right\rangle\left\langle\psi_1\right| + 2\left|\psi_2\right\rangle\left\langle\psi_2\right| - I^{\otimes n+1})R_1, \qquad (8.56)$$

which is calculated by the simulated program Code B. 88.

We consider a 128×128 color image shown in Figure 13 (a) as the second example. The set A of marked states of the second example is given by the binary image in Figure 13 (b). Other priori data are shown in Table 2.

We calculate $t=2$ using (8.46) and Table 2. Applying 2 iterations of the operator G_ψ on the state $\left|\psi_\chi(r)\right\rangle$, we obtain the target sub-image with the probability $P_t=0.9261$ (see Code B. 89). The retrieved target sub-image is shown in Figure 13 (c).

CONCLUSION

In this chapter, two quantum image segmentation algorithms are described. The complexity of the first algorithm is $O(n^2)$, which shows the algorithm is an efficient edge detection method. The second algorithm has used the generalized Grover search algorithm to efficiently retrieve a target sub-image of an image. The simulated results demonstrate that the two algorithm can be used to segment the target sub-image.

REFERENCES

Berthiaume, A., & Brassard, G. (1994). Oracle quantum computing. *Journal of Modern Optics*, *41*(12), 2521–2535. doi:10.1080/09500349414552351

Biron, D., Biham, O., Biham, E., Grassl, M., & Lidar, D. A. (1998). Generalized Grover search algorithm for arbitrary initial amplitude distribution. *NASA International Conference on Quantum Computing and Quantum Communications*, 140-147.

Datta, R., Joshi, D., Li, J., & Wang, J. Z. (2008). Image retrieval: Ideas, influences, and trends of the new age. *ACM Computing Surveys*, *40*(2), 5. doi:10.1145/1348246.1348248

Giovannetti, V., Lloyd, S., & Maccone, L. (2008). Quantum random access memory. *Physical Review Letters*, *100*(16), 160501. doi:10.1103/PhysRevLett.100.160501 PMID:18518173

Grover, L. (1996). A fast quantum mechanical algorithm for database search. *The 28th Annual ACM Symposium on the Theory of Computing*, 212-219.

Li, H. S., Zhu, Q., Zhou, R. G., Song, L., & Yang, X. J. (2014). Multi-dimensional color image storage and retrieval for a normal arbitrary quantum superposition state. *Quantum Information Processing*, *13*(4), 991–1011. doi:10.100711128-013-0705-7

Long, G. L., & Sun, Y. (2001). Efficient scheme for initializing a quantum register with an arbitrary superposed state. *Physical Review A.*, *64*(1), 014303. doi:10.1103/PhysRevA.64.014303

Nielsen, M. A., & Chuang, I. L. (2000). *Quantum Computation and Quantum Information*. Cambridge University Press.

Venegas-Andraca, S. E., & Ball, J. L. (2010). Processing images in entangled quantum systems. *Quantum Information Processing*, *9*(1), 1–11. doi:10.100711128-009-0123-z

Yao, X. W., Wang, H., Liao, Z., Chen, M. C., & Suter, D. (2017). Quantum image processing and its application to edge detection: Theory and experiment. *Physical Review X, 7*(3), 031041. doi:10.1103/PhysRevX.7.031041

Zhang, H., Fritts, J. E., & Goldman, S. A. (2008). Image segmentation evaluation: A survey of unsupervised methods. *Computer Vision and Image Understanding, 110*(2), 260-280.

Zhang, Y., Lu, K., & Gao, Y. (2015). Qsobel: A Novel Quantum Image Edge Extraction Algorithm. *Science China. Information Sciences, 58*(1), 1–13. doi:10.100711432-014-5158-9

Conclusion

This book has described quantum image representations, quantum geometric transformations, quantum tool algorithms, quantum image compression and quantum image segmentation algorithms, which are outlined as follows:

1. Quantum image representations solve how to store an image in a quantum system, and to retrieve the image from the quantum system, which are the necessary foundation for quantum image processing.
2. Quantum geometric transformations include the global operators and two-point swapping. These global operators in n-qubit quantum systems, such as symmetric flips, local flips, orthogonal rotations and translations, can be realized with the complexity $O(n^2)$ at most, which offer exponential speedup over their classical counterparts.
3. Quantum tool algorithms in the book include quantum Fourier transforms, quantum wavelet transforms and quantum wavelet packet transforms. These quantum tool algorithms all offer exponential speedup over their classical counterparts. Quantum wavelet packet transforms have been used to realize quantum image compression.
4. The efficient edge detection algorithm with the complexity $O(n^2)$ and quantum image segmentation based on generalized Grover search algorithm were provided. The latter algorithm can efficiently retrieve a target sub-image of an image.

The simulation codes of the above algorithms were provided in Appendix B. It is a notable feature of the book.

OPEN CHALLENGES AND FUTURE RESEARCH DIRECTIONS

Some open challenges and future directions in quantum image processing have been discussed (Ranjani, 2019; Yan, Iliyasu, & Le, 2017; Yan, Iliyasu, & Venegas-Andraca, 2016; Yan, & Venegas-Andraca, 2020). Combined them and works in this book, open challenges and future research directions are proposed as follows.

1. Quantum state estimation (QSE) is an important technique for quantum information processing (Zhang, Cong, Ling, & Li, 2018). The task of QSE is to retrieve the information of a quantum state by a series of measurements. Obtaining a quantum measurement is costly, because it has to prepare large number of identical copies of the quantum state (Zhang, Cong, Ling, & Li, 2018). There exist a number of QSE methods, such as the maximum-likelihood estimation (Hradil, 1997), self-learning algorithms (Fischer, Kienle, & Freyberger, 2000), and fast quantum state estimator with sparse disturbance (Zhang, Cong, Ling, & Li, 2018). However, these algorithms are used to retrieve the information of a quantum state with large number of measurements. For instance, recovering a low-rank density matrix of an n-qubit state needs $O(n2^{2n})$ measurements. Chapter 3 has described the $O(2^{2n})$ measurements are needed at least to retrieve a image from quantum systems. Therefore, one open question is how to design efficient QSE algorithms.

2. Chapter 3 shows that the circuits of quantum image representations can be designed with the complexity $O(2^n)$ at least. Therefore, the efficient implementation circuits or optimized circuit algorithms will be a research direction for quantum image representations.

3. So far, all of the so-called experimental implementation of quantum image algorithms has been restricted to classical computing resources and Matlab simulations. These offer a rather restrictive implementation of the expected power of quantum computation (Yan, & Venegas-Andraca, 2020). Practical quantum computing hardware is developing very fast in recent years. There are quantum devices available for users through the cloud (Google; Ibm; Microsoft). For instance, 5-qubit quantum device is provided by IBM Q Experience platform. It is likely some quantum algorithms may be implemented in these noisy intermediate-scale quantum (NISO) devices, such as, quantum chemistry (Yung, Casanova, Mezzacapo, Mcclean, Lamata, Aspuru-Guzik, & Solano, 2014; Wei, Li,

& Long, 2019), quantum machine learning (Wittek, & Gogolin, 2017; Hu, Wang, Wang, & Wang, 2019). Quantum image processing is also a promising area of these NISQ devices. In order to be implemented in NISQ devices, the influence of noises and gate errors must be studied in details. these topics will be important future research directions.

4. On digital computers, images and image processing underpinned advanced applications in videos and movies. The quantum movie framework provides a platform to ponder quantum movie representation and production, and it still requires refinement and expansion (Yan, & Venegas-Andraca, 2020).

CONCLUSION

It is hoped that the detail simulation codes have contributed to experience provided algorithms in this book for readers. Meanwhile, it is also hoped that open challenges and future directions proposed in the book can accelerate the development of quantum image processing.

REFERENCES

Fischer, D. G., Kienle, S. H., & Freyberger, M. (2000). Quantum-state estimation by self-learning measurements. *Physical Review A.*, *61*(3), 032306. doi:10.1103/PhysRevA.61.032306

Google ai quantum. (n.d.). https://ai.google/research/teams/applied-science/quantum-ai

Hradil, Z. (1997). Quantum-state estimation. *Physical Review A.*, *55*(3), R1561–R1564. doi:10.1103/PhysRevA.55.R1561

Hu, F., Wang, B. N., Wang, N., & Wang, C. (2019). Quantum machine learning with D-wave quantum computer. *Quantum Engineering*, *1*(2), e12. https://www.research.ibm.com/ibm-q/

Microsoft Quantum computer lab. (n.d.). https://www.microsoft.com/en-us/quantum/

Ranjani, J. J. (2019). Quantum Image Processing and Its Applications. In Handbook of Multimedia Information Security: Techniques and Applications. Springer.

Wei, S., Li, H., & Long, G. L. (2019). *Full Quantum Eigensolver for Quantum Chemistry Simulations*. arXiv:1908.07927

Wittek, P., & Gogolin, C. (2017). Quantum enhanced inference in Markov logic networks. *Scientific Reports*, *7*(1), 45672. doi:10.1038rep45672 PMID:28422093

Yan, F., Iliyasu, A. M., & Le, P. Q. (2017). Quantum image processing: A review of advances in its security technologies. *International Journal of Quantum Information*, *15*(03), 1730001. doi:10.1142/S0219749917300017

Yan, F., Iliyasu, A. M., & Venegas-Andraca, S. E. (2016). A survey of quantum image representations. *Quantum Information Processing*, *15*(1), 1–35. doi:10.100711128-015-1195-6

Yan, F., & Venegas-Andraca, S. E. (2020). *Quantum image processing*. Singapore: Springer Nature Singapore company.

Yung, M. H., Casanova, J., Mezzacapo, A., Mcclean, J., Lamata, L., Aspuru-Guzik, A., & Solano, E. (2014). From transistor to trapped-ion computers for quantum chemistry. *Scientific Reports*, *4*(1), 3589. doi:10.1038rep03589 PMID:24395054

Zhang, J., Cong, S., Ling, Q., & Li, K. (2018). An efficient and fast quantum state estimator with sparse disturbance. *IEEE Transactions on Cybernetics*, *49*(7), 2546–2555. doi:10.1109/TCYB.2018.2828498 PMID:29994018

Appendix 1

MATHEMATIC GROUNDS

This appendix is devoted to providing succinct mathematical grounds required in quantum image processing. For details on most of the ideas touched on here, you can consult basic probability theory (Ross, 2008), linear algebra (Friedberg, Insel, & Lawrence, 2003; Nielsen & Chuang, 2000), and wavelet theory (Ruch & Van Fleet, 2009).

Basic Probability Theory

Sample space is the set of all possible outcomes of an experiment, and is denoted by S. For instance, If the outcome of an experiment consists in the determination of the sex of a newborn child, then $S=\{g,b\}$, where the outcome g means that the child is a girl and b that it is a boy.

An event is any subset E of the sample space. If the outcome of the experiment is contained in E, then we say that E has occurred. For instance, if $E=\{g\}$, then E is the event that the child is a girl. For each event E of the sample space S, $n(E)$ is the number of times in the first n repetitions of the experiment that the event E occurs. Then the probability of the event E, $P(E)$ is defined as

$$P(E) = \lim_{n \to \infty} \frac{n(E)}{n}. \tag{1}$$

The basic notion of probability theory is that of a random variable. A random variable is a real-valued function defined on the sample space, which is determined by the outcome of the experiment. A random variable that can take on at most a countable number of possible values is said to be discrete. For a discrete random variable X, we define the probability mass function $p(a)$ of X by $p(a)=p(X=a)$. In this book we shall only be concerned with random variables which take their value from a finite set of values, and we always assume that this is the case. That is, if X must assume one of the values $x_1, x_2, \ldots, x_n$, then

$$\sum_{i=1}^{n} p(x_i) = 1, \tag{2}$$

where $p(x_1) \geq 0$.

The expression of a random variable X, denoted by E[X], is defined by

$$E(\mathrm{X}) = \sum_{i} x p(x). \tag{3}$$

Therefore, the expected value of X is a weighted average of the possible values that X can take on, each value being weighted by the probability that X assumes it.

The variance of a random variable X is defined by

$$Var(X) = E[(X - E(X))^2] = E(X^2) - E(X)^2. \tag{4}$$

The square root of the *Var(X)* is called the standard deviation of *X*, and we denote it by *SD(X)*. That is,

$$SD(X) = \sqrt{Var(X)}. \tag{5}$$

Suppose that an experiment, whose outcome can be classified as either a success or a failure is performed, a random variable X is said to be a Bernoulli random variable, if its probability mass function is given by

$$\begin{cases} p(0) = p(X = 0) = p, \\ p(1) = p(X = 1) = 1 - p, \end{cases} \tag{6}$$

where $X=1$ when the outcome is a success and $X=0$ when it is a failure.

The random variables X and Y are said to be independent if, for any two sets of real numbers A and B,

$$P(x \in A, y \in B) = P(x \in A)P(y \in B). \tag{7}$$

Theorem A.1 (The strong law of large numbers) Let X_1, X_2,... be a sequence of independent and identically distributed random variables, each having a finite mean $\mu = E(X_i)$. Then, with probability 1,

$$\lim_{n \to +\infty} \frac{X_1 + X_2 + ... X_n}{n} = \mu. \tag{8}$$

Linear Algebra

Linear algebra is the study of vector spaces and of linear operations on those vector spaces. A good understanding of quantum mechanics is based upon a solid grasp of elementary linear algebra. Some definitions and basic operations in linear algebra are defined as follows.

Definition A.2 (Group) A group is a set G, together with a map of $G \times G$ into G, denoted as $g*h$, with the following properties:

1. Associativity: For all $g,h,k \in G$, $g*(h*k) = (g*h)*k$.
2. There exists an identity element e in G such that for all $g \in G$, $g*e = e*g = g$.
3. For all $g \in G$, there exists $h \in G$, $g*h = h*g = e$. That is, h is the inverse of g, denoted as g^{-1}.

If $g*h = h*g$ for all $g,h \in G$, then the group is said to be commutative.

Definition A.3 (Field) A field $< \mathbb{F}, +, \cdot >$ is a set $\square$ with two operations, addition and multiplication, such that

1. $< \mathbb{F}, + >$ is a commutative group under addition, and its identity element is denoted as 0.
2. Let $\mathbb{F}^*$ be a set $\square$ without the element 0, then $< \mathbb{F}^*, \cdot >$ is a commutative group under multiplication, and its identity element is denoted as 1.
3. Distributivity: For all $a, b, c \in \mathbb{F}$, $a(b+c) = ab+ac$.

Definition A.4 (Vector Space) A vector space over $\square$ is a set V endowed with two operations: vector addition $V \times V \to V$, denoted by $(v,w) \to v+w$, and

274

scalar multiplication $\mathbb{F} \times V \to V$, denoted by $(a,v) \to av$, satisfying the following properties:

1. V is a commutative group under vector addition.
2.   2. Scalar multiplication satisfies the following identities:

$$\begin{cases} a(bv) = (ab)v, \text{ for all } v \in V \text{ and } a,b \in \mathbb{F} \ , \\ 1v = v, \text{ for all } v \in V. \end{cases} \tag{9}$$

3.   3. Scalar multiplication and vector addition are related by the following distributive laws:

$$\begin{cases} (a + b)v = av + bv, \text{ for all } v \in V \text{ and } a,b \in \mathbb{F} \ , \\ a(v + w) = av + aw, \text{ for all } v,w \in V \text{ and } a \in \mathbb{F}. \end{cases} \tag{10}$$

A subset $S \subseteq V$ is said to be linearly dependent if there exists a linear relation of the form $\sum_{i=1}^{k} a_i v_i = 0$, where $v_1, v_2, \ldots, v_k$ are distinct elements of S and at least one of the coefficients a_i is nonzero; S is said to be linearly independent otherwise. A basis for V is a subset $S \subseteq V$ that is linearly independent and spans V. If V has a finite basis, then V is said to be finite-dimensional, and otherwise it is infinite-dimensional.

The vector space of most interest to us is $\mathbb{C}^n$, the space of all n-tuples of complex numbers, $(c_1, c_2, \ldots, c_n)$. The elements of a vector space are called vectors, and we will sometimes use the column matrix notation

$$\begin{bmatrix} c_1 \\ \vdots \\ c_n \end{bmatrix} \tag{11}$$

to indicate a vector. There is an addition operation in $\mathbb{C}^n$ defined which takes pairs of vectors to other vectors, i.e.,

$$\begin{bmatrix} c_1 \\ \vdots \\ c_n \end{bmatrix} + \begin{bmatrix} z_1 \\ \vdots \\ z_n \end{bmatrix} = \begin{bmatrix} c_1 + z_1 \\ \vdots \\ c_1 + z_n \end{bmatrix}. \tag{12}$$

where the addition operations on the right are just ordinary additions of complex numbers. The scalar multiplication in is $\mathbb{C}^n$ defined by

$$a \begin{bmatrix} c_1 \\ \vdots \\ c_n \end{bmatrix} = \begin{bmatrix} ac_1 \\ \vdots \\ ac_1 \end{bmatrix}, \tag{13}$$

where a is a complex number, that is, $a \in \mathbb{C}$, and the multiplications on the right are ordinary multiplication of complex numbers.

In this book, we will use the standard notation of quantum mechanics for linear algebraic concepts. The standard quantum mechanical notation for a vector in a vector space is the symbol $|\psi\rangle$, where ψ is a label for the vector. The $|.\rangle$ notation is used to indicate that the object is a vector.

Suppose $|v_1\rangle, |v_2\rangle, ..., |v_n\rangle$ is a basis in $\mathbb{C}^n$, then any vector $|v\rangle$ in the vector space $\mathbb{C}^n$ can be written as a linear combination $|v\rangle = \sum_{i=1}^{n} a_i |v_i\rangle$ of vectors. For instance, a basis $|v_1\rangle, |v_2\rangle$ is a subset in $\mathbb{C}^2$ such that

$$\left|v_1\right\rangle = \begin{bmatrix} 1 \\ 0 \end{bmatrix}, \left|v_2\right\rangle = \begin{bmatrix} 0 \\ 1 \end{bmatrix}. \tag{14}$$

Since any vector

$$\left|v\right\rangle = \begin{bmatrix} a_1 \\ a_2 \end{bmatrix} \tag{15}$$

in $\mathbb{C}^2$ can be written as a linear combination $|v\rangle = a_1 |v_1\rangle + a_2 |v_2\rangle$ of the vectors $|v_1\rangle$ and $|v_2\rangle$, we say that the vectors $|v_1\rangle$ and $|v_2\rangle$ span the vector space $\mathbb{C}^2$.

Definition A.5 (Inner Product) Let *V* be a vector space, then a function (•,•) from *V*×*V* to $\mathbb{C}$ is an inner product if it satisfies the requirements that:

1.   1. (•,•) is linear in the second argument,

$$\left(|v\rangle, \sum_i \lambda_i |w_i\rangle \right) = \sum_i \lambda_i (|v\rangle, |w_i\rangle);$$ (16)

2. $(|v\rangle, |w\rangle) = (|w\rangle, |v\rangle)^*$, where $(\bullet)^*$ denotes complex conjugate of a complex number;
3. $(|v\rangle, |v\rangle) \geq 0$ with equality if and only if $|v\rangle = 0$.

For instance, an inner product in $\mathbb{C}^n$ is defined by

$$((v_1, \ldots, v_n), (w_1, \ldots, w_n)) = \begin{bmatrix} v_1^* & \cdots & v_n^* \end{bmatrix} \begin{bmatrix} w_1 \\ \vdots \\ w_n \end{bmatrix}.$$ (17)

Definition A.6 (Inner Product Space) An inner product space is a vector space equipped with an inner product.

Definition A.7 (Hilbert Space) In the finite-dimensional complex vector spaces that come up in quantum computation and quantum information, a Hilbert space is exactly the same thing as an inner product space.

Wavelet Theory

Here we introduce the discrete Haar wavelet transform, the discrete Daubechies D4 wavelet transform, and the discrete wavelet packet transform.

The Discrete Haar Wavelet Transform

Definition A.8 (The discrete Haar wavelet transform) Suppose that N is an even positive integer. We define the discrete Haar wavelet transform as

$$H_N = \begin{bmatrix} F_{N/2} \\ G_{N/2} \end{bmatrix} = \begin{bmatrix} \frac{\sqrt{2}}{2} & \frac{\sqrt{2}}{2} & 0 & 0 & \cdots & 0 & 0 \\ 0 & 0 & \frac{\sqrt{2}}{2} & \frac{\sqrt{2}}{2} & \cdots & 0 & 0 \\ \vdots & \vdots & \vdots & \vdots & \ddots & \vdots & \vdots \\ 0 & 0 & 0 & 0 & \cdots & \frac{\sqrt{2}}{2} & \frac{\sqrt{2}}{2} \\ \frac{\sqrt{2}}{2} & -\frac{\sqrt{2}}{2} & 0 & 0 & \cdots & 0 & 0 \\ 0 & 0 & \frac{\sqrt{2}}{2} & -\frac{\sqrt{2}}{2} & \cdots & 0 & 0 \\ \vdots & \vdots & \vdots & \vdots & \ddots & \vdots & \vdots \\ 0 & 0 & 0 & 0 & \cdots & \frac{\sqrt{2}}{2} & -\frac{\sqrt{2}}{2} \end{bmatrix}, \tag{18}$$

where the block $F_{N/2}$ is called the average block, and the block $G_{N/2}$ is called the detail block.

Suppose V is a vector in the N-dimensional vector space $\mathbb{R}^N$ of real numbers, where N is a positive integer divisible by 2^n. We compute the discrete Haar wavelet transform of V,

$$y^1 = H_N V = \begin{bmatrix} y^{1,a} \\ y^{1,d} \end{bmatrix}, \tag{19}$$

where the vector $y^{1,a}$ represents the $N/2$-length average portion of the transform, and $y^{1,d}$ denotes the $N/2$-length detail portion of the transform. The second iteration of the discrete Haar wavelet transform is

$$y^2 = \begin{bmatrix} H_{N/2} y^{1,a} \\ y^{1,d} \end{bmatrix} = \begin{bmatrix} y^{2,a} \\ y^{2,d} \\ y^{1,d} \end{bmatrix}, \tag{20}$$

where the vectors $y^{2,a}$ and $y^{2,d}$ are the $N/4$-length vectors that represent the average and detail portions, respectively, of the discrete Haar wavelet transformation applied to the vector $y^{1,a}$.

Since N is divisible by 2^n, we can iterate a total of n times, and the jth iteration of the discrete Haar wavelet transform, where $j=1,2,\ldots,n$, is

$$y^j = \begin{bmatrix} y^{j,a} \\ y^{j,d} \\ y^{j-1,d} \\ y^{j-2,d} \\ \vdots \\ y^{2,d} \\ y^{j1d} \end{bmatrix}, \tag{21}$$

where $y^{j,a} \in \mathbb{R}^{N/2^j}$, and $y^{k,d} \in \mathbb{R}^{N/2^k}$, and $k=1,2,\ldots,j$.

We can also write the iterated discrete Haar wavelet transform in terms of products of block matrices. Let I_n and O_n denote the $n \times n$ identity and zero matrices, respectively. We denote $H_{N,0}=H_N$ and

$$H_{N,j} = \mathrm{diag}[H_{N/2^j}, I_{N/2^j}, I_{N/2^{j-1}}, \ldots, I_{N/4}, I_{N/2}] \tag{22}$$

for $j=1,2,\ldots,n$, where $\mathrm{diag}[C_1,C_2,\ldots,C_n]$ is a matrix with blocks $C_1,C_2,\ldots,C_n$ on the main diagonal and zeros elsewhere. Then, we give the following definition:

Definition A.9 (The jth iteration of the discrete Haar wavelet transform) The jth iteration of the discrete Haar wavelet transform is expressed as $H_{N,j-1} \ldots H_{N,1} H_{N,0}$, that is,

$$y^j = H_{N,j-1} \ldots H_{N,1} H_{N,0} V . \tag{23}$$

Definition A.10 (The inverse of the jth iteration of the discrete Haar wavelet transform) Since $H_{N,j}^{-1} = H_{N,j}^T$, where $(\bullet)^{-1}$ and $(\bullet)^T$ are the inverse and transpose of matrix, we obtain the inverse of the iterated discrete Haar wavelet transform as $H_{N,0}^T H_{N,1}^T \ldots H_{N,j-1}^T$, i.e.,

$$H_{N,0}^T H_{N,1}^T \ldots H_{N,j-1}^T y^j = V . \tag{24}$$

The Discrete Daubechies D4 Wavelet Transform

Definition A.11 (The discrete Daubechies D4 wavelet transform) Suppose that N is an even positive integer. The discrete Daubechies D4 wavelet transform is defined as

$$D_N = \begin{bmatrix} h_0 & h_1 & h_2 & h_3 & 0 & 0 & \cdots & 0 & 0 & 0 & 0 \\ 0 & 0 & h_0 & h_1 & h_2 & h_3 & \cdots & 0 & 0 & 0 & 0 \\ \vdots & \vdots & \vdots & \vdots & \vdots & \vdots & \ddots & \vdots & \vdots & \vdots & \vdots \\ 0 & 0 & 0 & 0 & 0 & 0 & \cdots & h_0 & h_1 & h_2 & h_3 \\ h_2 & h_3 & 0 & 0 & 0 & 0 & \cdots & 0 & 0 & h_0 & h_1 \\ h_3 & -h_2 & h_1 & -h_0 & 0 & 0 & \cdots & 0 & 0 & 0 & 0 \\ 0 & 0 & h_3 & -h_2 & h_1 & -h_0 & \cdots & 0 & 0 & 0 & 0 \\ \vdots & \vdots & \vdots & \vdots & \vdots & \vdots & \ddots & \vdots & \vdots & \vdots & 0 \\ 0 & 0 & 0 & 0 & 0 & 0 & \cdots & h_3 & -h_2 & h_1 & -h_0 \\ h_1 & -h_0 & 0 & 0 & 0 & 0 & \cdots & 0 & 0 & h_3 & -h_2 \end{bmatrix}, \tag{25}$$

where $h_0 = \dfrac{1+\sqrt{3}}{4\sqrt{2}}$, $h_1 = \dfrac{3+\sqrt{3}}{4\sqrt{2}}$, $h_2 = \dfrac{3-\sqrt{3}}{4\sqrt{2}}$ and $h_3 = \dfrac{1-\sqrt{3}}{4\sqrt{2}}$.

Proposition A.12 (The Matrix T_N is Orthogonal) The matrix D_N given in Definition A.11 is orthogonal, that is, $D_N D_N^T = I_N$.

Definition A.13 (The jth iteration of the discrete Daubechies D4 wavelet transform) The jth iteration of the discrete Daubechies D4 wavelet transform is expressed as,

$$D_{N,j-1} \ldots D_{N,1} D_{N,0}, \tag{26}$$

where $D_{N,0} = D_N$, and

$$D_{N,j} = \mathrm{diag}[D_{N/2^j}, I_{N/2^j}, I_{N/2^{j-1}}, \ldots, I_{N/4}, I_{N/2}].$$

Definition A.14 (The inverse of the jth iteration of the discrete Daubechies D4 wavelet transform) Since the matrix $D_{N,j}$ is orthogonal, we have $D_{N,j}^{-1} = D_{N,j}^{T}$. The inverse of the iterated discrete Daubechies D4 wavelet transform is $D_{N,0}^{T} D_{N,1}^{T} \ldots D_{N,j-1}^{T}$.

The Discrete Wavelet Packet Transform

The only difference in performing i iterations of the discrete wavelet packet transform and i iterations of the discrete wavelet transform is that we apply a wavelet transformation matrix to both the averages and details portion at each packet iteration step.

Let W_N be a discrete wavelet transform, for instance, $W_N = H_N$ and $W_N = D_N$ are the discrete Haar wavelet transform and the discrete Daubechies D4 wavelet transform, respectively. We have the following definition.

Definition A.15 (The jth iteration of the one-dimensional discrete wavelet packet transform) The jth iteration of the one-dimensional discrete wavelet packet transform is defined as

$$W_N^j = W_{N,j-1} W_{N,j-2} \ldots W_{N,1} W_{N,0}, \tag{27}$$

where $W_{N,0} = W_N$ and

$$W_{N,j} = Diag(W_{N/2^j}, W_{N/2^j}, \ldots, W_{N/2^j})$$

is a matrix with 2^j blocks of $W_{N/2^j}$ on the main diagonal and zeros elsewhere.

Definition A.16 (The inverse of the jth iteration of the one-dimensional discrete wavelet packet transform) The inverse of the jth iteration of the one-dimensional discrete wavelet packet transform is defined as

$$(W_N^j)^{-1} = W_{N,0}^{T} W_{N,1}^{T} \ldots W_{N,j-1}^{T}. \tag{28}$$

Suppose that A is an $M \times N$ matrix where M, N are even positive integers. If we denote the columns of A by $a^1, a^2, \ldots, a^N$, then the matrix product $W_M A$ can be written

$$W_M A = W_M [a^1, a^2, \ldots, a^N] = [W_M a^1, W_M a^2, \ldots, W_M a^N], \tag{29}$$

and the product $W_M A$ simply applies the discrete wavelet packet transform to each column of A. In practice, both columns and rows of a digital grayscale image are processed. That is, the two-dimensional discrete wavelet packet transform of $M \times N$ matrix A where both M, N are even positive integers is defined as $W_M A W_N^T$. Therefore, we give the following definition.

Definition A.17 (The *j*th iteration of the two-dimensional discrete wavelet packet transform) The *j*th iteration of the two-dimensional discrete wavelet packet transform is defined as

$$W_M^j A (W_N^j)^T, \tag{30}$$

where W_M^j and $(W_N^j)^T$ are the *j*th iteration of the one-dimensional discrete wavelet packet transform and its inverse.

REFERENCES

Friedberg, S. H., Insel, A. J., & Lawrence, E. S. (2003). *Linear algebra* (8th ed.). Prentice Hall Press.

Nielsen, M. A., & Chuang, I. L. (2000). *Quantum Computation and Quantum Information*. Cambridge University Press.

Ross, S. (2008). *A first course in probability* (8th ed.). Prentice Hall Press.

Ruch, D. K., & Van Fleet, P. J. (2009). *Wavelet Theory: an elementary approach with applications*. John Wiley & Sons Press. doi:10.1002/9781118165652

Appendix 2

THE SIMULATION CODES

This appendix provides the simulation codes for the proposed algorithms, which are performed MATLAB R2017a, windows 7, and 64GB RAM with a classical computer.

The Codes for Qubit Gates in Chapter 2

Code B.1 Calculate n-qubit basis state $\left| j \right\rangle$ in (2.31)

```
function st = state(j,n)
f=dec2bin(j); % Convert from decimal to binary
[m1,m2]=size(f);
s=strcat(repmat('0',1,n-m2), f);
[m3,m4]=size(s);
a0=[1;0];
a1=[0;1];
for k=1:m3
    kj=1;
    for i=1:m4
        if s(k,i)=='0'
            t=a0;
        else
            t=a1;
        end
        kj=kron(kj,t);
    end
    st(:,k)=kj;
end
end
```

Code B.2 The implementation of multiple tensor product $U^{\otimes n}$

```
function Y=tenProduct(U,n)
  Y=0;
  if n>0
    Y=U;
    for i=1:n-1
      Y=kron(Y,u);
    end
  end
end
```

Code B.3 The implementation of the gate $V_n^i(U)$ in (2.32)

```
function P=Cun(n,i,U)
[m1,m2]=size(U);
k=log2(m1);
I=[1 0;0 1];
tj=state(i,n); % Calculate |i>
P=kron(U-tenProduct(I,k), tj*tj')+tenProduct(I, n+k);
end
```

Code B.4 The implementation of the gate $C_n^i(U)$ in (2.32)

```
function P=Cup(n,i,U)
[m1,m2]=size(U);
k=log2(m1);
I=[1 0;0 1];
tj=state(i,n); % Calculate |i>
P=kron(tj*tj',U-tenProduct(I,k))+tenProduct(I,n+k);
end
```

The Codes for NASS States in Chapter 3

Code B.5 Converting a 2D image *A2* to a column vector *A1*

```
function A1=d2tod1(A2)
[d1,d2]=size(A2);
A1=zeros(d1*d2,1);
m=0;
for i=1:d1
    for j=1:d2
            m=(i-1)*d2+j;
            A1(m)=A2(i,j);
```

```
        end
end
end
```

Code B.6 Converting a column vector *A1* to a 2D image *A2*

```
function A2=d1tod2(A1,d1,d2)
A2=zeros(d1,d2);
for i=1:d1
    A2(i,1:d2)=A1(1+(i-1)*d2:i*d2,1).';
end
end
```

Code B.7 The implementation of a NASS state for 2D grayscale images in (3.58)

```
% f is a grayscale image.
% The function GQ2 transforms the grayscale image f into a NASS
state, i.e., a vector Q.
function [G,Q]=GQ2(f)
[row,col]=size(f);
M=256;
fg=pi()*f/(2*M-2);% Convert colors to angles
dg=abs(fg).*abs(fg);
G=sqrt(sum(dg(:)));
%Normalize the image
g = fg/G;
%Convert a 2D image to a column vector
Q=d2tod1(g);
end
```

Code B.8 Retrieving a 2D grayscale image from a NASS sate

```
% Q is a vector for a NASS state.
% G is a normalization factor.
% The function QG2 converts a vector Q to a row*col grayscale
image f.
function f=QG2(Q, G, row, col)
g = Q*G;
f1=d1tod2(g, row, col);
% Convert angles to colors
f=f1*(2*256-2)/pi();
end
```

Code B.9 The implementation of a NASS state for 2D color images in (3.58)

```
% f is a color image.
% The function CQ2 transforms the color image f into a NASS
state, i.e., a vector Q.
function [G,Q]=CQ2(f)
[row,col,tem]=size(f);
%Convert colors to angles
M=2^24;
fg=pi()*(f(:,:,1)*256*256 + f(:,:,2)*256 + f(:,:,3))/(2*M-2);
dg=abs(fg).*abs(fg);
G=sqrt(sum(dg(:)));
%Normalize the image
g = fg/G;
%Convert a 2D image to a column vector
Q=d2tod1(g);
end
```

Code B.10 Retrieving a 2D color image from a NASS sate

```
% Q is a vector for a NASS state.
% G is a normalization factor.
% The function QC2 converts a vector Q to a row*col color image
f.
function gf =QC2(Q, G, row, col)
g = Q*G;
f=d1tod2(g, row, col);
% Convert angles to colors
M=2^24;
wginvac=f*(2*M-2)/pi();
gf(:,:,1)=fix(wginvac/(256*256));
gf(:,:,2)=rem(fix(wginvac/256),256);
gf(:,:,3)=rem(wginvac,256);
end
```

Code B.11 The implementation of a NASS state for a video in (3.60)

```
% f is a vedio.
% The function GQ3 transforms the video f into a NASS state,
i.e., a vector Q.
function [G,Q]=GQ3(f)
[row,col,st]=size(f);
% Convert colors to angles
M=2^8;
fg= pi()*f/(2*M-2);
dg=abs(fg).*abs(fg);
G=sqrt(sum(dg(:)));
```

```
% Normalize the image
g = fg/G;
% Convert a 3D image to a column vector
Q=[];
for i=1:row
    A=zeros(col,st);
    for j=1:col
        for k=1:st
            A(j,k)=g(i,j,k);
        end
    end
        Q=[Q;d2tod1(A)];
end
end
```

Code B.12 Retrieving a video from a NASS sate

```
% Q is a vector for a NASS state.
 % G is a normalization factor.
% The function QG3 converts a vector Q to a row*col*st vedio f.
function f =QG3(Q, G, row, col, st)
ghx=zeros(row,col,st);
for i=1:row
    i1=(i-1)*col*st+1;
    i2=i*col*st;
    A1=Q(i1:i2,1);
    A=d1tod2(A1, col, st);
    for j=1:col
        for k=1:st
            ghx(i,j,k)=A(j,k);
        end
    end
end
wginva=ghx*G;
% Convert angles to colors
  M=2^8;
  f=wginva*(2*M-2)/pi();
end
```

The Codes for Geometric Transformations in Chapter 4

Code B.13 The code of the two-point swapping for the grayscale image in (4.29)

```
% Two-point swapping for the grayscale image in (4.29)
function []=Two-pointSwapImage()
clear all
clc
% f is a 8*4 grayscale image
f=[1 2 3 4];
for i=1:7
    f=[f;i*4+1 i*4+2 i*4+3 i*4+4;];
end
[row, col]=size(f);
% Call the function GQ2 to create a NASS state
 [G,Q]=GQ2(f);
% Calculate the matrix TP of the circuit in Figure 4.1
W=[0 1; -1 0];
W1=[0 -1; 1 0];
X=[0 1; 1 0];
TP=Cun(4,15,X)*Cup(1,0,Cun(3,7,W))*Cup(2,0,Cun(2,3,W))*Cup(3,0,
Cun(1,1,W))*Cup(4,0,W);
TP=Cup(4,0,W1)*Cup(3,0,Cun(1,1,W1))*Cup(2,0,Cun(2,3,W1))*Cup(1,
0,Cun(3,7,W1))*TP;
%Implement the two-point swapping
TPQ=TP*Q;
% Retrieve the transformed image
Tf=uint8(QG2(TPQ, G, row, col));
end
```

Code B.14 The code of the two-point swapping for the video in Figure 4.21

```
% Two-point swapping for the video in Figure 4.21
function []=Two-pointSwapVideo()
clear all
clc
% f is a 4*2*4 video
f1=[1 5; 9 13; 17 21; 25 29];
f(:,:,1)=f1;
f(:,:,2)=f1+1;
f(:,:,3)=f1+2;
f(:,:,4)=f1+3;
[row,col,st]=size(f);
% Call the function GQ3 to create a NASS state
 [G,Q]=GQ3(f);
% Calculate the matrix TP of the circuit in Figure 4.1
```

```
W=[0 1; -1 0];
W1=[0 -1; 1 0];
X=[0 1; 1 0];
TP=Cun(4,15,X)*Cup(1,0,Cun(3,7,W))*Cup(2,0,Cun(2,3,W))*Cup(3,0,
Cun(1,1,W))*Cup(4,0,W);
TP=Cup(4,0,W1)*Cup(3,0,Cun(1,1,W1))*Cup(2,0,Cun(2,3,W1))*Cup(1,
0,Cun(3,7,W1))*TP;
TPQ=TP*Q; % Implement the two-point swapping
Tf=uint8(QG3(TPQ, G, row, col, st)); % Retrieve the transformed
image
end
```

Code B.15 The code of symmetric flip transformations for the image in Figure 4.22

```
% Symmetric flip transformations for the 128*128 color image
function []=FlipImage()
clear all
clc
X=[0 1; 1 0];
I=[1 0; 0 1];
% f is a 128*128 color image
f = double(imread('airplane.bmp'));
subplot(1,3,1),imshow(uint8(f));
[row, col,tem]=size(f);
r=log2(row);
c=log2(col);
% Call the function CQ2 to create a NASS state
 [G,Q]=CQ2(f);
% Flip along x axis
GFX=kron(tenProduct(I,r),tenProduct(X,c));
GFXQ=GFX*Q;
% Flip along y axis
GFY=kron(tenProduct(X,r),tenProduct(I,c));
GFYQ=GFY*Q;
% Retrieve  the transformed image
fx=QC2(GFXQ, G, row, col);
fy=QC2(GFYQ, G, row, col);
subplot(1,3,2),imshow(uint8(fx));
subplot(1,3,3),imshow(uint8(fy));
end
```

Code B.16 The code of symmetric flip transformations for the video in Figure 4.23

```
% Symmetric flip for the 128*128*2 video
function []=FlipVideo()
```

```
clear all
clc
X=[0 1; 1 0];
I=[1 0; 0 1];
% f is a 128*128*2 video
for i=1:2
    A=imread([num2str(i),'.bmp']);
    f(:,:,i)=double(A);
    subplot(2,4,i);
    imshow(A,[]);
end
[row, col,st]=size(f);
r=log2(row);
c=log2(col);
t=log2(st);
% Call the function GQ3 to create a NASS state
[G,Q]=GQ3(f);
% Flip along x axis
GFX=kron(tenProduct(I,r),tenProduct(X,c+t));
GFXQ=GFX*Q;
% Flip along y axis
GFY=kron(kron(tenProduct(X,r),tenProduct(I,c)),tenProduct(X
,t));
GFYQ=GFY*Q;
% Flip along t axis
GFT=kron(tenProduct(X,r+c),tenProduct(I,t));
GFTQ=GFT*Q;
% Retrieve  the transformed video
fx=QG3(GFXQ, G, row, col, st);
for i=1:2
    subplot(2,4,2+i);
    A=fx(:,:,i);
    imshow(uint8(A),[]);
end
fy=QG3(GFYQ, G, row, col, st);
for i=1:2
    subplot(2,4,4+i);
    A=fy(:,:,i);
    imshow(uint8(A),[]);
end
ft=QG3(GFTQ, G, row, col, st);
for i=1:2
    subplot(2,4,6+i);
    A=ft(:,:,i);
    imshow(uint8(A),[]);
end
  end
```

Code B.17 The code of local flip transformations for the image in Figure 4.24

```
% Local flip for the 128*128 color image
function []=LocalFlipImage()
clear all
clc
X=[0 1; 1 0];
I=[1 0; 0 1];
% f is a 128*128 color image
f = double(imread('airplane.bmp'));
subplot(1,3,1),imshow(uint8(f));
[row, col,tem]=size(f);
r=log2(row);
c=log2(col);
% Call the function CQ2 to create a NASS state
 [G,Q]=CQ2(f);
% Local flip along x axis for the left part of the image
m=0;
GFXL=kron(tenProduct(I,r),Cup(1,m,tenProduct(X,c-1)));
GFXLQ=GFXL*Q;
% Local flip along x axis for the right part of the image
m=1;
GFXR=kron(tenProduct(I,r),Cup(1,m,tenProduct(X,c-1)));
GFXRQ=GFXR*Q;
% Retrieve the transformed image
fl=QC2(GFXLQ, G, row, col);
fr=QC2(GFXRQ, G, row, col);
subplot(1,3,2),imshow(uint8(fl));
subplot(1,3,3),imshow(uint8(fr));
end
```

Code B.18 The code of local flip transformations for the video in Figure 4.25

```
% Local flip for the 128*128*2 video
function []=LocalFlipVideo()
clear all
clc
X=[0 1; 1 0];
I=[1 0; 0 1];
% f is a 128*128*2 video
for i=1:2
   A=imread([num2str(i),'.bmp']);
   f(:,:,i)=double(A);
   subplot(1,6,i);
   imshow(A,[]);
end
[row, col,st]=size(f);
% Call the function GQ3 to create a NASS state
```

```
[G,Q]=GQ3(f);
% Local flip along t axis for the left part of the image frames
temp=kron(Cun(1,0,tenProduct(X,7)),tenProduct(I,7))*Q;
GFTLQ=kron(tenProduct(I,7),kron(Cup(1,0,tenProduct(X,6)),I))*t
emp;
% Local flip along t axis for the right part of the image
frames
temp=kron(Cun(1,1,tenProduct(X,7)),tenProduct(I,7))*Q;
GFTUQ=kron(tenProduct(I,7),kron(Cup(1,1,tenProduct(X,6)),I))*t
emp;
% Retrieve the transformed video
fl=QG3(GFTLQ, G, row, col, st);
for i=1:2
    subplot(1,6,2+i);
    A=fl(:,:,i);
    imshow(uint8(A),[]);
end
fu=QG3(GFTUQ, G, row, col, st);
for i=1:2
    subplot(1,6,4+i);
    A=fu(:,:,i);
    imshow(uint8(A),[]);
end
end
```

Code B.19 The implementation of an *n*-qubit Swap gate in Figure 4.26.

```
% Swap gate with n qubits (n>=2)
function P=Swa(n)
I=[1 0;0 1];
X=[0 1; 1 0];
if n<2
    P=0;
else
    Im=1;
    if n>2
    Im=tenProduct(I,n-2);
    end
    P=Cun(1,1,kron(X,Im))*Cup(1,1,kron(Im,X))*Cun(1,1,kron(X,
Im));
end
end
```

292

Code B.20 The code of orthogonal rotation transformations for the image in Figure 4.27

```
% Orthogonal rotation for the 128*128 color image
function []=OrthogRotationImage()
clear all
clc
X=[0 1; 1 0];
I=[1 0; 0 1];
% f is a 128*128 color image
f = double(imread('airplane.bmp'));
subplot(1,4,1),imshow(uint8(f));
[row, col,tem]=size(f);
r=log2(row);
c=log2(col);
% Call the function CQ2 to create a NASS state
 [G,Q]=CQ2(f);
% Orthogonal rotation with pi/2
temp=kron(tenProduct(X,r),tenProduct(I,c))*Q;
temp=kron(Swa(r+1),tenProduct(I,c-1))*temp;
for i=r-2:-1:1
    temp=kron(tenProduct(I,r-i-1),kron(Swa(r+1),tenProduct(I,i)
))*temp;
end
GO1=kron(tenProduct(I,r-1),Swa(r+1))*temp;
% Orthogonal rotation with pi
GO2=tenProduct(X,r+c)*Q;
% Orthogonal rotation with 3*pi/2
temp=kron(tenProduct(I,c),tenProduct(X,r))*Q;
temp=kron(Swa(r+1),tenProduct(I,c-1))*temp;
for i=r-2:-1:1
    temp=kron(tenProduct(I,r-i-1),kron(Swa(r+1),tenProduct(I,i)
))*temp;
end
GO3=kron(tenProduct(I,r-1),Swa(r+1))*temp;
% Retrieve the transformed image
f1=QC2(GO1, G, row, col);
f2=QC2(GO2, G, row, col);
f3=QC2(GO3, G, row, col);
subplot(1,4,2),imshow(uint8(f1));
subplot(1,4,3),imshow(uint8(f2));
subplot(1,4,4),imshow(uint8(f3));
end
```

Code B.21 The code of orthogonal rotation transformations for the video in Figure 4.28

```
% Orthogonal rotation for the 128*128*2 video
function []=OrthogRotationVideo()
clear all
clc
X=[0 1; 1 0];
I=[1 0; 0 1];
% f is a 128*128*2 video
for i=1:2
    A=imread([num2str(i),'.bmp']);
    f(:,:,i)=double(A);
    subplot(2,4,i);
    imshow(A,[]);
end
[row, col,st]=size(f);
r=log2(row);
c=log2(col);
t=log2(st);
% Call the function GQ3 to create a NASS state
[G,Q]=GQ3(f);
% Orthogonal rotation with pi/2
GO1=kron(tenProduct(X,r),tenProduct(I,c+1))*Q;
GO1=kron(Swa(r+1),tenProduct(I,c))*GO1;
for i=r-2:-1:0
    GO1=kron(tenProduct(I,r-i-1),kron(Swa(r+1),tenProduct(I,i+1
))) *GO1;
end
% Orthogonal rotation with pi
GO2=kron(tenProduct(X,r+c),I)*Q;
% Orthogonal rotation with 3*pi/2
GO3=kron(kron(tenProduct(I,r),tenProduct(X,c)),I)*Q;
GO3=kron(Swa(r+1),tenProduct(I,c))*GO3;
for i=r-2:-1:0
    GO3=kron(tenProduct(I,r-i-1),kron(Swa(r+1),tenProduct(I,i+1
))) *GO3;
end
% Retrieve the transformed image
f1=QG3(GO1, G, row, col, st);
for i=1:2
    subplot(2,4,2+i);
    A=f1(:,:,i);
    imshow(uint8(A),[]);
end
f2=QG3(GO2, G, row, col, st);
for i=1:2
    subplot(2,4,4+i);
```

```
    A=f2(:,:,i);
    imshow(uint8(A),[]);
end
f3=QG3(GO3, G, row, col, st);
for i=1:2
    subplot(2,4,6+i);
    A=f3(:,:,i);
    imshow(uint8(A),[]);
end
end
```

Code B.22 The code for the circuit of T_k in Figure 4.18 (a)

```
function P=Tk(k) % k>1
X=[0 1; 1 0];
I=[1 0; 0 1];
if k==1
    P=X;
else
    P=Cun(k-1,2^(k-1)-1,X);
    for i=1:k-2
        P=kron(tenProduct(I,i),Cun(k-1-i,2^(k-1-i)-1,X))*P;
    end
    P=kron(tenProduct(I,k-1),X)*P;
end
end
```

Code B.23 The code of translation transformations for the image in Figure 4.29

```
% Translation for the 128*128 color image
function []=TranslationImage()
clear all
clc
X=[0 1; 1 0];
I=[1 0; 0 1];
% f is a 128*128 color image
f = double(imread('airplane.bmp'));
subplot(1,3,1),imshow(uint8(f));
[row, col,tem]=size(f);
r=log2(row);
c=log2(col);
% Call the fuction CQ2 to create a NASS state
 [G,Q]=CQ2(f);
% Call the function Tk to realize translation along x axis
TX=kron(Tk(r),tenProduct(I,c));
% TX is applied repeatedly 10 times to translate 10 pixels
along x axis
```

```
TXQ=TX*Q;
for i=1:9
    TXQ=TX*TXQ;
end
% Call the function Tk to realize translation along y axis
TY=kron(tenProduct(I,r),Tk(c));
% TY is applied repeatedly 10 times to translate 10 pixels
along y axis
TYQ=TY*Q;
for i=1:9
    TYQ=TY*TYQ;
end
% Retrieve the transformed image
fx=QC2(TXQ, G, row, col);
fy=QC2(TYQ, G, row, col);
subplot(1,3,2),imshow(uint8(fx));
subplot(1,3,3),imshow(uint8(fy));
end
```

Code B.24 The code of the translation transformation for the video in Figure 4.30

```
% Translation for the 128*128*2 video
function []=TranslationVideo()
clear all
clc
X=[0 1; 1 0];
I=[1 0; 0 1];
% f is a 128*128*2 video
for i=1:2
    A=imread([num2str(i),'.bmp']);
    f(:,:,i)=double(A);
    subplot(1,4,i);
    imshow(A,[]);
end
[row, col,st]=size(f);
r=log2(row);
c=log2(col);
t=log2(st);
% Call the function GQ3 to create a NASS state
[G,Q]=GQ3(f);
% Call the function Tk to realize translation
THQ=kron(tenProduct(I,r+c),Tk(t))*Q;
% Retrieve the transformed video
fq=QG3(THQ, G, row, col, st);
for i=1:2
    subplot(2,4,2+i);
    A=fx(:,:,i);
```

```
      imshow(uint8(A),[]);
end
end
```

The Codes for Quantum Fourier Transforms in Chapter 5

Code B.25 The code for the circuit of Γ_{2^n} in Figure 5.2 for n > 1

```
function SP=allpermutation(n)
 r=fix(n/2);
 I=[1 0;0 1];
 SP=Swa(n);
 if n>3
    for i=2:r
        In=tenProduct(I,i-1);
        SP=SP*kron(kron(In,Swa(n-(i-1)*2)),In);
    end
 end
end
```

Code B.26 The code for the circuit of $P_{2^{n-1},2}$ in Figure 5.3 for n > 1

```
function SP=Permutationn2(n)
I=[1 0;0 1];
if n==2
    SP=Swa(2);
else
  SP=allpermutation(n)*kron(allpermutation(n-1),I);
end
end
```

Code B.27 The code for the circuit of $P_{2,2^{n-1}}$ in Figure 5.3 for *n* > 1

```
function SP=Permutation2n(n)
I=[1 0;0 1];
if n==2
    SP=Swa(2);
else
    SP=kron(allpermutation(n-1),I)*allpermutation(n);
end
end
```

Code B.28 The code for the circuit of $S_{2^n}(R_n)$ in Figure 5.11 for $n > 1$

```
function P=S2N(n,Rn)
I=[1 0;0 1];
P=Cun(1,1,kron(Rn,tenProduct(I,n-2)));
for j=1:n-2
    Rn=Rn*Rn;
    P=kron(Cun(1,1,kron(Rn,tenProduct(I,n-2-
j))),tenProduct(I,j))*P;
end
end
```

Code B.29 The code for the circuit of $T_{2^n}(R_n)$ in Figure 5.12 for $n > 1$

```
function P=T2N(n,Rn)
I=[1 0;0 1];
P=kron(tenProduct(I,n-2),Cup(1,1,Rn));
for j=1:n-2
    Rn=Rn*Rn;
    P=P*kron(tenProduct(I,n-2-j),Cup(1,1,kron(tenProduct(I,j),
Rn)));
end
end
```

Code B.30 The code for the first circuit of 1D-QFT and its inverse in Figure 5.13 and Figure 5.14

```
% Rn=[1 0; 0 exp(2*pi()*i/2^n)] and Rn=[1 0; 0 exp(-
2*pi()*i/2^n)] correspond to 1D-QFT and its inverse,
respectively.
function F=ODQFT1(n,Rn)
H=sqrt(2)*0.5*[1 1; 1 -1];
I=[1 0;0 1];
if n==1
    F=H;
else
    F=kron(H,tenProduct(I,n-1))*S2N(n,Rn)*kron(I,ODQFT1(n-
1,Rn*Rn))*Permutationn2(n);
end
end
```

Code B.31 The code for the second circuit of 1D-QFT and its inverse in Figure 5.15 and Figure 5.16

```
% Rn=[1 0; 0 exp(2*pi()*i/2^n)] and Rn=[1 0; 0 exp(-
2*pi()*i/2^n)] correspond to 1D-QFT and its inverse,
respectively.
function F=ODQFT2(n,Rn)
H=sqrt(2)*0.5*[1 1; 1 -1];
I [1 0;0 1];
if n==1
    F=H;
else
    F=Permutation2n(n)*kron(I,ODQFT2(n-1,Rn*Rn))*S2N(n,Rn)*
kron(H,tenProduct(I,n-1));
end
end
```

Code B.32 The code for the test of 1D-QFT with n=4

```
% Rn=[1 0; 0 exp(2*pi()*i/2^n)] and Rn=[1 0; 0 exp(-
2*pi()*i/2^n)] correspond to 1D-QFT and its inverse,
respectively.
function F=ODQFT3(n,Rn)
H=sqrt(2)*0.5*[1 1; 1 -1];
I=[1 0;0 1];
if n==1
    F=H;
else
    F=kron(ODQFT3(n-1,Rn*Rn),I)*T2N(n,Rn)*kron(tenProduct(I,n-
1),H)*Permutation2n(n);
end
end
```

Code B.33 The code for the fourth circuit of the inverse of 1D-QFT in Figure 5.19 and Figure 5.20

```
% Rn=[1 0; 0 exp(2*pi()*i/2^n)] and Rn=[1 0; 0 exp(-
2*pi()*i/2^n)] correspond to 1D-QFT and its inverse,
respectively.
function F=ODQFT4(n,Rn)
H=sqrt(2)*0.5*[1 1; 1 -1];
I=[1 0;0 1];
if n==1
    F=H;
else
    F=Permutationn2(n)*kron(tenProduct(I,n-1),H)*T2N(n,Rn)*
```

```
kron(ODQFT4(n-1,Rn*Rn),I);
end
end
```

Code B.34 The code for the test of 1D-QFTs with n=4

```
function []=testODFT()
clear all
clc
% f is a 16*1 column vector
f=[1 2 3 4 5 6 7 8 9 10 11 12 13 14 15 16]';
n=4;
Rn=[1 0; 0 exp(2*pi()*i/2^n)];
IRn=[1 0; 0 exp(-2*pi()*i/2^n)];
% Apply inverse classcial Fourier transform on the column
vector
FT=sqrt(2^n)*ifft(f);
% Apply 1D-QFT for the first circuit in Figure 5.13 on the
column vector
QFT1=ODQFT1(n,Rn)*f;
disp('The first circuit');
norm(abs(FT-QFT1))
% Apply the inverse of 1D-QFT for the first circuit in Figure
5.14 on QFT1
IQFT1=ODQFT1(n,IRn)*QFT1;
% Compare IQFT1 with f
norm(abs(IQFT1-f))
% Apply 1D-QFT for the second circuit in Figure 5.15 on the
column vector
QFT2=ODQFT2(n,Rn)*f;
disp('The second circuit');
norm(abs(FT-QFT2))
% Apply the inverse of 1D-QFT for the sencond circuit in Figure
5.16 on QFT2
IQFT2=ODQFT2(n,IRn)*QFT2;
% Compare IQFT2 with f
norm(abs(IQFT2-f))
% Apply 1D-QFT for the third circuit in Figure 5.17 on the
column vector
QFT3=ODQFT3(n,Rn)*f;
disp('The third circuit');
norm(abs(FT-QFT3))
% Apply the inverse of 1D-QFT for the third circuit in Figure
5.18 on QFT3
IQFT3=ODQFT3(n,IRn)*QFT3;
% Compare IQFT3 with f
norm(abs(IQFT3-f))
% Apply 1D-QFT for the fourth circuit in Figure 5.19 on the
```

```
column vector
QFT4=ODQFT4(n,Rn)*f;
disp('The third circuit');
norm(abs(FT-QFT4))
% Apply the inverse of 1D-QFT for the fourth circuit in Figure
5.20 on QFT4
IQFT4=ODQFT4(n,IRn)*QFT4;
% Compare IQFT4 with f
norm(abs(IQFT4-f))
end
```

Code B.35 The code for the circuits of 2D-QFT and its inverse in Figure 5.25

```
function F=TDQFT(m,Rm,k,Rk)
F=kron(ODQFT1(m,Rm),ODQFT1(k,Rk));
end
```

Code B.36 The code for the test of 2D-QFT with a 128 × 128 image

```
function []=testTODFT()
clear all
clc
% f is a 128*128 image
f = double(imread('gclena128.bmp'));
subplot(1,2,1);
imshow(uint8(f),[]); %The original image
% Apply classical 2D inverse Fourier transform on the image
[row,col]=size(f);
m=log2(row);
k=log2(col);
FT=sqrt(2^m)*sqrt(2^k)*ifft2(f);
% Call the function GQ2 to create a NASS state
[G,Q]=GQ2(f);
% Apply 2D-QFT in Figure 5.25 on the image
Rm=[1 0; 0 exp(2*pi()*i/2^m)];
Rk=[1 0; 0 exp(2*pi()*i/2^k)];
QF=TDQFT(m,Rm,k,Rk)*Q;
% Retrieve the transformed image
QFI=QG2(QF, G, row, col);
% Display the amplitude spectrum of the transformed image
subplot(1,2,2);
mesh(abs(QFI))
% Compare classcial 2D inverse Fourier transform with 2D-QFT
norm(abs(FT-QFI))
% Apply the inverse of 2D-QFT on the transformed image QF
IRm=[1 0; 0 exp(-2*pi()*i/2^m)];
IRk=[1 0; 0 exp(-2*pi()*i/2^k)];
```

```
IQFI=TDQFT(m,IRm,k,IRk)*QF;
% Retrieve the image
IQFTI=QG2(IQFI, G, row, col);
% Compare IQFTI with f
norm(abs(IQFTI-f))
end
```

Code B.37 The code for the circuits of 3D-QFT and its inverse in Figure 5.26

```
function F=ThDQFT(m,Rm,k,Rk,h,Rh)
F=kron(kron(ODQFT1(m,Rm),ODQFT1(k,Rk)),ODQFT1(h,Rh));
end
```

Code B.38 The code for the test of 3D-QFT with a 64*32*8 video

```
function []=testThDQFT()
clear all
clc
% f is a 128*128*2 video
for j=1:2
    A=imread([num2str(j),'.bmp']);
    f(:,:,j)=double(A);
    subplot(1,4,j);
    imshow(A,[]);
end
% Apply classical 3D inverse Fourier transform on the video
[row, col,st]=size(f);
FT=sqrt(row)*sqrt(col)*sqrt(st)*ifftn(f);
% Call the function GQ3 to create a NASS state
m=log2(row);
k=log2(col);
h=log2(st);
[G,Q]=GQ3(f);
% Apply 3D-QFT in Figure 5.26 on the image
Rm=[1 0; 0 exp(2*pi()*i/2^m)];
Rk=[1 0; 0 exp(2*pi()*i/2^k)];
Rh=[1 0; 0 exp(2*pi()*i/2^h)];
QF=ThDQFT(m,Rm,k,Rk,h,Rh)*Q;
% Retrieve the transformed video
QFV=QG3(QF, G, row, col, st);
% Display the amplitude spectrum of the image frames of the
transformed video
for j=1:2
    subplot(1,4,2+j);
    A=QFV(:,:,j);
    mesh(abs(A))
end
```

```
% Compare classcial 3D inverse Fourier transform with 3D-QFT
for j=1:st
    norm(abs(FT(:,:,j)-QFV(:,:,j)))
end
% Apply the inverse of 3D-QFT on the transformed video QF
IRm=[1 0; 0 exp(-2*pi()*i/2^m)];
IRk=[1 0; 0 exp(-2*pi()*i/2^k)];
IRh=[1 0; 0 exp(-2*pi()*i/2^h)];
IQF=ThDQFT(m,IRm,k,IRk,h,IRh)*QF;
% Retrieve the video
IQFV=QG3(IQF, G, row, col, st);
% Compare IQFTI with f
for j=1:st
    norm(abs(f(:,:,j)-IQFV(:,:,j)))
end
end
```

The Codes for Quantum Wavelet Transforms in Chapter 6

Code B.39 The code for the Doppler function

```
function s=d(t)
    s=sqrt(t*(1-t))*sin(2*pi()*1.05/(t+0.05));
end
```

Code B.40 The code for the implementation of HQWT in Figure 6.3 and Figure 6.5

```
% k>=0 and n>k
function F=FHNK(n,k)
H=sqrt(2)*0.5*[1 1; 1 -1];
I=[1 0;0 1];
if k==0
    if n==1
        F=H;% The initial value in Figure 6.5
    else
        F=Permutationn2(n)*kron(tenProduct(I,n-1),H); % The
initial value in Figure 6.3
    end
else
    % The (k+1)-level HQWT
    F=Cup(1,0,FHNK(n-1,k-1))*Permutationn2(n)*kron(tenProduct(I
,n-1),H);
end
end
```

Code B.41 The code for the implementation of HQWT in Figure 6.4 and Figure 6.6

```
% k>=0 and n>k
function F=SHNK(n,k)
H=sqrt(2)*0.5*[1 1; 1 -1];
I=[1 0;0 1];
if k==0
    if n==1
        F=H;% The initial value in Figure 6.6
    else
        F=Permutationn2(n)*kron(tenProduct(I,n-1),H); % The
initial value in Figure 6.4
    end
else
    % The (k+1)-level HQWT
    F=Permutationn2(n)*Cun(1,0,SHNK(n-1,k-
1))*kron(tenProduct(I,n-1),H);
end
end
```

Code B.42 The code for the implementation of the inverse of HQWT in (6.16)

```
% k>=0 and n>k
function F=IFHNK(n,k)
H=sqrt(2)*0.5*[1 1; 1 -1];
I=[1 0;0 1];
if k==0
    if n==1
        F=H;% The initial value of  IFHNK(n,n-1)
    else
        F=kron(tenProduct(I,n-1),H)*Permutation2n(n); % The
initial value of IFHNK(n,k) with k<n-1
    end
else
    % The inverse of the (k+1)-level HQWT
    F=kron(tenProduct(I,n-1),H)*Permutation2n(n)*Cup(1,0,IFHNK
(n-1,k-1));
end
end
```

Code B.43 The code for the implementation of the inverse of HQWT in (6.17)

```
% k>=0 and n>k
function F=ISHNK(n,k)
H=sqrt(2)*0.5*[1 1; 1 -1];
I=[1 0;0 1];
```

```
if k==0
    if n==1
        F=H;% The initial value of  ISHNK(n,n-1)
    else
     F=kron(tenProduct(I,n-1),H)*Permutation2n(n); % The
initial value of ISHNK(n,k) with k<n-1
    end
else
    % The inverse of the (k+1)-level HQWT
    F=kron(tenProduct(I,n-1),M)^Cun(1,0,ISHNK(n-1,k-
1))*Permutation2n(n);
end
end
```

Code B.44 The code for the first 3 levels of HQWT with the input V in (6.46)

```
function []=testFirst3LevelHaar()
clc
clear all
for k=1:2048
    V(1,k)=d((k-1)/2048);
end
x=1:2048;
m=11;
V1=V';
 % 0 level
subplot(4,8,1:8);
plot(x,V1','.');
% 1 level
subplot(4,8,9:12);
V1=FHNK(m,0)*V';
x=1:1024;
plot(x,V1(x,1)','.');
subplot(4,8,13:16)
x=1025:2048;
plot(x,V1(x,1)','.');
 % 2 levels
V1=FHNK(m,1)*V';
subplot(4,8,17:18);
x=1:512;
plot(x,V1(x,1)','.');
subplot(4,8,19:20);
x=513:1024;
plot(x,V1(x,1)','.');
subplot(4,8,21:24);
x=1025:2048;
plot(x,V1(x,1)','.');
% 3 levels
```

```
V1=FHNK(m,2)*V';
subplot(4,8,25);
x=1:256;
plot(x,V1(x,1)','.');
subplot(4,8,26);
x=257:512;
plot(x,V1(x,1)','.');
subplot(4,8,27:28);
x=513:1024;
plot(x,V1(x,1)','.');
subplot(4,8,29:32);
x=1025:2048;
plot(x,V1(x,1)','.');
end
```

Code B.45 The code for all levels of HQWT with the input V in (6.46)

```
function []=testAllLevelHaar()
clc
clear all
for k=1:2048
    V(1,k)=d((k-1)/2048);
end
x=1:2048;
m=11;
V1=V';
% 0-11 levels
subplot(12,1,1)
plot(x,V1','.');
for j=1:m
    V1=FHNK(m,j-1)*V'; % Apply HQWT in Figure 6.3 and Figure
6.5 on the vector V
    subplot(12,1,j+1)
    plot(x,V1','.');
end
end
```

Code B.46 The code for the comparisons of HQWTs, their inverses, and classical Haar wavelet transform

```
function []=testComparisonHaar()
clc
clear all
for k=1:2048
    V(1,k)=d((k-1)/2048);
end
x=1:2048;
```

```
m=11;
% 0-11 levels
for j=1:m
    % Apply HQWT in Figure 6.3 and Figure 6.5 on the vector V'
    V1=FHNK(m,j-1)*V';
    % Apply HQWT in Figure 6.4 and Figure 6.6 on the vector V'
    V2=SHNK(m,j-1)*V';
    % Apply classical Haar wavelet transform on the vector V'
    [C2,L2] = wavedec(V',j,'haar');
    %The comparisons of HQWTs and classical Haar wavelet
transform
    err1(j,1) = norm(V1-C2);
    err2(j,1) = norm(V2-C2);
    % Apply the inverse of HQWT in (6.16) on the vector V1
    V3=IFHNK(m,j-1)*V1;
    %The comparisons of V3 and V'
    err3(j,1) = norm(V3-V');
    % Apply the inverse of HQWT in (6.17) on the vector V2
    V4=ISHNK(m,j-1)*V2;
    %The comparisons of V4 and V'
    err4(j,1) = norm(V4-V');
end
end
```

Code B.47 The code for the circuit of the downshift matrix Q_{2^n} in Figure 6.9 (a)

```
function P=Q2N(n)
I=[1 0;0 1];
X=[0 1; 1 0];
if n==1
    P=X;
else
    P=kron(tenProduct(I,n-1),X)*Cun(1,0,Q2N(n-1));
end
```

Code B.48 The code for the circuit of $(Q_{2^n})^{-1}$ in Figure 6.10 (a)

```
function P=IQ2N(n)
I=[1 0;0 1];
X=[0 1; 1 0];
if n==1
    P=X;
else
    P=Cun(1,0,IQ2N(n-1))*kron(tenProduct(I,n-1),X);
end
```

Code B.49 The code for the circuit of the matrix D_{2^n} in Figure 6.9 (b)

```
% n>1
function P=D2N(n)
I=[1 0;0 1];
a1=5*pi()/12;
a0=2*pi()/3;
S0=[sin(a0) cos(a0);cos(a0)  -1*sin(a0)];
S1=[-sin(a1) cos(a1);cos(a1) sin(a1)];
P=kron(tenProduct(I,n-1),S1)*Q2N(n)*kron(tenProduct(I,n-1),S0);
end
```

Code B.50 The code for the circuit of the matrix $(D_{2^n})^{-1}$ in Figure 6.10 (b)

```
% n>1
function P=ID2N(n)
I=[1 0;0 1];
a1=5*pi()/12;
a0=2*pi()/3;
S0=[sin(a0) cos(a0);cos(a0)  -1*sin(a0)];
S1=[-sin(a1) cos(a1);cos(a1) sin(a1)];
P=kron(tenProduct(I,n-1),S0)*IQ2N(n)*kron(tenProduct(I,n-
1),S1);
end
```

Code B.51 The code for the circuit of $D_{2^n}^P$ in Figure 6.11 (a)

```
% n>1
function P=D2NP(n)
P=D2N(n)*IQ2N(n);
end
```

Code B.52 The code for the circuit of $(D_{2^n}^P)^{-1}$ in Figure 6.11 (b)

```
% n>1
function P=ID2NP(n)
P=Q2N(n)*ID2N(n);
end
```

Code B.53 The code for the circuit of D4QWT $F_{2^n}^k$ in Figure 6.12

```
% k>=0 and k<=n-2
function F=F2NK(n,k)
if k==0
    F=Permutationn2(n)*D2NP(n); % The initial value
```

```
else
    % The (k+1)-level D4QWT
    F=Permutationn2(n)*Cun(1,0,F2NK(n-1,k-1))*D2NP(n);
end
end
```

Code B.54 The code for the circuit of the inverse of D4QWT $(F_{2^n}^k)^{-1}$ in Figure 6.13

```
% k>=0 and k<=n-2
function F=IF2NK(n,k)
if k==0
    F=ID2NP(n)*Permutation2n(n); % The initial value
else
    % The invese of the (k+1)-level D4QWT
    F=ID2NP(n)*Cun(1,0,IF2NK(n-1,k-1))*Permutation2n(n);
end
end
```

Code B.55 The code for the first 3 levels of D4QWT with the input V in (6.46)

```
function []=testFirst3LevelD4()
clc
clear all
% Call Doppler function d()
for k=1:2048
    V(1,k)=d((k-1)/2048);
end
x=1:2048;
m=11;
V1=V';
set(gcf,'color','white');
% 0 level
subplot(4,8,1:8);
x=1:2048;
plot(x,V,'.');
% 1 level
subplot(4,8,9:12);
V1=F2NK(m,0)*V';
x=1:1024;
plot(x,V1(x,1)','.');
subplot(4,8,13:16)
x=1025:2048;
plot(x,V1(x,1)','.');
% 2 levels
V1=F2NK(m,1)*V';
subplot(4,8,17:18);
```

```
x=1:512;
plot(x,V1(x,1)','.');
subplot(4,8,19:20);
x=513:1024;
plot(x,V1(x,1)','.');
subplot(4,8,21:24);
x=1025:2048;
plot(x,V1(x,1)','.');
% 3 levels
V1=F2NK(m,2)*V';
subplot(4,8,25);
x=1:256;
plot(x,V1(x,1)','.');
subplot(4,8,26);
x=257:512;
plot(x,V1(x,1)','.');
subplot(4,8,27:28);
x=513:1024;
plot(x,V1(x,1)','.');
subplot(4,8,29:32);
x=1025:2048;
plot(x,V1(x,1)','.');
end
```

Code B.56 The code for all levels of D4QWT with the input V in (6.46)

```
function []=testAllLevelD4()
clc
clear all
% Call Doppler function d()
for k=1:2048
    V(1,k)=d((k-1)/2048);
end
x=1:2048;
m=11;
V1=V';
 % 0-10 levels
subplot(11,1,1)
plot(x,V1','.');
for j=1:m-1
    % Apply D4QWT in Figure 6.12 on the vector V
    V1=F2NK(m,j-1)*V';
    subplot(11,1,j+1)
    plot(x,V1','.');
end
end
```

Code B.57 The code for the comparisons of D4QWT, its inverse, and classical D4 wavelet transform

```
function []=testComparisonD4()
clc
clear all
% Call Doppler function d()
for k=1:2048
    V(k,1)=d((k-1)/2048);
end
x=1:2048;
m=11;
% Set periodization extension mode
dwtmode('per');
% 0-10 levels
for j=1:m-1
    % Apply D4QWT in Figure 6.12 on the vector V
    V1=F2NK(m,j-1)*V;
    % Apply classical D4 wavelet transform on the vector V
    [C2,L2] = wavedec(V,j,'db2');
    %The comparisons of D4QWT and classical D4 wavelet
transform
    err1(j,1) = norm(V1-C2);
    % Apply the inverse of D4QWT in Figure 6.13  on the vector
V1
    V2=IF2NK(m,j-1)*V1;
    %The comparisons of V2 and V
    err2(j,1) = norm(V2-V);
end
end
```

The Codes for Quantum Wavelet Packet Transforms in Chapter 7

Code B.58 The code for 1D-HQWPT in Figure 7.3

```
% k>=0 and k<n
function R=ODHQWPT(n,k)
H=sqrt(2)*0.5*[1 1; 1 -1];
I=[1 0;0 1];
if k==n-1
    % 1-dimensional Haar quantum wavelet packet transform in
Figure 7.3 (c)
    R=allpermutation(n)*tenProduct(H,n);
elseif k==n-2
```

```
    % 1-dimensional Haar quantum wavelet packet transform in
Figure 7.3 (b)
    R=allpermutation(n)*kron(I,tenProduct(H,n-1));
else
    % 1-dimensional Haar quantum wavelet packet transform in
Figure 7.3 (a)
    R=allpermutation(n)*kron(allpermutation(n-k-
1),tenProduct(H,k+1));
end
end
```

Code B.59 The code for the inverse of 1D-HQWPT in Figure 7.4

```
% k>=0 and k<n
function R=IODHQWPT(n,k)
H=sqrt(2)*0.5*[1 1; 1 -1];
I=[1 0;0 1];
if k==n-1
    % The inverse of 1-dimensional Haar quantum wavelet packet
transform in Figure 7.4 (c)
    R=tenProduct(H,n)*allpermutation(n);
elseif k==n-2
    % The inverse of 1-dimensional Haar quantum wavelet packet
transform in Figure 7.4 (b)
    R=kron(I,tenProduct(H,n-1))*allpermutation(n);
else
    % The inverse of 1-dimensional Haar quantum wavelet packet
transform in Figure 7.4 (a)
    R=kron(allpermutation(n-k-1),tenProduct(H,k+1))*allpermuta
tion(n);
end
end
```

Code B.60 The code for 1D-D4QWPT in Figure 7.6

```
% k>=0 and k<n-1
function R=OD4QWPT(n,k)
I=[1 0;0 1];
if k==n-2
    % 1-dimensional D4 quantum wavelet packet transform in
Figure 7.6 (b)
    R=allpermutation(n);
    for j=2:n-1
        % Call the function D2NP(), which implements the
circuit in Figure 6.11 (a)
        R=R*kron(D2NP(j),tenProduct(I,n-j));
    end
```

```
    R=R*D2NP(n);
else
    % 1-dimensional Haar quantum wavelet packet transform in
Figure 7.6 (a)
    R=D2NP(n);
    for j=1:k
        R=kron(D2NP(n-j),tenProduct(I,j))*R;
    end
    R=allpermutation(n)*kron(allpermutation(n-k-
1),tenProduct(I,k+1))*R;
end
end
```

Code B.61 The code for the inverse of 1D-D4QWPT in Figure 7.6

```
% k>=0 and k<n-1
function R=IOD4QWPT(n,k)
I=[1 0;0 1];
if k==n-2
    % The inverte of 1-dimensional D4 quantum wavelet packet
transform in Figure 7.6 (d)
    R=allpermutation(n);
    for j=2:n-1
        % Call the function ID2NP(), which implements the
circuit in Figure 6.11 (b)
        R=kron(ID2NP(j),tenProduct(I,n-j))*R;
    end
    R=ID2NP(n)*R;
else
    % The inverte of 1-dimensional Haar quantum wavelet packet
transform in Figure 7.6 (c)
    R=ID2NP(n);
    for j=1:k
        R=R*kron(ID2NP(n-j),tenProduct(I,j));
    end
    R=R*kron(allpermutation(n-k-1),tenProduct(I,k+1))*allpermut
ation(n);
end
end
```

Code B.62 The code for the first 3 levels of 1D-HQWPT with the input V in (6.46)

```
function []=testFirst3LevelHaarPacket()
clc; clear all
for k=1:2048
    V(1,k)=d((k-1)/2048);
```

```
end
x=1:2048;
m=11;
V1=V';
 % 0 level
subplot(4,8,1:8);
plot(x,V1','.');
% 1 level
subplot(4,8,9:12);
V1=ODHQWPT(m,0)*V';
x=1:1024;
plot(x,V1(x,1)','.');
subplot(4,8,13:16)
x=1025:2048;
plot(x,V1(x,1)','.');
% 2 levels
V1=ODHQWPT(m,1)*V';
subplot(4,8,17:18);
x=1:512;
plot(x,V1(x,1)','.');
subplot(4,8,19:20);
x=513:1024;
plot(x,V1(x,1)','.');
subplot(4,8,21:24);
x=1025:2048;
plot(x,V1(x,1)','.');
% 3 levels
V1=ODHQWPT(m,2)*V';
subplot(4,8,25);
x=1:256;
plot(x,V1(x,1)','.');
subplot(4,8,26);
x=257:512;
plot(x,V1(x,1)','.');
subplot(4,8,27:28);
x=513:1024;
plot(x,V1(x,1)','.');
subplot(4,8,29:32);
x=1025:2048;
plot(x,V1(x,1)','.');
end
```

Code B.63 The code for the comparisons of 1D-HQWPT, its inverse, and classical Haar wavelet packet transform

```
function []=testComparisonHaarPacket()
clc
clear all
```

```
for k=1:2048
    V(1,k)=d((k-1)/2048);
end
x=1:2048;
m=11;
% 0-11 levels
for j=1:m
    % Apply 1D-HQWPT in Figure 7.3 on the vector V'
    V1=ODHQWPT(m,j-1)*V';
    % Apply classical 1D Haar wavelet packet transform on the
vector V'
    wt = wpdec(V',j,'db1');
    C2=[];
    for i=0: 2^j-1
        cfs=wpcoef(wt,[j,i]);
        C2=[C2; cfs];
    end
    %The comparison of 1D-HQWPT and classical Haar wavelet
packet transform
    err1(j,1) = norm(V1-C2);
    % Apply the inverse of 1D-HQWPT in Figure 7.4 on the vector
V1
    V2=IODHQWPT(m,j-1)*V1;
    %The comparisons of V2 and V'
    err2(j,1) = norm(V2-V');
end
end
```

Code B.64 The code for the first 3 levels of 1D-D4QWPT with the input V in (6.46)

```
function []=testFirst3LevelD4Packet()
clc
clear all
for k=1:2048
    V(1,k)=d((k-1)/2048);
end
x=1:2048;
m=11;
V1=V';
% 0 level
subplot(4,8,1:8);
plot(x,V1','.');
% 1 level
subplot(4,8,9:12);
V1=OD4QWPT(m,0)*V';
x=1:1024;
plot(x,V1(x,1)','.');
```

```
subplot(4,8,13:16)
x=1025:2048;
plot(x,V1(x,1)','.');
% 2 levels
V1=OD4QWPT(m,1)*V';
subplot(4,8,17:18);
x=1:512;
plot(x,V1(x,1)','.');
subplot(4,8,19:20);
x=513:1024;
plot(x,V1(x,1)','.');
subplot(4,8,21:24);
x=1025:2048;
plot(x,V1(x,1)','.');
% 3 levels
V1=OD4QWPT(m,2)*V';
subplot(4,8,25);
x=1:256;
plot(x,V1(x,1)','.');
subplot(4,8,26);
x=257:512;
plot(x,V1(x,1)','.');
subplot(4,8,27:28);
x=513:1024;
plot(x,V1(x,1)','.');
subplot(4,8,29:32);
x=1025:2048;
plot(x,V1(x,1)','.');
end
```

Code B.65 The code for the comparisons of 1D-D4QWPT, its inverse, and classical D4 wavelet packet transform

```
function []=testComparisonHaarPacket()
clc
clear all
for k=1:2048
    V(1,k)=d((k-1)/2048);
end
x=1:2048;
m=11;
% Set periodization extension mode
dwtmode('per');
% 0-10 levels
for j=1:m-1
    % Apply 1D-D4QWPT in Figure 7.5 on the vector V'
    V1=OD4QWPT(m,j-1)*V';
    % Apply classical D4 wavelet packet transform  on the
```

```
vector V'
    wt = wpdec(V',j,'db2');
    C2=[];
    for i=0: 2^j-1
        cfs=wpcoef(wt,[j,i]);
        C2=[C2; cfs];
    end
    % The comparison of 1D-D4QWPT and classical D4 wavelet
transform
    err1(j,1) = norm(V1-C2);
    % Apply the inverse of 1D-D4QWPT in Figure 7.5 on the
vector V1
    V2=IOD4QWPT(m,j-1)*V1;
    % The comparison of V2 and V'
    err2(j,1) = norm(V2-V');
end
end
```

Code B.66 The code for 2D-HQWPT in Figure 7.7 and Figure 7.78

```
% h>=0 and h<min(m,k)
function R=TDHQWPT(m,k,h)
R=kron(ODHQWPT(m,h),ODHQWPT(k,h));
end
```

Code B.67 The code for the inverse of 2D-HQWPT in Figure 7.7 and Figure 7.8

```
% h>=0 and h<min(m,k)
function R=ITDHQWPT(m,k,h)
R=kron(IODHQWPT(m,h),IODHQWPT(k,h));
end
```

Code B.68 The code for 2D-D4QWPT in Figure 7.7 and Figure 7.78

```
% l>=0 and l<min(m,k)-1
function R=TD4QWPT(m,k,l)
R=kron(OD4QWPT(m,l),OD4QWPT(k,l));
end
```

Code B.69 The code for the inverse of 2D-D4QWPsT in Figure 7.7 and Figure 7.8

```
% l>=0 and l<min(m,k)-1
function R=ITD4QWPT(m,k,l)
R=kron(IOD4QWPT(m,l),IOD4QWPT(k,l));
end
```

Code B.70 The code for the first 2 levels of 2D-HQWPT with a 256*256 image

```
function []=testFirst2Level2DHaarPacket()
clear all
clc
% f is a 256*256 image
f = double(imread('Cameraman.bmp'));
subplot(1,3,1);
imshow(uint8(f),[]); %The original image
[row,col]=size(f);
m=log2(row);
k=log2(col);
% Call the fuction GQ2 to create a NASS state
[G,Q]=GQ2(f);
% Apply 1-level 2D-HQWPT on the image
QH1=TDHQWPT(m,k,0)*Q;
% Retrieve the transformed image by 1-level 2D-HQWPT
QH1I=QG2(QH1, G, row, col);
subplot(1,3,2),imshow(uint8(QH1I));
% Apply 2-level 2D-HQWPT on the image
QH2=TDHQWPT(m,k,1)*Q;
% Retrieve the transformed image by 2-level 2D-HQWPT
QH2I=QG2(QH2, G, row, col);
subplot(1,3,3),imshow(uint8(QH2I));
end
```

Code B.71 The code for the synthesized matrix by wavelet packet coefficients

```
% A consists of wavelet packet coefficients of the j-level
wavelet packet transform
function B=Com(A,j)
if j > 0
    % The multi-level wavelet packet transform
    [x,y]=size(A);
    z=y/4;
    A1=A(:,1:z);
    A2=A(:,z+1:2*z);
    A3=A(:,2*z+1:3*z);
    A4=A(:,3*z+1:4*z);
    u1=Com(A1,j-1);
    u2=Com(A2,j-1);
    u3=Com(A3,j-1);
    u4=Com(A4,j-1);
    B=[u1 u3; u2 u4];
else
 % The single-level wavelet packet transform
    B=A;
    return;
```

```
end
end
```

Code B.72 The code for the comparisons of 2D-HQWPT, its inverse, and classical 2D Haar wavelet packet transform

```
function []=testComparison2DHaarPacket()
clear all
clc
% Ag is a 256*256 image
Ag = double(imread('Cameraman.bmp'));
[row,col]=size(Ag);
m=log2(row);
k=log2(col);
% Call the function GQ2 to create a NASS state
[G,Q]=GQ2(Ag);
h=min(m,k);
% 0-7 levels
for j=1:h
    % Apply 2D-HQWPT on the quantum image Q
    QH=TDHQWPT(m,k,j-1)*Q;
    % Retrieve the transformed image
    QHI=QG2(QH, G, row, col);
    % Apply classical 2D Haar wavelet packet transform on the
classical image Ag
    wpt = wpdec2(Ag,j,'db1');
    C2=[];
    for i=0: 4^j-1
        cfs=wpcoef(wpt,[j,i]);
        C2=[C2 cfs];
    end
    % Call the function Com() to create a matrix by using
coefficients of
    % (j+1)-level wavelet packet transform
    mdwt2=Com(C2,j);
    %The comparison of 2D-HQWPT and classical 2D Haar wavelet
packet transform
    err1(j,1) = norm(QHI-mdwt2);
    % Apply the inverse of 2D-HQWPT on the quantum image QH
    QH2=ITDHQWPT(m,k,j-1)*QH;
    % Retrieve the transformed image by the inverse of 2D-HQWPT
    QH2I=QG2(QH2, G, row, col);
    %The comparisons of QH2I and Ag
    err2(j,1) = norm(QH2I-Ag);
end
end
```

Code B.73 The code for the first 2 levels of 2D-D4QWPT with a 256*256 image

```
function []=testFirst2Level2DD4Packet()
clear all
clc
% f is a 256*256 image
f = double(imread('Cameraman.bmp'));
subplot(1,3,1);
imshow(uint8(f),[]); %The original image
[row,col]=size(f);
m=log2(row);
k=log2(col);
% Call the fuction GQ2 to create a NASS state
[G,Q]=GQ2(f);
% Apply 1-level 2D-D4QWPT on the image
QD1=TD4QWPT(m,k,0)*Q;
% Retrieve the transformed image by 1-level 2D-D4QWPT
QD1I=QG2(QD1, G, row, col);
subplot(1,3,2),imshow(uint8(QD1I));
% Apply 2-level 2D-D4QWPT on the image
QD2=TD4QWPT(m,k,1)*Q;
% Retrieve the transformed image by 2-level 2D-D4QWPT
QD2I=QG2(QD2, G, row, col);
subplot(1,3,3),imshow(uint8(QD2I));
end
```

Code B.74 The code for the comparisons of 2D-D4QWPT, its inverse, and classical 2D D4 wavelet packet transform

```
function []=testComparison2DD4Packet()
clear all
clc
% Ag is a 256*256 image
Ag = double(imread('Cameraman.bmp'));
[row,col]=size(Ag);
m=log2(row);
k=log2(col);
% Call the function GQ2 to create a NASS state
[G,Q]=GQ2(Ag);
h=min(m,k)-1;
% Set periodization extension mode
dwtmode('per');
% 0-6 levels
for j=1:h
    % Apply 2D-D4QWPT on the quantum image Q
    QD=TD4QWPT(m,k,j-1)*Q;
```

```
    % Retrieve the transformed image
    QDI=QG2(QD, G, row, col);
    % Apply classical 2D D4 wavelet packet transform on the
classical image Ag
    wpt = wpdec2(Ag,j,'db2');
    C2=[];
    for i=0: 4^j-1
        cfs=wpcoef(wpt,[j,i]);
        C2=[C2 cfs];
    end
    % Call the function Com() to create a matrix by using
coefficients of
    % j-level wavelet packet transform
    mdwt2=Com(C2,j);
    %The comparison of 2D-D4QWPT and classical 2D Haar wavelet
packet transform
    err1(j,1) = norm(QDI-mdwt2);
    % Apply the inverse of 2D-D4QWPT on the quantum image QD
    QD2=ITD4QWPT(m,k,j-1)*QD;
    % Retrieve the transformed image by the inverse of
2D-D4QWPT
    QD2I=QG2(QD2, G, row, col);
    %The comparisons of QD2I and Ag
    err2(j,1) = norm(QD2I-Ag);
end
end
```

Code B.75 The code for 3D-HQWPT in Figure 7.9 and Figure 7.10

```
% i>=0 and i<min(m,k,h)
function R=ThDHQWPT(m,k,h,i)
R=kron(kron(ODHQWPT(m,i),ODHQWPT(k,i)),ODHQWPT(h,i));
end
```

Code B.76 The code for the inverse of 3D-HQWPT in Figure 7.9 and Figure 7.10

```
% i>=0 and i<min(m,k,h)
function R=IThDHQWPT(m,k,h,i)
R=kron(kron(IODHQWPT(m,i),IODHQWPT(k,i)),IODHQWPT(h,i));
end
```

Code B.77 The code for the first 2 levels of 3D-HQWPT for a 64*32*8 video

```
function []=testFirst2Level3DHaarPacket()
clear all
```

```
clc
% Vg is a 64*32*8 video
for j=1:8
    A=imread([strcat('v',num2str(j)),'.BMP']);
    Vg(:,:,j)=double(A);
    subplot(3,8,j);
    imshow(A,[]);
end
[row, col,st]=size(Vg);
m=log2(row);
k=log2(col);
h=log2(st);
% Call the fuction GQ3 to create a NASS state
[G,Q]=GQ3(Vg);
% Apply 1-level 3D-HQWPT on the video
QH1=ThDHQWPT(m,k,h,0)*Q;
% Retrieve the transformed image by 1-level 3D-HQWPT
QH1I=QG3(QH1, G, row, col, st);
for j=1:8
    A=QH1I(:,:,j);
    subplot(3,8,8+j);
    imshow(A,[]);
end
% Apply 2-level 3D-HQWPT on the video
QH2=ThDHQWPT(m,k,h,1)*Q;
% Retrieve the transformed image by 2-level 3D-HQWPT
QH2I=QG3(QH2, G, row, col, st);
for j=1:8
    A=QH2I(:,:,j);
    subplot(3,8,16+j);
    imshow(A,[]);
end
end
```

Code B.78 The code for classical 3D j-level wavelet packet transform in (7.24)

```
% X is a video;
% wname is a wavelet name;
function B=WPT3(X,j,wname)
[row, col,st]=size(X);
% Applying 2D j-level wavelet packet transform on image frames
of the video X
for k=1:st
    wpt =  wpdec2(X(:,:,k),j,wname);
    C2=[];
    for i=0: 4^j-1
        cfs=wpcoef(wpt,[j,i]);
        C2=[C2 cfs];
```

```
      end
      % Call the function Com() to create a matrix by using
coefficients of
      % j-level wavelet packet transform
      mwpt2(:,:,k)=Com(C2,j);
end
% Applying the third dimensional wavelet packet transform on
the video mwpt2
for i1=1:row
    for i2=1:col
        V1=[];
        for i3=1:st
            tt=mwpt2(:,:,i3);
            V1=[V1;tt(i1,i2)];
        end
        wt = wpdec(V1,j,wname);
        C2=[];
        for i=0: 2^j-1
            cfs=wpcoef(wt,[j,i]);
            C2=[C2; cfs];
        end
        B(i1,i2,:)=C2;
    end
end
end
```

Code B.79 The code for the comparisons of 3D-HQWPT, its inverse, and classical 3D Haar wavelet packet transform

```
function []=testComparison3DHaarPacket()
clear all
clc
% Vg is a 64*32*8  video
for j=1:8
    A=imread([strcat('v',num2str(j)),'.BMP']);
    Vg(:,:,j)=double(A);
end
[row, col,st]=size(Vg);
m=log2(row);
k=log2(col);
h=log2(st);
% Call the function GQ3 to create a NASS state
[G,Q]=GQ3(Vg);
x=min(min(m,k),h);
% 0-2 levels
for j=1:x
    % Apply 3D-HQWPT on the quantum image Q
    QH=ThDHQWPT(m,k,h,j-1)*Q;
```

```
    % Retrieve the transformed image
    QHI=QG3(QH, G, row, col,st);
    % Apply classical 3D Haar wavelet packet transform on the
video Vg
    B= WPT3(Vg,j,'db1');
    %The comparison of 3D-HQWPT and classical 3D Haar wavelet
packet transform
    sum=0;
    for i3=1:st
        sum=sum+(norm(QHI(:,:,i3)-B(:,:,i3)))^2;
    end
    err1(j,1)=sqrt(sum);
    % Apply the inverse of 3D-HQWPT on the quantum image QH
    QH2=IThDHQWPT(m,k,h,j-1)*QH;
    % Retrieve the transformed image by the inverse of 3D-HQWPT
    QH2I=QG3(QH2, G, row, col, st);
    %The comparisons of QH2I and Vg
    sum=0;
    for i3=1:st
        sum=sum+(norm(QH2I(:,:,i3)-Vg(:,:,i3)))^2;
    end
    err2(j,1)=sqrt(sum);
end
end
```

Code B.80 The code for the first 2 levels of 3D-D4QWPT with a 64*32*8 video

```
function []=testFirst2Level3DD4Packet()
clear all
clc
% Vg is a 64*32*8 video
for j=1:8
    A=imread([strcat('v',num2str(j)),'.BMP']);
    Vg(:,:,j)=double(A);
    subplot(3,8,j);
    imshow(A,[]);
end
[row, col,st]=size(Vg);
m=log2(row);
k=log2(col);
h=log2(st);
% Call the fuction GQ3 to create a NASS state
[G,Q]=GQ3(Vg);
% Apply 1-level 3D-D4QWPT on the video
QD1=ThD4QWPT(m,k,h,0)*Q;
% Retrieve the transformed image by 1-level 3D-D4QWPT
QD1I=QG3(QD1, G, row, col,st);
```

```
for j=1:8
    A=QD1I(:,:,j);
    subplot(3,8,8+j);
    imshow(A,[]);
end
% Apply 2-level 3D-D4QWPT on the video
QD2=ThD4QWPT(m,k,h,1)*Q;
% Retrieve the transformed image by 2-level 3D-D4QWPT
QD2I=QG3(QD2, G, row, col,st);
for j=1:8
    A=QD2I(:,:,j);
    subplot(3,8,16+j);
    imshow(A,[]);
end
end
```

Code B.81 The code for the comparisons of 3D-D4QWPT, its inverse, and classical 3D D4 wavelet packet transform

```
function []=testComparison3DD4Packet()
clear all
clc
% Vg is a 64*32*8 video
for j=1:8
    A=imread([strcat('v',num2str(j)),'.BMP']);
    Vg(:,:,j)=double(A);
end
[row, col,st]=size(Vg);
m=log2(row);
k=log2(col);
h=log2(st);
% Set periodization extension mode
dwtmode('per');
% Call the function GQ3 to create a NASS state
[G,Q]=GQ3(Vg);
x=min(min(m,k),h)-1;
% 0-1 levels
for j=1:x
    % Apply 3D-D4QWPT on the quantum image Q
    QD=ThD4QWPT(m,k,h,j-1)*Q;
    % Retrieve the transformed image
    QDI=QG3(QD, G, row, col,st);
    % Apply classical 3D D4 wavelet packet transform on the
video Vg
    B= WPT3(Vg,j,'db2');
    %The comparison of 3D-D4QWPT and classical 3D D4 wavelet
packet transform
    sum=0;
```

```
    for i3=1:st
        sum=sum+(norm(QDI(:,:,i3)-B(:,:,i3)))^2;
    end
    err1(j,1)=sqrt(sum);
    % Apply the inverse of 3D-D4QWPT on the quantum image QD
    QD2=IThD4QWPT(m,k,h,j-1)*QD;
    % Retrieve the transformed image by the inverse of
3D-D4QWPT
    QD2I=QG3(QD2, G, row, col, st);
    %The comparisons of QD2I and Vg
    sum=0;
    for i3=1:st
        súm=sum+(norm(QD2I(:,:,i3)-Vg(:,:,i3)))^2;
    end
    err2(j,1)=sqrt(sum);
end
end
```

Code B.82 The code for quantum image compression based on h-level 2D-QWPTs

```
% A is a row*col grayscale images;
% Type is equal to 0  or 1, which denotes Haar wavelet or D4
wavelet
function [QHCI,Qr,psnr1]=QICQWPT(A,h,Type)
[row,col]=size(A);
m=log2(row);
k=log2(col);
% Call the function GQ2 to create four NASS states
[G,Q]=GQ2(A);
if Type==0
    % Apply h-level 2D-HQWPT on the image
    QH=TDHQWPT(m,k,h-1)*Q;
else
    % Apply h-level 2D-D4QWPT on the image
    QH=TD4QWPT(m,k,h-1)*Q;
end
% Get the threshold value
a=1.2*mean(abs(QH(:)));
% Retrieve the compressed vectors from QH
QH(abs(QH)<a)=0;
% Calculate quantum compression ratio
N=row*col;
B=(QH~=0);
Qr=N/sum(B);
% Retrieve the compressed images
if Type==0
    QHC=ITDHQWPT(m,k,h-1)*QH; % Apply the inverse of h-level
```

```
2D_HQWPT on QH
else
    QHC=ITD4QWPT(m,k,h-1)*QH; % Apply the inverse of h-level
2D_HQWPT on QH
end
QHCI=QG2(QHC, G, row, col);
% Call the function psnr() to calculate PSNR
psnr1=psnr(A,QHCI,max(max(A)));
end
```

Code B.83 The code for the examples of quantum image compression based on 3-level 2D-QWPTs

```
function []=testQICQWPT()
clear all; clc
% A stores four 256*256 grayscale images
A(:,:,1)= double(imread('Cameraman.bmp'));
A(:,:,2)= double(imread('glena.bmp'));
A(:,:,3)= double(imread('gbaboon.bmp'));
A(:,:,4)= double(imread('gairplane.bmp'));
for j=1:4
    subplot(3,4,j);
    imshow(uint8(A(:,:,j)),[]);
end
% Call the function QICQWPT to realize quantum image
compression  for 3-level 2D-HQWPT
Qrh=zeros(4,1);
Psnrh=zeros(4,1);
for j=1:4
    [QHCI,Qr,psnr1]=QICQWPT(A(:,:,j),3,0);
    Qrh(j,1)=Qr; % Get quantum compression ratio
    Psnrh(j,1)=psnr1; % Get peak signal-to-noise ratio
    subplot(3,4,4+j);
    imshow(uint8(QHCI),[]);
end
Qrhm=mean(Qrh); % Get the mean value of QRCs for 3-level
2D-HQWPT
Psnrhm=mean(Psnrh); % Get the mean value of PNSRs for 3-level
2D-HQWPT
% Call the function QICQWPT to realize quantum image
compression  for 2D-D4QWPT
dwtmode('per'); % Set periodization extension mode
Qrd=zeros(4,1);
Psnrd=zeros(4,1);
for j=1:4
    [QHCI,Qr,psnr1]=QICQWPT(A(:,:,j),3,1);
    Qrd(j,1)=Qr;
    Psnrd(j,1)=psnr1;
```

```
    subplot(3,4,8+j);
    imshow(uint8(QHCI),[]);
end
Qrdm=mean(Qrd); % Get the mean value of QRCs for 3-level
2D-D4QWPT
Psnrdm=mean(Psnrd); % Get the mean value of PNSRs for 3-level
2D-D4QWPT
end
```

The Codes for Quantum Image Segmentation in Chapter 8

Code B.84 The code for quantum Hadamard edge detection algorithm

```
% Ag is a 2^n*2^n binary image
function OutputI=QHED(Ag)
[row,col]=size(Ag);
 n=log2(row)+log2(col);
H=sqrt(2)*0.5*[1 1; 1 -1];
I=[1 0;0 1];
% Encode the image Ag into a quantum state Q;
fg=double(Ag);
dg=abs(fg).*abs(fg);
G=sqrt(sum(dg(:)));
g = fg/G; % Normalize the image
Q=d2tod1(g); %Convert the image to a column vector
% Create the input of the algorithm QHED
Qin=kron(Q,[1;0]);
% Apply the circuit in Figure 8.3 on the input Qin
R=kron(tenProduct(I,n),H)*Qin;
R=Q2N(n+1)*R;
R=kron(tenProduct(I,n),H)*R;
% Denormalize the vector R
DR=R*G;
% Read the values of the even positions of the vector DR
Qout=DR(2:2:end);
% Obtain the output image
OutputI=d1tod2(2*Qout, row, col);
end
```

Code B.85 The code for the example of quantum Hadamard edge detection algorithm

```
function []=testQHED()
clear all
clc
```

328

```
% Ag is a 128*128 binary image
Ag = imread('Cat.bmp');
subplot(1,2,1);
imshow(Ag); %The original image
% Call QHED function to perform quantum Hadamard edge detection
algorithm
OutputI=QHED(Ag);
% Display the edge of the image Ag
OutputI2=abs(OutputI);
OutputB=im2bw(OutputI2); % Converts the image OutputI2 to a
binary image
subplot(1,2,2);
imshow(OutputB);
end
```

Code B.86 The implementation of generalized Grover search algorithm in Figure 8.10

```
% A is the set of marked states
function Gph=GGrover(n,A)
I=[1 0;0 1];
X=[0 1; 1 0];
X1=-X;
H=sqrt(2)*0.5*[1 1; 1 -1];
[m1,m2]=size(A);
% The implementation of the operator U in Figure 8.8 (a)
U=kron(tenProduct(H,n),I);
for j=m1:-1:1
    U=Cup(n,A(j),X)*U;
end
% The implementation of the inverse of the operator U
IU=U';
% The implementation of R0 in Figure 8.9 (a)
R0=kron(tenProduct(I,n-1),X1*H)*Cup(n-
1,0,X)*kron(tenProduct(I,n-1),H*X);
% The implementation of R1 in Figure 8.9 (b)
R1=kron(tenProduct(I,n),H*X*H);
% The implementation of generalized Grover search algorithm in
Figure 8.10
Gph=U*kron(R0,I)*IU*R1;
end
```

Code B.87 The code for the first example of quantum image segmentation based on generalized Grover search algorithm

```
function []=testQISGGSA1()
clear all
clc
I=[1 0;0 1];
X=[0 1; 1 0];
State0=[1;0];
% S is a 135*1 vector which stores the positions of the image
edge
S= [964;965;966;967;968;1028;1033;1034;1092;1099;1156;1164;1221
;1229;1286;
    1294;1350;1359;1414;1424;1478;1489;1543;1554;1607;1619;1620
;1640;1641;
    1642;1643;1644;1645;1646;1647;1648;1649;1671;1685;1686;1687
;1688;1691;
    1692;1693;1695;1696;1697;1698;1699;1700;1701;1702;1703;1714
;1715;1735;
    1753;1754;1758;1780;1781;1798;1846;1847;1848;1849;1860;1861
;1914;1915;
    1916;1924;1981;1982;1983;1984;1988;2031;2032;2033;2034;2035
;2036;2037;
    2038;2039;2040;2041;2042;2043;2044;2053;2054;2055;2094;2120
;2158;2185;
    2186;2187;2188;2189;2190;2191;2199;2215;2216;2217;2218;2219
;2220;2221;
    2256;2257;2262;2264;2265;2267;2268;2269;2270;2271;2272;2273
;2274;2275;
    2276;2277;2278;2322;2323;2324;2325;2330];
[m1,m2]=size(S);
% Ag is a 64*64 grayscale   image
Ag = double(imread('airplane64.bmp'));
subplot(1,2,1);
imshow(uint8(Ag));
[row, col]=size(Ag);
m=log2(row);
k=log2(col);
n=m+k;
% Call the function GQ2 to create a NASS state
[G,Q]=GQ2(Ag);
% Create a NAQSS state
Q1=kron(Q,State0);
for j=1:m1
    Q1=Cup(n,S(j),X)*Q1;
end
% Calculate N, r, the averages of the amplitudes, and the
variances of the amplitudes
```

```
N=row*col;
r=m1;
A1=Q1(1:2:end);
A2=Q1(2:2:end);
La0=sum(A1)/(N-r);% The average of the amplitudes of unmarked
states
Ka0=sum(A2)/r;% The average of the amplitudes of marked states
% The variance of the amplitudes of unmarked states
Dtal0=sum(abs(A1-La0).*abs(A1-La0))/(N-r);
% Calculate the optimal iterations of Grover in (0.10)
ph=atan(Ka0*sqrt(r/(N-r))/La0);
w=acos(1-2*r/N);
t=round((pi()/2-ph)/w);
% Apply the t iterations of generalized Grover search algorithm
on  the NAQSS state Q1
Gr=GGrover(n,S);
for j=1:t
    Q1=Gr*Q1;
end
% Calculate the average of the amplitudes of marked states of
Q1
A3=Q1(2:2:end);
Kat=sum(A3)/r;
% Calculate the probability of success
Pt= sum(abs(A3).*abs(A3));
% Retrieve the target sub-image
A3(A3~=0) = A3(A3~=0)-Kat+Ka0;
QI=QG2(A3, G, row, col);
subplot(1,2,2);
imshow(uint8(QI));
end
```

Code B.88 The implementation of the generalized Grover search algorithm in (8.56)

```
function Gph=GGrover2(n,A) % A is the binary image of a target
sub-image
I=[1 0;0 1];
X=[0 1; 1 0];
t0=[1;0]; % The state |0>
t1=[0;1]; % The state |1>
H=sqrt(2)*0.5*[1 1; 1 -1];
[m1,m2]=size(A);
N=2^n;
B1=double(A);
B2=double(~A);
V1=d2tod1(B1); % Convert the image B1 to a column vector
V2=d2tod1(B2); % Convert the image B2 to a column vector
```

```
Ph1=(kron(V2,t0)+kron(V1,t1))/sqrt(N); % Calculate the state in
(8.29)
Ph2=(kron(V2,t1)+kron(V1,t0))/sqrt(N); % Calculate the state in
(8.54)
R1=kron(tenProduct(I,n),H*X*H); % Calculate R1 in Figure 8.9
(b)
% The implementation of generalized Grover search algorithm in
(8.56)
Gph=(2*Ph1*Ph1'+2*Ph2*Ph2'-tenProduct(I,n+1))*R1;
end
```

Code B.89 The code for the second example of quantum image segmentation based on the generalized Grover search algorithm

```
function []=testQISGGSA2()
clear all
clc
% Ag is a 128*128 color image
Ag = imread('airplane128.bmp');
subplot(1,3,1);
imshow(Ag);
Ag=double(Ag);
[row,col,tem]=size(Ag);
m=log2(row);
k=log2(col);
n=m+k;
% Tar is the 128*128 binary image of a target sub-image
Tar=imread('airplaneBin.bmp');
subplot(1,3,2);
imshow(Tar);
% Call the function CQ2 to create a NASS state Q
[G,Q]=CQ2(Ag);
% Create a NAQSS state Phx
t0=[1;0]; % The state |0>
t1=[0;1]; % The state |1>
B1=double(Tar);
B2=double(~Tar);
V1=d2tod1(B1); % Convert the image B1 to a column vector
V2=d2tod1(B2); % Convert the image B2 to a column vector
Q1=Q.*V1;
Q2=Q.*V2;
Phx=kron(Q2,t0)+kron(Q1,t1);
% Calculate N, r, the averages of the amplitudes, and the
variances of the amplitudes
N=row*col;
r=nnz(Tar); % Number of nonzero elements
A1=Phx(1:2:end);
A2=Phx(2:2:end);
```

```
La0=sum(A1)/(N-r);% The average of the amplitudes of unmarked
states
Ka0=sum(A2)/r;% The average of the amplitudes of marked states
 % The variance of the amplitudes of unmarked states
Dtal0=sum(abs(A1-La0).*abs(A1-La0))/(N-r);
% Calculate the optimal iterations of Grover in (8.46)
ph=atan(Ka0*sqrt(r/(N-r))/La0);
w=acos(1-2*r/N);
t=round((pi()/2-ph)/w);
% Apply the t iterations of generalized Grover search algorithm
on the NAQSS state Phx
Gr=GGrover2(n,Tar);
for j=1:t
    Phx=Gr*Phx;
end
% Calculate the average of the amplitudes of marked states of
Phx
A3=Phx(2:2:end);
Kat=sum(A3)/r;
% Calculate the probability of success
Pt= sum(abs(A3).*abs(A3));
% Retrieve the target sub-image
A3(A3~=0) = A3(A3~=0)-Kat+Ka0;
QI=QC2(A3, G, row, col);
subplot(1,3,3);
imshow(uint8(QI),[]);
end
```

About the Author

HaiSheng Li is an Associate Professor and Master's Supervisor at College of Electronic Engineering at Guangxi Normal University, China. He received the M.S. degree in computer science from Chongqing University and the Ph.D. degree in computer science from the University of Electronic Science and Technology of China. He worked as a visiting scholar at University of Technology, Sydney, Australia, and Tsinghua University, China. His research interests include quantum image processing, quantum signal processing, and quantum algorithm.

Index

L

lattice 32-33, 37, 46, 128

O

orthogonal rotation 132, 143, 145-149, 153-154

P

postulates 10, 27

Q

quantization hypothesis 1
quantum algorithms 157, 251
Quantum Circuit 13, 21, 63, 76, 133-134, 136-137, 176, 182, 188, 197-198, 200, 210, 213, 227, 237
quantum computation 1-3, 8, 27, 31
Quantum Image Processing 31, 129, 158, 246
Quantum Images 31-32, 46, 83, 157
quantum mechanics 1, 10-11, 13, 27
quantum representation 32, 68, 74, 88, 95, 99
Quantum Wavelet 111, 193-196, 201, 207, 213, 217, 221-223, 225-226, 228, 230, 233, 243
quantum wavelet packet transform 221-223, 225, 228, 243
Qubit Lattice 32-33, 37, 46, 128
Qubits 2-3, 5, 15-16, 18, 23-24, 26, 33, 38, 46, 53-54, 66, 76-77, 88, 92, 94-95, 99-100, 111-112, 117, 120, 122-123, 128-129, 208, 211

S

Segmentation 66, 246-247, 250, 261, 263-265
Shuffle Permutations 102, 158-159, 180, 182, 191, 195
Sub-Image 66, 251, 263, 265-266
superposition state 8, 10, 32, 37, 49, 61, 66, 71-72
Symmetric 132, 139-142, 149-151, 155, 178

T

target objects 247
Tensor Products 1-3, 27, 158, 162, 165, 191
transformations 132, 135, 139-141, 146, 149-155
two-point swapping 132-133, 136-139, 149-150, 155
typical image 246
typical image processing 246

W

wavelet packet 221-223, 225-228, 230, 232-241, 243
Wavelet Transform 88, 94, 106, 110-111, 193-197, 201, 205, 212, 214, 216-217, 225

Z

zonal bit reversal 197, 199

Ensure Quality Research is Introduced to the Academic Community

Become an IGI Global Reviewer for Authored Book Projects

Premier Reference Source

Emerging GIS Applications for Emergency and Disaster Management

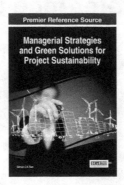
Premier Reference Source

Managerial Strategies and Green Solutions for Project Sustainability

Premier Reference Source

Comparative Approaches to Using R and Python for Statistical Data Analysis

Premier Reference Source

Solutions for High-Touch Communications in a High-Tech World

The overall success of an authored book project is dependent on quality and timely reviews.

In this competitive age of scholarly publishing, constructive and timely feedback significantly expedites the turnaround time of manuscripts from submission to acceptance, allowing the publication and discovery of forward-thinking research at a much more expeditious rate. Several IGI Global authored book projects are currently seeking highly-qualified experts in the field to fill vacancies on their respective editorial review boards:

Applications and Inquiries may be sent to:
development@igi-global.com

Applicants must have a doctorate (or an equivalent degree) as well as publishing and reviewing experience. Reviewers are asked to complete the open-ended evaluation questions with as much detail as possible in a timely, collegial, and constructive manner. All reviewers' tenures run for one-year terms on the editorial review boards and are expected to complete at least three reviews per term. Upon successful completion of this term, reviewers can be considered for an additional term.

If you have a colleague that may be interested in this opportunity, we encourage you to share this information with them.

IGI Global
DISSEMINATOR OF KNOWLEDGE
www.igi-global.com

Publisher of Peer-Reviewed, Timely, and
Innovative Academic Research Since 1988

IGI Global's Transformative Open Access (OA) Model:
How to Turn Your University Library's Database Acquisitions Into a Source of OA Funding

In response to the OA movement and well in advance of Plan S, IGI Global, early last year, unveiled their OA Fee Waiver (Offset Model) Initiative.

Under this initiative, librarians who invest in IGI Global's InfoSci-Books (5,300+ reference books) and/or InfoSci-Journals (185+ scholarly journals) databases will be able to subsidize their patron's OA article processing charges (APC) when their work is submitted and accepted (after the peer review process) into an IGI Global journal.*

How Does it Work?

1. When a library subscribes or perpetually purchases IGI Global's InfoSci-Databases including InfoSci-Books (5,300+ e-books), InfoSci-Journals (185+ e-journals), and/or their discipline/subject-focused subsets, IGI Global will match the library's investment with a fund of equal value to go toward subsidizing the OA article processing charges (APCs) for their patrons.

   Researchers: Be sure to recommend the InfoSci-Books and InfoSci-Journals to take advantage of this initiative.

2. When a student, faculty, or staff member submits a paper and it is accepted (following the peer review) into one of IGI Global's 185+ scholarly journals, the author will have the option to have their paper published under a traditional publishing model or as OA.

3. When the author chooses to have their paper published under OA, IGI Global will notify them of the OA Fee Waiver (Offset Model) Initiative. If the author decides they would like to take advantage of this initiative, IGI Global will deduct the US$ 1,500 APC from the created fund.

4. This fund will be offered on an annual basis and will renew as the subscription is renewed for each year thereafter. IGI Global will manage the fund and award the APC waivers unless the librarian has a preference as to how the funds should be managed.

Hear From the Experts on This Initiative:

"I'm very happy to have been able to make one of my recent research contributions, 'Visualizing the Social Media Conversations of a National Information Technology Professional Association' featured in the *International Journal of Human Capital and Information Technology Professionals*, freely available along with having access to the valuable resources found within IGI Global's InfoSci-Journals database."

– **Prof. Stuart Palmer**,
Deakin University, Australia

For More Information, Visit: www.igi-global.com/publish/contributor-resources/open-access or contact IGI Global's Database Team at eresources@igi-global.com

CPSIA information can be obtained
at www.ICGtesting.com
Printed in the USA
BVHW010046300820
587630BV00013B/156